ReFocus: The Films of Larisa Shepitko

ReFocus: The International Directors Series

Series Editors: Robert Singer, Gary D. Rhodes and Stefanie Van de Peer

Board of advisors:
Lizelle Bisschoff (Glasgow University)
Stephanie Hemelryck Donald (University of Lincoln)
Anna Misiak (Falmouth University)
Des O'Rawe (Queen's University Belfast)

ReFocus is a series of contemporary methodological and theoretical approaches to the interdisciplinary analyses and interpretations of international film directors, from the celebrated to the ignored, in direct relationship to their respective culture – its myths, values and historical precepts – and the broader parameters of international film history and theory.

Titles in the series include:

ReFocus: The Films of Susanne Bier Edited by Missy Molloy, Mimi Nielsen and Meryl Shriver-Rice
ReFocus: The Films of Francis Veber Keith Corson
ReFocus: The Films of Xavier Dolan Edited by Andrée Lafontaine
ReFocus: The Films of Pedro Costa: Producing and Consuming Contemporary Art Cinema Nuno Barradas Jorge
ReFocus: The Films of Sohrab Shahid Saless: Exile, Displacement and the Stateless Moving Image Edited by Azadeh Fatehrad
ReFocus: The Films of Pablo Larraín Edited by Laura Hatry
ReFocus: The Films of Michel Gondry Edited by Marcelline Block and Jennifer Kirby
ReFocus: The Films of Rachid Bouchareb Edited by Michael Gott and Leslie Kealhofer-Kemp
ReFocus: The Films of Andrei Tarkovsky Edited by Sergey Toymentsev
ReFocus: The Films of Paul Leni Edited by Erica Tortolani and Martin F. Norden
ReFocus: The Films of Rakhshan Banietemad Edited by Maryam Ghorbankarimi
ReFocus: The Films of Jocelyn Saab: Films, Artworks and Cultural Events for the Arab World Edited by Mathilde Rouxel and Stefanie Van de Peer
ReFocus: The Films of François Ozon Edited by Loïc Bourdeau
ReFocus: The Films of Teuvo Tulio Henry Bacon, Kimmo Laine and Jaakko Seppälä
ReFocus: The Films of João Pedro Rodrigues and João Rui Guerra da Mata Edited by José Duarte and Filipa Rosário
ReFocus: The Films of Lucrecia Martel Edited by Natalia Christofoletti Barrenha, Julia Kratje and Paul Merchant
ReFocus: The Films of Shyam Benegal Edited by Sneha Kar Chaudhuri and Ramit Samaddar
ReFocus: The Films of Denis Villeneuve Edited by Jeri English and Marie Pascal
ReFocus: The Films of Antoinetta Angelidi Edited by Penny Bouska and Sotiris Petridis
ReFocus: The Films of Ken Russell Edited by Matthew Melia
ReFocus: The Films of Kim Ki-young Edited by Chung-kang Kim
ReFocus: The Films of Jane Campion Edited by Alexia L. Bowler and Adele Jones
ReFocus: The Films of Alejandro Jodorowsky Edited by Michael Newell Witte
ReFocus: The Films of Nuri Bilge Ceylan Edited by Gönül Dönmez-Colin
ReFocus: The Films of Claire Denis Edited by Peter Sloane
ReFocus: The Films of Steve McQueen Edited by Thomas Austin
ReFocus: The Films of Yim Soon-rye Edited by Molly Kim
ReFocus: The Films of Annemarie Jacir Iqra Shagufta Cheema with Stefanie Van de Peer
ReFocus: The Films of Joachim Trier Anne Gjelsvik
ReFocus: The Films of Agnieszka Holland Elżbieta Ostrowska
ReFocus: The Films of Larisa Shepitko Edited by Lida Oukaderova

edinburghuniversitypress.com/series/refocint

ReFocus:
The Films of Larisa Shepitko

Edited by Lida Oukaderova

EDINBURGH
University Press

Edinburgh University Press is one of the leading university presses in the UK. We publish academic books and journals in our selected subject areas across the humanities and social sciences, combining cutting-edge scholarship with high editorial and production values to produce academic works of lasting importance. For more information visit our website: edinburghuniversitypress.com

© editorial matter and organisation Lida Oukaderova, 2024 , 2025
© the chapters their several authors 2024, 2025

Grateful acknowledgement is made to the sources listed in the List of Illustrations for permission to reproduce material previously published elsewhere. Every effort has been made to trace the copyright holders, but if any have been inadvertently overlooked, the publisher will be pleased to make the necessary arrangements at the first opportunity.

Edinburgh University Press Ltd
13 Infirmary Street
Edinburgh EH1 1LT

First published in hardback by Edinburgh University Press 2024

Typeset in 11/13 Ehrhardt MT by
IDSUK (DataConnection) Ltd
A CIP record for this book is available from the British Library

ISBN 978 1 3995 2403 2 (hardback)
ISBN 978 1 3995 2404 9 (paperback)
ISBN 978 1 3995 2405 6 (webready PDF)
ISBN 978 1 3995 2406 3 (epub)

The right of Lida Oukaderova to be identified as the editor of this work has been asserted in accordance with the Copyright, Designs and Patents Act 1988, and the Copyright and Related Rights Regulations 2003 (SI No. 2498).

Contents

List of Figures vii
Notes on Contributors ix

    Introduction 1
    Lida Oukaderova

Part I Late Socialism: Cinema, Ideology, Subjectivity

1 Larisa Shepitko at VGIK and in Soviet / Post-Soviet Archives and Press 19
   Nina Sputnitskaya
2 Larisa Shepitko, Aleksei German, and the Trials and Tribulations of Post-Thaw Soviet Filmmaking 38
   Tim Harte

Part II Intermediality: From Word to Image

3 Ghosts of the Present Past: *Wings* (1966), from the Script by Natalia Riazantseva and Valentin Ezhov to the Film by Larisa Shepitko 57
   Eugénie Zvonkine
4 *The Ordeal* and *The Ascent* 77
   Karla Oeler

Part III The Materiality of Moving Images

5 The Revolutionary Past as Environment: Rain, Dust, and Faces in *The Homeland of Electricity* 97
   Viktoria Paranyuk
6 The Senselessness of the Heroic Act and the Experience of War in *The Ascent* 116
   Elizabeth A. Papazian

Part IV Time, Memory, Temporality

7 *White on White* and *The Black Square*: Shepitko's *The Ascent*, Stan Brakhage, and Cinematic Abstraction 139
   Anne Eakin Moss

8 Liquid Time: *The Homeland of Electricity* as Unprocessed Trauma 158
   Lilya Kaganovsky

Part V Landscape and Environment

9 Methods of Conquest: Larisa Shepitko's *Heat*, Soviet Russian Colonialism, and the Representation of the Virgin Lands Campaign in Soviet Cinema of the 1950s–60s 179
   Zdenko Mandušić

10 Larisa Shepitko's Ecologies 200
    Lida Oukaderova

11 The Shepitko Sky: Larisa Shepitko's Meteorological Cinema of Immersion, Wonder, and Openness 223
    Raymond De Luca

Part VI Shepitko in Post-Soviet Cinema

12 The White, the Black, and the Gray: The Problem of Choice in Larisa Shepitko's *The Ascent* and Sergei Loznitsa's *In the Fog* 247
    Sergey Toymentsev

Index 269

Figures

2.1	Petrukhina listening to "The Steel Squadron" in *Wings*.	41
2.2	The Soviet prisoner-of-war barge in *Trial on the Road*.	48
2.3	The Christ-like Sotnikov in *The Ascent*.	51
3.1	Nadia's reminiscence of flying.	66
3.2	Nadia in front of the museum stand.	70
3.3	Nadia in the plane. Her eyes fill up with tears.	72
4.1	Sotnikov's face in the landscape.	86
4.2	Graphically, Portnov's smaller head seems to sink into Sotnikov's larger one.	89
4.3	The back of Rybak's head blocking Demchikha's face.	91
5.1	The hero meets a new environment.	102
5.2	The religious procession enveloped in a dust cloud.	103
5.3	The young man carries the old woman across the barren landscape.	104
5.4	The rain commingles with the tears of the villagers.	111
6.1	A snowman in front of Demchikha's house, as seen through the window by Sotnikov and Rybak.	121
6.2	Shot seven: Credit sequence and mobile camera.	122
6.3–6.5	Close-ups of people in the forest receiving their portion of grain.	125
7.1	Man in the snow, *Dog Star Man*, dir. Stan Brakhage, 1964.	141
7.2	A composite of shots from the four opening shots of *The Ascent*.	143
7.3	Branches suggesting a swastika in front of Sotnikov's face.	148
7.4	Blood on the doorframe to fool the angel of death.	149
7.5	Malevich's *Black Square* as framed in the cellar door.	150
8.1	The village of Rogachevka in the 1920s.	160

8.2	Grinya (Sergei Gorbatiuk).	164
8.3	The Opera, *The Homeland of Electricity*, Voronezh, 2017.	171
9.1	Low-angle, low-horizon silhouette shots, clockwise from the top: *The First Echelon*, *Restless Spring*, *Heat*, and *Alenka*.	185
9.2	Kemel' underneath the tractor in *Heat*.	189
10.1	Rybak in the landscape's all-consuming whiteness.	210
10.2	Landscape without any coordinates or scale.	211
10.3	Rybak in a state of psychic collapse.	214
10.4	The camera looking closely at the natural world.	217
10.5	The estranged land at the end of *Farewell*.	219
11.1	Characters backdropped by nothing but sky.	227
11.2	Neuro-images of the sky.	231
11.3	Sotnikov looking at the moon.	238
12.1	Sotnikov's close-up during the execution.	255
12.2	Rybak's close-up during his suicide attempt.	255
12.3	Portnov's close-up when he confronts Sotnikov's gaze.	256
12.4	Sushenya sits between the bodies of Burov and Voitik.	264

Notes on Contributors

Tim Harte is Provost and Professor of Russian at Bryn Mawr College. His academic research is focused on early 20th-century Russian literature, film, and art. Harte is the author of *Faster, Higher, Stronger, Comrades! Sports, Art, and Ideology in Imperial Russian and Early Soviet Culture* (2020) and *Fast Forward: The Aesthetics and Ideology of Speed in Russian Avant-Garde Culture, 1910–1930* (2009), as well as over 10 articles and book chapters, and he is co-editor (with Marina Rojavin) on *Soviet Films of the 1970s and Early 1980s: Conformity and Non-Conformity Amidst Decay* (2021) and *Women in Soviet Film: The Thaw and Post-Thaw Periods* (2018).

Lilya Kaganovsky is Professor of Slavic, East European & Eurasian Languages & Cultures at the University of California, Los Angeles. Her publications include *The Voice of Technology: Soviet Cinema's Transition to Sound, 1928–1935* (2018) and *How the Soviet Man was Unmade* (2008); the edited volumes *Arctic Cinemas and the Documentary Ethos* (with Anna Stenport and Scott MacKenzie, 2019); *Sound, Speech, Music in Soviet and Post-Soviet Cinema* (with Masha Salazkina, 2014), and *Mad Men, Mad World: Sex, Politics, Style and the 1960s* (Lauren M. E. Goodlad, Lilya Kaganovsky and Robert A. Rushing, 2013); as well as numerous articles on Soviet and post-Soviet cinema. She is a member of the editorial board of the journal *Studies in Russian and Soviet Cinema*, and the Associate Editor for film and media at *The Russian Review*. She is currently working on a book on Soviet women's cinema.

Zdenko Mandušić is Assistant Professor in the Department of Slavic Languages and Literatures at the University of Toronto. His work focuses on issues of cinematic authenticity, reality effects, the imaginary conceptualization of technology, and the influence of discourse on the production and reception of art. He is currently working on a book project, titled *Revising Reality: The Documentary Turn in Soviet Cinema after Stalin*, which focuses on the mobilization of documentary elements in Soviet fiction films of the 1950s and 1960s.

Anne Eakin Moss is Associate Professor in the Slavic Department at the University of Chicago, where she is also affiliated faculty in the Department of Cinema and Media Studies and the Center for the Study of Gender and Sexuality. Her first book, *Only Among Women: Philosophies of Community in the Russian Imagination, 1860–1940* (2019), examines the privileged place of women's relations in Russian literature and cinema. She is currently working on a book tentatively titled *The Special Effects of Soviet Wonder*. Essays from the project have been published in *Screen*, *Film History*, *Die Zeitschrift für Medien- und Kulturforschung*, and *Andrei Tarkovsky: ReFocus* (ed. Sergey Toymentsev, Edinburgh University Press, 2021).

Karla Oeler teaches in the Film & Media Studies Program in the Department of Art & Art History at Stanford University. Her research and teaching take a comparatist approach to film and literary history, theory, and criticism. She is the author of *A Grammar of Murder: Violent Scenes and Film Form* (2009). Her work has appeared in various publications including *Cinema Journal*, *The Journal of Visual Culture*, *Kinokultura*, *Screen*, and *Slavic Review*. She is currently working on a book called *The Surface of Things: Cinema and the Devices of Interiority*.

Lida Oukaderova is an Associate Professor of Film Studies in the Department of Art History at Rice University. She is an author of *The Cinema of the Soviet Thaw: Space, Materiality, Movement* (2017). Currently she is working on a book titled *In Pursuit of the Common: Soviet and Russian Cinema Since the 1960s*.

Viktoria Paranyuk is a lecturer in Film and Screen Studies at Pace University and freelance film curator in New York City. She is currently at work on *Modern Soviet Cinema: Realism, Modernism, and the Aesthetics of Sincerity*. Viktoria's work has been published in *Slavic Review*, *Film History*, and *Senses of Cinema*.

Mariia Pankova is a graduate student at the Center for Human Rights and the Arts, Bard College. She is a documentary filmmaker and artistic researcher with an interest in the intersection of traditional and contemporary art and the formation of the post-Soviet identities in her native Kyrgyzstan.

Elizabeth Astrid Papazian is Associate Professor of Russian and Cinema & Media Studies at the University of Maryland, College Park. Her research interests include literary and cinematic modernism, documentary modes in literature and cinema, and the intersection between art and politics, focusing in particular on early Soviet culture. She is the author of *Manufacturing Truth: The Documentary Moment in Early Soviet Culture* (2009), and co-editor of *The Essay Film: Dialogue, Politics, Utopia* (2016). She is currently working on a book project on realism in Soviet cinema.

Raymond De Luca is an Assistant Professor in the Department of Russian and East Asian Languages and Cultures at Emory University. Raymond received his Ph.D. from Harvard University in Slavic Languages and Literatures in 2022. His research and teaching interests include Soviet culture, animal studies, film theory, and critical race studies. He is currently working on a book entitled *The New Soviet Animal*, which examines how the human-animal divide was re-imagined in revolutionary Russia as Soviet artists and ideologues turned to animals as allies of the working class in the building of communism.

Nina Sputnitskaia holds a doctorate in art history from the All-Russian State University of Cinematography (VGIK), where she currently works as a senior researcher in the Department of Information and Analytics. She has published on gender issues in cinema; on the work of Aleksandr Ptushko; and on Soviet and Russian animation. Her articles have appeared in English and French publications, including *Studies in Russian and Soviet Cinema*. She is also a senior editor of the academic journal *Telekinet*, contributor to the journal *The Art of Cinema* (Iskusstvo kino), *VGIK's Bulletin* (Vestnik VGIK), and others. Her authored monographs include *The Problem of Gender in Modern Russian Cinema and TV Series* (2016), *Multitrend. Trends in Modern Animation Russia* (2016), *Ptushko. Rou: Masterclass of Russian Fantasy Cinema*, and a number of edited volumes.

Sergey Toymentsev is Assistant Professor of Russian at Saint Louis University. He is the editor of *ReFocus: The Films of Andrei Tarkovsky* (2021). His articles and reviews appeared in *Novoe literaturnoe obozrenie*, *CLCWeb: Comparative Literature and Culture*, *Comparative Literature Studies*, *Journal of Philosophy: A Cross-Disciplinary Inquiry*, *Film Criticism*, *French Studies*, *Studies in Russian & Soviet Cinema*, *Film International*, and *Kinokultura*.

Eugénie Zvonkine is an Associate Professor in the Film Studies Department at the University of Paris 8. She writes on history and aesthetics in Soviet and post-Soviet cinema from the 1960s to the present day. She has published three monographs, including *Kira Mouratova: un cinéma de la dissonance* (2012) and a translation of Muratova's unrealized script *Regardez attentivement vos rêves* (2019) with comments. She (co-)edited the collective volumes *Cinéma* *russe, (r)évolutions* (2017), *Ruptures and Continuities in Soviet/Russian Cinema: Styles, Characters and Genres Before and after the Collapse of the USSR* (with Birgit Beumers, 2019), and the volume *Serguei͏̈ Loznitsa, un cinéma à l'épreuve du monde* (with Céline Gailleurd and Damien Marguet, 2022).

Introduction

Lida Oukaderova

The present volume on the cinema of Soviet Ukrainian filmmaker Larisa Shepitko is being completed at a time of war between Russia and Ukraine, which began with the Russian army's invasion of Ukrainian territories on February 24, 2022. As of the writing of this introduction in the spring of 2023, the war continues to rage on with no clear end in sight, bringing death, destruction, dislocation, and suffering to millions of Ukrainian citizens. In the meantime, it has become impossible to ignore calls from journalists, artists, academics, and Ukrainians across the globe to confront and grapple with the history of Russia's imperial ambitions and consciousness before, during, and after the Soviet period. In a March 2023 article, *The New York Times* reported on how such an historical reckoning might transpire, describing recent efforts by museums to acknowledge and accurately label as Ukrainian those artists and works that had been previously designated as Russian or Soviet. A failure to do so would amount to "stealing a heritage," making it ever more difficult for modern-day Ukraine to account for its historical lineage and protect a shared cultural memory.[1] The process is anything but simple, given the extreme ethnic diversity of the territories of Russia, the former Russian Empire and the Soviet Union; the shifts in borders over centuries; and the history of colonization, annexation, and population resettlements. Furthermore, Moscow's long-standing role as an epicenter of opportunity, drawing and appropriating talent from the surrounding territories, complicates attempts to assign clear ethnic and national alliances and identities.

In light of these discussions, I want to simply state that Larisa Shepitko was born and spent the first sixteen years of her life in Ukraine, which was then a Federal Republic within the Soviet Union. Her city of birth, Artiomovsk, is present-day Bakhmut in Ukraine's Donbas region. Although Shepitko moved after the war with her family to Kyiv and then Lviv, in Western Ukraine, where she finished high school, Bakhmut has in recent years made claims to her legacy. In 2016, the city commemorated the director's birth by renaming its "Klara Zetkin Street" to "Larisa Shepitko Street" and in 2018 installed a plaque in her honor on the walls of the local movie theater eerily named "Pobeda"—"Victory."

Just a few months ago, Bakhmut was unlikely to be known to anybody outside of Ukraine and perhaps Russia. Since August 2022, however, it has continuously occupied international headlines, after the Russian army intensified its military assault on the city.[2] The fighting for Bakhmut has been described as one of the bloodiest in the 21st century, with conditions reminiscent of trench warfare.[3] Although of little strategic value, the battle has become a "defining moment" in the war, "a marathon contest to see which army can break the other."[4] It is unclear, in the face of current Russian atrocities, how much has remained of the "Victory" movie theater with Larisa Shepitko's plaque, or of her street. But if war significantly shaped Shepitko's life—she experienced occupation, evacuation, and the full extent of war and postwar material deprivations in the 1940s —it continues to haunt her after her death, her birth city destroyed as part of a military aggression she was unlikely to have ever imagined. Shepitko's meditation on war, resilience, and betrayal in her most celebrated film *The Ascent* (Voskhozhdenie, 1977), depicting Soviet partisan struggles against Germans during World War II, has acquired a new meaning in this violent stage of Ukraine-Russia relations.

We can only surmise how much Shepitko's Ukrainian roots shaped her thinking and filmmaking. She was educated at the most reputable Soviet film school VGIK—The All-Union State Institute of Cinematography—in Moscow, beginning her directorial studies under the guidance of another Ukrainian-born director, Oleksander Dovzhenko, one of the most influential figures of the Soviet 1920s–30s cinematic avant-garde. She lived in the Soviet capital and made all but one of her films at the USSR's most renowned film studio Mosfilm. Like other prominent Soviet filmmakers of her generation, she had to negotiate between Soviet cultural bureaucracy and her intellectual interests and creative intuition. She faced criticism, censorship, and limitations on the distribution of her films when stretching beyond the accepted Soviet representational paradigms, while at the same time succeeding in producing films that strongly resonated with Soviet and international audiences.

But unlike, say, her contemporary Andrei Tarkovsky, whom she deeply admired and with whom she claimed an affinity, she found it acceptable to work within the Soviet system, seeing no need to leave, even after being invited to direct in Hollywood after the international success of *The Ascent*. Soviet institutions, in turn, while frequently making her work difficult in minor and major ways, consistently supported her productions, acknowledged her talent, and rewarded her successes. They also understood her representative importance, inviting her to be the face of Soviet feminism within an emerging international feminist cinema.[5] Shepitko's cinematic career, in other words, cannot be neatly characterized as specifically Ukrainian or generally Soviet: she produced a distinct body of work which was undoubtedly inflected by her Ukrainian origins and broader Soviet culture but which remained unmistakably her own, pervaded by the desire to explore the human condition through the potentialities of moving images.

It is nevertheless important to note that while Shepitko lived her adult life in Moscow, she continually sought to escape the capital in her work, gravitating towards peripheral locations. Of the six feature films that she made over the course of her short career, only one, *You and Me* (Ty i ia, 1971), is filmed and situated in Moscow, but even then, a good half of it steers clear of the capital, as we follow the main protagonist on his flight to Siberia, while he attempts to reflect on his present and past.[6] Otherwise, Shepitko shoots the Kyrgyz/Kazakh steppe in *Heat* (Znoi, 1963); the Crimean Sevastopol in *Wings* (Kryl'ia, 1966)—her only film set and shot in Ukraine; a small village in the Astrakhan region in *The Homeland of Electricity* (Rodina elektrichestva, 1967); Belorussian landscapes in *The Ascent* (which is also shot in Murom, in the woody areas between Moscow and Petersburg); and a fictional island on a Siberian river, filmed in the rural areas around Lake Seliger, also located between Moscow and Petersburg, in *Farewell* (Proshchanie, 1981). Having moved to Moscow from Lviv, a city near the Polish border, Shepitko continued to activate not only peripheral Soviet territories but also a particular *kind* of territory, marked by desolate steppes, pristine snow-covered landscapes, natural waters, and historical ruins, all of which, in their otherness and emptiness, implicitly questioned meanings and meaning-making practices generated by the capital's prevailing values and hierarchies.

By the time of her untimely death in a car accident in 1979, Shepitko had achieved a legendary status among filmmakers and audiences in the Soviet Union and select cinematic circles abroad. The reasons for this legendary status are manifold: the new kinds of characters, stories, and spaces her films brought on screen; the Soviet cultural bureaucracy's often aggressive criticism of her work; her film crews' accounts of the dramatic working conditions on set; and the fact that she was one of the few female directors in the USSR (essentially the only one in the 1970s) to have relatively regular access to the international film community. Shepitko's personal life complemented if not amplified her professional reputation, with her assertive personality, "film star" physical appearance, and marriage to another exceptional figure in Soviet film, Elem Klimov, contributing to the allure of the auteur. Yet between her death and 2008, when the Criterion Collection released two of her films on

DVD, her figure and work largely disappeared and were rarely considered in international historical and theoretical debates—precisely at the time when much of cinematic history and theory were being written.[7]

This disappearance can be attributed to several individual and interconnected factors. The Soviet film culture of the 1950s–70s, including its new wave, has not achieved the same canonical status as other cinematic new waves, despite Soviet directors' constant participation and frequent prizes at international film festivals. Shepitko's films, furthermore, did not reach broad international distribution during her lifetime, circulating mostly within specialized screening venues and thus remaining unknown to most historians (or regular moviegoers). More generally, with the exception of perhaps Andrei Tarkovsky, rarely did a Soviet postwar director manage to "transcend" the specifically Soviet contextualization of their work, being treated instead as artists addressing local interests and thus examined within the field of "area studies." Shepitko did attain a broader international recognition with *The Ascent* in 1977: her film was shown at film festivals and other venues across the globe, gaining praise from such figures as Werner Herzog, Susan Sontag, and Francis Ford Coppola. However, her death in 1979 brought an abrupt stop to this momentum. With no more films to follow up on the success of *The Ascent* and no continuous circulation of her previous work, her name and films were essentially forgotten, until the Criterion's DVD release of *Wings* and *The Ascent* in 2008.

This volume is the first collection of scholarly essays on Shepitko's work in English, taking as its goal a rigorous exploration of her oeuvre's aesthetic and political depth. Looking at her work as—necessarily—a part of late socialist Soviet culture, this volume engages extensively with contemporary and historical debates in film history and theory. Over the last decade and a half, a body of Shepitko scholarship has developed with a significant focus on gender and visual representation in her work, especially her film *Wings*. This book, while building on these essential preceding studies, moves beyond them, opening her cinema to a number of questions sparked by historical and contemporary concerns. While discussing Shepitko's films as part of the intellectual, artistic and ideological currents of the 1960s and 1970s, the volume's chapters focus on Shepitko's workings through of trauma and history; study the formal ways by which she visualizes interiority and subjectivity; examine her links to the Soviet visual and literary avant-gardes; discuss her cinema's imbrication into the history of Russian colonialism; interpret her films as an ecological, environmental, and atmospheric practice; and consider her influence on contemporary film. Through these analyses, the collection offers interpretations of Shepitko's oeuvre that are relevant for our times, while it also enriches contemporary film studies' theoretical concerns by thinking them through in connection to a still-marginal director.

Shepitko's cinema grew out of a more liberal political climate in the late 1950s and early 1960s (more liberal, that is, by comparison to Stalinism) and is best understood within the context of the shifts and contradictions of late Soviet culture, including within cinematic institutions. When Shepitko began her studies at VGIK in 1955, the Soviet Union was on the cusp of a significant turn in its political and cultural existence. Joseph Stalin died in 1953. In 1956, the Soviet leader Nikita Khrushchev delivered his historic speech at the Twentieth Communist Party Congress in Moscow, in which he denounced Stalin's totalitarianism, cult of personality, and crimes against Soviet citizens, opening up a space for historical reflection and social reorganization. What followed was a period known as the Soviet Thaw, lasting until the mid-1960s and marking a process of significant liberalization in all spheres of life, from politics, to economics, to everyday life.

The period's designation as a "thaw" seeped into public and historical discourse from Ilya Ehrenburg's novel *The Thaw* (1954), generating an image of melting ice as a metaphor of the transition from the punishing Stalinist system to Khrushchev's more tolerable and tolerant governing practices. Yet if Ehrenburg's novella associated a thaw with optimistic images of spring, renewal, and freedom, the metaphor—considered within the history of Russian and Soviet culture—also evoked contradictory interpretations. As the historians Denis Kozlov and Eleonory Gilburd noted, specifically for Khrushchev, a thaw "suggested nothing but slush and mud, sickly confusion and instability—a reading that reflected the word's longstanding connotations of disarray, slackening and enfeeblement."[8]

The Thaw's contradictions, indeed, were everywhere, as reforms towards more democratic governance were often accompanied by reactionary measures. As far as progressive measures go, economic decentralization took partial hold under Khrushchev, as the management of production was transferred to regional authorities in an attempt to revive the Soviet economy. It was also following Khrushchev's lead that ethnic groups that were deported by Stalin were allowed, partially, to return to their original areas, in a political endeavor to right a historical wrong.[9] Massive numbers of the Gulag prisoners were freed and expressions of political discontent were more tolerated.[10] An increase in mobility, manifested in the flourishing of tourism from, to, and within the Soviet Union, led to broader possibilities for the Soviet population to encounter other cultures, which had become nearly impossible for the average citizen during the Stalinist decades.[11]

Yet it was also during Khrushchev's reign that some of the most lasting, reckless, and oppressive measures were undertaken: from the sending of the Soviet troops to Hungary in 1956 to suppress public opposition; to the construction of the Berlin Wall in 1961; to the buildup of nuclear weapons in Cuba leading to the 1962 missile crisis; to the exploitation of natural resources and development of Virgin Lands that irreparably damaged Soviet landscapes.[12] If, in the realm of culture, artists, writers and filmmakers enjoyed a newly-found freedom to create, experiment, and reflect on Soviet history, collectivity, and subjecthood, they also found that this freedom could easily vanish at the whim of institutional forces or, worse, Khrushchev's own desires and taste.[13]

Khrushchev's replacement with Leonid Brezhnev in 1964, followed by the Soviet invasion of Prague in 1968, brought all hopes for a renewal of the socialist project to a screeching halt, leading to a period known as "stagnation," which lasted until Mikhail Gorbachev's arrival in 1985. Originally used to describe slow or negative economic growth, "stagnation" came to connote a general sense of decay and conservatism in the entirety of Soviet political and intellectual life. The Brezhnev era was resistant to change: it stiffened institutional bureaucracy, refused to yield power to a younger generation, and excluded "people with initiative, independent judgment, and integrity" from positions of authority from which productive reforms might be initiated—thus paralyzing movement forward.[14] The era was also plagued by trials of prominent artists and scientists, markedly squelching attempts at a non-conformist culture.

Nevertheless, the last two Soviet decades encompassed varying forms of engagement with official Soviet ideology, its principles and morals, which is necessary to keep in mind when considering Shepitko's cinema. The accounts of these engagements challenge the perception of Soviet ideology as a unidirectional force consuming all spheres of life and ordering Soviet experiences into binary oppositions of "progress" and "decay," or "conformism" and "resistance."[15] Sergey Yurchak in particular has argued that while the formulaic discourse of state ideology became emptied of its original meaning, it continued to be reproduced performatively, "*enabl[ing]* the emergence of diverse, multiple, and unpredictable meanings in everyday life, including those that did not correspond to the constative meanings of authoritative discourse."[16] Accordingly, a separation of Soviet citizens into those who simply conformed or resisted does not do justice to the complexities of individual agency and circulations of power in the last decades of the Soviet regime.

This applies as much to everyday practices as to artistic production. The historian and prominent party and government member Anatoliy Chernyaev went so far as to suggest that Soviet literature and the arts "liberated themselves from the dictum of politics (and politicians) and acquired a logic of their own, a logic of critical and independent reflection of reality."[17] Not everyone would agree with this statement. In the realm of cinema—which was funded fully by the state and subject to expansive institutional checks—the question of independence is particularly difficult. As Catriona Kelly describes, corrections and re-editing of films could be demanded "at every stage from the original proposal . . . up to clearance of the finished film for screening. Even once films were signed off, their makers' travails continued, since distribution categories based on 'ideological and artistic quality' could be used to condemn releases to the smallest possible audience."[18]

A significant number of late Soviet films were "shelved"—that is, not allowed any distribution (or removed immediately after the initial release) and put in storage, to be rediscovered only with the fall of the USSR. The most notable of these films include Aleksandr Askoldov's *Comissar* (Kommissar, 1967), Mikhail Kalatozov's *I am Cuba* (Ia Kuba, 1964), Kira Muratova's *Long Goodbyes* (Dolgie provody, 1971), and Shepitko's own *Homeland of Electricity*. The latter was a short, commissioned as part of an almanac entitled *The Beginning of the Unknown Century* (Nachalo nevedemogo veka) to celebrate the 50th anniversary of the 1917 revolution. However, upon its completion, it was deemed unsuitable for release. What is noteworthy however, is that all these shelved films (along with many others) *were* at least completed, having passed through multiple stages of control, indicating that the system was flexible enough to allow for a "critical and independent reflection of reality" within the arts.

Such flexibility came from different sources. One of them was a lack of clear guidelines as to what constituted proper artistic and ideological content. Ideological thought, when part of cinematic representations, could obtain nuances which made their appropriateness debatable and difficult to assess. Further complicating any clear orthodoxy, the final decisions were made not through written formulas but by individual figures, with varied film knowledge and artistic sensibilities. Furthermore, different people and institutions got involved at various stages of production, and what was good for one might not have been good for another, and vice versa. As Kelly explains, "state bodies frequently funded . . . the production of films that other state bodies (or sometimes the very same state body) proclaimed were unsuitable for public display."[19] And increasingly, market forces and international reception gained credence within Soviet bureaucracy, allowing "questionable" films to be released or, at least, to survive.

In many ways, as Shepitko's own history with censorship demonstrates, shelved works had (eventually) a better fate than the films that were severely "corrected" in the process of production or passed the final approval only after extensive re-editing. The latter often meant deep cuts and changes to an already completed film, which could be done even without the original director, distorting—and often destroying—the intended work. The most notorious case was Marlen Khutsiev's *Ilyich Gate* (Zastava Il'icha)—finished in 1962 only to be sent back to the editing room and released anew in 1964 with significant changes. But Shepitko's *You and Me* too went through extensive censorship troubles. In the words of the film's assistant director Valentina Khovanskaia, Shepitko faced a hostile environment from the approval committees, starting with the script that she co-wrote with Gennadii Shpalikov, who himself had a history of scripts being denied. Describing the process of making *You and Me*, Khovanskaia writes:

> we were asked to show the material to the editing committee (*redaktura*) almost every day. And every time, inevitably, we were reprimanded, given instructions and demands, and, as the result, asked to re-film. [. . .] Larisa had a difficult task: she had not only to imagine a new scene but to create something of an equivalent to what was rejected [. . .] The work did not follow a developed, thought-through script . . .; rather it was reshaping, remaking, patching.[20]

As a result of these interventions, Shepitko felt that her film was "mutilated," that she "lost it."[21] And yet, Khovanskaia suggests, it was a learning process during which Shepitko developed strategies to prevent such violent intrusions into her future productions. Whatever these strategies were, she implemented them successfully with her next film *The Ascent*, creating a work behind which she stood in full and which became the pinnacle of her career, celebrated nationally and internationally after winning the Golden Bear Prize at the Berlin Film Festival in 1977.[22]

* * *

Shepitko's career coincided with a wave of transnational feminist movements, which rose in the wake of the 1960s social uprisings, to which women's rights were central. The USSR at the time did not experience the same level of political activism related to gender equality as the United States and Europe. However, Soviet ideology and institutions had actively promoted gender equality since the 1917 revolution, with results that alternated between sweeping progress and hapless regression.[23] "The woman question" remained central to public discussions in the late Soviet period as well. Shepitko, as one of very few Soviet female directors at the time, spoke frequently of the difficulties of being a woman in what was largely understood to be a male profession. In 1975, for instance, she wrote,

> yes, our profession is masculine, harsh, and a woman is advised to enter it only if she has the capacity to rise above the purely 'feminist' problems. At the same time, a particular spiritual structure and fine neurological organization (nobody, not even men, would doubt this) give women an ability to penetrate into the deepest secrets of the human soul.[24]

Shepitko's insistence on a biologically determined female experience might sound outdated for a contemporary audience; however, in general, it mirrors Soviet feminist discussions during late socialism, which took for granted naturally defined gender differences while seeking to advance women's rights on paper and in everyday life. Yet she also moves beyond this standard position in her awareness that legally established rights are only one step towards a lived experience of social equality, stating:

> for fifty-eight years, our country's laws have protected women's judicial and social rights. But no law or decree will immediately change men's psychology and the mechanics of men's attitudes towards women, which have been created over centuries.[25]

Although she does not necessarily articulate what *would* initiate a change in the psychology and "mechanics" of male behaviors, it can be argued that her cinema—whether explicitly about women or not—took up this task. In exploring the structures of filmic representation, questioning the hierarchies of vision, and generating unconventional and, at times, radically different temporal and spatial perceptions and experiences, her cinema posed a challenge to calcified "behavior" and subjectivity, masculine and otherwise. Her films displace masculinity as the dominant generating force of worldviews and open up a space for differing gazes and sociability. As such, they run parallel to and intertwine with the cinema of the two most canonized female filmmakers working at the same time, Agnès Varda and Chantal Akerman. Yet, while Varda and Akerman's work, along with several other female directors of the 1970s, has served as a foundation for feminist film theory and history, Shepitko, along with Kira Muratova (one of the most thought-provoking Soviet Ukrainian directors who also started her career in the 1960s), has, until recently, remained marginal to feminist theory and history, despite her profoundly innovative formal and narrative ways to think about gender on screen.[26]

The last decade and a half have seen a broader acknowledgement of Shepitko's cinema, and her feminist aesthetics, among international film critics and goers. Her films, for instance, make an appearance in the first minutes of Mark Cousins' 14-hour documentary *Women Make Film: A New Road Movie Through Cinema* (2019) that brings to life the work of 183 women filmmakers, traversing the globe and all of cinematic history. The documentary features a sequence from *You and Me* accompanied by Tilda Swinton's earnest voiceover, commenting that the film "was made by one of the cinema's greatest tragedians and visual thinkers, Ukrainian Larisa Shepitko. *You and Me* is a masterpiece, but it's almost never shown." *The Ascent* appears in this documentary as well.

The present volume's essays do not extensively examine questions of gender in Shepitko's cinema, although passing discussions of gender-related concerns are present throughout. This is not an omission but a recognition that film historians have recently produced a relatively comprehensive feminist subsection in the interpretation of her work, which is essential for this and any future Shepitko studies. As a background for this volume, the following is a brief summary of this scholarship.

Lilya Kaganovsky's "Ways of Seeing: on Kira Muratova's *Brief Encounters* and Larisa Shepitko's *Wings*" initiates a discussion of Soviet female auteurs, positioning them at the center of critically transformative 1960s Soviet visual practices. If the cinema of the Soviet Thaw manifested itself in general as "counter-cinema" in its fundamental departure from Stalinist filmic genres and conventions, Kaganovsky argues that the work of Shepitko and Muratova moved beyond this, developing a set of narrative and visual strategies to examine patriarchal forms of cinematic representation and question the "*gendered ways of seeing and structures of looking.*"[27] What matters in Shepitko's *Wings* is not only the presence of a female protagonist, whose alienation as a woman and a former war pilot is strongly felt throughout, but that the film, through its non-linear narrative, use of freeze-frames and unmoored points of view allows for "a dizzying look at the world from a non-subject position liberated from gravity and all other forms of constraints."[28]

Wings is also at the center of my own book chapter "A Walk Through the Ruins: Larisa Shepitko's *Wings*," which examines the practice of walking, and what it means to create a specifically *Soviet* female flaneur, especially when considered alongside other postwar cinematic walkers of the period, Michelangelo Antonioni's female protagonist in *La Notte* (1961) in particular.[29] For both women, walking works to mobilize their agency and subjectivity and to get in touch with their respective cities—Sevastopol and Milan—despite their sense of a profound disconnect. For Shepitko, the sensory embrace of the environment taking place during selected walking sequences shatters both Soviet linear historical time and spatial order, filling it with intimate memories and unhealed traumas that Soviet institutional commemorative practices preferred to forget.

Olena Dmytryk closely examines the physical and social attributes of the protagonist of *Wings*—her gestures, language, clothes, beer-drinking, and more—to suggest that she "can be considered a 'queer' character, as her behavior is a dissent from the hegemonic gender and sexual norms of the Thaw."[30] And Marina Rojavin notes a significant shift away from the typical Soviet female protagonist in *You and Me*, where the main character diverges from conventional Soviet representations of womanhood. Rojavin asserts that she is "not associated with a woman-hero or mother, nor [. . .] with sacrifice or moral standards."[31] Yet she is not a thriving embodiment of feminism either. Desiring self-sufficiency and independence, she is shown as having no means to achieve these, remaining a figure through which the film's men seek to address their emotional and professional crises.

Most of these studies are referenced in the present collection, creating a foundation for new questions and analyses that this book undertakes and that are organized as follows.

The volume begins with the section "Late Socialism: Cinema, Ideology, Subjectivity," which locates Shepitko's work and career within the Soviet 1960s and 1970s. Nina Sputnitskaya's chapter provides a window into Soviet and post-Soviet critical literature, press, and archival documents on Shepitko, emphasizing shifts in the reception of her work and concluding with an extensive Soviet and post-Soviet bibliography of texts debating her films. Tim Harte's chapter brings into focus the work of another prominent Soviet director, Alexei German, whose films, especially his *Trial on the Road* (Proverka no dorogakh, 1971, also shelved upon its completion) overlaps aesthetically with Shepitko's. Harte argues that both are auteurs who, having trained to become filmmakers during the Thaw, significantly departed from the established Soviet visual and narrative conventions, especially in their nuanced reworkings of World War II Soviet heroism, paving the way for the critical historical and ethical reflections in the cinema of 1970s socialism.

The second section, "Intermediality: From Word to Image" addresses Shepitko's translation of the literary word into moving images. Eugénie Zvonkine's chapter "Ghosts of the Present Past" examines the script by Natalia Riazantseva, who wrote scripts for some of the most compelling Soviet films of the 1960s and 1970s. Scriptwriting in the Soviet Union was an art practice in its own right, understood as akin to literary production, and Riazantseva's text for *Wings* presents a cohesive, completed narration comparable to novelistic writing. Zvonkine carefully walks us through Shepitko's cinematic re-mediation, showing how Riazantseva's novelistic unity turns here into an open-ended, as if "incomplete" film, in which individual memory and the past "win over" the unfulfilling reality of the present. In a similar vein but with a different focus, Karla Oeler's chapter examines Shepitko's adaptation of Vasil' Bykov's novel *Sotnikov* (1970). The novel consistently alternates between the subjective perceptions and points of view of the two main protagonists, and includes extensive passages of their inner thoughts and moral doubts. Oeler demonstrates the complex process by which Shepitko renders individual thinking and interiority on screen—specifically, how the inwardness of literary free indirect discourse is externalized, cinematically, within the spaces, bodies, and dialogues of film.

The following section, "The Materiality of Moving Images" continues with a discussion of Shepitko's material filmic surfaces to address her interest in revolutionary history and experiences of war. Viktoria Paranyuk's chapter "The Revolutionary Past as Dust, Rain, and Face in *The Homeland of Electricity*" reads Shepitko's short not as a discursive and emplotted representation of history but an *atmosphere* through which history is animated as experience, a multisensory and embodied phenomenon, reconsidering how the Soviet past can be imagined and accessed in the wake of the 1960s historical re-evaluations. Elizabeth Papazian's chapter "The Senselessness of the Heroic Act and the

Experience of War in *The Ascent*" takes us on a step-by-step exploration of *The Ascent*'s extraordinary opening sequence to examine the film's material realism. Papazian argues that Shepitko's images exceed the film's narrative purpose, generating a nearly documentary reality that asks viewers to "co-suffer" through the war's ordinary—rather than heroic—acts and experiences.

The fourth section takes on the issues of "Time, Memory and Temporality" in Shepitko's work. Anne Eakin Moss's chapter "*White on White* and *The Black Square*: Shepitko's *The Ascent*, Stan Brakhage, and Cinematic Abstraction" begins with a discussion of Stan Brakhage, who took a great interest in Shepitko's *The Ascent*. Moss brings forth visual parallels between these directors' work to examine the underlying presence of 1910s–20s Russian/Soviet avant-garde artistic practices (Kazimir Malevich's suprematism in particular) in *The Ascent*, questioning what place visual—and specifically cinematic—abstraction might have in the aesthetics of the 1970s. Lilya Kaganovsky's chapter "Liquid Time: *The Homeland of Electricity* as Unprocessed Trauma" turns to Shepitko's short to examine its relation to the early Soviet avant-garde, this time cinematic (Dovzhenko's and Sergei Eisenstein's films) and especially literary (Andrei Platonov's story "The Homeland of Electricity" on which Shepitko's film is based). While these past works served to imagine a communist future, Kaganovsky argues that Shepitko's films transform them into images of a nation's traumatic and unworked-through past.

The three chapters in the section "Landscape and Environment" examine Shepitko's steady interest in filming natural environments throughout her career. Zdenko Mandušić's chapter situates Sheptiko's first feature film *Heat* within the Soviet genre of "natural conquest" films, which flourished during Nikita Khrushchev's Virgin Land campaign, carefully tracing how *Heat*'s visual rhetoric departs from earlier Soviet films on this topic. He also examines the film's history of production and postproduction as part of Soviet colonial practices. The latter encompass both the colonization history of Kazakh/Kyrgyz environments by Moscow's economic forces and the colonization of the Kyrgyz film industry as manifested especially in the film's being dubbed into Russian, eliminating the presence of Kyrgyz language and voices, against Shepitko's will. My own chapter "Shepitko's Ecologies" examines *Heat*, *The Ascent*, and *Farewell* as part of emerging Soviet and international ecological debates, arguing that environmental justice in these films appears repeatedly at odds with what is understood as morally and historically progressive human subjectivity. And Raymond DeLuca's chapter "The Shepitko Sky: Larisa Shepitko's Meteorological Cinema of Openness, Immersion, and Flux" shifts our attention from the ground to the sky to examine the latter's expansive presence throughout Shepitko's oeuvre. DeLuca reads this presence as an immaterial but all-encompassing condition that pervades Shepitko's cinematic space, shaping not only movements and landscapes but also characters and narrative structures, asking us to consider the sky's open-endedness as a way of being in, and viewing, the world.

The volume concludes with the section "Shepitko in Post-Soviet Cinema," with Sergey Toymentsev's chapter "The Problem of Choice in Sergei Loznitsa's *In the Fog* and Larisa Shepitko's *Ascent*." While both films are literary adaptations of Vasil' Bykov's fiction, Loznitsa critiques the Soviet mythology of war in his 2012 work, especially its glorification of sacrifice, while mourning the possibility of authentic choice which, Toymentsev argues, was still possible in Shepitko's drama. (As a side note, Loznitsa has become one of the most astute cinematic observers of Ukrainian history, excavating archival footage to document the region's history of subjugation in such films as *Babi Yar. Context* [2021], while creating new visual archives by filming Ukraine's independence movement of Maidan in *Maidan* [2014].)

While the book is organized in distinct sections around specific categories, individual chapters resonate with one another across conceptual boundaries and engage with contemporary and historical debates in film history and theory. The goal is to offer a more comprehensive, historically grounded understanding of Shepitko's cinema and to situate her as a director whose artistic practices speak to our times—be it in relation to history, ethics, politics, or the environment.

NOTES

1. Robin Pogrebin, "Museums Rename Artworks and Artists as Ukrainian, not Russian," *The New York Times*, March 17, 2023. Accessed April 25, 2023. https://www.nytimes.com/2023/03/17/arts/design/museums-relabel-art-ukraine-russian.html?searchResultPosition=2
2. At the moment of writing these lines, more than sixty percent of the city lies in ruins, and its prewar population of about 70,000 has dwindled by about ten times, while hundreds of soldiers—Ukrainian and Russian—have been wounded or are dying there daily in battles.
3. Christopher Miller, "Hell. Just hell: Ukraine and Russia's war of attrition over Bakhmut," FT.com, London, Dec. 9, 2022. The Financial Times Limited.
4. Carlotta Gall, "Ukrainian Soldiers, Nearly Encircled, Push Russians Back," *New York Times*, March 6, 2023. Accessed April 28. https://www.nytimes.com/2023/03/06/world/europe/ukraine-bakhmut-battle.html
5. See, for instance, Shepitko's discussion of her trip to the UNESCO-sponsored symposium "Women in the Media" in Saint Vincent, Italy, in 1975: Larisa Shepitko, "Zhenskie problemy i muzhskoe kino," *Sovetskii ekran*, 19 (1975): 1.
6. Shepitko also produced a "film-concert" *13 PM* (V trinadtsatom chasu nochi), which was supposed to be shown on TV on New Year's Eve, 1968 but was ultimately not casted.
7. On Soviet and post-Soviet criticism and scholarship of Shepitko's work see Nina Sputnitskaya's chapter in this volume.

8. Denis Kozlov and Eleonory Gilburd, "The Thaw as an Event in Russian History," in Kozlov and Gilburd, eds., *The Thaw: Soviet Society and Culture During the 1950s and 1960s* (Toronto, Buffalo, London: University of Toronto Press, 2013), 20.
9. Viktor Zemskov, *Spetsposelentsy v SSSR 1930–1960*, (Moscow: Nauka, 2005).
10. On the history of the Gulag prisoners' release in the 1950s, see Miriam Dobson, *Khrushchev's Cold Summer: Gulag Returnees, Crime, and the Fate of Reform after Stalin* (Ithaca: Cornell UP, 2011).
11. On travel under socialism, see Anne E. Gorsuch and Diane P. Koenker, eds. *Turizm: The Russian and East European Tourist Under Capitalism and Socialism* (Ithaca and London: Cornell University Press, 2006).
12. An excellent account of these events, with a focus on Khrushchev's decision-making see his biography by William Taubman, *Khrushchev: The Man and His Era* (New York and London: W.W. Norton & Co, 2003).
13. For more on the Thaw culture, see: Kozlov and Gilburd's *The Thaw: Soviet Society and Culture during the 1950s and 1960s*, and Anne E. Gorsuch and Diane P. Koenker, *The Socialist Sixties: Crossing Borders in the Second World* (Bloomington and Indianapolis: Indiana UP, 2013).
14. Stephen Kotkin, *Uncivil Society: 1989 and the Implosion of the Communist Establishment* (New York: Modern Library, 2009), 14.
15. For a historical and cultural reconsideration of the stagnation period see Dina Fainberg and Artemy Kalinovsky, *Reconsidering Stagnation in the Brezhnev Era: Ideology and Exchange* (New York: Lexington Books, 2016).
16. Alexei Yurchak, *Everything Was Forever, Until It Was No More: The Last Soviet Generation* (Princeton and Oxford: Princeton UP, 2006), 25.
17. Anatolij Cherniaev, *Sovmestnyi iskhod: dnevnik dvukh epoch*, 1972–1991 (Moscow: ROSSinPEN, 2008), 373.
18. Catriona Kelly, "Beyond Censorship: Goskino USSR and the Management of Soviet Film, 1963–1985," *Slavonic and Eastern European Review*, Vol. 99, Number 3, July 2021, 432–463, 434.
19. Kelly, 437.
20. Khovanskaia, *Kinoveedcheskie zapiski*, 69 (2004): 1071–32.
21. Elem Klimov, ed. *Larisa: Kniga o Larise Shepitko. Volspominaniia. Vystupleniia. Interviv'iu. Kinoscenarii. Stat'ii.* (Moscow: Iskusstvo, 1987), 73.
22. For more on Shepitko's history with censorship authorities see V. Fomin, "Larisa Shepitko: Ia razbilas' v krov'," *Rodina*, 14 (2004). Fomin notes that essentially all her films had a complicated history with censorship—*Heat* was understood as "a horrific ideological diversion," *Wings* "just barely made it into theaters," and after *You and Me*, "her reputation as a seditious director was cemented."
23. Histories of transnational circulation of feminist thinking are just beginning to be written. As Myra Marx Ferree and Alili Mari Tripp write, "In spite of the common perception that feminism originated in the West and diffused to the rest of the world . . . the influences have historically been multidirectional and a product of transnational mutual learning and sharing." Myra Marx Ferree and Aili Mari Tripp, eds., *Global Feminism: Transnational Women's Activism, Organizing, and Human Rights* (New York: New York UP, 2006), 9.

24. Larisa Shepitko, "Zhenskie problemy i muzhskoe kino," *Sovetskii ekran*, 19 (1975): 1.
25. Shepitko, ibid.
26. Yet Shepitko, as a specifically female director, appears to have had an impact on filmmakers in the non-Western world, becoming an inspirational force to advance women in film industries. Masha Salazkina writes, for instance, of the Indian director Basu Bhattacharya, a frequent visitor to Uzbekistan's Tashkent film festival, who commented that after seeing Shepitko's *Wings*, he became much more committed to supporting female filmmakers in his own country. Salazkina, *World Socialist Cinema: Alliances, Affinities and Solidarities and the Global Cold War* (Berkeley: University of California Press, 2023).
27. Lilya Kaganovsky, "Ways of Seeing: on Kira Muratova's *Brief Encounters* and Larisa Shepitko's *Wings*," *Russian Review* 71, no. 3 (2012): 482–499, 486.
28. Kaganovsky, 497.
29. Lida Oukaderova, *The Cinema of the Soviet Thaw: Space, Materiality, Movement* (Bloomington: Indiana UP, 2017), 116–149.
30. Olena Dmytryk, "Difficult Cases: Communist Morality, Gender and Embodiment in Thaw Cinema," *Studies in Russian and Soviet Cinema* 11, no. 1 (2017), 3–19, 7–8.
31. Marina Rojavin, "What Can Be Done About It? I'm a Woman, not a Pet": The Non-Heroic Heroines in Romm's *Nine Days of One Year* and Shepitko's *You and Me*," in Marina Rojavin and Tim Harte, eds., *Women in Soviet Film* (London and New York: Routledge, 2018): 155–175, 160.

PART I

Late Socialism: Cinema, Ideology, Subjectivity

CHAPTER I

Larisa Shepitko at VGIK and in Soviet / Post-Soviet Archives and Press

Nina Sputnitskaya
Translated: Mariia Pankova

Entering the All-Russian Institute of Cinematography (VGIK) in 1955, Larisa Shepitko had little prior professional experience in cinema. A sixteen-year-old young woman attached a recommendation letter from the director of Kyiv Film Studio to her admission documents, where during her school years she was acquiring the basics of filmmaking. According to her school certificate received after studying in Lviv and Kyiv, she achieved the best academic results in the subject of history, with her knowledge being evaluated as "excellent." Her proficiency in Russian and Ukrainian languages, as well as Ukrainian literature, was marked as "good." However, due to a medical condition with her lungs, Shepitko was unexpectedly denied admission to the exam, and only after receiving a new certificate from a tuberculosis dispensary did the rector of VGIK, Vladimir Golovnya, approve her admission.

At the entrance exams, Shepitko demonstrated an excellent command of the subject of foreign languages and the committee credited her high level of erudition in cinema. A draft of a film review preserved in Shepitko's file in the VGIK archive testifies to her determination to stand up against authorities. For the exam, for instance, she was assigned to review the film *Devotion* (Ispytanie vernosti, 1954) by Ivan Pyryev, who at the time served as the director of Mosfilm and was known for his aggressive temper and misogynist attitude in the workplace. The young Shepitko's judgment on the film and its protagonist was quite daring: "The stereotypical scholar Sheksnin is a kind of chubby old man in glasses, most likely with a beard, who loves to remember the old days. When you see Sheksnin, you just feel sorry for the director!"[1] Despite this critical commentary, she passed the entrance examinations and enrolled in the program, studying first in the group of Olexander Dovzhenko, who passed away a year later, and then Mikhail Chiaureli.[2] In 1961, she completed the full course of study; the examination committee awarded her degree in June 1963, after she presented her diploma film *Heat* (Znoi).³

During her studies, the passion and uncompromising nature of the young director became evident, along with her desire to fully immerse herself in the material, which consisted in finding both the characters' authentic psychologies and the corresponding cinematic techniques to express them. As a student, inspired by Dovzhenko's passion for the origins and unique folk culture of Ukraine, she began working in the house museum of the giant of Ukrainian literature Vasyl Stefanyk before adapting his story into a film—one of her earliest film projects while at VGIK. Afterwards, she produced the cinematographic sketch *The Window is Opening Wide* (Okno raspakhnulos'). Like other representatives of this new cohort of Soviet filmmakers such as Andrei Tarkovsky, Andrei Konchalovsky, Elem Klimov, and Mikhail Kalik, she was interested in a childlike, unclouded view of reality, which she explored in this film, deploying a well-known metaphor of an open window in a story about a transformation of the world taking place before the eyes of a five-year-old boy. Following this project, she directed a film based on a novella by Konstantin Paustovsky, *The Blind Cook* (Slepoi povar, 1960), and worked on the documentary film *Living Water* (Zhivaia voda, 1962), about the Pomors, an ethnic group living in Russia's north on the White Sea coast. Her graduation film *Heat* (1963), shot in the steppes of Kyrgyzstan, received wide acclaim, with prizes at film festivals in Central Asia, at the All-State Film Festival in Leningrad, and culminating with the Grand Prix at the International Film Festival in Karlovy Vary, and the jury diploma in Frankfurt am Main. In Kyrgyzstan, for some time, she was informally called the "mother of Kyrgyz cinema."⁴ Many years later Larisa would recall this time as having a "fascinating feeling of brotherhood."⁵

On January 1, 1965, Mikhail Romm, a prominent Soviet filmmaker of an older generation, wrote about Shepitko's *Heat* in a column titled "Wishing Courage," commenting that "the film [*Heat*] she directed was courageous. There was nothing of feminine handicraft in it: sharp conflict, largely sculpted characters, powerful episodes."⁶ He wished Larisa success on her creative path and announced the beginning of her work in the Third Creative Association of the Mosfilm studio, which he was overseeing at the time.

On the eve of International Women's Day on March 7, 1965, Shepitko—then a 26-year old young director—published an article in the newspaper *Moskovskaia Nedelia* (Moscow Week), in which she shared her experience as a student of Dovzhenko and noted her plans for making a film about a female war pilot, which would eventually become her feature film *Wings*. As part of this article, she addressed difficulties faced by women working in cinema and creating female characters: "The protagonist is full of life. I am aspiring to express it from a different position than male directors do. I hope that I will manage to penetrate the world of women, to reveal the causes and origins of many actions."[7] The text ends with a message to young female directors:

> The global film industry tries to persuade repeatedly that directing is not a woman's job. Unfortunately, there are few female directors, especially of the younger generation. There are many reasons for that. I only want to touch upon some qualities that sometimes hinder women directors from 'conquering' cinema. As soon as a fresh VGIK student graduates, even the most capable one, she is left alone with the studio, script, and production, she loses that reserve of courage, energy, and initiative, which male directors never lack. On the International Women's Day, I want to wish my colleagues, female directors, more cheerfulness, confidence, dare, and courage. I wish the most talented female filmmakers to dispel forever the unfair myth and declare creative equality in principle.[8]

Her position as a young female director brought her visibility: the same year, 1965, her portrait adorned the cover of the widely circulated monthly journal *Sovetskii Ekran* (Soviet Screen). Lev Kulidzhanov, the director and head of the Union of Cinematographers, included Shepitko as a young director on the board of the USSR-Uruguay Society, where she represented Soviet cinema overseas along with renowned filmmakers, such as Alexander Stolper and Alexander Ivanov.[9]

When Shepitko's *Wings* was released in 1966, the press received it with mixed, but overall warm reactions. The film provided a new perspective on war, women's role in it, and the generational trauma that the director personally experienced, drawing on her mother's biography to create the character of Nadezhda Petrukhina. However, the film sparked discussions and received ambiguous evaluations in certain circles, as evidenced by the October issue of *Iskusstvo kino* [The Art of Cinema] in 1966. For instance, Vladimir Kardin while generally positive about the film, was dissatisfied with the protagonist. Kardin noted that Shepitko depicted "not the tragedy of the time, but of a bad character."[10] A former commander of a fighter aviation regiment Agniya Polyantseva praised Maya Bulgakova's performance (the actress playing the protagonist), but based on discussions with female veterans, noted that they did not recognize themselves in Petrukhina: "We were not soldiers like Nadezhda Stepanovna."[11] Regarding the portrayal of a lost generation and teenagers' hatred towards a female front-line soldier, she remarked: "It is unnatural and completely unacceptable in our socialist society."[12] However, the presenters, including critics, director Aleksandr Zarkhi and actress Tamara Makarova rated *Wings* as an excellent work. The editorial staff of *Iskusstvo kino*, citing the publication of the script in their earlier issue, indicated how Shepitko's film transformed a cliché story about a female pilot into a drama tied to "certain features of the past time" rather than the character of a woman.[13]

Wings could be called a forgotten masterpiece, as this film's theatrical run was a measly three days. While it wasn't entirely banned, it remained stored away on a shelf for most of the Soviet period. Sometimes it was shown in film clubs and theaters for repeated screenings. But the film's story didn't fit into any generally accepted canons. It was only in post-Soviet times that the film was re-evaluated and called "one of the most humanistic films of the 60s."[14]

In May 1967, Shepitko, as a Ukrainian (which she emphasized in her report), together with the Lithuanian Vitas Zalakavicius, attended the Week of Work by Young Directors of National Republics, organized by the director of the Cinémathèque Française, Henri Langlois in Paris. She presented films of emerging directors from Kyrgyzstan, Lithuania, Latvia, Turkmenistan, Georgia, and Russia. Upon her return, she published "Travel Notes" on the pages of *Sovetskii Ekran*, discussing her trip, reactions in Paris to *Wings*, and meetings with foreign colleagues working in the film industry. Shepitko's fears that foreigners would miss the social context of the film and only read it as a drama about an aging woman did not prove true: according to Shepitko, the film's translator, Lyuda Schnitzer, played an important role in the film's successful international reception. Otherwise, Shepitko expressed regret that her long-awaited meeting with Agnès Varda and Jean-Luc Godard did not happen, although she shared her excitement about getting to know other filmmakers and writers, such as Louis Aragon, Elza Triolet, Georges Simenon, Yuri Annenkov, Sasha Pitoev, Marina Vlady, and other representatives of the "'cream of the crop' of the progressive Russian community living in Paris."[15] And although Shepitko described with enthusiasm how Paris was drowning in red flags (their trip coincided with Alexei Kosygin's visit to France),[16] the notes end with a criticism of the Soviet film distribution process: "I am convinced that we could help sell many of the films we brought. But there wasn't even the smallest detail – brochures, leaflets, photographs. Nothing that any shabby Western firm, interested in spreading its products as widely as possible, would do, and most importantly, almost immediately."[17]

The first success was followed by a series of difficulties. The short film *Motherland of Electricity*, which Shepitko shot in the Kalmyk steppes and which was eagerly awaited by critics, was immediately shelved, with no release. This was followed by a complicated process of making *You and Me*, with constant intrusion of censorship demanding corrections. None of the challenges she faced were reported in the press, and it is worthwhile looking at some of the unpublished responses to *You and Me*, from critics and audiences.

The history of censorship of *You and Me* started with the screenplay, two versions of which were reviewed by the critics Mikhail Bleiman and Rostislav Yurenev, whose comments are preserved in the Russian State Archive of Literature and Art (RGALI). In September 1968, Bleiman compared the film novella to attempts to work "a là Michelangelo Antonioni" and noted that, unlike the works of the Italian master, there was "no logic in the narrative form" in Gennadii Shpalikov's script. However, a year and a half later, responding to another version of the script, he noted Shepitko's ability to chart the characters' development, indicating thus that the script was being edited according to institutional expectations.[18] Yurenev was less critical in his judgments, retaining hopes that Shepitko would be able to realize the screenplay that, according to him was "casual, yet aesthetically pleasing, [written] with great skill."[19] In the studio's final verdict, the director's script was commended for the preclusion of the possibility of interpreting the characters' lives as a dream.[20] Shepitko herself valued the script as "a journey into her extraverted self," thinking of it as a story of awakening, success, and reassessment of values. She was captivated by the task of adapting a plot that consisted of impressions, moods, relationships, collisions, and connections between the film's main protagonists.[21]

Despite the attention that the film received at the Venice Film Festival in 1972, the director considered *You and Me* to be a disappointment. A meeting with viewers, however, might have lessened her dissatisfaction. The following remarks are from the young audience attending a meeting at Moscow State University (MGU) in 1972, the record of which is also preserved in the RGALI archive.[22]

- *The film is much-needed, it can't be expressed in words, in the note, it is life itself!*
- *I didn't believe the girl who attempted suicide.*
- *Thank you for your thought-provoking film.*
- *Life itself!*
- *You were sincere and tried to express emotions with words (I'm not talking about thoughts – it's easier). And your films are so unusual and intense because they reflect your emotional nature.*
- *I didn't get to see the film "You and Me", but even this excerpt gives a general idea, makes you "shake yourself up" and try to start living anew.*
- *Come back to us again. It is interesting to listen to you and there is no need to prepare in advance. You jump from topic to topic but think in front of us. Thank you!*
- *Taking the square root of the degree to which you elevated your film and opening the brackets of the multidimensionality of this film, you conclude that the viewer suffers ONLY because you wanted to see yourself "in a good light" on the screen.*
- *It is impossible!*
- *Do not listen to the math department. The film is brilliant.*
- *I liked the film, thank you. But running away to the tundra is not a solution.*
- *The film reminded me of "Everything for Sale."*[23]
- *Why make this film? I don't understand anything. Why do we care about the problems of 30-year-olds?*
- *Thank you for the film! I am leaving because it doesn't benefit from the explanations. Explain it to 20-year-olds!*

During the conversation, it became clear that although the film excited particularly "the thirty-year-olds," younger viewers were also not indifferent. They voiced contradictory opinions, gave varying ratings to the film, asked to clarify the meanings of certain scenes, and expressed confusion about the open ending. Overall, the discussion was lively and the archived fragments allow us to have a fuller picture of the immediate reception of *You and Me*.

Despite difficulties with censorship in the 1960s and early 1970s, Shepitko gained a reputation as an exemplary Soviet female director, which, in turn, became an important asset for the state agencies. In July 1975, she was sent on a trip to Italy to participate in the UNESCO International Colloquium "Women in Cinema."[24] At the colloquium, she spoke about the keen interest of Europeans in the Soviet experience; reported about the problems of social discrimination against women in film industries and about the difficulties of financing film productions. After the screening of several films and the following discussion, Shepitko noted that the women's movement in cinema had gone beyond specifically feminist issues, it was becoming more serious and all-encompassing.

The meeting led to the establishment of the International Association of Women in Cinema under UNESCO's auspices. Shepitko was one of eight original members of this inaugural council. As reported by the director, the council was supposed to meet in six months at the headquarters in Stockholm to elect the president of the International Association of Women in Cinema. Shepitko then reported on the activities and goals of the international organization, its progressive views, and how she was advised to decline participation in the council, for the reason that out of 30 delegates, only three were representatives of the socialist camp, and only one candidate, Shepitko, was nominated for the council. However, as Shepitko wrote, it was precisely for this reason that she did not risk refusing the position, in order not to incur "the loss of our influence on the directions and development of this organization." At the end of the report, Shepitko announced that the election of the organization's president was postponed until the meeting in Stockholm and concluded her message by stating that the delegates expressed interest in holding the second colloquium meeting in Moscow.

Shepitko's next big endeavor was *The Ascent* (1977), which marked a new phase in her creative production, with her career reaching its apex. Despite its religious undertones, the film, depicting Soviet partisan fighting during World War II, complied with the rhetoric of Soviet war representations. Boris Pavlenok, then the director of the Belorussian State Film Committee, proudly mentioned the film in the January issue of the journal *Iskusstvo kino* in an article that preceded the 60th anniversary of the October Revolution.[25] For him, the protagonist of *The Ascent*, the partisan Sotnikov, was an example of a new kind of Soviet man—a man of independent thinking, who lives according to the communist moral principles, and is "always ready to fight for his convictions," even in the most difficult and deadly circumstances.[26] The film's broad impact captivated viewers and critics, drawing them to explore every aspect of it, including the music by Alfred Schnittke and production design by Yuri Raksha. The film's global reach not only gave Shepitko opportunities to travel abroad but also enabled her to demonstrate proactive involvement in international initiatives. This was reflected in the press, as shown by an article in the newspaper *Vechernyaya Moskva* (Evening Moscow*)*, "Miss Mira iz SSSR" (Miss Peace from the USSR), published on March 7, 1978.

Soviet government agencies again took advantage of the opportunity to turn a female director into an emissary of Soviet ideology abroad by sending her on trips to Western Europe, the United States, and Canada. One of the reports stored at RGALI, co-authored by Shepitko and a senior inspector of "Sovexportfilm" Igor Semeryakov, describes her travel to the United States and Canada.[27] She visited the United States from August 31st to September 6th, 1977, on the special invitation of Telluride International Film Festival's management to show *The Ascent*. The film was screened on the closing day and was recognized as the "best film of all screenings" as per the attendees' reports.[28] For Shepitko, it was an occasion to meet with many prominent international filmmakers, including Martin Scorsese, Liza Minnelli, Agnès Varda, Ellen Burstyn, and Werner Herzog. Following Telluride, an extensive discussion of *The Ascent* took place in Berkeley, where the director met with teachers, students, and cinephiles. She was also invited to meet Francis Ford Coppola, who "was very excited, sincerely congratulated the production team, and expressed readiness to help with the distribution of the film in the United States."[29] Later, another screening took place at the Museum of Modern Art in New York, followed by an invitation to Hollywood to direct a film based on the book *Silence of the North*, the screenplay for which was written specifically for the actress Ellen Burstyn, who presented Shepitko with the novel.

The report on Shepitko's North American trip shows that two distribution companies, "660 NY-films" and "Cinema 5," offered to buy *The Ascent*; another distribution company, "Amikos-film," which had acquired the distribution rights to Shepitko's film two months earlier, also discussed its plans for the film's theatrical release. A hope was expressed that Shepitko's three other films – *Heat*, *Wings*, and *You and Me* would be scheduled for a retrospective screening, parallel to an event taking place in West Berlin. Furthermore, it was proposed that *The Ascent* be submitted for an Oscar nomination in the category of "Best Foreign Film of the Year," and a telegram confirming this fact was received upon Shepitko's return to Moscow. Another report briefly talks about the Toronto Film Festival which Shepitko attended from September 15th to 19th, and during which she apparently was struck by the West's "catastrophic ignorance of our contemporary life, the complete lack of accurate information about the democracy, fulness, and spiritual life of our society."[30]

Archival materials document the significant attention paid to the reaction of Francis Ford Coppola to *The Ascent*, who shared with Shepitko the details of his working process on the film *Apocalypse Now* and expressed interest in collaboration with Soviet filmmakers. Interestingly, a separate paragraph in the report is dedicated to Milos Forman, who allegedly assured the delegation from the Soviet Union of his "normal and loyal relationship with [his] homeland, Czechoslovakia," and expressed his dream of visiting the USSR for the Moscow International Film Festival. The report concludes with a complaint about the limited resources allocated for the trip.

It is worth noting another publication about the "Shepitko-Coppola Case." In 1985, the art and film historian Ilya Vaisfeld published a letter from Karina Mukaseeva, a graduate of the VGIK and a friend of Shepitko, about Shepitko's impression of her meeting with Coppola, especially his complaints about how film production was structured in the United States. The letter states,

> He had heard about *The Ascent* and wanted to see it. Nothing was impossible for him. He arranged for both the film and the director to be brought to him. I don't remember how the introduction happened. What's important is something else. He dismissed everyone and decided to watch it only with Larisa. He had several screening rooms. They sat down, and the film began. He watched it eagerly. When the lights came on, he immediately started passionately lauding and celebrating Larisa's achievement. Then he fell silent. And he cried in front of Larisa. Not during the film. After. He cried intensely, desperately. It shook him. As he explained it, it was out of envy. He started shouting, 'How did you manage this – so complete! Everything – the plot, the characters!' He cried and shouted, 'You are lucky!!! You can afford this perfection, completeness. But in *Apocalypse Now*, I got confused and didn't know the ending. I had to make eight different endings, you see?' Shepitko vividly described this encounter, with her hands shaking – spilling coffee, her voice lower than usual, almost fading away. I have never seen her so excited in my life.[31]

The letter goes on to mention that Coppola is currently on the verge of bankruptcy, and the author concluded that *The Ascent* became not only Shepitko's triumph but also an ideological victory for the USSR.

The documents regarding the participation of Soviet cinema at the London International Film Festival, held from November 22 to December 1, 1977, in which Shepitko took part, also contain some intriguing information. Written on December 2, 1977, it recounts the screening of *The Ascent* on November 23 in the Royal Festival Hall, and its "unanimous adulation."[32] Shepitko described the film's positive public reception, as well as a 40-minute broadcast on November 30 on BBC television, dedicated to contemporary reflections on the struggle against fascism in art and cinema, including in films by Bernardo Bertolucci, Thodoros Angelopoulos, and Shepitko. Unlike other filmmakers, Shepitko was invited not for three but seven days, which, in her opinion, indicated an interest in Soviet cinema from the "English representatives." Furthermore, Shepitko was invited to deliver a series of lectures at the National Film Institute, but she did not "take responsibility for resolving this matter."

Shepitko also noted the great interest in distributing *The Ascent* expressed by the representatives of international distribution companies, who she referred to the Soviet delegation in London. But she remarked that she never saw the Soviet delegation representative, Comrade Yartsev, at the festival, and he did not carry out the necessary work with the distributors. In the report's conclusion, the author highlighted the absence of "complete and accurate information regarding the state of contemporary Soviet cinema" abroad and advocated for the development of intercultural contact between the USSR and Great Britain. This unplanned trip required additional financial expenses and efforts, but Shepitko considered them justified.

An interest in Shepitko's work further intensified after her tragic death. Her works were thoroughly analyzed in publications by accomplished Soviet film scholars, in textbooks, and specialized sections of academic publications dedicated to the cinema of the 1960s and 1970s. Aleksandr Macheret, in his book *O poetike kinoiskusstva* [*On the Poetics of Cinematic Art*], provides a detailed analysis of how an authentic image is achieved in Shepitko's *Wings*. The researcher finds a basis for constructing the character of Petrukhina in Chekhov's *Ivanov* and characterizes Shepitko's film as one of the most significant in the cohort of the 1960s films, one that addressed viewers without an authoritative dictum and stimulated an independent reflection.[33]

Yakov Varshavsky considers Shepitko's films among the best in Soviet cinema.[34] The Lithuanian writer Eduardas Mezhelaitis, in a conversation with Elga Lyndina, speaks highly of Shepitko's work with the literature on war.[35] The film scholar Valentin Mikhalkovich, in his article "Sounds and Meanings," examines the peculiarities of the visual representation of the world inhabited by Shepitko's characters. He identifies the primacy of the elements [*stikhia*] over narrative logic, the "expressiveness of sounds" of the "collective soul," a "fierce spatiality," and a distinctive rhythmic organization in Shepitko's adaptation of Andrei Platonov's prose in *Motherland of Electricity*. He argues that together with other filmmakers of the 1960s, she brought about a "restructuring of the cinematic language."[36] Furthermore, the Bureau of Film Propaganda published the brochure *Larisa Shepitko* with a print run of 100,000 copies in 1982, prepared by the prominent Soviet film critics Victor Demin and Vera Shitova.[37]

Another set of publications are dedicated to Shepitko's colleagues, allowing for a detailed examination of all aspects of Shepitko's creative imagination. One of the most interesting is the collection *Khudozhnik kino Yuri Raksha* [Film Artist Yuri Raksha], which features photographs of Shepitko taken during the production of *The Ascent*.[38] A significant body of publications is dedicated to the memory of Larisa Shepitko. Among them are newspaper articles, particularly those related to the premiere of the two-part film *Farewell* [Proshchanie], completed by her husband Elem Klimov. He also compiled the book *Larisa*, featuring memories, scripts, and critical texts on Shepitko.

On May 12, 1983, several newspapers featured articles about the unveiling of a memorial at the Novokuznetsk Cemetery in Moscow, dedicated to a group of filmmakers who died during the filming of *Farewell*. The memorial honored the director, cinematographer, production designer, and other staff members from the Mosfilm studio. To commemorate the unveiling, an evening event dedicated to Larisa Shepitko's work took place at the Central House of Cinema, where the film *Farewell* and excerpts from her other works were screened. In the summer of 1990, there were reports about the opening of a memorial plaque in Lviv on the building of School No. 13 on Spartak Street, "where the Laureate of the State Prize – Larisa Shepitko – studied."[39]

Yuri Vizbor, in his memoirs "Kogda vse byli vmeste . . ." (When All Were Together . . .) provides a detailed account of their collaboration in *You and Me*, complementing his narrative with Shepitko's personal statements.[40] Director Gleb Panfilov recalls her triumph at the Berlin International Film Festival in West Berlin and her incredible beauty, stating, "I couldn't make any sense of it. Why? Why isn't she an actress, a movie star? And, in the end, I understood: not even the biggest role could express her as much as an author's film could."[41] In the newspaper *Knizhnoe obozrenie* [Book Review] on August 7, 1987, the prominent Kyrgyz writer Chingiz Aitmatov and Belarusian writer Vasil Bykov remembered Shepitko's fervent dedication to art, describing her as an "intensely thinking artist."[42] Aitmatov especially admired her ability to work in difficult steppe conditions during the shooting of *Heat*, as well as her willpower and stoic character. Both writers recognize Shepitko's special talent, her ability to rejoice in the success of friends and colleagues. In the same publication, writer Valentin Rasputin, the author of *Farewell to Matyora* [Proshchanie s materoi], on which Shepitko/Klimov's *Farewell* is based, notes her uniqueness and spirituality, stating that the memory of such individuals "helps to retain our conscience." Bykov further notes that Shepitko never tried to persuade others of her opinions but merely shared her vision, and it was through her fervor that she captivated writers whose work she adapted. It was her determination and commitment from the very outset of the work, that amazed Bykov.

Furthermore, the poet Bella Akhmadulina characterized Shepitko as "Charming, delicate, and defenseless, yet somehow spartan." According to her, many mistook Shepitko's restraint, her "concealment of sorrows and passions" for strength and invulnerability, which, however, only disguised her problems. Remembering their joint work on Akhmadulina's role in *You and Me* (which never materialized, as Akhmadulina was not approved for this role by the authorities), she paid tribute to the director's ability to manipulate actors: "Everything Larisa wanted from me, she could get, and I was somehow not involved in the process." In 1988, the readers of *Sovetskii Ekran* were treated to the actor Yuri Vizbor's detailed account of his work with Larisa Shepitko, and the actress Alla Demidova on the set of *You and Me*. Vizbor shared previously unknown details of the production, including Shepitko's serious illness during the film shooting.

Significant attention was given to Shepitko's cinema when her films became more accessible after the Perestroika and the Fifth Congress of Cinematographers taking place in May 1986.[43] Her work was reassessed and reinterpreted with the reliance on archival materials. Viktor Demin, during a memorial evening for Shepitko in 1988, recalled that "in her terms, nine years is equivalent to three films. Three films that do not exist"—referring to the nine years that passed since her death during which she could have produced another body of work. He believed that she would have been an active participant in the Fifth Congress of Cinematographers because she had a special trait: "She constantly sought to reinvent herself in order to correspond to a new stage of her ever-changing surroundings."[44] It was also during these years that the broader public learned about the existence of *The Homeland of Electricity*. Reviews of this short appeared in the pages of the journals *Sputnik kinokritika* in 1987 and *Iskusstvo kino* in 1988. The official newspaper *Pravda* revealed the information about the film even earlier, in January of 1986.[45]

Oleg Kovalov and Alexander Lipkov, as well as Algimantas Kundialis wrote about Shepitko with great enthusiasm in their reviews of the essay collection *Larisa*, emphasizing the timeliness of Shepitko's cinema, the possibility of rediscovering her well-known films, and seeing the works that were rejected by censorship.[46] The 1980s became a time when a more accurate and comprehensive portrait of the director was created, with critics paying particular attention to her anticipation of change and her desire to resist the official discourse, which was visible in her images. A series of publications dedicated to the 50th anniversary of her birth in 1988 also points to new explorations in the field of Shepitko's studies. This includes the article "She Taught Us Not to Step Back" (Ona uchila ne otstupat') in *Sovetskaia Kultura* (Soviet Culture). Furthermore, on December 25, 1987, Central Television began a retrospective screening of Shepitko's films in honor of her anniversary.

A new chapter in Shepitko's criticism begins in the 1990s when the era of discoveries of victims of the Soviet censorship was replaced by a low rate of new film releases. With an increasing urgency, questions concerning the future of the film industry in the territories of the former Soviet Union were debated in the pages of film journals. These publications frequently recalled the 1960s and its filmmakers, who, after a fleeting moment of freedom during the Thaw period, had to confront the harsh censorship of the Brezhnev era. Nevertheless, they survived many trials and tribulations. Among this group of texts are such books as Ales' Adamovich's *My—shestidesiatniki* [We, the Sixtiers], Lev Annensky's *Shestidesiatniki my* [The Sixtiers and Us], and Valerii Fomin's *Kino i vlast'. Sovetskoe kino, 1965–1985 gody: dokumenty, svidetel-staval, razmushleniia* [Cinema and Power. Soviet Cinema, 1965–1985: Documents, Testimonies, Reflections] among many others.

A separate category of literature about Shepitko consists of memoirs about key episodes in her life and her role in the lives of other artists. For example, the actress Alla Demidova, who played the main female protagonist in *You and Me*, recalls her time working with Shepitko on the film.[47] Natalya Bondarchuk, in her book *Edinstvennye dni* [The Only Days], writes about Shepitko's friendship with Andrei Tarkovsky and about their mutual influence on each other. Shepitko apparently approved Bondarchuk for a role in *You and Me*, after her unsuccessful auditions for Tarkovsky's *Solaris*. After seeing Shepitko's film footage, Tarkovsky apparently reconsidered his verdict and invited the actress to audition for the role of Hari in *Solaris* once again, ultimately confirming her for the role. Furthermore, the actress recalls a horrifying episode when, as a guest at Klimov and Shepitko's, she attempted to take her own life, apologizing to the participants of those events for the incident. Shepitko also often appears in recollections about mystical events and tragic destinies in the lives of famous people, or as a figure that adds vivid colors to less prominent, non-artistic individuals. For example, N. Andreev in the article "Podvig partapparatchika Kunitsyna" [The Great Deed of The Party Apparatchik Kunitsyn] recalls the role of the bureaucrat Kunitsyn in defending important films during the period of stagnation, concluding his article with the following anecdote:

> Larisa Shepitko showed her famous film *The Ascent* at the House of Cinema Veterans, which is about the fate of the partisan Sotnikov, who remains unbroken in the face of death. After the screening, someone from the audience shouted at her, 'Where have you seen such Sotnikovs in real life?' And she, pointing at Kunitsyn, said, 'There he is, Sotnikov.'[48]

Important details about Shepitko's life can be found in the book *Elem Klimov: Nesniatoe kino* [Elem Klimov: Unfilmed Cinema] and in various materials dedicated to the family of these two prominent filmmakers, ranging from academic works to popular TV adaptations by Fyodor Razzakov, which are easily accessible to the average viewer.[49]

Shepitko has been often the subject of publications by film historian Valery Fomin, who has chronicled in detail Soviet filmmakers' struggles in the 1960s and 70s against Soviet censors. The publicist Dal' Orlov, however, takes a more critical stance towards Shepitko. In his autobiography *Replika v zal: zapiski dejstvuiushchego litsa* [*Replica in the Hall: Notes of an Acting Participant*], he adds his insights to the production and postproduction history of *The Ascent*. He denies, for instance, the possibility of any obstacles to the film's release and recalls Shepitko's intense—and not necessarily ethical—work with actors. Relying in particular on Boris Plotnikov's recollections (Plotnikov played one of the two main protagonists in *The Ascent*), Orlov relays a story of the actor receiving urotropine drops in his eyes to help generate the character's stunning gaze, and reporting that "his full vision only returned after six months."[50] Orlov also describes how Plotnikov had to "lay on the ground, while they poured frozen ice into his hair. Since then, he [has] started going bald . . ."[51]

The press's interest in Shepitko's works, particularly in *The Ascent*, was reignited after the release of Sergei Loznitsa's film *V tumane* [*In the Fog*, 2012]. Thus the film critic Anton Dolin argues that Loznitsa's film, which, like *The Ascent*, is based on Vasil' Bykov's prose, reproduces the text more accurately, noting that Loznitsa tells "a story of the innocent, just as *The Ascent* was a story of the guilty." The 80th anniversary of Shepitko did not go unnoticed either. In January 2018, her autobiographical novella was published in the newspaper *Ekran i stena* [*Screen and Stage*]. Articles and archival materials describing Shepitko as an outstanding graduate of VGIK also appeared in publications of VGIK dedicated to the centenary of the film institute, such as in Vladimir Malyshev's collection *Mechtaiu uchit'sia vo VGIKe . . .!* [*Dreaming of Studying at the VGIK . . .!*].

In conclusion, it is worth noting the main trends in how Shepitko's work has been discussed in today's Russia. Her creative output is frequently analyzed in regard to gender questions and in the context of Russian religious existentialism and Christian dogmas. Shepitko's films are repeatedly understood as anti-war films, "depicting the tragic nature of war, which is destructive to human spirituality."[52] Great attention is paid to the musical and sound textures of her films (I. Shilova, Yu. Mikheeva, E. Rusinova, A. Miroshkina, A. Mukhamadeeva).

In recent years, Russian educational television channels have released and frequently broadcasted films about Shepitko. Among them are such TV programs as *Razgovor s Larisoi* [*A Conversation with Larisa*, 1999], *Zachem perezhila tebia liubov' moia* [*Why My Love Survived You*, 2007], *Voskhozhdenie Larisy Shepitko* [*The Ascension of Larisa Shepitko*, 2008], *Ia zaveshchaiu tebe . . . Yuri Raksha* [*I Bequeath to You . . . Yuri Raksha*, 2008), and *Vstrechi s Vladimirom Gostiukhinym* [*Encounters with Vladimir Gostyukhin*] at the Boris Yeltsin Presidential Center. Additionally, there are television episodes from the series *Ostrova* [Islands], titled "Larisa Shepitko" (dir. T. Skabard, 2012) and a documentary film *The Golgotha of Larisa Shepitko* (dir. A. Kazakevich, and K. Golenchik, 2017).

TEXTS PUBLISHED ON SHEPITKO IN RUSSIAN

1960s

Dautova, L. "Svetloe pobezhdaet." *Sovetskii ekran* 15 (1963): 14.
"Kryl'ia". Podrobnyj razgovor» [Lazarev Lazar', Kardin Vladimir, Polyanceva A., Papava Mikchail, Zarkhi Alexander, Makarova Tamara, Shitova Vera, Shtein Alexander]. *Iskusstvo kino* 10 (1966): 12–30.
Maksimenko V. "Zakonomernosti talanta". *Molodoi kommunist* 9 (1967): 116–119.
"Nachalo. Larisa Shepitko". *Iskusstvo kino*, 6 (1965): 49.
Romm, Mikhail. "Zhelaiu muzhestva." *Sovetskoe kino*, January 1, 1965, 7.
Shepitko, Larisa. "Raskazyvaet Larisa Shepitko." *Moskovskaia nedelia*, March 7, 1965.
Shepitko, Larisa. "Nedelia dlinoiu v dva mesiatsa. Putevye zapiski." *Sovetskii ekran* 5 (1967): 16–17.
Shepitko, Larisa. "Dlia kogo stavitsia fil'm?" *Iskusstvo kino* 6 (1968): 31–33.

1970s

Ashimov, K. and V. Furtichev, eds., *Kino Sovetskoi Kirgizii*. Moscow: Iskusstvo, 1979.
Laskina, Alla. "Derevo zhizni". *Literaturnaya gazeta*, August 22. 1979.
Pavlenok, Boris. "Vstupaia v iubileinyi god". *Iskusstvo kino* 1 (1977): 6–14.
Pokarin V. "Saga o dvoikh v lesu." *Sovetskii fil'm* 8 (1977): 35–37.
Posadskii, Evgenii. "Voskhozhdenie." Ivanovo, May 7, 1977
Rubina, M. "Vybor. *Sovetskaia Sibir', Novosibirsk*, April 26, 1977.
Shilova, Irina. *Fil'm i ego muzyka*. Moscow: Sovetskii kompozitor, 1973.
Shiriaev Yurii. "O vremeni i o sebe". *Moskovskaia kinonedelia*, October 4, 1970.
Smirnov P. "Voskhozhdenie." *Izvestiia*, February 21, 1977.
"V muromskikh leash". *Komsomol'skaia iskra*, January 25, 1976.
Vasil'kova I. "Miss mira" iz SSSR." *Vecherniaia Moskva*, March 7, 1978.
Shepitko, Larisa "Chuvstvo udivitel'nogo bratstva". *Sovetskii ekran* 22 (1978): 8–9.
"S'iomochnaia gruppa priglashaet . . ." *Muromskij rabochii*, January 9, 1976.
Shepitko, Larisa "Voskhozhdenie. Poslednee interv'iu Larisy Shepitko." *Literaturnoe obozrenie* 9 (1979): 98–101.

1980s

Abdullaev, Bayram. *Vstrechnoe dvizhenie. Opyt vzaimodeistviia literatury i kino na materiale sredneaziatskogo regiona*. Ashkhabad: Institut Istorii im. Sh. Batyrova,1986.
Ashimov, Kaarman. *Kino Kirgizii*. Moscow: Soiuzinformkino, 1981.

Bazavliuk Marina, and Vladimir Gostyuhin, Victor Demin, Vera Shitova, eds. *Larisa Shepi'ko*. Moscow: Vsesoyuznoe byuro propagandy kinoiskusstva, 1982.
Berman, Boris. "Kniga o Larise." *Moskovskie Novosti*, Nobember 16, 1987.
Demin, Victor and Vera Shitova. *Larisa Shepitko*. Moscow: All-Union Bureau of Film Propaganda, 1982.
Demin, Victor. "Tri fil'ma, kotoryh net . . ." *Moskovskii komsomolets*, January 14, 1988.
Kapralov, Georgii. "'Rodina elektrichestva.' Neizvestnyi fil'm Larisy Shepitko." *Pravda*, January 28, 1986.
Kapralov, Georgii. "Svidanie s sovest'iiu. Vspominaia Larisu Shepitko." *Pravda*, January 11. 1988.
Kovalov, Oleg. "Iz smireniya ne pishutsya stihotvoreniya." *Sovetskii ekran* 23 (1987): 4–5.
Kovalev, Oleg and Aleksandr Lipkov, Algimantas Kyndialis. "Larisa." *Kino* 1 (1988): 10–11.
Klimov, Elem, ed. *Larisa*. Moscow: Iskusstvo, 1987.
Kundyalis Algimantas. "Vspominaya Larisu. . . ." *Kino. Vil'nyus* 1 (1988): 10–11.
"Larisa." *Knizhnoe obozrenie*. 32 (1987): 3.
"Larisa. Kniga o Larise Shepitko." *Sovetskii ekran*. 5 (1987): 18–19.
Lipkov, Alexander. "Po maksimumu." *Literaturnoe obozrenie* 6 (1987): 92–95.
Lipkov, Alexander. "Vremia nadezhd." *Kino. Riga* 4 (1987): 4–5.
Macheret, Alexander. *O poetike kinoiskusstva*. Moscow: Iskusstvo, 1981.
Makarov, Alexander. "Nachalo nevedomogo veka." *Sputnik kinozritelia* 11 (1987): 4.
Medvedev, Armen. *Chto chelovek dolzhen*. Moscow: Vsesoyuznoe byuro propagandy inoiskusstva, 1986.
Miagkova, Irina. "Ni vyrazit' slovom, ni kriknut'." Sovetskaia kul'tura, Febrary 13, 1988.
Mezhelaitis, Eduardas. "Khhleb dushi." Iskusstvo kino. 1 (1984): 6–17.
Mikhalkovich, Valentin. "Zvuchaniia i znacheniia." *Iskusstvo kino* 1 (1988): 39–43.
Ognev, Vladimir. "20 let nazad . . .". *Iskusstvo kino* 1 (1988): 32–39.
Panfilov, Gleb. "Ona s nami." *Smena* 5 (1986): 23, 25.
Plakhov, Andrei. *Kinoletopis' podviga. Informatsiia № 2*. Moscow: Soyuzinformkino, 1985.
Raksha, Irina, ed. *Khudozhnik kino Yuri Raksha*. Moscow: Vsesoyuznoe byuro propagandy kinoiskusstva. 1983.
Rasputin, Valentin. "Svetonosnost'." *Smena* 5 (1986): 23.
Seregina, Natalia. "Khudozhestvennoe obobshchenie temy." *Sovetskaia muzyka*, 6 (1980): 11–16.
Shepitko, Larisa. "Obiazana pered soboj i pered liud'mi . . ." [Dva poslednih interv'yu L. Shepitko 1977–1978]. K 50-letiyu so dnya rozhdeniya L. E. Shepitko." *Iskustvo kino* 1 (1988): 93–98.
Vaisfel'd, Iliya. "Ispoved' v prosmotrovom zale." *Sputnik kinofestivalia*, 2 (1985): 7.
Varshavskii, Yakov. *Esli fil'm talantliv*. Moscow: Iskusstvo, 1984.
Vizbor, Yrii. "Kogda my byli vmeste . . ." *Yunost'* 4 (1983): 104–110.
Vylegzhanina Svetlana and Imran Melikov. *Nashi sovremenniki na ekrane*. Frunze: Ilim, 1983.

1990s

Adamovich Ales', ed. *My – shestidesyatniki: stat'i.* Moscow: Sovetskii pisatel', 1991.
Annenskii, Lev. *Shestidesyatniki i my: Kinematograf, stavshii i ne stavshii istoriei.* Moscow: Vsesoiuznoe tvorcheskoe proizvodstvennoe ob`edinenie "Kinotsentr," 1991.
Fomin. Valerii. "Te, chto pliashut i poyut po dorogam." *Ekran i stsena* 44 (1997): 8–9.
Krashevskaya O. "Pamiati Larisy." *Sovetskaia kul'tura*, July 23, 1990.
Vlasov, Marat. *Sovetskoe kinoiskusstvo 50-kh-60-kh godov: Uchebnoe posobie.* Moscow: VGIK, 1993.

2000s

Batenina, Elena. "Elem i Larisa." *Observatoriia kul'tury* 5 (2008): 74–83.
Bogdanova, Galina and Kruglikova, Elena. *Velikie zhenshchiny XX veka.* Moscow: Martin. 2002.
Bondarchuk, Natalia. *Edinstvennye dni.* Moscow: AST Astrel', 2009.
Fomin, Valerii. "Ya razbilas' v krov'." *Rodina* 6 (2005): 54–61.
Margolit, Evgenii. "Tikhoe kino." *Kinovedcheskie zapiski*, 92/93 (2009): 238–248.
Klimov, German and Marina Murzina, eds. *Elem Klimov. Nesnyatoe kino. Scenarii. Interv'iu. Vospominaniya.* Moscow: Izdatelskii dom "Hronikyor," 2008.
Muhamadeeva, Alfia. "Poeziya i tragediya narodnoj zhizni." *Iz naslediya otechestvennyh kompozitorov XX veka. Sb. statej po materialam tvorcheskih sobranij molodyh issledovatelej.* Romanshchuk, Inna, ed. Moscow: ROO "Soyuz moskovskih kompozitorov," 2007, 130–143.
Orlov, Dal'. *Replika v zal: zapiski deistvuiushchego litsa.* Moscow: Novaya elita, 2001.
Razzakov, Fedor. *Zvezdnye pary: suprugi, liobvniki, liubovnitsy.* Moscow: Eksmo-Press, 2000.

2010s

Demidova, Alla. *Zerkal'nyi labirint.* Moscow: Proza i K, 2013.
Dolin, Anton. "Dal'she v les". May 25. 2012. https://www.gazeta.ru/culture/2012/05/25/a_4601025.shtml
Fomin, Valerii. "Letopis' nashego Soyuza. God 1978." *Sk-novosti*, January 21. 2013.
Fomin, Valerij *Peresechenie parallel'nykh-2.* Moscow: Ministry of Culture of the Russian Federation, NII kinoiskusstva (VGIK), Kanon +. 2014.
Malyshev Vladimir and Dmitriy Karavaev, Maksim Kazyuchits, Nina Sputnitskaya, eds. *Mechtayu uchit'sya vo VGIKe . . . Iz lichnyh del vypusknikov VGIKa.* Moscow: OOO "Veche," 2019.
Mikhailik, Elena, "Sovetskii ekzistentsializm: Put' geroia k sebe (Na materiale avtorskikh fil'mov 1960–1980–kh godov.)" *Yaroslavskij pedagogicheskij vestnik*, 6 (2015): 252–256.
Miroshkina, Alfia. *Kinomuzyka Al'freda Shnitke: opyt issledovaniya.* Dissertatsia na soiskanie uchenoi stepeni kandidata iskusstvovedeniya, Magnitogorsk, 2017.

Plakhov, Andrei. *Kino na grani nervnogo sryva*. Saint Petersburg: Knizhnye masterskie. Masterskaya "Seans," 2014.

Razzakov, Fedor. *Kak ukhodili kumiry: pamiat' sogrevaiushchaia serdtsa*. Moscow: Eksmo-Press, 2010.

Shepitko, Larisa. "Dvoe." *Ekran i stsena*, 2 (2018): 6–7, 14–15.

Zaitseva, Lidia. *Ekrannyi obraz vremeni ottepeli*. Moscow: VGIK; Sankt-Peterburg: Nestor-Istoriya, 2017.

2020s

Andreev, Nikolai. "Podvig partapparatchika Kunicyna." *Rodina*, 10 (2022): 60–64.

Piskunovskaya, Daria "Obraz zhenshchiny-tvortsa v sovremennom dokumental'nom kino." In *World Science: Problems and Innovations. Sbornik Statei LIII Mezhdunarodnoi nauchno-prakticheskoj konferentsii*. Penza, 2021: 276–278.

NOTES

1. Personal file of Larisa Shepitko, the VGIK archive, p. 17.
2. Shepitko also made her acting debut in *Poem of the Sea* (Poema o more, 1958), Dovzhenko's last film, finished by his wife, Yuliya Solntseva, after Dovzhenko's death.
3. RGALI, file 3095, p. 791.
4. On the Role of Shepitko in the development of Kyrgyz Cinema, see K. Ashimov, V. Furtichev, eds., *Kino Sovetskoi Kirgizii* (Moscow: Iskusstvo, 1979), 121–125; and Svetlana Vylegzhanina and Imran Melikov, eds., *Nashi sovremenniki na ekrane*, (Frunze: Ilim, 1983), 44.
5. Larisa Shepitko, "Chuvstro udivitel'nogo bratstva," *Sovetskii ekran*, 22 (1978): 8–9.
6. Mikhail Romm, "Zhelaiu muzhestva," *Sovetskoe kino*, January 1, 1965, 7.
7. Larisa Shepitko, "Rasskazyvaet Larisa Shepitko," *Moskovskaia Nedelia*, March 7, 1965, 11.
8. Ibid.
9. RGALI, File 2936, Opis'1, delo. 2213, p. 1.
10. "'Kryl'ia.' Podrobnyii razgovor," *Iskusstvo kino*, 10 (1966): 12–30, 12.
11. Ibid., 18.
12. Ibid., 18.
13. Ibid., 30.
14. Andrei Shemiakhin, https://www.culture.ru/live/movies/3067/krylya-larisa-shepitko-1966
15. Larisa Shepitko, "Nedelia dlinoiu v dva mesiatsa. Putevye zapiski," *Sovetskii ekran* 5 (1967): 16–17.
16. The Chairman of the Council of Ministers of the USSR under Stalin and Brezhnev, he set a record for the longest tenure in that position. The Eighth Five-Year Plan (1966–1970), which took place during the era of Kosygin's

economic reforms, became the most successful in Soviet history and earned the nickname "golden."
17. Shepitko, 17.
18. RGALI, File 2944. Opis'4, delo 2039.
19. Ibid., p. 7.
20. Ibid., p. 22.
21. Ibid., p. 11.
22. RGALI, File 3223, Opis' 1, delo 163 [Notes sent for the discussion of the film "You and Me" at Moscow State University].
23. The film by Andrzej Wajda from 1968.
24. RGALI, file. 2944, opis' 13, delo 2581.
25. Boris Pavlenok, "Vstupaia v iubileinyi god," *Iskusstvo kino*, 1 (1977), 6–14.
26. Ibid., 9.
27. State organization engaged in foreign economic activity in the field of cinema, including distribution of Soviet films abroad and acquisition of foreign films for screening in Russia.
28. RGALI, file. 2944, Opis' 13. delo 3138, p. 43.
29. Ibid.
30. Ibid., 45.
31. Il'ia Vaisfeld, "Ispoved' v prosmotrovom zale," *Sputnik kinofestivalia* 2 (1985), 7.
32. RGALI, File 294, Opis'13, delo 3053.
33. Aleksandr Macheret, *O poetike kinoiskusstiva* (Moscow: Iskusstvo, 1981), 157–167.
34. Yakov Varshavsky, *Esli fil'm talantliv* (Moscow: Iskusstvo, 1984).
35. Eduardas Mezhelaitis, "Khleb dushi," *Iskusstvo Kino* 1 (1984): 6–17.
36. Valentin Mikhalkovich, "Zvuchaniia i znacheniia," *Iskusstvo Kino*, 1 (1988): p. 39.
37. Victor Demin and Vera Shitova, *Larisa Shepitko* (Moscow: All-Union Bureau of Film Propaganda, 1982).
38. Irina Raksha, ed. *Khudozhnik kino Yuri Raksha* (Moscow: All-Union Bureau of Film Propaganda, 1983).
39. O. Krasheskaya, "In Memory of Larisa," *Sovetskaia kul'tura* July 23, 1990, 6.
40. Yuri Vyzbor, "Kogda vse byli vmeste," *Youth*. 4 (1983): 104–110.
41. Gleb Panfilov, "Ona s nami," *Smena* 5 (1986): pp. 23, 25.
42. Chingiz Aitmatov and Vasil Bykov "Larisa," *Knizhnoye Obozreniye*, August 7, 1987. p. 11.
43. The Revolutionary Congress, where a series of fundamental decisions were made, particularly regarding the removal of films from the "shelf," the revision of censorship restrictions, and the condemnation of the policies of the Union of Cinematographers' leaders.
44. Victor Demin, "Tri fil'ma, kotorykh net," *Moskovsky komsomolets*, January 14, 1988, 9.
45. Kapralov G. "Rodina elektrichestva. Nezivestnyi fil'm Larisy Shepitko," *Pravda*, January 28, 1986, 6.
46. Oleg Kovalov, Aleksandr Lipkov, and Algimantas Kyndialis, "Larisa," *Kino* 1 (1988): 10–11.
47. Alla Demidova, *Zerkal'nyj labirint* (Moscow: Proza, 2013), esp. the chapter "Penie obozzhonnym gorlom ili Larisa Shepitko, pp. 504–515.

48. Nikolai Andreev, "Podvig partapparatchika Kunitsyna," *Rodina*, 10 (2022): 60–64.
49. Fedor Razzakov, *Zvezdnye pary: suprugi, liubovniki, liubovnitsy* (Moscow: EKSMO-Press, 2000); Razzakov, *Kak ukhodili kumiry. Pamiat- sogrevaiushchaia serdtsa* (Moscow: Eksmo, 2010).
50. Orlov, 405.
51. Ibid.
52. Lidia Zaitseva, *Ekrannyi obraz vremeni ottepeli* (Moscow: VGIK; Sankt-Peterburg: Nestor-Istoriya, 2017), 50–52, 54–56, 89–95, 185–189.

CHAPTER 2

Larisa Shepitko, Aleksei German, and the Trials and Tribulations of Post-Thaw Soviet Filmmaking

Tim Harte

Two of the more distinctive cinematic voices to emerge at the tail end of the Soviet Thaw were, without a doubt, those of Larisa Shepitko and Aleksei German. Along with Kira Muratova, Shepitko and German came of age in the late 1960s as prominent, innovative filmmakers boasting unique visions and auteur sensibilities shaped by the early Thaw period and that period's potent sense of artistic possibility. Shepitko would subsequently enjoy a successful, albeit brief filmmaking career tragically cut short by a fatal automobile accident; German would outlive the Soviet Union but encounter severe mid-career censorship that limited his productivity as a filmmaker. Both, however, would make their mark on post-Thaw Soviet cinema. It is the overlapping film work of Shepitko and German that constitutes the focus of this chapter, which will probe the ways in which the parallel artistry of these two celebrated filmmakers reflected broad aesthetic tendencies and themes in post-Thaw Soviet cinema as well as the challenges faced by film directors within the Soviet system. Although possessing divergent artistic sensibilities, Shepitko and German—both born in 1938—together encapsulated a defiant response to and revision of Stalinist cinematic tropes while offering a resolute path forward for late Soviet cinema.

The films of Shepitko and German overlapped in both conspicuous and inconspicuous ways. The stultifying, small city setting of Shepitko's first major film, *Wings* (*Krylia*, 1966), would, for instance, be replicated in much of German's work, most notably his *Twenty Days Without War* (*Dvadtsat' dnei bez voiny*, 1976) and *My Friend Ivan Lapshin* (*Moi drug Ivan Lapshin*, 1983, released 1986), while both *Wings* and *Lapshin* featured protagonists having to contend with their wartime pasts, their own heroics, and varying degrees of psychological damage. On a more practical level, both Shepitko's work, particularly her second feature-length film, *You and Me* (*Ty i ia*, 1971), and German's Soviet-era output encountered stifling censorship. Regardless, the most glaring intersection of work by Shepitko and German can be found in *The Ascent* (*Voskhozhden*ie, 1977), Shepitko's last film, and *Trial on the Road* (*Proverka na dorogakh*, 1971, released 1985), a film directed early on by German in 1971 that did not reach Soviet screens until the mid-1980s. Highlighting issues of valor, betrayal, and patriotic sacrifice through their World War II plots and mutual reliance on religious allegory, these two films share similar settings, similar opening scenes in the snow, stark black and white aesthetics, and even a prominent actor (Anatoly Solonitsyn). Although *The Ascent* can arguably be seen as Shepitko's creative response to *Trial on the Road*, the two films show two filmmakers grappling in different, yet equally powerful ways with the Soviet past and the Soviet present.

SHEPITKO'S *WINGS*, GERMAN'S *LAPSHIN*, AND THE DAMAGED POST-THAW HERO

A contemporary malaise permeates Shepitko's *Wings*. Whereas German situated all of his films in a bygone Soviet era (or a medieval-like future, as is the case in his last film, *Hard to Be a God* [*Trudno byt' bogom*, 2013]), Shepitko placed the bulk of the action in *Wings* within the everyday present, shooting the film's outdoor scenes in Crimea. Following up on her debut film, *Heat* (*Znoi*, 1963), the action of which transpires on the dusty steppe of Kyrgyzstan, the young Ukrainian-born filmmaker opted for a subdued, gray Chekhovian setting in which the central protagonist—Nadezhda Petrukhina—finds herself isolated and out of step with Soviet contemporaneity. As a former World War II pilot, Petrukhina, played by the actress Maya Bulgakova, languishes amidst her day-to-day duties as the principal of a vocational school and City Soviet deputy and in her dormant love life. *Wings* may begin with a view through a large glass window onto a crowded, motion-filled city street, yet the film's out-of-the-way setting translates into a series of slowly unfolding events and a portrait of a Soviet heroine increasingly hemmed in by her quotidian environment. As conveyed through wistful flashbacks and a brief scene in a local museum before a Great Patriotic War display, Petrukhina had enjoyed a successful, heroic stint as a World War II pilot but had also witnessed the death of her lover and fellow pilot, Mitya (Leonid Dyachkov), during air combat; it is the loss of this lover—along with Petrukhina's own past glories as a pilot—that casts a shadow over her present-day existence. Petrukhina wallows in restrained despair amidst her stifling small-city life, even though her neighbor Pasha (Panteleimon Krymov), director of the local museum, has taken a distinct interest in her. Meanwhile, Petrukhina's adopted daughter, Tanya (Zhanna Bolotova), is for all intents and purposes estranged from her awkwardly formal mother, as the two struggle to communicate. At work, moreover, Nadezhda Stepanovna may have the respect of her colleagues, yet she stumbles when it comes to punishing a wayward young man at the school. Nadezhda does discover some comforting solidarity with Shura (Rimma Nikitina-Markova), a friendly middle-aged woman who serves beer to costumers at the local watering hole, yet their playful solidarity ends when they realize that a crowd of men has been observing them streetside through a window. With everyday existence closing in on her, Nadezhda finds herself not only trapped, but also unable to cope with her present prospects and thus in desperate need of some form of escape, whereby she takes off in a self-commandeered airplane at the elliptical conclusion of the film.

A similar, albeit more indirect and retrospective sense of stifled prospects and even doom hangs over the head of the central protagonist of German's *My Friend Ivan Lapshin*. Likewise living in a small, out-of-the-way Soviet city, the eponymous Lapshin (Andrei Boltnev) is a veteran of the Russian Civil War who serves as the local police chief in a town rife with crime and ominously poised on the cusp of the 1930s Stalinist purges. Under Lapshin's leadership, the police in this fictional city of Unchansk pursue a shady band of criminals headed by an elusive leader, Solov'ev. Much like Petrukhina, however, Lapshin proves unlucky in love, for he is clumsy and awkward in the presence of a local theater actress, Natasha (Nina Ruslanova), to whom he takes a concerted yet futile liking. Lapshin does succeed in hunting down Solov'ev at the end of the film, yet he does so with a ferocity that does not bode well for anyone involved, as the era's utopian ideals, casually spouted by Lapshin and his men from time to time, increasingly come across as both unfeasible and ironic amidst the brutal law-enforcement methods at play.[1] It is implied that these methods will soon come back to bite German's hero.

The two central protagonists of *Wings* and *Lapshin*, it becomes clear, are bolstered yet haunted by their heroic, military pasts. Along these militaristic lines, it is aviation that tellingly links the two films. Although airplanes as well as the effects of air combat plague both Petrukhina and Lapshin to varying degrees, the implicit thrill of flight provides a much-needed diversion from the uncomfortable, deflated present. When in need of a respite from her daily toil, Nadezhda wanders over to the local airfield or daydreams about her own past flights. In *Lapshin*, meanwhile, aviation figures as a unifying cultural marker. With the film's opening credits rolling, German highlights the playful reenactment of a popular comedic sketch from the 1930s of an aerial fight involving an Italian fascist pilot who must parachute from his plane over Abyssinia. The two minor characters acting out this aviator routine provide sound effects and gestures that mimic aerial bombardment and the fierce combat between fighter planes. Further underscoring the aviation link between *Wings* and *Lapshin* are respective diegetic renditions of the popular

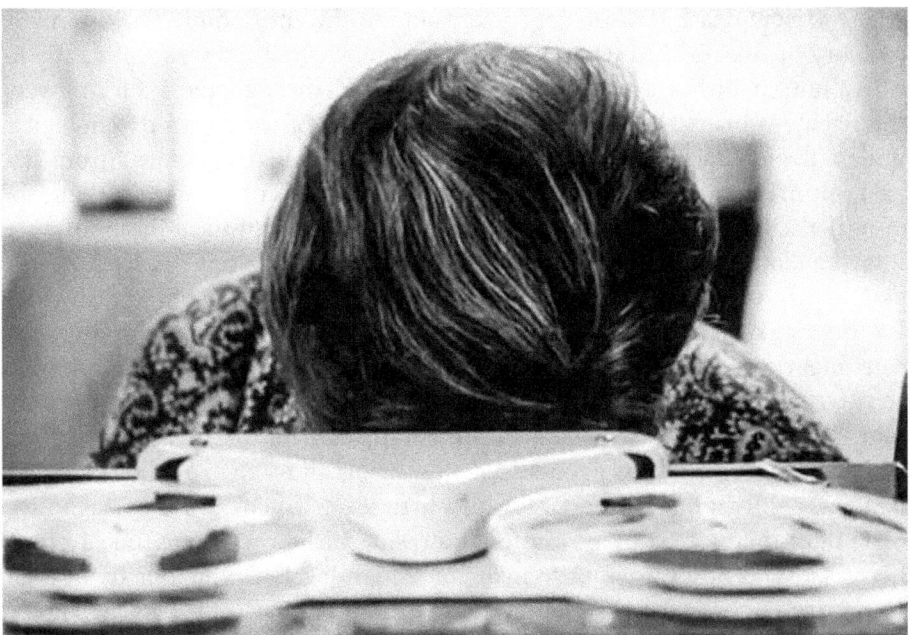

Figure 2.1 Petrukhina listening to "The Steel Squadron" in *Wings*.

Soviet war song "The Steel Squadron" ("Stal'naia eskadril'ia"). A military march, or air march (*aviamarsh*), "The Steel Squadron" was composed in the late 1920s to glorify the Soviet Air Forces ("Where the infantry can't pass/And the armored train can't rush/The gloomy tank can't crawl/There flies the steel squadron . . .").² Petrukhina, her head hung sadly low over a reel-tape device, listens to the singing of "The Steel Squadron" via a recording that her former wartime comrades have sent her to raise her spirits (**see Figure** 2.1), while Lapshin and his fellow police officers sing a slightly different, more ominous version of the song—"For the last time/Into mortal combat/Flies the steel squadron"—as they disperse following Lapshin's birthday party at the start of the film. A fascination with modern flight indeed pervades the everyday. Elsewhere in German's film, moreover, the journalist Ganin (Andrei Mironov) mentions that he is working on the life story of an aviator. In both films, flight offers an attractive alternative to the earthbound dreariness of everyday Soviet life, be it in the 1930s or 1960s.

Aviation and airplanes, however, also torment the protagonists of *Wings* and *Lapshin*. Petrukhina, sitting in a hall at the local museum, cannot help but notice that she has become an outdated relic of the past, featured as a bygone flying hero in the city museum exhibit that schoolchildren dutifully observe. And there is, of course, the flashback to the fatal crash of her lover, Mitya, whose violent death lurks in the background of the entire film. The traumatic memory of this death, shown through point-of-view shots is, as Lilya Kaganovsky puts it in her analysis of *Wings*, "filtered through the subjectivity of the female protagonist," thus informing so much of the film's psychological undercurrent.[3] Petrukhina, as if to revisit this traumatic moment from her past, ultimately returns to the air and to all the inherent danger of flight, for even if the film's final scene ends with the heroine's elliptical disappearance into the cloudy distance, it is implied that Petrukhina's final ascent into the clouds may very well be her last earthly flight. In German's film, meanwhile, Lapshin wakes up in tears from a disturbing seizure-like dream and cryptically mentions dreaming of an airplane. Later in the film, following a similar seizure that has caused him to fall out of bed, it is explained by the narrator that Lapshin had served as a squadron commander in the Russian Civil War and come out of it severely concussed after being hit by an exploding shell, yet had never sought out treatment for his wartime shellshock. Both protagonists, one might therefore contend, suffer as a result of their past war-time aviating heroics, even as they attempt to maintain a high level of functionality in their respective work.

The events underlying *Lapshin* may transpire in the 1930s, but the film nevertheless reflects a post-Thaw reckoning with Soviet heroism, as does *Wings*, with both doing so, to varying degrees, in an explicitly Chekhovian manner that calls into question traditional notions of the dramatic hero. Chekhov's turn-of-the-century fiction and drama, in fact, would prove well-suited to the post-Thaw period, its reevaluation of Soviet heroics, and the far-reaching malaise that came over stagnating Soviet society at the time. In the 1970s, for example, Chekhov's mid-career play *Ivanov* (1887), with its middle-aged protagonist unable to replicate his past successes and ultimately succumbing to suicide, "was seen as a forecast of the current mood and enjoyed multiple revivals," according to Laurence Senelick and Sergei Ostrovsky.[4] The era's increasingly Chekhovian outlook would accordingly resonate throughout both films under discussion. In *Wings*, Petrukhina's heroic days have come and gone, akin to the twilight years of a quickly fading Chekhov hero or heroine, while the semicomical Lapshin, as if the central protagonist in some sad Chekhovian comedy, stumbles about as he fights crime with a self-defeating ferocity, a ferocity that will, it is implied, ultimately befall him and many others as well.[5] Akin to a Chekhov play set on the cusp of great historical upheaval (e.g., *The Cherry Orchard*), German's film depicts a world soon to be torn apart by the Stalinist Purges of the 1930s and the era of Great Terror. The valiant Lapshin will not survive, it can be assumed, what ensues.[6] Meanwhile, *Wings* similarly undermines the prototypical Soviet (i.e., Stalinist) hero, albeit somewhat unconventionally through its despairing female protagonist and her wistful nostalgia for past glory and love.

Behind the Chekhovian, post-Thaw malaise in *Wings* and *Lapshin* would lurk a poignant critique of Stalinism. *Wings*, with its emphasis on a heroic, female protagonist at odds with contemporary Soviet society, ultimately leans toward a reappraisal of Stalinist, socialist realist ideology and its reliance on the resolute (i.e., one-dimensional) Soviet hero.[7] Petrukhina, it is safe to say, is out of step with her times. "Nadezhda," Kaganovsky contends, "is a Stalinist character displaced from her position of cultural dominance by the changes brought on by the Thaw."[8] In a similar yet more critical vein, German's Stagnation-era film establishes a version of Soviet history that, although not entirely bereft of intrepidness, uses its complex protagonist to call into question the conventional socialist realist trope of the Soviet hero. In the words of Russian film critic Anton Dolin, German's protagonists are "non-heroes," foremost among them being Lapshin.[9] Hence, both Petrukhina and Lapshin emerge as characters trapped by circumstances and their respective eras, unable to realize their potential and thus quite fitting prototypes for late Soviet cinema. Although filmed some seventeen years apart and focused on quite disparate time periods, *Wings* and *Lapshin* epitomize post-Thaw artistic responses to the dark legacy of Stalinism, simultaneously conveying the stifling stagnation that had taken root in Soviet society by the early 1970s.

GERMAN'S *TRIAL*, SHEPITKO'S *ASCENT*, AND MARTYRDOM IN WORLD WAR II

The heroic and its converse, treason, lie at the heart of the two films by German and Shepitko that most vividly intersect: in both German's *Trial on the Road* and Shepitko's *The Ascent*, Stalinist notions of heroism are not only probed, but also thoroughly reevaluated and, to varying degrees, recalibrated. Shepitko's last film and German's early film (which reached Soviet screens only a year before the release of *Lapshin*) feature a heightened preoccupation with bravery as well as a historical resonance that goes far beyond the everyday, out-of-the-way grayness of *Wings* and *Lapshin*. Taking place during World War II amidst desperate, fierce partisan resistance to Nazi troops in occupied territory of the Soviet Union, the two films run parallel in many striking respects, yet philosophically diverge. Both filmmakers have turned to the seemingly firm patriotic ground of World War II (specifically 1942, in the Pskov region in *Trial* and Soviet Belorussia in *Ascent*), albeit at very different stages of their careers, when German was emerging as a filmmaker in his own right with *Trial* and Shepitko was sadly concluding her career with *Ascent* and its poignant depiction of sacrifice, cowardice, and martyrdom. *Trial* and *Ascent* both grapple with intersecting ideological and aesthetic questions, even as they vividly underscore their respective directors' divergent methods and viewpoints.

A literary orientation, for one thing, links *Trial* and *Ascent*. Both films draw upon relatively short works of Soviet fiction that probed Soviet notions of bravery and devotion to the country's victorious fight against Fascism during the Great Patriotic War (as World War II commonly became known in the Soviet Union). German loosely based *Trial on the Road* on the 1965 short story "Operation 'Happy New Year!'" ("Operatsiia 'S Novym godom!'"), written by his father, the well-known Soviet writer Yuri German, and adapted for film by Edward Volodarsky, while Shepitko based *The Ascent* on the 1970 novella *Sotnikov* by the celebrated Soviet/Belorussian writer Vasil' Bykaŭ (Bykov), whose prose Yuri Klepikov transformed into a relatively faithful screenplay for Shepitko.[10] The literary origins of both films, it stands to reason, provided the two directors with a good amount of artistic and ideological leeway as they delved into contentious matters of Soviet valor and perfidy during the war.

The decision by both German and Shepitko to situate their respective films within the ostensibly safe parameters of World War II does make sense, especially given how some of the most daring Soviet filmmaking, particularly during the Thaw, addressed aspects of the Soviet Union's monumental efforts in the fight against Nazi Germany (Mikhail Kalatozov's *The Cranes are Flying* [*Letiat zhuravli*, 1957] and Andrei Tarkovsky's *Ivan's Childhood* [*Ivanovo detstvo*, 1962] immediately come to mind). For with the Thaw's loosening of artistic restrictions came a willingness on the part of the nation's filmmakers to undermine or ignore Stalinism's heavy-handed, myopic emphasis on Soviet heroism and the like. Amidst the Thaw, Denise Youngblood explains, "Soviet filmmakers were able to show the emotional costs of the war, without the need for heroics to offset the suffering."[11] Directors such as German and Shepitko, moreover, eagerly waded into such a popular, prevalent subject matter for cinema, given that the war remained quite germane to a Soviet society still coming to terms with the country's costly, harrowing victory over the Germans. "Given the centrality of war and wartime to Soviet history," Youngblood explains, "war films gave filmmakers the opportunity to subvert official history in the guise of art or entertainment, a luxury that Soviet historians did not have."[12] So well suited to the big screen, war and its historical significance, along with its ethical implications, preoccupied a new generation of Soviet film directors that included Shepitko and German.

Both filmmakers were especially drawn to the theme of World War II. Two of German's more celebrated films—*Trial* and *Twenty Days Without War*—would delve into aspects of the war period, as the filmmaker probed a key event from the Soviet past in a resolutely detailed, humane way.[13] As German himself would clarify in 1979, "War is a time of inhuman circumstances in which the human is fully revealed. War is an unmediated drama, the drama of life, that reveals in a person such depths that this person could not have even imagined at a time of peace."[14] Although the heightened, often violent action of suspenseful combat scenes in *Trial* would virtually disappear in *Twenty Days Without War*, the amplified emotions of wartime life occupied center stage in both of these war films directed by German. For Shepitko, the war likewise linked her films. She herself would explain that the theme of war on display in *Ascent* continued a motif initially broached in *Wings*:

> [The war theme] was, in my opinion, completely natural. It was not even a sharp turn, but rather a return. For *Wings*, at least for me, is also war themed. To understand and show on screen the persona of the school director Petrukhina, not taking into account her wartime biography, was simply impossible. The war signified too much in her life.[15]

So central to the work of both German and Shepitko, World War II and its heroic parameters provided a powerful means through which to explore the Soviet past, establish their respective cinematic visions, and delve into a post-war Soviet ethos.

In seizing upon the opportunity to revisit the Soviet war experience, both German and Shepitko would cite Aleksandr Stolper's 1964 war film *The Living and the Dead* (*Zhivye i mertvye*) as inspiring their respective films. Based on a novel of the same name by Konstantin Simonov, whose fiction also provided the basis for German's *Twenty Days Without War*, *The Living and the Dead* has often been seen and cited as the quintessential Thaw-era World War II film in that it did not obscure Soviet mistakes and disarray at the start of the Nazi invasion of the Soviet Union in 1941 (while the novel also highlighted the way any Soviet soldier caught behind enemy lines was deemed a traitor by the Stalinist state). *The Living and the Dead* appealed, in particular, to German, who remarked, "It seems to me that watching this picture, many filmmakers felt embarrassed: why had they not up to then told at least part of this truth. In this movie I understood and felt the rigid dependency of mastery on realism and on comprehending the truth."[16] Such realism would become a crucial aspect of German's filmmaking. Meanwhile, in a 1976 interview, Shepitko cited a specific battle scene from the first half of *The Living and the Dead* that features a weaponless Soviet soldier throwing a rock at a Nazi tank and then tragically perishing.[17] Shepitko recalls shedding tears over this scene but also her amazement at how two Soviet officers in the movie theater barely reacted to this tragic moment in the film. Shepitko thus vowed in her own World War II film to convey the profundity of a soldier's choice between life and death. The reactions of the two filmmakers to *The Living and the Dead* would therefore be quite telling: for Aleksei German, cinema could reveal some greater truth about the war, whereas for Larisa Shepitko, there was a desire to reveal the heightened emotions and spiritual quandaries inherent in war.

Beginning scenes of both *Trial on the Road* and *The Ascent* feature abundant snow, as if blank canvases upon which the two filmmakers can sketch their respective heroes. In *Trial*, following an opening credits scene of German soldiers either ruining or requisitioning Soviet produce and livestock, a fierce skirmish in a snowy field ensues followed by the unexpected appearance of two lone figures: the partisan commander Ivan Lokotkov (Rolan Bykov), who limps up to the entrance of a wooden peasant house, and Aleksandr Lazarev (Vladimir Zamanskii), who walks out of the wintry woods dressed in a German military uniform but is intent, it soon becomes clear, on joining the ranks of the Soviet partisan fighters. A former Red Army sergeant, Lazarev will be taken in by the partisan brigade under the command of the stern, yet compassionate Lokotkov, who initially harbors suspicions of Lazarev and his entreaties to fight for the Soviet partisans, given that Lazarev had not only surrendered to the enemy, but also served in the ranks of the Nazi army. Even more skeptical of Lazarev is Major Petushkov (Solonitsyn), a party commissar who wants to see the now repentant Lazarev shot. An ingenious plan, however, is hatched by the judicious Lokotkov to raid the Nazi-controlled rail station where Lazarev had previously worked and to hijack a supply train so as to resupply the beleaguered partisan brigade. In preparing for this raid, Lazarev has a chance to prove himself by ambushing some Nazi officers on a snowy road and stealing their car, the film's eponymous "trial" that proves successful yet results in the death of one partisan fighter (Oleg Borisov). Upon learning of this death, Petushkov rashly blames Lazarev, who once imprisoned yet again by the partisans attempts to hang himself out of shame. Ultimately, however, the raid is launched and, although the heroic Lazarev perishes amidst fierce fighting at the enemy-controlled rail station, the partisan infiltrators succeed in hijacking the supply train. The film subsequently ends by jumping ahead to 1945, with the humane, humble Lokotkov, ultimately Lazarev's defender, working on his broken-down truck in a German town before being recognized and then thanked for his past leadership by an officer passing by en route to Berlin at the very end of the war. Amidst the commotion and victory celebrations, the two men warmly embrace.

Shepitko's *Ascent* likewise begins in the snow, as a group of partisans that includes women and children emerges from hiding in a white field and scurries to safety in the woods. From this group of starving partisans—and out of the woods—come two soldiers, Rybak (Vladimir Gostiukhin), a local partisan, and Sotnikov (Boris Plotnikov), a school-teacher-turned-soldier, both of whom have volunteered to go in search of food that they hope to find in a nearby village occupied by the Nazis. Rybak helps along the ailing, depleted Sotnikov before they reach the house of a village elder (Sergei Iakovlev), whom they contemplate shooting (at Sotnikov's urging), given that he appears to have willingly collaborated with the enemy. Instead, Rybak and Sotnikov requisition and shoot a sheep and then begin their return to the brigade; along the way, however, they fall into a skirmish with a handful of enemy soldiers, whereby one enemy soldier perishes and Sotnikov is wounded. Sotnikov attempts to kill himself so as not to be captured by the Nazis, yet Rybak drags him away to temporary safety. The two men eventually find refuge in the wooden house of Demchikha (Liudmila Poliakova), but the coughing of the unwell Sotnikov gives them away to the Nazi soldiers who have arrived to search the premises. Taken into custody and dragged before a local collaborator, Portnov (Solonitsyn), the two partisan soldiers soon reveal their true colors: Sotnikov refuses to submit to the interrogation and never wavers during the subsequent torture, as he steadfastly resists giving away any information about himself or the brigade; Rybak, on the other hand, proves much more forthcoming, avoids torture, and, following a harrowing night in a cell with his fellow captives, decides to save his own skin by collaborating with the Nazis. Conversely, Sotnikov makes an unsuccessful attempt to free the others by confessing to everything. In the film's climactic scenes, Portnov and the Nazis orchestrate a public execution, with Sotnikov, along with the village elder, Demchikha, and a young Jewish girl all led up a hill to the village square and hung on the gallows before a crowd of onlookers. The tearful, distraught Rybak, having realized the perfidy of his actions as the public execution transpires, attempts to hang himself in a nearby outhouse, yet he ultimately resigns himself to working with the enemy.

As the two synopses of *Trial* and *Ascent* suggest, both German and Shepitko grappled in their respective films with the issue of Soviet patriotism. German, boasting a directness that surely compelled the authorities to shelve his film, criticizes in *Trial* the black-and-white certainty of Stalinist mores surrounding World War II and Soviet soldiers' devotion to the Soviet cause.[18] Party commissar Petushkov's dogmatic view of the conflicted, repentant Lazarev offers the basis of German's reevaluation of Stalinism, a critique of past Soviet leadership that would continue in subsequent films by German, including *Lapshin*. As Emil Draitser contends in his analysis of *Trial*, "[Petushkov's] suspicion of Lazarev is not so much a personal idiosyncrasy, as a reflection of Stalinist attitudes and behavior in the Soviet Union. Suspicion is the sole basis of his condemnation of Lazarev."[19] Such a questioning of Stalinist certitude—and flimsy suspicion—would be deemed unacceptable by the censors in 1971, for German's critique of official Soviet attitudes during the war permeates the entire film. In one lengthy flashback scene in the film, Lokotkov harkens back to a previous situation in the fight against the Nazis when he refused to blow up a rail bridge under which a barge full of Soviet prisoners-of-war was passing (**see Figure** 2.2), thus incurring the rage of Petushkov, who demanded the completion of the mission despite the loss of Soviet life that would have ensued had the bridge been detonated. As *Trial* suggests, Stalinism did not allow for any ethical ambiguity or wavering.

Figure 2.2 The Soviet prisoner-of-war barge in *Trial on the Road*.

Whether the ideological situation in 1977 had become that much different from what existed in 1971 remains to be seen, yet Shepitko was clearly prompted to take a different tack in *Ascent* than that which German probed in the initially shelved *Trial*. In what might appear at some level to be a return to the certitude associated with Stalinism, Shepitko elevates questions of valor and steadfast ideals to a broadly universal, human level, thus attempting to sidestep any focus on Stalinist dogma. Instead, she contrasts Rybak's desperate lust for life and Portnov's soulless, self-serving cynicism with Sotnikov's resolute, sacrificial decision not to collaborate with the Nazis. Whereas earlier in the film, Rybak proved the more resolute of the two as he led Sotnikov toward the village, once the two men are in captivity it immediately becomes clear that Rybak's and Sotnikov's positions have shifted, for Sotnikov is the one who leads by example while Rybak grovels and follows. In one day-dreaming scene, Rybak imagines himself racing away from the Germans through the snow and getting shot, while in a second daydreaming scene following the hanging of his compatriots, he conjures up an image of himself slipping away yet immediately shot down. Nevertheless, Rybak, unlike Sotnikov, lacks the imagination, foresight, and moral fortitude to see that collaboration with the enemy will lead to misery and shame. Indeed, once captured by the Nazis, Sotnikov refuses to give the location of the partisan unit, their hideouts, and their contacts. "I won't betray anyone," says Sotnikov, "for some things matter more than one's skin." Interrogating Sotnikov, the cynical Portnov retorts, "Everything ends with our death, and you won't die a heroic death, either." That the actor, Solonitsyn, best known for his performances in a handful of films directed by Tarkovsky (e.g., *Andrei Rublev*, *Solaris*, and *Stalker*), plays both German's Petushkov and Shepitko's Portnov makes Shepitko's scene all the more telling and powerful, for it is as if she has upended German's script, whereby party commissar becomes feckless Nazi collaborator and Stalinist certitude gives way to a betrayal of humanistic principles. Feckless, amoral collaboration with the Nazis overshadows past Stalinist sins.

Although both shot in stark black and white (as are *Wings* and most of *Lapshin*), *Trial* and *Ascent* feature dissimilar cinematic styles and techniques. In *Trial*, for instance, German homes in on small particulars of the World War II era, an attention to historical detail that would expand in the filmmaker's subsequent films. With the help of his *Trial* cinematographer Yakov Skliansky, German also tends to film striking outdoor scenes through which the narrative action transpires, be it a wintry field, a river running under a bridge, or a snowy road. His brushstrokes are both detailed and vivid. In *Ascent*, however, Shepitko increasingly deemphasizes details from the past and striking landscapes, instead focusing intently on the human face. In the overnight cell sequence, during which Sotnikov and the others await their fate, Shepitko conveys the fierce discussion between Rybak and Sotnikov primarily though close-ups of the prisoners' physiognomies, whereby the emphasis falls not on any period minutiae or accurate reconstruction of the era but rather on the inner anguish of the two protagonists, who argue fiercely about the wisdom and ethics of their shared trial. Sotnikov warns Rybak not to wade into "shit" ("der'mo"); conscience, Sotnikov emphasizes, is what is most important, while Rybak stresses that he simply wants to live. Their faces inches apart and often together in the same close-up, Sotnikov and Rybak question each other's innermost beliefs. It is through this reliance on the close-up that Shepitko strives to establish some objective truth surrounding questions of honor and treason in World War II. The early film theorist Béla Balázs, exploring the use of the close-up in cinema and its unprecedented perspective on the human face, has argued that "this most subjective and individual of human manifestations is rendered objective in the close-up."[20] Just such a sense of objectivity emerges in Shepitko's final film through its abundant close-ups, as the filmmaker's attention to human physiognomy underscores her investigation of Soviet World War II ethics and allows her to expand the scope of this investigation to a more universal level.

The contrast between Shepitko's use of the close-up to establish an objective, universal truth and German's more subjective, retrospective search for historical truth can be seen throughout both films. Take, for instance, a scene early on in *Trial*, when a limping Lokotkov enters the wooden home of a female villager and questions her. Played by Maya Bulgakova, who had appeared several years earlier as Petrukhina in Shepitko's *Wings* (Shepitko, one could contend, gets a better, more understated performance from Bulgakova than does German in his early film), this village woman, tending to her three children, bemoans her plight as an abandoned mother (her husband has run off, she says) and beseeches Lokotkov, who sits across from her in the dark abode, to leave the premises ("Go to hell! I never asked you to come in," she wails). Their interaction proves confrontational, fraught, and never clear cut. One might then compare this early village scene in *Trial* to the one in *Ascent* when Rybak and Sotnikov take refuge in the home of Demchikha, who also has three children and is husbandless. Shepitko's village woman is just as wary of the male intruders—and she has good reason to fear that the two partisan soldiers will land her in trouble with the Nazis—yet the filming of the scene underscores a human intimacy that prevails throughout the film. Shepitko includes multiple shots in which Demchikha is together with the two men, as she kneels besides the supine and ailing Sotnikov while Rybak looks on, and in other shots Rybak questions Demchikha, with his face inches away from hers. Whereas German uses the close-up quite sparingly and in fact highlights a certain wariness and distrust between people during wartime (particularly in that suspicious atmosphere generated by Stalinist attitudes, one might contend), Shepitko amplifies human connection and a universal set of ethics. Through her use of the close-up, Shepitko succeeds in transcending the everyday parameters of a given scene, as she delves into the deeper human—and spiritual—dimensions of a situation, be it soldiers seeking refuge in the house of a compatriot or prisoners awaiting their fate in a dark, overnight cell.

Religious motifs, odd as it may seem for two relatively late Soviet films, figure quite significantly in both *Trial* and *Ascent*, albeit in somewhat divergent ways. With his surname, Lazarev in *Trial* of course evokes the Biblical Lazarus of Bethany, contrasted as a beggar to a rich man in the Gospel of Luke and then, in the Gospel of John, as the brother of Mary and Martha (Mary's sister) who dies of an illness but whom Christ resurrects from the dead after four days, proving the miraculous power of faith in God. German's resurrected Lazarev thus serves as a modern-day Lazarus who redeems himself through his valor during the raid on the rail station, offering an oblique nod to rehabilitation (i.e., resurrection) within the Soviet system. Lazarev may die at the end of the film, yet he has already risen from his proverbial death as collaborator. Lazarev's ordeal therefore constitutes an earthly "trial" made possible by the film's other protagonist, Lokotkov, whose compassion allows for the debased Lazarev to resurrect and redeem himself.

Whereas the religious allusions were already quite explicit in Yuri German's short story "Operation 'Happy New Year!'" and thus easily adaptable to screen, in Bykaŭ's *Sotnikov* the religious subtext was less than evident; Shepitko and Klepikov, therefore, had to extrapolate from the novella, creating extensive religious meaning within the film, not only via their telling replacement of the title *Sotnikov* with *The Ascent*, but also through much of the film's narrative and imagery. With the film title already broaching obvious religious and spiritual connotations, the opening shots in *Ascent* of wooden telephone poles within a snowy landscape introduce visual associations with the crucifixion cross, while early images of the wide-eyed Sotnikov resting in the woods with branches hanging over his head conjure up notions of Christ and his crown of thorns (see **Figure** 2.3). And Sotnikov ever more directly assumes his Christ-like role once Portnov begins to interrogate him in a manner akin to Pontius Pilate questioning Christ, just as the treasonous Rybak emerges as a Judas-like character. Furthermore, the subsequent procession to the gallows of the condemned Sotnikov along with the village elder, Demchikha, and the Jewish girl suggests a modern-day Procession to Calvary, where Christ was crucified outside of Jerusalem. As the Christ-like Sotnikov is hanged, he locks eyes with a young boy in a pointed "Budenovka" hat, which further accentuates his role as a modern-day martyr, and when the Judas-like Rybak is led back to the German command center, this boy joins in with other villagers and glares disapprovingly at the now distraught, shamed Rybak, whereby one elderly female villager even goes so far as to call Rybak a Judas under her breath. And lastly, in a final Judas-like act, the tearful Rybak attempts to hang himself (as does a tearful Lazarev in *Trial*), but to no avail. So while German focuses in on Lazarev's resurrection and earthly trial, Shepitko shifts her focus to metaphysical questions of eternal salvation, as Sotnikov implicitly ascends from his earthly state of suffering while Rybak remains in the purgatory of his shameful, debased existence.

Figure 2.3 The Christ-like Sotnikov in *The Ascent*.

Discussing the religious parable created in *Ascent*, Aleksandr Shpagin has argued that "it is precisely a firmness of attitudes that links [Shepitko's religious parable] to Soviet myth."[21] Religion and Soviet myth overlap in Shepitko's film, Shpagin contends, for, "the Soviet myth turns out to be a wonderful receptacle for religious consciousness, even though in reality they are totally opposed to one another."[22] Despite being at ideological odds with Soviet culture, the religious parable presented by Shepitko entails a moral dogmatism that proves familiarly unyielding in its certitude as the filmmaker trumpets via her religious motifs the Soviet myth of selfless sacrifice in the service of the nation's fight against the Nazis. So whereas German undermines the Stalinist Soviet myth vis-à-vis his reliance on religious allegory, Shepitko in essence reinforces this Soviet myth and, if not Stalinist attitudes, then at least a Stalinist certitude during World War II via her religious parable.

A close link, or more tenuous link, to the Soviet present (i.e., the 1970s) further distinguishes the two films. Whereas German delved into the wartime past and its fraught ideology in *Trial*, Shepitko would emphasize that the character portrayal in *Ascent* could in fact be linked to the present day. In a 1977 interview, Shepitko states:

> Making a film about the war, we have not striven to transform ourselves into historiographers scrupulously investigating the events of the past. More than anything we have wanted to answer today's questions, to think about the contemporary need for lofty ideals, for the spiritual richness of life. That is why we have not tried to create heroes who are in every way like those people who lived thirty years ago. On the contrary, we have striven to ensure that in our heroes, in their mannerisms, in their actions, in their ability to assess a situation, viewers recognize themselves, today.[23]

Shepitko proves far less interested in recreating the past than she is at addressing important questions of the day regarding honor and moral fortitude, concepts that had as much relevance in 1970s Soviet culture as they did in 1942. Per Shpagin's reading of the film, Shepitko has extended a Soviet myth and Stalin-era ethos into her present, post-Thaw era. Hence, whereas German's emphasis falls on memory and the past, Shepitko brings that same past quite deliberately into the post-Thaw present, with much less of a concern for the everyday minutiae and reckoning with the nation's Stalinist legacy that German would place at the forefront of his films.

Given the fact that neither director spoke or wrote at length about the other, it is hard to say whether Shepitko's *Wings* directly informed German's *Lapshin*, or that Shepitko intentionally evoked German's *Trial* in her *Ascent*. Although it can safely be assumed that Shepitko was aware of German's Lenfilm production and its unceremonious shelving in 1971, there is nothing to indicate whether Shepitko saw *Trial on the Road* prior to making *The Ascent*. Conversely, in a long 1979 interview in the Soviet film journal *The Art of Cinema* (*Iskusstvo kino*), cited earlier in this chapter, German discusses contemporary Soviet cinema yet makes absolutely no mention of Shepitko's work. What is clear, however, is that they both drew upon similar themes and concerns in post-Thaw Soviet cinema. *Trial on the Road* and *The Ascent* start virtually in the same place and culminate with the deaths of their respective protagonists, who in both cases sacrifice themselves willingly for the Soviet cause. Nevertheless, these deaths—and the implied deaths of the central protagonists in *Wings* and *My Friend Ivan Lapshin* as well—point to a final important distinction between the two filmmakers: whereas in German's work, death comes in a matter-of-fact way, with hardly a fuss, for Shepitko pathos emerges out of the mortality, as is clearly the case with Mitya's traumatic expiration and Nadezhda's potential demise in *Wings* along with the hanging of Sotnikov and the others in *Ascent*. This pathos in turn fosters spiritual reflection but also a resolute belief in sacrifice for the sake of the Soviet cause and, implicitly, humanity. German returns to the past and stoically reflects on both life and death through the film image, whereas Shepitko transcends the past to explore and even extend, albeit with significant modification and sorrow, a stern, yet resolute Soviet ethos.

NOTES

1. As J. Hoberman notes, *Lapshin* "represents Bolshevik idealism as a lost dream." J. Hoberman, "Exorcism: Aleksei German Among the Dark Shadows," *Film Comment* January-February 1999: 154.
2. "The Steel Squadron" was featured in and made especially famous by the 1955 Soviet film *Maksim Perepelitsa*, directed by Anatolii Granik.
3. Lilya Kaganovsky, "Ways of Seeing: On Kira Muratova's Brief Encounters and Larisa Shepit'ko's Wings," *The Russian Review*, vol. 71, no. 3 (July 2012): 495.
4. Laurence Senelick and Sergei Ostrovsky, eds., *The Soviet Theater: A Documentary History* (New Haven, CT: Yale University Press, 2014), 556.
5. German, discussing his decision to have the relatively unknown actor Andrei Boltnev play the role of the film's central protagonist, remarked, "He had to have the face of a man from the Red List, a man who would soon be killed." Cited in Anton Dolin, "No Surrender: The Strange Case of Russian Maverick Aleksei German, and His Stubborn Battle to Overthrow Cinematic Orthodoxy and Correct the Historical Record," translated by Oleg Dubson, *Film Comment* 48/2 (March/April 2012): 30. Dolin's article on German initially appeared in the Russian newspaper *Moskovskie novosti*.
6. In *Lapshin*, other Chekhovian details stand out. At the end of German's film, following Solov'ev's demise and the lengthy recovery of the journalist Khanin, whom Solov'ev stabbed, the narrative concludes in undramatic Chekhovian

fashion with a departure. Khanin, who at several points in the film asks Lapshin to travel across the country with him, leaves for Moscow, whereas both Lapshin and the actress Natasha remain in Unchansk; they are Chekhovian characters wasting their potential by refusing to challenge their fate. And Natasha, staying put despite the impending departure of Khanin, tellingly remarks that she is not like one of Chekhov's famous three sisters. For other Chekhovian elements in Lapshin, see Julian Graffy, "Unshelving Stalin: After the Period of Stagnation," in Richard Taylor and Derek Spring, eds., *Stalinism and Soviet Film* (London: Routledge, 1993), 224.

7. For more on the central gender dynamics in *Wings*, see Tatiana Mikhailova and Mark Lipovetsky, "Flight without Wings: The Subjectivity of a Veteran in Larisa Shepit'ko's *Wings*," in Rimgaila Salys, ed., *The Russian Cinema Reader*, vol. 2 (Boston: Academic Studies Press, 2013), 70–83.
8. Kaganovsky, 491.
9. Dolin, 28.
10. In 1971, German intended for his film to keep the title of *Operation "Happy New Year!" (Operatsiia "S Novym godom!")* but following the film's long period of dormancy, it was retitled *Trial on the Road (Proverka na dorogakh)* in 1986.
11. Denise Youngblood, *Russian War Films: On the Cinema Front, 1914–2005* (Lawrence, KS: University Press of Kansas, 2007), 118.
12. Youngblood, 3.
13. German's first film, *The Seventh Companion (Sed'moi sputnik*, 1968), which he co-directed with Grigori Aronov, features battle scenes from the Russian Civil War.
14. Aleksei German, "Pravda—ne skhodstvo, a otkrytie," *Iskusstvo kino*, no. 12 (December 2001): 79. This interview was originally published in *Iskustvo kino* in 1979.
15. Lev Karakhan, "Krutoi put' *Voskhozhdeniia*," *Iskusstvo kino*, no. 10, 1976: 86.
16. See German, 82. Also cited in Youngblood.
17. See Karakhan, 86.
18. *Trial on the Road* was shelved until 1986 because, according to internal memos of the state film agency Goskino, it "suffers from extreme conceptual failings" and "distorts the image of a heroic time and the image of the Soviet people who rose up in the occupied territories in mortal battle with the German fascist occupier. The film's main subject, the subject of the heroic battle with the occupiers, fades into the background." Cited in Graffy, 218.
19. Emil Draitser, "*Trial on the Roads*, Trial Indeed," *Studies in Comparative Communism*, vol. xxi nos. 3/4: 296.
20. Béla Balázs, *Theory of the Film: Character and Growth of a New Art*, trans. Edith Bone (New York: Dover Publications, 1970), 60.
21. Aleksandr Shpagin, "Religiia voiny. Sub'ektivnye zametki o bogoiskatel'stve v kinematografe o voine," *Iskusstvo kino* no. 6, June 2005: 86. Shpagin also mentions German's *Trial on the Road* in this article, yet he does not compare *Trial* with *Ascent*.
22. Ibid, 87.
23. Cited in Karakhan, 87.

PART II

Intermediality: From Word to Image

CHAPTER 3

Ghosts of the Present Past: *Wings* (1966), from the Script by Natalia Riazantseva and Valentin Ezhov to the Film by Larisa Shepitko

Eugénie Zvonkine

The first publication of the script that would eventually give birth to *Wings* (*Krylia*, 1966) by Larisa Shepitko was published in the journal *Iskusstvo kino*, under the title "The Tale of a Pilot" (*Povest' o letchitse*).[1] It would have other titles, such as "Guards Captain," (*Gvardii kapitan*[2]) before the final one, *Wings*, is finally chosen. The script by Valentin Ezhov and Natalia Riazantseva presents several substantial differences with the film, but at the same time it foreshadows, in its writing, some of the important traits of the film to be.

Of course, there is always a significant difference between the written word and the film, not only on a phenomenological level, but also because the script, or the script*s*, since there are always several versions of those for a single film, are but intermediate steps in the filmmaking.[3] In *Wings*, Shepitko shows that she is more than aware of the difference between the written word and the image and sound by introducing the character of a young journalist, absent from the original script by Riazantseva. This young woman has written an article on the protagonist of the film, Nadia (or Nadezhda Stepanovna), who is the director of a professional school and a war veteran. But when Nadia reads the paper, she immediately discards it as completely inaccurate. She reads out loud her own description: "I am greeted by a tired, modestly dressed woman with wrinkles." The spectator can only agree with Nadia's reaction – dressed in a manly suit and a severe skirt, always holding herself upright, talking in an authoritative tone, she does not resemble this description in the slightest.

Moreover, Shepitko admitted to strongly changing the script from its first version throughout the entire shooting:

> It has always been important to me whether the story fits into the main thing that I personally care about [. . .]. If the plot suited me, fine.

At first, the script "The Tale of a Pilot," which later became "Wings," was written about something else entirely. The authors Valentin Ezhov and Natalia Riazantseva agreed to changes that I asked for, and later, even during the shooting, I adapted the dramaturgy to myself, to my idea, and the script was remade up to the last second. Ezhov, when he came to watch the film, didn't recognize his script . . .[4]

But still, a comparative analysis appears useful for several reasons: the scriptwriter Natalia Riazantseva (co)writes here her first feature while Shepitko directs her second feature film, but one that she really considers as her first serious work, since her 1963 *Heat* (*Znoi*) was her VGIK diploma.[5] Riazantseva would become one of the important scriptwriters of the stagnation era: she wrote not only the script for Kira Muratova's *Long Goodbyes* (*Dolgie provody*, 1972), entitled "How to Become a Man" (*Stat' muzhchinoi*) and "About Women and Children" (*O zhenshinakh i detiakh*)[6] at different stages of fabrication, but also scripts for many other important films of this period, such as *Private Life of Kuzyaev Valentin* (*Lichnaya zhizn' Kuzyaeva Valentina*, 1967) by Ilya Averbakh and Igor Maslennikov, *Other People's Letters* (*Chuzhye pis'ma*, 1975) and *The Voice* (*Golos*, 1982) by Ilya Averbakh. Riazantseva's second marriage with Ilya Averbakh explains their frequent collaborations.[7] These filmographic and biographical details place Riazantseva at the heart of this artistic period and according to interviews and documents, it seems that Riazantseva was the principal author of the *Wings* script.

Another reason to analyze the script in detail in regard to the film is the tradition of literary scripts (*literaturnye stsenarii*), specific to the Soviet context. Whereas in the West, screenplays were traditionally written in the present tense, with very few descriptions and no incursions in the character's feelings and thoughts (unless they are heard as a voice over), and dialogues were signaled very clearly, in the Soviet literary script of the 1960s, the main text was presented as a novel.[8] As Riazantseva puts it herself: "Inexperienced readers – I many times verified this myself – are completely unable to tell a novel from a script."[9] Thus in a literary script, the dialogues are not always fully written, and not always clearly assigned. The authors gladly use the past tense, descriptions, *apartés*, and sometimes even describe their characters' emotions or thoughts. Moreover, many directors as well as screenwriters defended this literary tradition as crucial to the Soviet cinema. In his foreword to Riazantseva's book of screenplays, Soloviov writes:

> Natalia Riazantseva, as cliché as it sounds, is a typical representative of the Soviet screenwriting school. The Soviet scriptwriting school always understood the script as literature. [. . .] [M]eanings, images, the future appearance [of the film] are embedded in these letters, they magically grow out of them.[10]

One could even argue that this specific tradition of screenwriting is one of the reasons why many recent studies have shown the importance of the sensory, haptic quality of Soviet cinema,[11] since the idea behind this tradition is that the literary qualities of the written text are to inspire a cinematic "translation" into cinematographic language. Thus, the screenplay should be not just a notation of actions and dialogues, but be as expressive as possible, using adjectives and detailed descriptions that would eventually inspire the *mise-en-scène*.[12] We will see in Riazantseva's writing several striking examples of an authentic literary writing.[13] Moreover, even if she complains that "talented directing has always trumped literary efforts"[14] and that it is quite rare to find a person who would read a script as a literary text, at the same she time completely contradicts herself by recounting the following episode:

> I received one author's copy with my script in the *Iskusstvo kino* editorial office. One is not enough; I had to buy more at the newsstands [. . .]. At one kiosk near metro station Belorusskaya a girl is sitting, reading something under the counter. I ask: do you have this issue? "Oh, she says, it's the last one left, I'm reading it now, there's such an interesting script, I can't tear myself away, can I finish it and then leave it for you? Come back tomorrow, I'll hide it, I'll remember you." I ran away without revealing that it was *my* script she was reading![15]

As a matter of fact, in the USSR, there was a solid tradition for publication of scripts, and it had little to do with whether the film would be realized or not. Thus, *Iskusstvo kino* boasted in its presentation that it published 16 scripts per year. Since its foundation in the 1930s, the journal has published numerous scripts and texts on the training of screenwriters. In the 1960s and 1970s, the journal published screenplays by Evgenii Yevtushenko, Andrei Tarkovsky and many others. The version of the script we are going to analyze here is a perfect example of such a publishing tradition, since it had been published two years before the film was finished.

A COMPLEX CHARACTER, FROM TEXT TO SCREEN

The dialogue between the script and the film is particularly interesting in what concerns the description and characterization of the main character.

The first description of Nadia in Riazantseva and Ezhov's script emphasizes her ordinary and underwhelming looks—in the middle of a crowd composed of boys who intend to jump in the water, "a woman slipped in the middle, not very young, starting to gain weight, in a faded, polka-dot bathing suit."[16] The next descriptions convey the same impression. The reader is reminded of her being overweight when she helps a waitress of a canteen to move bottle crates: "They were two fat women after all."[17] These reminders accentuate the contrast between her silhouette of the present time and that of her past self, in the flashbacks, where she is described as "a thin sixteen-year-old girl."[18]

She is always described by the authors of the script as quite unappealing: "She began to brush her unattractively curled hair, and it became tangled again in the wind."[19] She seems to have poor choice in clothing and no knowledge whatsoever of how to spruce herself up: "Anyone who knows anything about fashion would find her clothes appalling: the skirt was out of age, the blouse was out of fashion, and the brooch was out of place, but she didn't seem to care."[20]

She is awkward and rigid in her gestures: "Nadezhda Sergeyevna[21] awkwardly pulled on her wool sweater and buttoned her collar high with a shiny brooch;"[22] "Nadezha Sergeyevna, upright, stiff, in a dress with a starched collar, walked to her classroom."[23] But this rigidity is compensated by her corpulence and her very feminine appearance—kids call her 'auntie' (*teten'ka*).

In the film, Shepitko and the actress Maya Bulgakova significantly changed the image of the protagonist. In particular, the beginning of the film strongly conveys two impressions: her almost complete lack of femininity and her apparent lack of individuality. The film opens with a sequence absent from the script, at a sewing shop. We observe people passing in the street without any diegetic sound.[24] Then we hear footsteps, and a tailor appears in the frame, while the camera travels back, revealing that the passers-by were observed through the window of the shop. The tailor has a dark tissue, that looks quite rigid, hanging over his shoulder, and enters a cabin where someone is standing whom we do not immediately identify as male or female. The person (we only see their back) is wearing a dark suit and has short hair. Their voice does not provide a completely clear indication either. "This one?" asks the tailor. "This one," confirms the person. "Let's start," says the tailor. We then see a series of close ups where we see only a part of the client's upper body (shoulders, back, neck) and the centimeter, while the tailor's voice measures the client and proceeds to a presentation of the character through numbers: "105, 35, 39, 48, 35, 55, 42, 14, 19, 91, 78, 60, 56, 5." Usually, an opening sequence introduces the main character by displaying his physical appearance, manners, and behavior. But this count and these shots deliver to us no such information whatsoever. When the count is done, we finally see the protagonist's face and discover that she is in fact a woman. As for the tailor, he doesn't really look at her and lets out inadvertently: "It is a standard size 48." So, after presenting her as someone with masculine attitude and appearance or, at least, someone that no one would ever dream to call 'auntie,' the film emphasizes her dullness, her ordinary, nondescript personality: she is 'standard,' she can be reduced to a series of numbers. In the following sequence, when her students are trying to eavesdrop on a formal event she is attending, and fail to hear what she is saying, noteworthy dialogue between them takes place:

- One, two, three, four, five . . . That's a lot of decorations!
- These are medals.
- And the sound. What is she saying?
- Why, is it so hard to guess?

Once again, she is described through numbers (this time it is the number of her war medals). The following discussion indicates that she is probably saying run-of-the-mill platitudes in a typical late-Soviet style, but it also goes to show how predictable she is—it is not hard to guess what she must be saying. (An indication of that aspect of her personality was already present in a short comment in the script about the fact that she would always have the radio on in her room, as if she could never stay alone with her own thoughts and was only comfortable with a continuous stream of Soviet platitudes that most radio programs would broadcast.)

As Olena Dmytryk points out, Nadia offers "to the audience a representation of female masculinity,"[25] since she "does not strive to conform to Thaw gender conventions of femininity"[26] (she is not a biological mother, doesn't want to cook her meals anymore, prefers eating in a man-populated bar, does not marry her suitor). Dmytryk even goes as far as suggesting that Nadia could be considered as "a 'queer' character, as her behavior is a dissent against the hegemonic gender and sexual norms of the Thaw."[27]

But the character is also both "hard and soft." This feminine softness does appear in the film, especially when Nadia suddenly displays her fragility: when she tenderly whispers to call her friend-suitor Pasha, then her daughter, asking them to come back after they've closed the door behind them, or when we suddenly see her beautiful and fit body lying on the beach and stretching in the warm sun. Lida Oukaderova pointed out this permanent tension between the protagonist's image and how she perceives herself or how she *feels* in the world: she "cannot avoid being framed as an object," while she is being filmed "as a mute, framed face on a local television channel; as an inhibited figure standing in a café, stared at by a group of men; and in a photograph nailed to a wall in a museum,"[28] but she seeks a haptic, sensory relationship to her surroundings.

This binary feminine-masculine quality of the protagonist is most probably inspired by Riazantseva and Shepitko's position in the Soviet film industry. Riazantseva writes:

> We have been so afraid of sentimentality, so often demonstrated our courageous attitude toward life, because in our profession women are

regarded with suspicion, and sentimentality is somehow considered a sign of a woman's world view, although this is not true at all.[29]

Shepitko also said on several occasions that because of her gender, she felt herself "as a guest"[30] in her own profession. It is also quite striking that Soloviov for instance, would even analyze Riazantseva's script (he also considered Riazantseva as the main author of the script), with the same concepts: "an endlessly delicate web of psychological details, which only a woman can discern in characters and human relationships, is spread around or hidden (all in the right proportions) in the rigid, masculine framework of the dramaturgical scheme."[31]

The other side of the character that is very important in both the script and the film is Nadia's awkwardness. It is underlined several times in the script, by descriptions as well as by actions: she often behaves strangely, out of tune with everybody else, and seems to suffer from it. But whereas the script mostly stands on her side and shows that she is right in her behavior and decisions, even if a little extreme, the film shows otherwise. One of the most striking examples is the sequence when she goes to visit her adoptive daughter as it is described in the script and filmed and edited in the film. Her daughter has left to live with her husband/lover and has not invited her mother over, or even really warned her beforehand.

In the script, Nadia buys a cake and goes to visit her daughter. They have guests over, who welcome and surround Nadia when she says: "Well, young people, shall we have a drink?" (*Nu chto, molodezh, vypiem?*) and then "You are all a bit dull" (*Kakie-to vy skuchnye*). The young crowd seems to rather appreciate her, responding to her, making jokes, one of them remembering that he is her former student. Her daughter however is very reticent with her and she is in a bad mood because of a fight with her recent husband. When Nadia tries to reason with her, Tanya answers: "Everything in life is more complicated, and you would never understand it. Thank you for my happy childhood. That's enough."[32] Then her behavior becomes even more offensive:

> Tanya twirled in front of Nadezhda Sergeyevna, spread her arms, smiled indulgently, as if she were talking to a child, and Nadezhda Sergeyevna stood there, lost, at first not even understanding Tanya's words. But with each of Tanya's movements, it became clearer and clearer to her that there was an unknown and unkind person in front of her, and that she could not change anything however hard she would try.[33]

Then, desperate to see eye to eye with this ungrateful child, Nadia admits that she has adopted her and leaves without looking back, even though Tanya feels bad and timidly calls her "mom".

In the film, Shepitko manages to make the situation much more complex, sometimes by slight changes in the *mise-en-scéne* or choice of actors. For instance, Tanya's fiancé is her former teacher (he admits being 37 years old) and the crowd assembled in their small flat is around thirty or even forty years old. Nadia exclaims with an awkward laughter: "Well, young people, why aren't you cheerful, why are you so sad? Put on your woogie-boogie (*sic*)." But this time, it is painfully obvious how wrong these sentences sound in this context. These men are not really young, they are quite adult, and she has just interrupted a serious artistic discussion (in a short episode Evgenii Evsitgneev is telling a theatrical story that sounds like improvisation). The guests then try to flee under various pretenses, but Nadia stops them on the doorstep, makes them come back to eat the cake and have a drink with her. When they all surround her and tell her that "Igor is so lucky to have such a great stepmother," the spectator perfectly understands what is going on, while Nadia seems genuinely pleased. Another element of this scene discretely points at Nadia's desynchronization with the others. She wants to make a toast to the married couple and starts reciting a poem by Stepan Shipachev, "Love is to be treasured."[34] The poem is from 1939, it is quite naïve, and the poet is mainly known for his wartime poems. This idea of outdated references was already present – quite early in the script as well as in the film – when Nadia teaches a song to her neighbor's kids: "The Steel Squadron,"[35] a march that was mostly popular during the Second World War. When Nadia tries to remember the love poem, the only one to catch up with her is Evstigneev's character, who is obviously the eldest in the room apart from Nadia. As to the daughter, she is annoyed by her mother, but throughout the entire passage tries to behave well towards her. Nadia also behaves less radically (one might say, less cruelly) in the film than in the script: her complaints about her adoptive daughter are not addressed to the daughter herself but only to her friend Pasha.

Of course, Nadezhda's painfully preposterous behavior, which almost hurts the spectator, reminds us of the film that will be made in the USSR some years later, also based on a script by Natalia Riazantseva—Kira Muratova's *Long Goodbyes*. Just as in Muratova's case later, Shepitko takes a brilliantly depicted middle-aged woman that struggles to fit the role society has cast for her and is at pains to have relationships with others; she accentuates her traits and her risibility. In both cases, the protagonists' jobs were upgraded so that they would seem more respectable: Nadia was a schoolteacher in the script, she is a professional school director in the final version, whereas Muratova's Evgeniia is transformed from a typist into a chief translator.[36]

But both Shepitko and Muratova, while showing us how their characters are misfits, make it possible for the spectator to feel at the same time their humanity and their interior fragility, which makes them loveable. This is how Jane Taubman described Muratova's protagonist: "Muratova subjects her heroine to a steely-eyed, penetrating gaze that reveals her worst faults. But [. . .] Evgeniia is no caricature. Sharko makes her sufficiently sympathetic for us to cringe in embarrassment"[37] when she ridicules herself. When she was preparing for the shooting of *Wings*, Shepitko said that conveying the complexity of Nadia's contradictory behavior was essential to the success of the film.[38] The proximity of these two characters created and cocreated by Riazantseva is coherent with the screenwriters' tastes and predilections. As Dmitrii Bykov put it, the "beauty of defeat, the existential courage of the doomed (. . .) becomes the main theme of her scripts."[39]

Just as will be the case for Evgeniia (who is divorced), Nadia (whose great love has died during the war) is courted by a man and could make a new sentimental life for herself, but it doesn't work out. Nadia's suitor is a long-time friend, and in the script, they go as far as making an appointment at the registry office for their marriage, but in the last scene, Pasha tells her: "You think, I really believe you are going to marry me?"[40] and she welcomes this acknowledgment with gratitude and relief. In the film, this plotline is reduced to its minimum since Nadia's sudden question to Pasha: "Will you marry me?" is understood by both of them as nothing more than a last-ditch effort to fit into contemporary life. Nadia immediately drops the subject and Pasha does not even answer her question.

It may be the director herself that gave the most interesting hint on how Nadia's difficulty in her interactions with others should be viewed:

> She was always in a tense *mise-en-scène* towards herself, time, and society, and she was very sensitive to social demands. She sincerely met these demands, but times were changing, and her and her peers' assessments of her own position in life were, of course, reconsidered. But a human being cannot be multiplied. It is possible to revise an opinion, but it is impossible to revise life.[41]

Thus, Nadia is always in a self-representation mode, almost never acting naturally. Hence the strictness and the unvoluntary cruelty. One of the most striking moments of the film is when Nadia makes a denigrating comment to the student that had run away from professional school and then come back, thus provoking his violent reaction (he tells her that he hates her). The way Bulgakova performs this scene shows how Nadia instantly realizes that it was a big mistake to say what she said. Such brisk changes from happiness to bitterness and disappointment can be observed several times in the film, as was already foreshadowed in the script, through her falsely enthusiastic announcements ("I am going to eat at the restaurant every day starting from now on"[42]) but also when she was trying to make herself pretty by changing her hairstyle and then by feeling ashamed.[43] The same happens when she refused to participate in the end of school class party, and we stay with her, while joyful speeches and applause are heard from afar.[44] Like Evgeniia, Nadia could be characterized by the French film critic Serge Daney as one of those "characters whose narrow horizon is coupled with a useless lucidity."[45]

REMINISCENCES OF THE PAST

On the whole, the script appears much more cohesive and understandable, narration-wise, than the film, which clearly opts for a more fragmented story. One of the reasons for that is the way the scriptwriters and the director use images and sounds of the past. In the script, there are three flashbacks. The first one appears on page 25 (of 57) of the archival copy, almost in the middle of the screenplay. After it, the flashbacks take up more and more space in the narration. After two pages dealing with the present, we immediately go to the second flashback, one-page long. Afterwards, memories take more and more space in the narration, ending the script with one long flashback that allows us to fully understand the protagonist's story.[46] While in the first two flashbacks we learn about her training and her feelings for her instructor, in this long final flashback, we witness her first accident during the war and how, afterwards, she is found by Soviet soldiers ("Wow, it's a chick," "She's just a girl"[47]), then how she meets her instructor, who has also been injured, in the hospital, how he courts her, and finally how they decide to enroll in the same unit, never to be separated again, but then he perishes in an attack that she witnesses. After these flashbacks we now fully understand the protagonist's trauma and bereavement, and why it is so hard for her to live in the present. Moreover, this unusual structure—two short flashbacks in the middle and a very long one that takes up almost all the final third of the script—makes us experience an overwhelming *presence of the past*, as if the narration, just as its protagonist, struggles to remain in the present. One could even argue that this last flashback is the most intense part of the narration since there are two action scenes (Nadia's first accident and Mitia's death) and because several months of a lifetime are squeezed into a few pages. The diegetic present, by contrast, is much less eventful; there are many scenes where Nadia just walks around, talking with Pasha or alone (Oukaderova qualified her as "the Soviet flaneur"[48]), and the diegetic duration of the present segment is only a few days.

In the film, the sudden emergence of the images from the past is rather short, even though, here too, the two final flashbacks are longer. The director keeps only fragments from the sequences described in the script even though we know many of them have been shot or at least prepared (as the storyboard from the first flashback of the script proves, when Nadia is in training and almost kills a nearby goat[49]). Most of them are filmed from the protagonist's subjective point of view. Unlike the script, we almost never *see* the young version of Nadia, but we see *through* her eyes – there is a permanent "juxtaposition and tension between objectivity and subjectivity, between looking at and looking with the protagonist."[50]

For instance, twice, images from the past do not even appear as flashbacks because they completely lack any narrative consistency: they rather appear as visual reminiscences that suddenly emerge in front of the protagonist's eyes or inside her head, by association with what she sees. The first one appears only 12 minutes into the film (out of 81 minutes) and thus much earlier than in the script. After taking her neighbor's kids to the beach and then to the aerodrome, Nadia is in her kitchen, peeling potatoes. The camera pans from her busy hands to her face. She stops her activity and forgetfully gazes out the window. The diegetic sounds disappear, and we hear extradiegetic music played by a violin. Then we see what seems to be in front of Nadia's eyes, as if we were on a plane: the clouds and the earth cross the frame diagonally, as if the plane was flying lopsided **(see Fig. 3.1)**. Then the image gets blurry, and the yard of her house appears. First it is out of focus, but quickly the focus is reestablished, while the diegetic sound returns with her neighbor calling her and pulling her out of her reverie. An identical moment happens once again in the 38th minute of the film. We see Nadia standing in a corridor of the professional school she directs. When

Figure 3.1 Nadia's reminiscence of flying.

the cleaning lady addresses her with a question about the runaway student, Nadia does not respond. Instead, we see her face in a close-up. Then, once again, we see the shot of the sky. Then the image gets blurry, and the shot of the school yard appears, while the diegetic sound returns (the cleaning lady is still calling: "Nadezhda Stepanovna!"). Each of these episodes is very brief: only 15 seconds for the first one and 14 seconds for the second (counting from the start to the interruption of the music), but they are nonetheless strangely haunting. Oukaderova quite accurately notes that these reminiscences "completely defy the kind of framing of Nadia's body prevalent in the representations of her current life,"[51] which partially explains this "haunting" effect on the spectator.

Here, the music also deserves our special attention. It is a poignant melody played by a single violin and it is always interrupted mid-way, creating an even stronger effect of emotional strain on the spectator. This unfinished melody is a metaphor of the protagonist's heartbreaking loss of the life she could have lived with Mitia. Such an approach to extradiegetic music is quite typical of this cinematographic epoch. It is the same kind of music that we find in Muratova's *Long Goodbyes*. The composer Oleg Karavaichuk recounted that during his collaboration on this film with Muratova, he composed a musical score for an orchestra, but she transformed it to into a piano solo which was, moreover, slightly out of tune.[52]

In *Wings*, the beginnings and the ends of these reminiscences are signaled to us by the music, which starts before the image of the past appears, as if the visual snippets of Nadia's memories imposed themselves, almost against her will. This state of mind—being swept away by an involuntary influx of memories or past sensations—was already hinted at by the script: "She was thinking about something of her own. She had been distracted all day today. She often seemed distracted."[53]

The spectators then feel that what they observe are not memories but rather reminiscences, not as violent as post-traumatic involuntary retrieval of unwanted memories, but also unavoidable. While memory and remembrance signify the capacity to remember as well as the content of the memory, the *reminiscence*, a word that I find more accurate in this context, is centered on feeling, on the senses and on the process of remembering rather than the contents. Reminiscence comes from the late Latin *reminiscentia* (reminiscence, recollection) and from the verb "reminsci" which means "recall to one's memory, make an act of remembrance."[54] In his *In Search of Lost Time*, Marcel Proust called the effect of apparition of memories due to a sensation such as taste (the famous madeleine) a "reminiscence."[55] By the way, in a text about Shepitko written after her death, Riazantseva confirms that this is exactly how she experiences memory, as overwhelming, sensorial waves: "Am I remembering? No, no effort of memory, no recall – I remember anyway, excessively, with an overabundance of detail, color, light. It is dazzling."[56]

The loss of any narrative value of these 'images of the past' is a valuable addition to the elegiac style of the film. In the script, the moments where Nadia watches the planes are those where this intonation is most noticeable in the text. For instance, when Nadia and the boys on the beach are looking at a plane making loops in the air, this is how it is described in the script: "The woman stood up and looked up at the sky, too. In the sunlight, barely visible, a white feather was somersaulting."[57] On the aerodrome, Nadia's ecstasy at the sight of the planes is again conveyed through metaphor:

> She never took her eyes off the rising plane. [. . .] Nadezhda Sergeyevna followed the young woman with her eyes as she walked toward the plane, and then she followed the plane, which was rapidly gaining speed, and she flinched as it took off from the ground and squinted and squinted until it turned into a dot and melted into the sun.[58]

The same music is also used by Shepitko in other sequences of the film, with no obvious image from the past but which she wants to show as moments of reminiscence. For instance, when a plane makes loops in the sky it is accompanied by the same music, even though this time the diegetic sound also stays in the soundtrack. The penultimate flashback of the film is introduced by a metaphoric shot. Nadia wanders around the city, buys some berries but cannot wash them before eating them because there is no water in the nearby faucet. She then starts walking, her hands full with berries, and—as if answering her secret wish—it starts pouring down. The street empties while everybody takes cover and Nadia finds herself alone in the middle of a large empty street. The same music starts again, this time played by a piano and a violin. Once again, the close-up of her face is followed by a subjective shot of the empty street that strangely resembles a take-off runway. A new shot of Nadia's face is followed by another shot of the street. But this one is imaginary: in a diving shot, the camera travels forward above the wet cobblestones then pans up and leaves the ground as if taking off. It goes up and up until most of the frame is occupied by the sky and we hear her calling out: "Mitia!" The next shot makes us 'land' in the penultimate flashback, that lasts for three and a half minutes (the final flashback of the script is cut into two in the film).

But instead of a cohesive long narration about Nadia's youth and love during the war what we get here are again only snippets. They do come from the script, but they are barely recognizable. For instance, the first shot brings us to the countryside, as Mitia is walking towards Nadia (through whose eyes we are watching the scene), while she tells him: "Let's go back." The spectator at this point cannot know what Nadia is talking about. But we can clearly situate this moment with the help of the script: when they are both at the sanatorium, Mitia and Nadia leave it on the sly in an attempt to get to the seaside on foot. They get lost on the way, sleep out in the middle of nowhere and have their first kiss during this escapade. The conversations they have during this episode of the film, such as their discussion about a long-forgotten people that left stone art behind them before disappearing, or else the suggestion that Mitia makes about asking to join her squadron, as well as their confessions of love, all come from the script. However, whereas in the script they were very easy to understand and to follow because they were linked to other parts of the screenplay, here, we can barely situate them in a narrative continuity since we get only short and disconnected bits of these conversations and miss the larger context.

This way of abandoning large parts of the context that was present in the script and leaving in the finished film only short bits of it also reminds us of Muratova's *Long Farewells*: in the script, along with the main storyline of the mother and her son Sasha trying (and failing) to understand each other and to communicate normally, there is a second storyline, about Sasha's teacher, Anna Danilovna, who is very awkward and insecure. She is mocked by Sasha's class, and it is partly through his decision to help her that Sasha matures enough to understand that he needs to be supportive of his mother.[59] Muratova filmed the sequences of this storyline but finally decided to cut them from the final edit (there even was an important disagreement between Riazantseva and Muratova because of this decision[60]). But Muratova put in the final version of the film a very enigmatic three-minute sequence that is actually composed of snippets from these cut sequences; we even see the face of the actress who played the teacher, Natalia Ralleva. Here again there is something common between both Shepitko and Muratova who "basically took a finished script and started to damage it as [they] needed to,"[61] according to Muratova's words.

In the flashback of Mitia, each one of the five shots that compose it ends in a freeze frame. These mental 'photographies,' snapshots of Mitia, at the same time underline Nadia's loss and grief and discontinuity of her memories that seem to escape her. The philosopher Paul Ricoeur considered that forgetting was one of the intrinsic characteristics of private memory, as opposed to the official and collective memory.[62] By dealing in this elliptic way with the flashback of the script, by creating a character that "is in the 'time trap' between collective and individual memory, between ideological clichés/historical myths and everyday life/real experience,"[63] Shepitko fully takes her place among other important Soviet film directors obsessed with individual, private memories, such as Alexey German Sr. But let us remember that *Wings* was made in 1966, while *Trial on the Roads* (*Proverka na dorogakh*, 1972), *Twenty Days without War* (*Dvadzat' dney bez voyny*, 1976) and *My Friend Ivan Lapshin* (*Moy drug Ivan Lapshin*, 1983) would not be directed until the 1970s and the beginning of the 1980s.[64]

The film's last flashback is very different from the others even though it is once again introduced by Nadia's gaze: she stands in front of the museum stand dedicated to Mitia's heroic death, she lowers her head and then suddenly raises it, her eyes above the stand (**see Fig. 3.2**).

Figure 3.2 Nadia in front of the museum stand.

But this time she is not facing the camera which already hints at the different quality of the sequence to come. The flashback shows Mitia's final battle where he perishes. Here the *mise-en-scène* is "objective," exterior to Nadia's point of view: we see Mitia alone in his aircraft as well as Nadia alone in hers. This time we see her face. We also see both planes from afar when Mitia's plane, hit by enemy fire, descends to the ground, and Nadia's plane makes tender and desperate circles around it. Here once again, Shepitko has found a cinematographic way to convey the tenderness and repetition expressed in words in the screenplay, where Nadia communicates by radio with Mitia until the end: "Yes, my treasure! . . . (*Da, moy rodnoy*) Yes, my darling! . . . Hold on! . . . Hold on. Just a little bit more, just a little bit further."[65] When Mitia's aircraft is hit, the same extradiegetic music intervenes once again, replacing the more conventional music that accompanied the beginning of the scene. It is this time reinforced by an orchestra. It takes us out of the present of the event (the deadly combat) and places us in the present of Nadia's contemporary life, from where she is remembering this moment. After Mitia's plane crashes and explodes, we go back to the subjective camera: we fly over the burning remains, and then forward, above small silhouettes in the field and over a church in the distance. In the script, this moment is described as a subjective camera shot: "Nadia did not hear the explosion. She only saw a hole – from the height of it – a small hole. Nadia threw the machine down, in a dive, and almost crashed into the hole herself . . . Like a candle, she soared high up into the bright sky."[66] Whereas in the previous flashback, every shot ended with a freeze frame, here there are two freeze frames inside the same shot: one of the burning remnants and one of the church. The editing then brings us back to the museum stand and to Mitia's photography pinned on it. The camera then pans down and finds Nadia's photograph, young, with very short hair and a large smile. This link between individual memory and photography will be developed again by German Sr. in *Twenty Days without War*. The main hero of the film, the war journalist and writer Lopatin, is in Tashkent for a few days and visits the cinema studio where they are filming a short film based on one of his war novels. The novel was about a civilian woman and some of Lopatin's comrades who perished during an air attack near Stalingrad. Not convinced by the intradiegetic *mise-en-scène*, Lopatin suddenly remembers this episode as he witnessed it. We see everyone—his close friend, the woman and others—getting ready to be photographed when the airstrike happens, and they get buried under a fallen wall. Mikhail Yampolsky analyzed this moment as a "radical, violent" way to be transported "from the reality into the past" because "both the people and the ruins against which they were photographed, cease to exist in the most literal sense only a moment after Lopatin has triggered the shutter. Here, fixation and annihilation coincide. What remains of the disappearing reality?"[67] Shepitko's Nadia seems to ask herself the same question: after the story about the people "that just left one day" that she shares with Mitia during their walk in her memory, and the story her friend Pasha (the director of the museum) tells her about a frozen mammoth that was discovered by the scientists and that was "perfectly edible," she suddenly tells him: "I am your exhibit. [. . .] You know, earlier today, a girl asked about me: 'Did she die, too?' By the way, what do you think: did she die?" The connection with her past self, the one smiling at us from the photograph on the stand, and her present self is not obvious even to herself.

Yampolsky argues that German works "to restore the individual memory of unspeakable facts."[68] The same could be said of *Wings*. In Shepitko's film, the photographs appear as disappointing documents since they do not reveal all the amplitude of the protagonists' feelings, but they also represent the effort of the individual memory to retain the past (the freeze frames tried to "stop the instant" in Nadia's private memories of Mitia) as well as its incapacity to do so, and thus the finitude and fragmentation. Just as it will be for German, for Shepitko in 1966, the individual memory and the subjective sensations and reminiscences are infinitely more precious than the official version of history: before the last flashback Nadia observes an unwell, bored guide, who tells her story in a few formal and dry words in front of a class of school kids also bored out of their wits.

The end of the film takes a sequence situated initially quite far from the end of the script and transforms it. In the script, Nadia comes to the aerodrome once again, and an old friend of hers who has become a flight instructor suggests taking her on a flight with him. He has invited her before, but she has refused. This time she accepts. It is during this flight that the long final flashback of the script is triggered. This is how this flight is described by Riazantseva and Ezhov: "Nadezhda Sergeyevna leaned back in her seat. Her face was changing with every minute of her flight. It came alive, became youthful. Nadezhda Sergeyevna smiled a broad, childlike, ingenuous smile, the way people smile only when no one sees them. [. . .] She had a happy face that we had never seen before."[69] What she sees from the window is described exactly as we see it in the film in the two reminiscences: "And suddenly the Earth stood as a wall on one side, and on the other side was a wall of sky and below there was the horizon."[70] But in the film, this flight does not happen by invitation. Very unhappy, Nadia ends up (once again) on the aerodrome where she looks for her friend, nowhere to be found. Left alone on the field near a plane, she suddenly hesitates, then painfully climbs inside the aircraft. Her friend then appears, surrounded by his students. He says it is too late to take her on a ride, but the students suggest to just give her a ride on the field. While rolling on the field, she already starts laughing like a kid ("She glowed with joy, like a schoolgirl, and then laughed happily"[71]), but then her face grows suddenly serious. Her eyes fill up with tears (**see Fig. 3.3**).

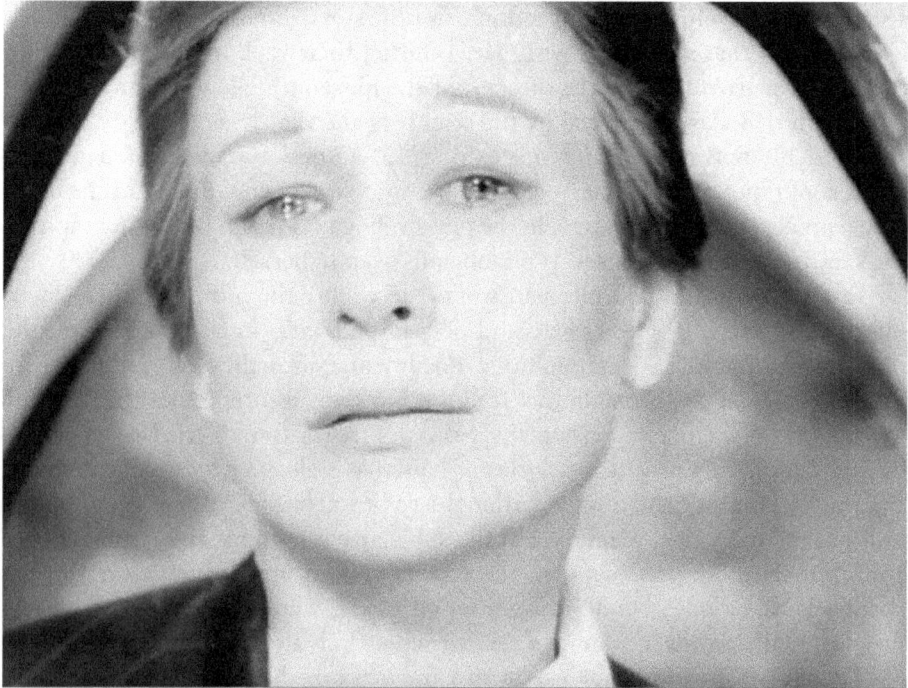

Figure 3.3 Nadia in the plane. Her eyes fill up with tears.

When the students are ready to park the plane, Nadia suddenly starts the engine, escapes the students and her friend trying to stop her, rolls away on the runway and takes off in the distance. The final shot of the film, that lasts for thirty seconds, looks like the two reminiscences in the first part of the film, though it is just slightly longer: it is a subjective camera shot from the plane, of the sky and earth, spinning. The extradiegetic music appears when the plane drives on the take-off runway, but this time it is harmoniously supported by additional instruments.

Even though in the script this moment was situated far from the end, the poetics developed by the authors underlined the importance of this moment: Nadia "got used to the plane, it became easier for her, and the wings of the plane became her wings. She soared up, tumbled, fell, bathed in the sky."[72]

This final sequence has been questioned by all the scholars who have studied the film as well as by the redactors at the time. Olena Dmytryk underlines that the script's finale is much more conventional, whereas the "film ending is more open and thus much more provocative."[73] Danijela Lugarić considers that the last scene can be read as the protagonist's suicide.[74] The redactors of the script commission considered that the finale could be understood as an "act of rebellion."[75] But one could argue that it is simply the past 'winning over' the film. The resemblance of this last shot with the reminiscences that appeared out of nowhere in the middle of Nadia's everyday life and this unrealistic and poetic ending create the sensation that the "present past" of individual memories and reminiscences has taken over the film. The past has become present (and the present has become the past) in this dreamlike escape from her disappointing reality.

NOTES

1. Valentin Ezhov, Natalia Riazantseva, "Povest' o liotchitse", *Iskusstvo kino* 12 (1964), 119–156.
2. Larisa Shepitko, *Gvardii kapitan. Rezhissiorskaia razrabotka fil'ma*, RGALI, file 3223 opis 1, delo 15.
3. Apart from all the versions of a script demanded by the Soviet system of production and censorship, Riazantseva was famous for writing and re-writing her scripts many times: "she writes slowly, laboriously, painfully, so that each episode exists in a huge number of versions . . ." Sergei Soloviov "Predislovie" in Natalia Riazantseva, *Golos, Kinoscenarii* (Moscow: Amfora, 2007) 9–11, 9.
4. Larisa Shepitko, "Poslednee interv'iu", interview with Lev Rybak, in Elem Klimov (ed), *Larisa. Kniga o Larise Shepitko* (Moscow: Iskusstvo, 1987), 179–194, 185.
5. "In my opinion, *Heat* is nothing more than an exercise that should have been made within the walls of the VGIK, and even not in the last year." Larisa Shepitko, "Poslednee interv'iu" 180.

6. Eugénie Zvonkine, 2012, *Kira Mouratova, un cinema de la dissonance*, Lausanne : L'Âge d'Homme, 72.
7. She was married first to Gennaii Shpalikov, director and scriptwriter, who, too, wrote the scripts for such unmissable films of the end of the Thaw as *I am Twenty* (*Zastava Il'icha*, released as *Mne dvadtsat' let*, 1964) by Marlen Khutsiev, where Riazantseva holds a small part as an actress, and *Walking the Streets of Moscow* (*Ya shagayu po Moskve*, 1964) by Georgii Daneliya. He would also write the script of Shepitko's later film, *You and I* (*Ty i ya*, 1971).
8. There are, however, some noticeable counterexamples, such as Michelangelo Antonioni's screenplays.
9. Natalia Riazantseva, "Ot avtora", in Natalia Riazantseva, Golos, 12–16, 13.
10. Soloviov, 11.
11. Emma Widdis, *Socialist Senses, Film, Feeling and the Soviet Subject, 1917–1940* (Bloomington : Indiana University Press, 2017); Oukaderova Lida, *The Cinema of the Soviet Thaw, Space, Materiality, Movement* (Bloomington: Indiana University Press, 2017); Toropova Anna, *Feeling Revolution, Cinema, Genre, and the Politics of Affect under Stalin* (Oxford: Oxford University Press, 2020); Ana Hedberg Olenina, *Psychomotor Aesthetics: Movement and Affect in Modern Literature and Film* (Oxford: Oxford University Press, 2020).
12. This idea was already championed by Sergei Eisenstein in "The Form of the Script," transl. into English by Richard Taylor (ed.), *S.M. Eisenstein, Writings, 1922–1934* (London: BFI Publishing, 1988), 34–136; Sergei Eisenstein, "O forme scenariia," *Biulleten' kinokontory torgpredstva SSSR v Germanii* Berlin, 1929, Nos. 1–2, 29–32.
13. It is noteworthy that Evgenii Gabrilovich, who stands at the origins of the literary screenwriting tradition, was Riazantseva's professor in VGIK. Riazantseva, "Ot avtora," 12. During the first half of the 1930s, Nathan Zarkhi, one of the most important screenwriters of the time, recounts his discussion with the writer Evgenii Gabrilovich in which he was convincing him to devote himself to screenwriting. He argued that "the screenplay was, or at least should become, a literary genre in its own right, 'authentic pure-blooded literature'; that in ten years' time film scripts would be written by 'the Tolstoys and Turgenevs of our time' and that cinematurgy (as Zarkhi called it) would be high on the list of libraries." Luda & Jean Schnitzer, « Cinématurgie », *La maison où je vis et autres scénarios littéraires soviétiques*, Paris : Les éditeurs français réunis, 1969, 45.
14. Riazantseva, "Ot avtora,"13.
15. Riazantseva, 13–14.
16. Natalia Riazantseva, Valentin Ezhov, "Krylia" in Natalia Riazantseva, *Golos. Kinoscenarii*, 511–568, 511.
17. Riazantseva, Ezhov, 540.
18. Riazantseva, Ezhov, 536.
19. Riazantseva, Ezhov, 513.
20. Riazantseva, Ezhov, 513.
21. She becomes Nadezhda Stepanovna in the film.
22. Riazantseva, Ezhov, 518.
23. Riazantseva, *Ezhov*, 530.

24. Lida Oukaderova accurately points out that, "As the establishing shot of the feature, it is sorely lacking in any concrete coordinates to situate the image in time and place." Oukaderova, 120.
25. Olena Dmytryk, "Difficult cases: Communist morality, gender and embodiment in Thaw cinema," *Studies in Russian and Soviet Cinema*, 11:1 (2017), 3–19, 9.
26. Dmytryk, 7.
27. Dmytryk, 7–8.
28. Oukaderova, 117.
29. Natalia Riazantseva, "Prednaznachenie," in Elem Klimov (ed.), *Larisa*, 142–146, 143–144.
30. Larisa Shepitko, "Kogda my ne naprasny," Meeting with the audience, Kazan, 27.09.1979, in E. Klimov, *Larisa*, 168–176, 170.
31. Soloviov, 9–10.
32. Riazantseva, Ezhov, "Krylia," 527.
33. Riazantseva, Ezhov, 527–528.
34. "Lubov'iiu dorozhit' umeite".
35. "Stal'naia èskadril'ia," 1929, composed at the end of the 1920s, based on a poem by Boris Kovynev.
36. Delo fil'ma *Dolgie provody (Byt' muzhchinoi)*, avtor scenariia N. Riazantseva, rezzhissior- postanovstschik K.G. Muratova, proizvodstvo Odesskoi kinostudii, 05.03.1970 – 12.07.1971, RGALI, Goskino, f. 2944, op. 4, 2054, 39p.
37. Zinaida Sharko is the actress performing the part of Evgeniia Vasilievna. Jane Taubman, *Kira Muratova* (New York, Tauris, 2005), 20.
38. "The difficulty is that we seek to explore the character of a human being in detail. But it is not a cold, dispassionate analysis, but a struggle for the individual, an assertion of her rights to a place in life." Larisa Shepitko, "Vtoroi fil'm Larisy Shepitko," *Moskovskaja Pravda*, 07.09.1965.
39. Dmitrii Bykov, "Posleslovie," in E. Klimov (ed.), *Larisa*, 668–669, 668.
40. Riazantseva, Ezhov, "Krylia," 567.
41. Larisa Shepitko, "Poslednee interv'iu," 182.
42. Riazantseva, Ezhov, "Krylia," p. 518.
43. Riazantseva, Ezhov, 543.
44. Riazantseva, Ezhov, 533.
45. Serge Daney, « L'archipel Muratova », *Libération*, 17.08.1987.
46. Riazantseva, Ezhov, 552–567.
47. Riazantseva, Ezhov, 553.
48. Oukaderova, 116–149.
49. Storyboard of the episode "Aerodrom of the aeroclub" ("Aèrodrom aèrokluba") drawn by Elem Klimov, RGALI, f. 3223, op. 1 d. 13. 1965, 35–37.
50. Adam Bingham, "No Angels: Larisa Shepitko's Wings." *Senses of Cinema*, issue 53, 2009, consulted on http://sensesofcinema.com/2009/cteq/no-angels-larisa-shepitkos-wings/#fn-337-2
51. Oukaderova, 126.
52. Oleg Karavaichuk, interview by Pavel Sirkes, "Poriadok not," *Iskusstvo kino*, 2 (1995), 107–111.
53. Riazantseva, Ezhov, "Krylia," 516.

54. Centre National de Ressources Textuelles et Lexicales, cf. <https://www.cnrtl.fr/etymologie/r%C3%A9miniscence>.
55. Marcel Proust, *Le Temps retrouvé*, Paris : Gallimard, 1927, 878.
56. Riazantseva, "Prednaznachenie," in E. Klimov (ed.), *Larisa*, 142–146, 144.
57. Riazantseva, Ezhov, "Krylia," 512.
58. Riazantseva, Ezhov, 514–515.
59. Natalia Riazantseva, *Byt' muzhchinoi (o zhenshinakh i detiakh), literaturnyi stsenarii*, Odessa, 1970, 62 pp.; Natalia Riazantseva, *Byt' muzhchinoi, rezhissiorskaia razrabotka*, Odessa, 1970, 145 pp.
60. Natalia Riazantseva, interview by Jackie Buet, « Mouratova et les scénarios » in the Catalogue of the 10th International Women Film Festival, 12–20.03.1988, 67.
61. Kira Muratova, quoted by Viktor Bozhovich, « Rentgenoskopiia dushi », *Iskusstvo kino*, 9 (1987), 51–70, 59.
62. Paul Ricoeur, « Histoire et mémoire », in Antoine de Baecque and Christian Delage (eds.), *De l'histoire au cinéma*, Paris : Editions complexe, IHTP CNRS, coll. Histoire du temps présent, 1998, 17–28, 18.
63. Danijela Lugarić, "'I'm beginning a new life': the (im)possibility of beginning or ending in Larisa Shepitko's *Wings* and Pavel Chukhrai's *The Thief*", *Studies in Russian and Soviet Cinema*, 14:1 (2020), 37–56, 38.
64. About individual memory in German's cinema, cf. Alexander Graham, "Immersion in time: history, memory and the question of readability in the films of Aleksei German," *Studies in Russian and Soviet Cinema*, 6: 2 (2012), 177–216.
65. Riazantseva, Ezhov, "Krylia," 566.
66. Riazantseva, Ezhov, 566.
67. Mihail Jampolskii, « Front i tyl », *Kinovedcheskie zapiski*, 96 (2010), 180–181.
68. Ibid.
69. Riazantseva, Ezhov, "Krylia," 550.
70. Riazantseva, Ezhov, 550.
71. Riazantseva, Ezhov, 551.
72. Riazantseva, Ezhov, 551
73. Dmyrtyk, 10.
74. Danijela Lugarić, 42.
75. Valerii Fomin, "Skvoz' stroi," *Kinostsenarii*, 2 (1997), 170–174.

CHAPTER 4

The Ordeal and *The Ascent*[1]

Karla Oeler

The task of showing thinking and feeling that characters choose to keep to themselves—interiority—has long challenged filmmakers to innovate. Vasily Bykov's *The Ordeal* (1970), originally published with the title *Sotnikov*, presents Larisa Shepitko with precisely this challenge. The novel juxtaposes two protagonists, partisan fighters Rybak and Sotnikov, as they seek food for desperate comrades; skirmish with German soldiers; and ultimately suffer capture and punishment in a wintry World-War-II Soviet Union. Throughout the novel, from chapter to chapter, the dominating focalization alternates from one to the other. As Lazar Lazarev writes, "This principle is consistently maintained throughout the work. There is no neutral voice of the author . . ."[2] Through this alternating focalization, the novel contrasts two theories of morality, which moral philosophers might call consequentialist and deontological. Following a consequentialist logic, Rybak chooses to cooperate with the Germans once they are captured, rationalizing, fearfully, that this will allow him to live to fight Nazis and collaborators in the future. Sotnikov, in contrast, refuses, on principle, to give his captors any information; he assumes the deontological stance that any betrayal is impermissible, futile, and repugnant. Bykov relies on the technique of free indirect discourse to stage this conflict of moral viewpoints, realizing the unreliable and indeterminate ways it can play out under stark, wartime circumstances.

In adapting Bykov's novel, Shepitko acknowledges the challenge it poses: "Many warned that our ideological construction could be conveyed only in literature, where there is room for internal monologues, authorial digressions, etc. To tell the truth, I myself was afraid of this."[3] Her film *The Ascent* (1977) adapts Bykov's novel almost scene for scene, but it excludes the protagonists' memories and dreams, and does not easily lend itself to the crisply alternating focalization of the novel. While concerned about her ability to convey the novel's "ideological construction" through the filmic medium, Shepitko, even while still working on the film, professes satisfaction that the inwardness detailed in the novel is nevertheless making itself felt:

> And now, when more than half of the material has already been filmed, we suddenly noticed – and most importantly, others noticed it – that those numerous layers of memories, reflections of the characters, which were of help to the actors, turned out to be tangible on the screen. The invisible movement of the inner life of the characters one way or another comes through in their actions.[4]

She attributes this to a "miracle of cinema": "There is something that you can't see with your eyes on the set, but on the screen this invisible is felt, exists." This chapter aims to explore some of that "miracle" through close analysis. More specifically, in rendering Bykov's narrative as film, Shepitko must adapt his key device, free indirect discourse, but the constraints and affordances of film change its qualities and uses. Thirteen years before the release of *The Ascent*, Pier Paolo Pasolini identified and described what he considered to be a cinematic free indirect, which he defined as "the immersion of the filmmaker in the mind of his character and then the adoption on the part of the filmmaker not only of the psychology of his character but also of his language."[5] For Pasolini, this adoption of a character's language meant the adoption of a "style" of seeing: "The fundamental characteristic of the 'free indirect point-of-view shot is not linguistic, but stylistic," he writes. This shift in style can be subtle, as in "the sequential juxtaposition of two insignificantly different points of view of the same image."[6] As we'll see, moments in Shepitko's film resemble the cinematic techniques Pasolini isolated as evocative of the free indirect. At other moments, however, she transforms Bykov's free indirect into unusually blocked and edited scenes of conversation. Together these scenes demonstrate Shepitko's innovativeness, as well as the strengths and limitations of the cinematic free indirect theorized by Pasolini. To build this argument, this chapter will describe Bykov's novel (and specifically what his wielding of the technique of free indirect discourse accomplishes), analyze some of Shepitko's strategies for adapting the free indirect, and reflect on the ways Shepitko's methods illuminate the medium specificity of film in regard to the representation of inwardness.

The novel consists of nineteen chapters, the first and last of which are focalized through Rybak. Sotnikov's subjectivity thus dominates the even-numbered chapters and Rybak's the odd. This structural oscillation establishes patterns that, but for the intricacies of the protagonists' musings, verge on the schematic. Most schematically, before their arrest the novel contrasts Rybak's competent strength with Sotnikov's fevered, weakened state, which ultimately leads to their capture. After their arrest, Sotnikov proves unyielding while Rybak gives in to fearful rationalization and betrayal. Overlaying this irony of the strong becoming weak and the weak becoming strong, the free indirect establishes characterological continuities: Rybak repeatedly shifts responsibility onto others while Sotnikov consistently reflects on his own answerability and guilt. We see this from the beginning: in Chapter 1, Rybak muses, "They'd be back in camp by morning. Or at least they should be . . . But they were being held up by Sotnikov;"[7] whereas in Chapter 2, "The thought that most troubled Sotnikov was that he might become a burden to his companion" (13). Both assessments prove correct; they are realistic and initially without ethical valence. But as their situation worsens, the pattern deepens, developing into a moral habit. Three times the novel mentions Rybak's tendency to clear his own conscience—first about a woman with whom he had an affair earlier in the war (42); second about Pyotr the Headman, arrested for being a collaborator after Rybak and Sotnikov appropriate his sheep (109–110); and finally, upon succumbing to German pressure, when he reasons, "At all events he had no intention of serving the Germans. He was just waiting for the right moment to come along. It could be now, it could be later, and he would see it when it came" (156). Sotnikov, in contrast, is "preoccupied by his own responsibility for what had happened." When he sees Demchikha about to be arrested because he and Rybak hid in her house, endangering her and her children, his sense of responsibility and shame is so great that he would rather "have sunk into the ground" than face her (87). After standing up to torture, he makes up his mind to confess to everything to protect her and the others; whereas Rybak "realized that perhaps the time had come to abandon the impossible task of protecting Demchikha. It was up to Demchikha now to get herself out of it if she could" (117). In the cellar, on the uncertain and fearful eve of their likely impending execution, Rybak reflects on his fellow prisoners, "The hell with the lot of them. They were no concern of his" (138); whereas Sotnikov, sure of his coming death, realizes "If anything now remained in life to concern him, it was only his final responsibilities toward the people around him" (143).

The novel's original title, "Sotnikov," suggests he is the privileged character, even though Rybak's focalization dominates more chapters. But various details complicate the valorization of Sotnikov. Both Sotnikov and Rybak's expectations for their chosen courses of action utterly collapse. Sotnikov's admirable sense of responsibility for others leads him unwisely to accept a mission for which his health renders him unfit, setting in motion events that lead to the demise of many in addition to himself. He thinks his confession will save others, but, excepting Rybak, they all hang futilely and with little recognition. Rybak, meanwhile, thinks he'll continue fighting Germans and collaborators until it slowly dawns on him that his only future lies in working *for* them. His rationalizations for preserving his own life and freedom lead to his soul-destroying cooptation by the enemy. In addition to showing how the consequences of both protagonists' actions do not necessarily match their intentions, the novel also subverts its schematic contrast of the two when Sotnikov entertains moral reflections that could just as easily be Rybak's:

> No, death certainly resolved nothing and justified nothing. Only life gives people a definite opportunity, which they either make something of or waste completely. Only life can stand up to evil and violence. Death is deprived of everything . . . Yet he could not agree with Rybak's action, which contradicted his entire humanity. (160–61)

Ironically, he cannot agree with Rybak's action, but finds himself more articulate in justifying it than in explaining why he rejects it. His conflicting judgment of Rybak amplifies this mental facility to take both sides:

> Turned over to the other side, the bastard! Sotnikov thought viciously, almost enviously, and then had a sudden doubt—should he think of Rybak in that way? Now, in the last instants of his life, he had unexpectedly lost his former conviction of his right to demand the same standard from others as he demanded of himself. Rybak was a good partisan . . . but as a man and as a citizen he clearly lacked something. But how could he have filled that gap? After he had left school at 12, he had probably read no more than a dozen or so decent books. He could hardly have reached a level of morality in his spiritual development which would allow his actions to be judged by mankind's highest standards. (162)

The phrase "almost enviously" emphasizes the unsettled nature of Sotnikov's moral reflections. His thinking is in motion, seemingly changeable, and so is the thinking of the narrative as a whole: Sotnikov's softening toward Rybak's betrayal on account of his lack of education, for instance, is contradicted by Demchikha's scornful emphasis on the collaborator and interrogator Portnov's elite education, which does not prevent him from torturing Sotnikov and hanging them all. And lest we believe Sotnikov's strong principles are always right, the narrative reveals their flaw. Sotnikov's involuntary repugnance for any sort of betrayal almost leads him, mistakenly, to shoot the German-appointed headman Pyotr Sych, for which he subsequently feels guilty when he learns the partisans had asked Pyotr to accept the position of headman because the alternative would have been worse for the village. Sometimes principle works, sometimes it doesn't. Even the principle of loyalty to one's side comes into question when we learn Sotnikov's revered father fought for both the tsarist army and the Red Army, suggesting there can be reasons for switching sides.

The novel produces the effect of vital, sinuous thinking by establishing the dominant attitudes of its juxtaposed protagonists and then rendering them unsteady and changeable through afterthoughts, qualifiers, contradictions, and judgments later recognized as mistakes—a challenging terrain on which Shepitko's film is sometimes unsteady, or, ironically, overly steady. The changing titles of the novel—"Sotnikov," "The Ordeal," "Liquidation"—suggest the tenuousness of any "moral of the story." Shepitko's film title, "The Ascent," as she understands it, stabilizes meaning. She says of it:

> The ascent is not to just anywhere, but to oneself. To the best in us, which makes us human. In the moments of the highest trials, we either destroy the human in ourselves, or ascend to its heights. Sotnikov ascended. Rybak, though he remained alive, destroyed the self within himself.[8]

Novel and film share this valorization of Sotnikov's death, especially the way he connects with a child forced to witness his hanging and tries to set a brave example. But Shepitko's more emphatic moralizing of this scene corresponds with her filming of it. Bykov writes:

> Among the faceless multitude his eyes fell on the thin figure of a boy of twelve or so . . . It was hard to tell from here what he felt about them, but Sotnikov suddenly felt a desire that he should not think badly of them. But when Sotnikov caught his eye, he saw in it so much inconsolable grief and so much sympathy that he could not help himself from smiling at the boy, just with his eyes—don't worry, lad. (164)

Shepitko says of this moment in her film:

> Sotnikov, deprived of any strength for physical struggle, will gain the most important strength – love for people. He gives them, people, a clear example of how to become better than they are. Sotnikov is not finite. Sotnikov bequeaths himself, his moral strength to a weak child. And he understood it.[9]

While Bykov initially writes of Sotnikov's perception of the boy, "It was hard to tell from here what he felt about them" (164), Shepitko transforms the scene into a shot-reverse shot structure featuring facial closeups of the weeping boy and Sotnikov, whose image is suffused with light as he manages one last heroic smile (with his mouth, and not only his eyes) to which the boy manages an answering smile. In his last long closeup, the sun hits Sotnikov's forehead and there is ramping of the film speed so that when he swings forward to die, it is in slow motion. Sotnikov's dark clothing fills the frame, momentarily turning the screen black before he swings back and leaves nothing but white sky in the shot. The final closeup shows the boy, his face registering understanding and resolve as he wipes his tears. Shepitko thus transforms the uncertainty that distance imposes in Bykov's narrative: she gives what transpires between Sotnikov and the boy a greater decisiveness by registering it in closely framed reverse shots. Loud, somber, momentous non-diegetic music underscores the emotional qualities of Sotnikov's execution and the boy's easily visible tears. Bykov's muted, tentative prose becomes Shepitko's melodramatic scene.

The strategies Shepitko uses to adapt the novel's free indirect discourse to the film medium result in a less complex representation of Sotnikov's heroism, and they also more pointedly emphasize the mechanics of Rybak's self-destruction. These strategies include the ostentatious set pieces where Rybak (Vladimir Gostyukhin) imagines himself attempting, fatally, to escape. These sequences, where the film literally pictures Rybak's inward thinking, can be read as illustrations of the adage that a coward dies many deaths, although their function far exceeds this: their concatenation with Rybak's final scene works effectively to communicate his horrified recognition of his error. The movement of thinking—the ironies of thinking—represented by the verbal free indirect, which is more abstract and less beholden to the immediately perceptible world, challenges a medium restricted to showing the surface of things. At the same time, the surface of things—the inexhaustible and changing details of the external world—elude and exceed verbal comprehension, and sometimes create a far more vivid sense of inward experience, as in the sleigh-ride sequence, where the *politsai* transport the captured partisans to German headquarters. In what follows, I will consider this sequence along with Rybak's other scene of imagined escape and his final scene, and I will juxtapose these with another tactic Shepitko deploys to transpose Bykov's intricate prose: externalizing the novel's free indirect discourse by transforming it into scenes of conversation. The two key conversations I will analyze are the one between Rybak and Demchikha (Lyudmila Polyakova), when he asks her to accept the fatal risk of sheltering Sotnikov (Boris Plotnikov), and the one between Sotnikov and the traitorous interrogator Portnov (Anatoli Solonitsyn). This latter conversation, I argue, restages the novel's inward workings of conscience as outwardly visible morality play. At key moments in both conversations, Shepitko eschews the more typical shot-reverse shot structure, adopting unusual and expressive framings that register the pressure of inwardness on the graphic qualities of the shot.

Unmarked in the novel, the sleigh ride is a set piece of the film. In the novel, the free indirect discourse continues unabated, overlaying the transport of the captives by sleigh from Demchikha's house to the German headquarters. Thus obscured by the free indirect, the sleigh ride itself does not stand out as a scene.

Instead, Rybak's reflections, which fill three and a half pages, mostly crowd out the immediate external circumstances. Rybak rues the mistakes that led to their capture; thinks about how it's Sotnikov's fault; imagines their comrades, hungrily awaiting their return; remembers the battle where he met and befriended Sotnikov; tries in vain to see a way to escape and live; and finally despairs. The sleigh ride continues into the next chapter, which presents Sotnikov's thinking. We read of his concern for Demchikha, the way he's trying to signal to Rybak that they should establish her innocence, and, finally, his perceptions of the external world, one of which finds its way into the film: "A lank-haired girl [. . .] was throwing slops on to the snow. And before she turned back fearfully into the house, she too peered curiously at the road. [. . .] Life was going on—uneasy, difficult, but at all events normal life which Rybak and Sotnikov had not known for so long and now would never know again" (97). The film's realization of the sleigh ride begins with Demchikha begging her captors to let her return to her small children and Sotnikov telling them she's innocent. A captor punches him in the face and stuffs a cloth in Demchikha's mouth. The *mise-en-scène* helps to communicate Sotnikov's concern for Demchikha and her children by placing him supine, next to her in the sleigh. Lying shoulder to shoulder with her, Sotnikov meets her gaze despite his distress at having placed her and her children in this dire situation. Rybak appears alone in a separate frame, glancing around with an expression of anguish and desperation. This formal separation of him from his fellow captives helps mark his isolating concern for himself. The camera tilts down to show him trying to loosen the ties that bind his hands. We get a sharper sense of the captives' inward experience through the dissonance of the external world. In a two-shot, Sotnikov and Demchikha look into one another's eyes as one of their captors casually begins to whistle a tune. We know *that* they are thinking and feeling and can surmise their alarm and dismay, but we do not know precisely *what* they are thinking and feeling. When Sotnikov closes his eyes in this shot, it seems meaningful, but it's also ambiguous, or underdetermined. Does he close them to signal his shame and regret at putting Demchikha into this situation? Does he also close them because his fever and wound are making him feel faint? Nothing is clear except the incongruity between his feelings when he opens his eyes again, and the offscreen singing and guffaws of the captors at that very moment. The pressure of the exterior evokes a contrary interior. A shadow moves over Sotnikov's face as the camera comes to rest only on him, the singing swells, and he looks toward the camera with an expression utterly at odds with the song. The film more explicitly visualizes Rybak's thinking. In the novel we read:

> Perhaps it would be worth trying his luck even with his hands tied? But if he were to do so, he would need a more suitable place, somewhere not so flat, a turn in the road maybe, or a steep valley with bushes at the

bottom, a sharp dip, or some trees. Unfortunately, here it was all flat and open . . . Rybak kept as sharp a watch as he could . . . and found nothing. (95–96)

In the midst of the sleigh-ride sequence, Shepitko stages Rybak's subjective visualization of his failed escape in a way that conveys his panicked distress and despair more strikingly than Bykov's prose. A point of view sequence begins with a shot of Rybak turning his head to look at the snowy terrain. At the end of the shot he sits up straighter, more alert, as if having noticed something. Following this medium close-up of Rybak looking, the film cuts to an extreme long shot of the landscape, in which a running man, his back to the camera, suddenly appears from behind a rise. This image appears to be from Rybak's point of view. What seems to be a reverse shot returns to the sleigh, showing only the edge of it, where the captors sit, dangling their feet off the end. One of the captors, Stas (Nikolai Sektimenko), jumps off the sleigh and looks in the direction of the running man. A point-of-view shot shows the man glance back and try desperately to climb a slippery precipice. Stas, in medium close-up, smiles and takes aim. Again we see his target, now closer, in medium shot, his back still to the camera. Stas begins to fire his automatic rifle, and the subsequent shot shows the bullets hit their mark. When the dying man turns toward the camera, we clearly see that it is Rybak. A non-diegetic musical chord crescendos and stops abruptly in the next shot, which returns to the close-up of Rybak on the sleigh, looking toward the camera, but seemingly without seeing anything, lost in thought. His captors' laughing and singing fill the soundtrack as he turns away from the snowdrifts across which he had imagined himself fleeing. The sequence thus surprises by having him see his imaginary self in the landscape into which he gazes. This stylized realization of Rybak's imagination draws attention to itself. So do the mundane details of this wintry prisoner transport, which just as effectively, if more subtly, evoke a distraught inwardness. When, for instance, we return to the living Rybak, we see to his left part of the horse's haunches moving inexorably onward toward the German headquarters. A captor harshly asks Rybak what he's staring at, another laughs, and a third continues to sing. These offscreen voices again render interiority vivid by providing it with the contrast of a discordant perceptible world.

The sleigh-ride sequence features one of two stylistically marked moments of subjective imagining associated with Rybak and his desire to break free. The second occurs after the hanging as Rybak trudges back to the German headquarters under the cold stare of the villagers who witnessed his betrayal. A woman calls him a Judas. As in the first instance, but in a briefer, more condensed way, Rybak imagines himself making a run for it and getting shot. The two imagined escape sequences rhyme in several ways: both feature images of Rybak, shot in the back by Stas and his machine gun (shown in close-up).

In both he slowly turns to face the camera with a similar dying posture. Both feature a crescendo followed by sudden silence as Rybak stops imagining and returns to reality, and both include the offscreen voice of a military policeman asking Rybak what he's staring at. This poetic repetition gives depth and meaning to Rybak's final scene. Here he exits the latrine where he tried unsuccessfully to hang himself; and for the first time since his capture, he finds himself alone and unwatched. The wooden gate of the German barracks has been left open and swings in the wind; the guard dog pays him no mind; the yard is empty. It's the perfect opportunity to escape, but there's nowhere to go. Rybak can no longer imagine himself fleeing into the landscape because he no longer has anyone, or anywhere, to flee to: he has alienated himself from everyone, including himself. Through, and across, the visual and aural repetitions, and differences, of these three sequences, the film gives depth, force, and precision to this final recognition scene.

After Rybak imagines himself escaping for the first time, the sleigh-ride sequence continues with a long shot that shows the sleigh moving across the screen from right to left. A sustained, high-pitched note begins to sound in conjunction with the snow-muted clop of the horse's hooves. The camera then returns to Sotnikov in a shot that lasts over 25 seconds. The sustained note of the previous shot leads into melancholic, non-diegetic music. This long tracking shot (the camera appears to be on the sleigh) begins with an in-focus close-up of Sotnikov's face against the snowy ground, in soft focus behind it. Sotnikov slowly turns his head to look up at the sky and sunlight falls diagonally across his shadowed face. The camera tilts up slightly, so that only his nose and eyes are in the frame and the landscape appears in soft focus, with a smudged dark line of woods on the distant horizon (**see Fig. 4.1**). The camera holds here for a few seconds, and then racks focus so that Sotnikov's face is soft, the distant landscape clearer. These subtle, but expressive cinematographic choices (the tilt, the rack focus) are akin to Pasolini's examples of a cinematic free indirect subjectivity, which include, for instance, "the sequence of two shots which frame the same piece of reality, first from nearby, then from *a bit* further; or first frontally and then *a bit* more obliquely; or finally, actually on the same axis but with two different lenses." Pasolini calls this "'obsessive framing'" (the scare quotes are his) and associates it with the auteur's (in this case, Antonioni's) "immersing himself in his neurotic protagonist."[10] Shepitko's framing, because of its closeness, similarly involves immersion in Sotnikov's character. Formally, the shot is unusual even as it is also realistic: few shots in cinema place the nostrils of a protagonist at the bottom center of a moving frame. Sotnikov's face is moved like an inanimate object across a landscape, the passivity of his head countered by the thoughtfulness of his eyes. His head contains this indistinct world through which he is pulled against his will. And when the camera racks focus, blurring his face to articulate the

Figure 4.1 Sotnikov's face in the landscape.

lines of the trees in middle ground, we also sense, perhaps together with him, the independence of the world from him, its indifferent continuation without him. Through this literal blurring first of the world that contains him, then of his head, which contains his experience of the world, the filmic enunciation creates a sensibility attributable to both character and narration. Purely expressive, providing no new narrative information, this subtle shift from distinction to indistinction seamlessly belongs to character and film: it is the free indirect.

From captives and captors on the sleigh, the film turns to the world and the people who stop what they're doing to watch it pass. We see a group of boys playing in the street, a woman throwing out slops (as in the novel), a man with a bundle of firewood. These shots seem to be from the point of view of the sleigh, except that their frames are static. To whose perspective do they belong? They are reminiscent of the shots designed by Shepitko's influential first teacher at VGIK, Oleksandr Dovzhenko, in his 1929 film *Arsenal*, where characters, statically framed, directly address the camera with questions about the Ukrainian Civil War. This direct gaze at the camera in Dovzhenko's film lifts the characters slightly out of the story world, making them function more as statements about the senseless waste of war. As in *Arsenal*, but not as decisively, Shepitko's still framings of people pausing their daily activities to watch the passing prisoners differentiate this series of shots from more perspectival, and hence more immersive images; this makes them function as a kind of commentary on the action, like a chorus: the villagers' sympathies lie with the captives, not the captors; and they know the captives are doomed.

The end of the sleigh-ride sequence, with its extremely low-angle tracking shots, adopts Sotnikov's supine perspective. The camera, like Sotnikov and Demchikha, is looking up as it passes by icicles hanging from eaves and open fortochkas with their connotation of inward warmth and comfort. Displacing these suggestions of a familiar world, an official stone building with a Nazi flag enters the frame. We see the fateful rectangular iron archway from which, at the end of the film, all of the captives, save Rybak, are hanged. An unlit electric light dangling from a wire against the gray sky is also activated as a spatial marker that appears in subsequent scenes. The film conveys the subjective experience of this dreary place through the repetition and condensation of subjective meaning around such ordinary objects. The sleigh-ride sequence wordlessly, forcefully, evokes a sense of the captives' sensory and emotional experience and forebodings. The intricacies of moral reasoning under duress, however, pose a greater challenge. Shepitko meets this challenge by transforming Bykov's free indirect into dialogue, or, more precisely, into unusually stylized scenes of interrogation and argument.

The film transposes Sotnikov's thinking into a medieval morality play. The interrogator Portnov plays the devil, trying to tempt him and Rybak; and he also competes with Sotnikov over the soul of Rybak. The effect, I will argue, is to make Sotnikov a more static character and Portnov, played by Anatoly Solonitsyn—Andrei Rublev himself—more complex than in the novel. Shepitko distinguishes her film from Bykov's story, saying of her film, that Sotnikov:

> ... comes into conflict with Portnov, who believes that if there is no [immortality], then that means everything is permitted. In [Bykov's] story, everything is decided on the Rybak-Sotnikov axis. We decided to go deeper with Portnov's image. Because Portnov and Sotnikov understand each other and decide questions at the highest level.[11]

Reprising Dostoevsky's, "If there is no God, then everything is permitted," to describe Portnov's stance, Shepitko gestures at the literary and philosophical tradition in which she sees herself working. The uneducated Rybak's moral recognition that he destroyed his life by saving it can be effectively communicated on a sensory, nonverbal level by the sequence of two failed imaginary escapes and the final unblocking of an escape route, with the irony that he no longer has anywhere to go. But "deciding questions at the highest level" requires, for Shepitko, the use of language, leading her at key points to transform Bykov's free indirect technique into cinematic conversation. While there is a continuum between thinking and feeling, the questions that Portnov and Sotnikov discuss also require the precision of words. "Free indirect discourse," when claimed for cinema, becomes the "free indirect point of view shot" (Pasolini), or "free indirect affect" (Homay King),[12] but sometimes the cinematic representation of a thought process requires the specificity of language.

The scene that introduces Portnov begins with a fire in a fireplace that almost fills the frame. The light of the flames flickers on his gaunt face, in his first facial close-up, along with a slight smile. The angle and lighting of his head in his first close-up follow the principles of Russian icon painting: his prominent forehead creates the base of a triangle ending in his chin, which is in a different plane.[13] He is like a fallen angel. The early blocking of Portnov's initial conversation with Sotnikov is unusual: the camera does not film the actors facing one another from an angle, but instead films from directly behind Sotnikov, who, in turn, sits directly in front of Portnov in the middle ground so that the camera and two actors are on the same axis. Portnov's smaller head thus hovers above Sotnikov's larger one (see **Fig. 4.2**). When Portnov recedes even further into the background, stepping behind his desk and sitting, on a graphic level he disappears behind, or descends into Sotnikov's larger figure, just as—in the interrogation itself—he tries to get inside the latter's head. When the editing returns to a more typical shot-reverse shot structure, Sotnikov's face appears against a softly focused background that is half dark and half light, accentuating the temptation and hard decisions he faces. Shepitko replaces with dialogue Bykov's free indirect discourse (quoted above) where Sotnikov reflects on the uselessness of death: in the film, this is not Sotnikov's own passing thought, but rather the interrogator's lure. Sotnikov staunchly says, "There are things more important than one's own hide." Portnov pauses at these words, then he starts to laugh: "Where? What is it? With death everything ends for us. The entire world." Sotnikov's struggle with himself in the novel thus becomes a struggle with the interrogator in the film. The morality play externalizes the novel's inward thought. Performance details such as the timing of pauses, silences, or one's slight turn of the head away from the other suggest each hears things from his opponent that he himself has also thought. This is especially true of Solonitsyn's performance, of which Shepitko says, "an extremely subtle, sensitive actor, he, like a medium, accepted all my sometimes unspoken feelings about this image. All the nuances, all the details, the whole array of tools with the help of which we opened up Portnov."[14] Shepitko's description of Solonitsyn's performance points to the persistent importance of the unspoken. Although his character is necessary to externalize as conversation what remains a single character's tortuous, inward considerations in Bykov's novel, Portnov's own misgivings about whether "all is permitted" are communicated gesturally, not verbally, as in the scene in the yard of the barracks before the execution.

THE ORDEAL AND THE ASCENT   89

Figure 4.2 Graphically, Portnov's smaller head seems to sink into Sotnikov's larger one.

Here, Boris Plotnikov's Sotnikov is less complex, more straightforwardly heroic. The morning of the execution, when the prisoners emerge from the cellar, Sotnikov confesses to killing the German soldier in a last-ditch effort to save the others. He reveals his true name and tells Portnov, "I have father, mother, country." Portnov, who has forsaken his country for Germans who treat him as an outsider (the blocking always situates him slightly outside the German circles), turns away at these words, takes off his hat, and wipes his face before refusing Sotnikov the satisfaction of saving anyone else. Sotnikov has no time to savor his small moral victory over Portnov because Rybak, upon realizing that Sotnikov's confession won't save him, tells Portnov he's willing to join the collaborators. That Rybak represents an object of contention in the moral battle between Portnov and Sotnikov is indicated by the shots, which leave Rybak out of frame after he makes this fateful decision. Instead we see a medium close-up of Portnov who lifts his chin, attentive to this turn; a reverse shot of Sotnikov, appearing distressed; and a medium close-up of Portnov, a slight smile starting across his lips as he recognizes Rybak's caving has given him a victory in his struggle with the unyielding Sotnikov. In sum, the moral reasoning that transpires in free indirect discourse in the novel is realized by this older structure of the medieval morality play in the film, and this externalization of thinking makes Sotnikov appear heroic in a less fraught way than in the novel: the film's Sotnikov suffers nobly, does not question himself, and the narrative, mostly, does not question, or undercut him.

The visual association between the night in the cellar and the agony in the garden further reinforces Sotnikov's statically heroic image. In the agony in the garden, Jesus prays, "My father! If it is possible, let this cup pass from me. Yet not as I will, but as you will" (Matthew 26:39) and paintings depicting this often show both cup and sleepy apostles. Sotnikov tells Rybak not to let him die of his wounds before morning so that he can confess and take the blame. To keep him alive they give him water. A close-up shows Sotnikov sipping from the proffered cup with his big eyes raised and his face brightly lit (in general he often has the brightest face in the frame and at key moments, the air around his face seems diffused with light). The liner notes of the Criterion edition call the film, "at once a visceral, earthy evocation of life on the ground during World War II and a momentous, spiritual Christian allegory."[15] Shepitko explains and qualifies her use of the Christian imagery:

> In all times there were Rybaks and Sotnikovs, there were Judas and Christ. I'm not religious, but, since this legend entered people, it means it's alive, it is in each of us. Since the time of Christ, people have appeared who gave themselves to others, but did Christ's feat teach humanity much?[16]

Making Sotnikov Christlike and transforming his inward doubts into a debate with Portnov flattens him as a character. He becomes allegorical. Emanuela Patti distinguishes allegory from Erich Auerbach's concept of *figura*, which inspired Pasolini's early filmmaking. She writes, "Allegory differs from *figura* in that, in allegory, a figure is feigned to illustrate a given proposition; in *figura*, the figure and the figured are thought to be real."[17] A key example for her is Pasolini's 1961 film *Accatone*, where the title character, in his death, is Christlike even though, throughout the film, he also appears as an utterly self-referential, or non-transcendent, sub-proletarian pimp. The liner notes are right to call *The Ascent* allegorical: Sotnikov's comparison to Christ is unironic. Unlike in the novel, we do not have to contend with his moral failings or doubts; he "illustrates a proposition" about heroic self-sacrifice. Accatone, on the other hand, is an unrepentant criminal who dies riding a motorcycle he steals to get away from the police after helping his friends steal sausages. He's at such an unbridgeable distance from the Christlike that he—and the figure of Christ—become more real through the simultaneous strangeness and aptness of the comparison. In externalizing Sotnikov's inner debates, Shepitko does not diminish the realism with which she shows the theater of war, but she removes the inner doubt that makes Sotnikov's character more intricate and realistic in the novel.

The innovative blocking of Portnov's interrogation of Sotnikov stylistically resonates with the blocking of Rybak and Demchikha's dialogue earlier in the film, just before the Germans arrive to arrest them. With his comrade incapacitated, Rybak desperately wants Demchikha's help. He straightens, smooths his hair, and smiles as she enters her home to discover him and Sotnikov. As she takes off her scarf and coat, she begins to scold, telling them she has no food to give them. She moves toward Rybak and Sotnikov and discovers the bloodied cloth that had been wrapped around Sotnikov's wounded leg. She pauses and stares at it as Rybak tries to gather it up in his hand. She looks at the wound and sits by Sotnikov's head. Then she dashes into the next room, leaving Sotnikov and Rybak still seated in the frame. She reappears ripping cloth for dressing the wound and tosses it to Rybak. She tells them the old women in the village were talking about the shooting of a German soldier. Rybak's voice, off frame, says "Old women know everything." He enters the frame where Demchikha stands in medium close up, his back to the camera. Her two youngest children peer from behind her over the top of the shelf that serves as a room divider as Rybak asks, "But now what?" As he asks this, the back of his head blocks the view of Demchikha's face except for its lower left corner; and the view of her son's face, except for its upper right corner (**see Fig. 4.3**). He leans over her, importunate, but also somewhat threatening.

Figure 4.3 The back of Rybak's head blocking Demchikha's face.

Demchikha, looking him in the eye, moves to her left becoming again visible to the camera as she turns Rybak's question back on him: "How should I know what you should do?" A medium close-up of Sotnikov, supine, intervenes: his face—not Rybak's—functions as the reverse shot even though he's not yet a participant in the conversation, but rather an onlooker. He moves his lips as if to speak just as Rybak continues, "You understand—he can't walk. That's for sure." Again, as he implores her, the back of his head moves to block the view of her face; and once again, in a way that is quietly, stylistically astounding, no face is visible in this medium-close-up two shot of an intense conversation. Again, Demchikha moves leftward past the obstructive back of Rybak's head before she speaks. "You got here, didn't you?" she asks. And again, it's Sotnikov who gets the reaction shot. He lowers his eyes as if to acknowledge the risk they're asking Demchikha to take for herself and her children. This time he manages to speak, not to Demchikha, but Rybak: "Stop, Rybak. Let's go." He starts moving to get up, as Rybak angrily turns, telling him to "Hold it," and turns back again to Demchikha, now visible in soft focus behind him. At this moment, Sotnikov looks out the window, sees approaching Germans, and the conversation becomes moot as the three of them scramble for a way to hide all trace of Sotnikov and Rybak's presence.

This brief conversation stylistically resembles Sotnikov's contentious interactions with Portnov in two ways: first, as in the interrogation scene, Shepitko rejects the usual shot-reverse shot structure in favor of momentarily filming the actors on the same axis so that one of them obstructs, either fully or partially, the view of the other; second, as in the scene where Rybak agrees to work with the Germans in order to save his own life, the key reaction shots belong not to him, but to Sotnikov, even though Rybak is the one speaking. The significance of these formal choices are, however, different in this scene. Rybak's graphic obstruction of Demchikha in the blocking literalizes the way he's obscuring her needs—indeed, her very existence—in favor of his own. The tripartite nature of this dialogue, where Sotnikov gets the reactive reverse shots that should belong to Rybak, allows Shepitko to contrast not just Sotnikov's face with the back of Rybak's head, but Sotnikov's capacity for understanding others and his responsibility to them with Rybak's inability to see himself as he narrowly focuses on his mission. Again, Shepitko's transformation of the free indirect into a scene of conversation flattens and simplifies the character by putting his inward thoughts into the mouths of others. In Bykov's scene, Rybak is fully aware of the risk he's asking Demchikha to take:

> 'Well, what next? . . .'
> 'How should I know what you're going to do next?'
> 'Well, it's obvious he can't move. That's a fact.'
> 'He got here all right.'

> But all the same she was probably aware of what he was hinting at. They eyed each other steadily and cautiously. These prolonged looks said more than words could have done. Once again Rybak felt himself uncertain of what he was doing. The burden that he was trying to shift on to the shoulders of this woman was too heavy. It was clear that she was just as aware as he of the risk that she would be exposing herself to if she did what he wanted, and she was resisting the idea. (81)

By depriving Rybak of these thoughts to have them register instead on Sotnikov's face (and in Sotnikov's verbal intervention), Shepitko's film makes Rybak more heedlessly inconsiderate; just as, by rendering as Portnov's spoken words Sotnikov's inner doubts about whether his death will serve any purpose, Shepitko's film renders him more perfectly, and predictably, heroic. Turning the free indirect into dialogue scenes can flatten a character. The inward debates of the novel give the characters depth and the realistic vitality of an undecided mind contending with itself. The characters' choices do not always seem guaranteed. Shepitko's film displaces this inner uncertainty with the vivid plastic realization of the same debates, externalized. She makes Bykov's muted realism melodramatic.

Shepitko's *The Ascent* is in the tradition of post-World-War-II cinematic modernism that is at issue when Pasolini describes the "free indirect point of view shot" in "The Cinema of Poetry." Beyond that, she is also working in the older, and simultaneously formalist and realist tradition of her teacher Dovzhenko. Her grounding in these traditions, and her literary source, which uses free indirect discourse throughout, is what makes her film so illuminating as a case study for considering the difference between the proclaimed cinematic adaptation of the technique of the free indirect, and the actual adaptation of a story written in the free indirect style. Scenes where Shepitko uses Pasolinian free indirect point-of-view include the false point-of-view shots when Rybak sees himself running away, or the tilt and rack focus of Sotnikov's supine head moving through the landscape. These scenes communicate the sensation and emotion—the inward experience—that are plausible for these characters, in these circumstances. An open gate and an empty yard suddenly become distressing because they force Rybak's recognition that just when his path is clear there's no longer any escape. A landscape that suddenly comes into focus and an open fortochka help build Sotnikov's recognition of a world outside his own wartime travails that will continue without him once he dies. Such adaptations of the free indirect technique, with their marked stylization, powerfully convey a blending of the characters' sensory, emotional, and reflective processing of wartime experience. But to adapt the undercutting irony and uncertainty with which Bykov riddles his protagonists' more abstract moral reasoning, Shepitko must externalize the novel's self-dividing inwardness as outward debate. She redistributes the self-questioning that renders Bykov's protagonists multifarious; assigning each character a consistent, fixed standpoint. This is not to say the film eliminates the inward uncertainty of Bykov's characters. Rather, it displaces it onto their outward vulnerability to the unforgiving cold, the weakness of the body, and the brutality and callousness of the Nazis and their collaborators.

NOTES

1. I'm very grateful to Lida Oukaderova and Elizabeth Papazian for directing my attention to important secondary sources; to the Stanford Humanities Center Working Group in Literary & Visual Culture, especially Harleen Kaur Bagga and Maria Shevelkina, for a productive discussion of an earlier version of this essay; and to Alex Woloch, for his unfailingly helpful feedback.
2. Lazar Lazarev, *Vasil Bykov*, trans. Amanda Calvert (Moscow: L. Raduga Publishers, 1987), 94–95.
3. Karakhan, L. "Krutoi put' 'Voskhozhdeniia'," *Iskusstvo kino*. 1976. No. 10, 85–101, 93.
4. Ibid.
5. Pier Paolo Pasolini, *Heretical Empiricism*, trans. Ben Lawton and Louise K. Barnett (Washington, D.C.: New Academia Publishing, 2005), 175.
6. Ibid., 178, 179.
7. Vasily Bykov, *The Ordeal*, trans. Gordon Clough (London: The Bodley Head, 1972), 6. Hereafter I will give all page numbers from this edition parenthetically in the text.
8. Shepit'ko, L., "Voskhozhdenie k pravde. Stenogramma obsuzhdeniia posle prosmotra fil'ma 'Voskhozhdenie'," *Sovetskii ekran*. 1978. No. 1, https://chapaev.media/articles/8936
9. Ibid.
10. Pasolini, *Heretical Empiricism*, 179.
11. "Kogda my ne naprasny . . ." (iz vystupleniia v Kazansckom molodezhnom tsentre 27 ianvaria 1979 goda), Larisa: vospominaniia, vystupleniia, interv'iu, kinostsenarij, stat'i: Kniga o Larise Shepit'ko (Moskva: Iskusstvo, 1987), 172.
12. Homay King, "Free Indirect Affect in Cassavetes' *Opening Night* and *Faces*," *Camera Obscura* 19, no. 2/56 (2004), 105–139.
13. See Clemena Antonova, *Space, Time, and Presence in the Icon: Seeing the World with the Eyes of God* (London: Routledge, 2010), 41: "The principle of simultaneous depiction of different planes . . . lies at the heart of a typical facial type with a disproportionately wide forehead. The total shape of the face becomes triangular . . ." (I am grateful to Maria Shevelkina for directing my attention to Antonova's text in relation to this shot.)
14. Shepit'ko, L., Voskhozhdenie k pravde.
15. Larisa Shepitko, *The Ascent* (1977) [DVD] (2008). USA: The Criterion Collection, Eclipse Series 11, Larisa Shepitko.
16. «Когда мы не напрасны . . .», 171–72.
17. Emanuela Patti, *Pasolini after Dante: 'The Divine Mimesis' and the Politics of Representation* (London: Routledge, 2016), 39.

PART III

The Materiality of Moving Images

CHAPTER 5

The Revolutionary Past as Environment: Rain, Dust, and Faces in *The Homeland of Electricity*

Viktoria Paranyuk

Commissioned by the Experimental Creative Film Studio in early 1967, Larisa Shepitko's short film *The Homeland of Electricity* (Rodina elektrichestva) was to be one among five contributions to *Beginning of an Unknown Century* (Nachalo nevedomogo veka), an omnibus film conceived to commemorate the 50th anniversary of the October Revolution.[1] One of the studio's senior creative associates, Vladimir Ognev, proposed the idea of adapting for the project writers who had witnessed and written about the maelstrom of the revolutionary era.[2] The list comprised Isaak Babel, Yuri Olesha, Konstantin Paustovsky, Aleksandr Malyshkin, and Andrei Platonov, authors whose work had suffered varying degrees of censorship during the Stalin years.[3] The short films were to be directed by recent graduates of the All-Union State Institute of Cinematography (VGIK) – Andrei Smirnov, Genrikh Gabai, Elem Klimov, Dzhemma Firsova, and Shepitko. In the end, the State Film Commission under the Council of Ministers greenlighted the four out of five proposals for production in late April.[4]

For her film, Shepitko chose Platonov's short story "The Homeland of Electricity," which focuses on an episode set during the devastating famines of 1921–22 in the Lower Volga basin. In the early 1920s, Platonov had worked as a land reclamation engineer at the Voronezh branch of Regional Agency for Land Management, overseeing projects for drought prevention, and in that capacity had travelled the area extensively.[5] Written in 1926 and possibly reworked as late as 1939, "The Homeland of Electricity" is a fictionalized account based on the author's firsthand experiences in the famine-stricken countryside.[6] Like the short story, the film seems to have the requisites of a postrevolutionary narrative of modernization: the plot concerns an agent of the new regime delivering progress to the backwoods. An engineering student, who in the film's script is referred to as Grinya but otherwise unnamed, is sent by a regional Bolshevik boss to a remote village in southern Russia to alleviate the consequences of a severe drought by installing an electric water pump. Shepitko's adaptation remains mostly faithful to Platonov's text save for a few crucial divergences, which will be discussed later. Rhetorically, Shepitko's short, as does *Beginning of an Unknown Century* overall, falls within the celebratory tradition of affirming the Soviet state's founding myths: the revolution and turbulent times that followed. The film and its treatment of the period, however, should be approached as a product of the 1960s, when public debate was greatly preoccupied with the country's past, giving rise to post-Stalin historical consciousness.

The creators of *The Homeland of Electricity* did not set out to analyze sociohistorical processes, provide objective accounts, or establish the facts of what had occurred based on archival records, all activities with which a professional historian is involved. But it is undeniable that Shepitko's work is concerned with history, particularly if considered in the frame of what Denis Kozlov has called the historical turn in post-Stalin culture.[7] The film was made during a time when intellectuals, artists, and many other groups in Soviet society turned to history as a source of inspiration for creating new accounts of continuity between the past and the present, attempting to bridge the gaps between them. Interpretations of history were under scrutiny. Entrenched narratives about the past became unacceptable. Doubt took over many segments of the population. Kozlov describes this widespread retrospective activity as "a collective search for origins and identities."[8] What "started as the public reevaluation of Stalinism gradually resulted in a much broader historical self-questioning," he writes.[9] By making *The Homeland of Electricity*, Shepitko and her colleagues, themselves historically situated, participated in the process of the production of historical knowledge.[10] As such, the film touches upon shared areas of interest with those of the historian – the role of human agency, of material circumstances, and the possibility of ever comprehending a historical event.

In this chapter, I examine Shepitko's film as a site of the production of history that stages an engagement with the past that is sensorially and atmospherically oriented. As a work of cinematic art, *The Homeland of Electricity* casts into relief what might be involved in historical knowing and whether this kind of knowing offered by the cinema points beyond facts, names, places, language, narratives. The film pursues affective, nonrepresentational, and embodied contours of a historical episode, and derives its validity from the overlap between "what happened and that which is said to have happened," to use the phrase of the anthropologist and historian Michel-Rolph Trouillot.[11] Shepitko's film makes deeply resonant questions about the nature of historical knowledge and truth, collective memory and narrative, access to the past, by way of the material-affective affordances particular to the medium. I propose to analyze *The Homeland of Electricity* as an example of cinema that figures history as an environment rather than an emplotted story. I argue that this film reimagines an episode from the immediate postrevolutionary era not as an event conveyed by the paradigmatic plot that had been established in socialist-realist literary fiction and cinema, but as a changeable environment that gives this history an immersive and sensorially resonant form. The atmospheres that are inseparable from this environment decenter the role of the standard narrative of revolutionary progress, draw attention to the material circumstances through objects and surfaces, weather events and faces, and ask the spectator of the 1960s to share in the reassessing and re-visioning of the mythologized past.

I shift my approach to onscreen figuration and signification of history as environment and its atmospheres from the linguistic, discursive, and representational conception of figuration and signification to embodied, situated, and ecological perspectives, drawing in part on Steffen Hven's theory of diegesis in cinema. Hven frames cinematic signification in environmental rather than textual terms. The scholar adopts what he calls a material-affective approach and reconceptualizes the diegesis as environment, bringing front and center the often-neglected aspects of the narrative film, namely, "the nonrepresentational, affective, atmospheric, material, kinesthetic, multisensorial, rhythmic, and sonic."[12] One of the several ramifications of this theory of the diegesis as environment is the receptive dimension, which posits viewers not as decoders of linguistic signs or builders of a mental representation of a filmic world, but as an embodied presence (Hven uses the term "organism"), lending their perceptual and cognitive capacities to the film, making it come "alive as a lived, felt space-time."[13] Similar to the diegesis, history in a conventional narrative film has primarily relied on creating meaning through language and narrative. The framework of history as environment, on the other hand, opens richer avenues into cinematic investigations of the past. It might ask questions such as, what can a narrative film do differently from written accounts and archival records in order for us to form a greater connection to the past? Can a film about a slice of history make us feel this history? How might the approach to cinematic figuration of history as environment change our understanding of historical knowledge and perception of history? And what is to be gained from it?[14]

ATMOSPHERES

The film's entry into the past lies through an affectively charged environment. While in keeping with the story's electricity plot, the film creates the environment that greatly exceeds the plot rather than being contained by it. Indeed, the environment takes over the narrative peripetia, enveloping, as it were, both the main character and the narrative itself. For this environmental aesthetic Shepitko's cinematic revisioning is partly indebted to Platonov's prose, which is famously unorthodox, bending grammar and lexis to fit his imaginative visions of a utopian society.[15] Thomas Seifrid has called Platonov's writerly traits the "weird deformations of the Russian language," which, moreover, occur "in the course of narrating a series of bizarre events within a loose, anti-novelistic form."[16] Shepitko's script contains several evocative descriptions of the landscape taken almost verbatim from Platonov's text. It is likely that the author's disregard for standard language, and especially his resistance to the Soviet anthropocentrism, imparted an initial impulse to the screen adaptation where the centrality of the human protagonist is questioned. But the film takes the environment, in which the story is set, further, rendering it gloriously atmospheric.

The film visualizes and voices the revolutionary past by playing with the medium's immersive and affective capacities. It plunges the hero into the atmospheres of the place – sounds, weather events, and inhabitants – which attunes his entire body to the environment where he is a stranger. In turn, the resonances and intensities created by the movement of and within the film modulate our embodied experience of viewing accordingly and attune us to this double coil of history, which represents the turbulent years of the Russian Civil War as seen from the vantage point of the unstable 1960s.

The film figures history as environment in several, specifically cinematic ways. The physical location in which the story is set overlaps with the historical geography of the famines in southern Russia. In the summer of 1967, Shepitko, cinematographer Dmitri Korzhikhin, and a small crew installed themselves in a village by the Volga River, near the southern city of Astrakhan, where most of the filming took place. Soviet cinema of the late 1950s and 1960s, similar to other cinemas in the postwar years, reclaimed on-location shooting as a means, among other things, of capturing the character of a real place and enhancing the realism of representation. The use of nonprofessional actors, often native to the locale, was part of this drive toward creating a more genuine cinematic reality. Shepitko reportedly insisted on the accuracy of the geography and cast local residents as peasants, which gives a certain claim to truth inasmuch as such a claim is possible in a fictional narrative. But I would argue that in *The Homeland of Electricity*, the overlap of the shooting location with the historical site of the famines lends the film a layered, ghostly quality, which is further intensified by how the moving images and sounds constitute the screened world and its inhabitants.

It is an active, unstable, spirited world, alive with weather phenomena, such as dust, heat, wind, rain. The many sounds – speaking and singing voices, breath, electronic and analogue music, the noise generated by the weather – are inseparable from the images. These auditory and visual elements construct an atmosphere that intercedes between the unnamed protagonist and the surroundings as soon as he arrives at the proverbial backwoods.

The philosopher Gernot Böhme defines atmosphere as a mediator between one's body and the environment. Neither subjective nor objective, atmosphere derives from our interactions with one another and with the world around us. Atmospheres are spatially extended and emotionally charged.[17] They exist out there, semi-objectively, and yet they are immaterial, unstable, and more the condition of perception than its object.[18] Atmosphere is felt personally but can also be imparted intersubjectively, making it an embodied, situational, and social phenomenon. Böhme finds stage design, or scenography, particularly useful in his articulation of the aesthetic theory of atmospheres as a way of pinpointing atmosphere's wide political, commercial and social reach.[19] In examining *The Homeland of Electricity*, I merge Böhme's affective theory of atmospheres with the anthropologist Tim Ingold's more environmentally capacious, phenomenological conception at the heart of which are weather and air.

Air encompasses weather and its elements – sunshine, rain, mist, wind, and so on. Moreover, the aerial medium enwraps us and everything around us and therefore it enwraps our encounters with things and each other. In other words, we exist inside the medium. By virtue of its composition and lack of resistance, the air, which we need to live, allows us to see, hear, smell, and feel – it allows us to be perceiving subjects.[20] For Ingold, this "common immersion" of people and things in the medium is what gives rise to all resonant interactivity and activity and reveals an environment-in-formation – "a world of becoming, of fluxes and flows . . . a weather world."[21] If Böhme's take emphasizes the man-made aspect of the atmospheric, which can be readily manufactured and manipulated, Ingold draws attention to the unpredictability and change that underlie our environment. Both scholars note how the atmosphere is foundational to our social existence.

I suggest that Shepitko's film, by calling attention to the haptic, visual, and sonic capacities of the cinematic technology, activates and brings to prominence the affective and meteorological articulations of the atmospheric. The film does not just foreground atmospheres; it fills all planes of the screened space with a weather-world. The protagonist is caught in dust, blazing sunshine, and finally rainfall. Moreover, electricity, which is at the center of the narrative, resides in the air: it transmits electromagnetic radiant energy, allowing us to see.[22] Shepitko's film creates this enveloping environment, with its fluctuating atmospheres, through specific devices and stylistic choices. Among them are the manipulation of duration, the mixing of extreme shot scales, direct cuts, fading to white rather than the more conventional black, the visual rhyming of the texture of the peasants' faces and the texture of the cracked earth, and above all, the staging of meteorological circumstances by way of wind machines, the use of tulle fabric, and creation of perpetual dust.

THE CUT

Editing tunes the viewer immediately into the particular character of the remote village of Verchovka, where the hero finds himself. The film does not track the young engineer's journey from his home town to his destination. He is suddenly there, transported from the regional party headquarters to a dusty, barren landscape. This is also the moment when his voiceover narration stops, indicating a shift in his own experience of the events. The cut between the two spaces – from the medium shot of the young man framed by a semicircular alcove like a saint to the extreme closeup of his face in profile, asleep – is straight, startling. Here, as elsewhere in the film, a cut seems to do more than indicate spatial and temporal change. The act of editing does not merely join, interweave, attach, or fold images and sounds together but literally cuts, exerting an abrupt, almost physical force upon the character's body as well as the spectator's. It is an Eisensteinian collision – of scale, rhythm, composition. The cut enacts a dislocation that lands the hero, who is now an outsider, in the new environment, whose particular physiognomy is signaled by the shot scale, the tactility of the image, and the wheezing of the wind (**see Fig. 5.1**). A beetle ambling across the character's brow awakens him. This extreme closeup is followed by a wide shot of a religious procession on the horizon that materializes out of the white dust kicked up by the wind. The engineer soon learns that singing, which he strains to hear, emanates from the procession. Once again a straight cut pushes us into the middle of this thin crowd: some people clutch icons, some banners and crosses – furrowed faces entranced, emaciated bodies bending frenziedly to the ground, praying for rain.

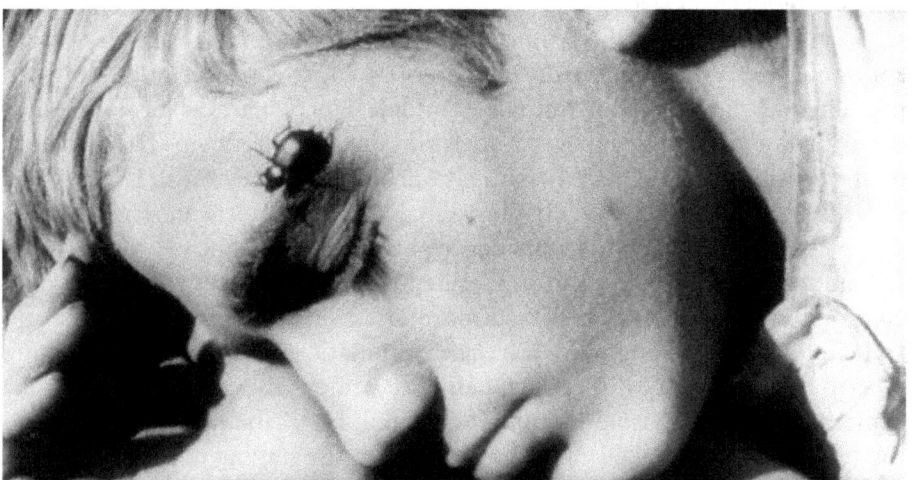

Figure 5.1 The hero meets a new environment.

Figure 5.2 The religious procession enveloped in a dust cloud.

The initial encounter between the young bearer of progress and what seems like the inhospitable place is haptically and aurally orchestrated. In Platonov's text, the journey takes three days on foot. In the continuity script, it was to comprise a day and a night, and to be filmed mostly in extreme long shots, panning across the landscape: the scorched steppe and "the billows of dust, rising upwards and stilling into white caps"[23] (**see Fig. 5.2**). The film foregoes the duration of the voyage and instead shows the character's awakening in a remote destination to give prominence to the new surroundings and his sense of displacement. The sudden cut, together with the dramatic scale of the adjacent shots, implies that the village is cut off from a wider world, imparting it a somewhat utopian aspect. The visual tactility and sonic vibrations that underlie the environmental aesthetic continue from this moment on.

When the worshippers take shelter from the sun in the meager shade offered by a stone outcropping, the newly arrived stranger, barefoot, clumps of earth falling away under his step, approaches the group; his eyes are drawn to an icon propped against a rock. He looks at the Mother of God image and her sorrowful countenance answers via short-reverse-shot. The following closeup rests on an ancient woman-worshipper, mouthing a prayer. "Granny," the engineer says, "Why are you praying? There is no God, and there will be no rain." "There probably isn't. The truth is yours," she agrees. As the two talk – he about nature being deaf to prayer and fearing only reason and work, and she about her hard life, work having consumed her flesh – the camera moves closely and slowly along the bodies of the elderly peasants resting nearby. The calloused hands and wrinkled features set against the rock rhyme with its rough surface. Their bodies are embedded in this landscape as much as the stone outcropping. The editing and camerawork connect the compositional triangle of the peasants, the Mother of God icon, and the rock.

When it is time for the procession to move on, the engineer carries the old woman in his arms to the village, a sequence that forms a separate vignette with no dialogue and relies on a visual rhythm. In contrast to the initial trip to the godforsaken place, this walk, accompanied by the musical score and enacted through straight cuts, unfolds in a series of shots taken from different angles and distances. Once again, editing functions not to logically connect the images but to underline a sense of spatial disjointedness and the desolate, bleached-out surroundings. In one of the shots, the young stranger and his fragile cargo pass by a body lying prone on the ground, a direct reference to the victims of the famine. This moving sequence is imbued with grace, bringing to the fore the place of religion and devotional imagery in Shepitko's film (see Fig. 5.3).

According to the recollection of a film critic who was present on set, the director conceived of the adaptation as a gospel parable in which the young savior brings light to the people.[24] Early in the filming process, the cinematographer suggested an anamorphic attachment to the camera lens that compressed the image horizontally. This resulted, when projected, in slightly elongated figures that recall Byzantine icons. The visual effect accorded with Shepitko's idea. Indeed, the sacred aspect of *The Homeland of Electricity* – from the procession of the worshippers to the striking shots of the engineer carrying the old woman across the wind-swept landscape – is undeniable. Ognev has noted that the first appearance of the hero to the peasants is reminiscent in its expansive composition and iconography of the painter

Figure 5.3 The young man carries the old woman across the barren landscape.

Alexander Ivanov's large canvas *The Appearance of Christ before the People* (1837–57).²⁵ The mixture of sacredness and paganism in the imagery conceivably warrants a separate essay. Here, I simply touch upon this aspect and read the film against the idea of the parable as regards the young hero: his mission as the savior who brings light and truth to the masses does not go as planned. This, moreover, diverges from Platonov's text, in which the protagonist fulfills his revolutionary duty. If examined from the position of the environmental approach this article employs, his mission in effect fails, or more accurately, dissolves into the atmosphere.

The optical elongation of figures introduces an additional element to the visual field and therefore alters the overall look of the screened space. The vertical orientation of the icon and the horizontal orientation of the landscape together create an environment seemingly unbounded by the screen. Electricity, which is found everywhere, is an integral element of this unboundedness, and as such, undermines the hero's role.

ELECTRICITY

In the film's opening shot, the camera pan over the frontpage of a newspaper reveals that the story takes place in September of 1921, during the Civil War, when the new Soviet state was staring into an abyss that stretched between the revolutionary dreams and the existing material conditions.²⁶ At this time, Lenin announced the Bolshevik program of rapid electrification and establishment of the State Commission for the Electrification of Russia (GOELRO) to implement the herculean plan.

Anindita Banerjee identifies the origins of Lenin's ambitious project and his slogan "Communism is equal to Soviet power plus the electrification of the entire country" in the utopian narratives of creation that arose in the late 19th and early 20th centuries. Similar to Western Europe, perceptions of electricity in imperial Russia were split between rational, scientific views and vitalist, mesmerist explanations.²⁷ But if in the West, by the first decade of the 20th century, the transformative impact of electricity became part of everyday life and thus attenuated electricity's magical connotation, in Russia, electric power, inaccessible to the majority of the population into the late 1920s, remained largely in the realm of utopian speculation. This dual vision of electricity as natural phenomenon that can be technologically harnessed and as unconquerable mystical life force took hold of the Russian creative imagination, especially in millenarian philosophies and emerging modernist literature, which turned electricity into the vital instrument for envisioning a singularly Russian model of modernity – a model that never abandoned the occult half of the equation.²⁸ Lenin's revolutionary slogan reflects the fusion of the technological and metaphysical potentials of electricity. In the absence of empirical knowledge and infrastructure, the Soviet vision of technological and social progress tapped into the indigenous cultural imagination that, Banerjee writes, "recuperated 19th-century perceptions of electricity, conflated them with mechanical applications recognized in the early 20th century, and emphasized its potential cosmogony and poesis rather than its ability to transform the environment."[29]

Platonov's short story fits in this utopian paradigm derived from the dual perception but with an ironic slant, as noted by Banerjee, in its highlighting of the gap between material reality and idealistic rhetoric.[30] Shepitko's film likewise presents the rational and mystical views of electricity as often inseparable, but Platonov's irony gives way to a more weighted reassessment of the revolutionary era grounded in the Soviet 1960s. The film, moreover, suggests other visions that are not easily subsumed by the bivalent frame. These stem from figuring history as environment rather than a narrative. As electricity constitutes a big part of this environment, it is only fitting that its representation takes on many varied forms in the film.

At one point, the protagonist inspects the local DIY methods of harnessing electrical power in another sequence constructed as a vignette. He sets out on a walk through the village that consists of some dozen ramshackle wooden houses spread across a desolate landscape howling with the wind. The village comes across as both virtually deserted, dying out, and alive with the many eyes peering from the crooked windows. The often-restless camera investigates the surrounding space, sometimes taking on the engineer's perspective, sometimes its own, following the phrasing of the non-diegetic, 1960s jazz-inflected music written by Roman Ledenev. Mainly closeups and wide shots comprise the sequence.

The closeups frame the visitor's inspection as being observed by the villagers whose stares, set in windows like icons, interrupt his movement. At the start of the sequence, an old man blinks at the outsider through the window of his shack. Immediately after, a follow shot, conveying the intensity of an offscreen stare aimed at the protagonist's back, makes him suddenly turn around to find the wrinkled face of a woman ensconced by a window. As he follows a cluster of wires, the camera dollies in rapidly from above the ground to a dugout and halts at a young woman's face in tight focus. The last encounter in the vignette begins with a circular camera move on the ground and ends with the camera leaving the earth to show us – and the visitor, who once again is compelled to swing around – a tableau featuring a lone elder standing like a guard in middle of a fenced-in area. He greets the engineer with a simple hello, who mumbles hello in reply, the only two words in the sequence. The electric lines are presumably enmeshed in the twigs and branches of the wattle fence.

The shot-reverse shot choreography and the nervous camerawork produce the sensation of being watched. But it is not a one-way relationship: the visitor too watches the villagers and their way of life. Although the faces are immobile and their expressions melancholy – similar to the icons we see earlier during the procession – their stillness is offset by much movement in their environment: the play of light, the quiver of a cobweb, the swaying of a spindly tree reflected in the glass, the unstable shadows. In other words, the images of the impoverished village represented by the severe visages of its residents contain multiple signs of life. As the stranger walks on, he is immersed in the same environment, the same weather-world in flux – a breeze ripples his hair and the occasional tufts of vegetation; the entire sequence is sundrenched as if to remind us of the effects of heat, fading to white in the end.[31]

I consider these movements in the film and of the film as generators of an atmosphere that involves the story's main concern, at least at the level of content: electricity and its significance to the revolutionary project. It is rendered both visible and invisible. Initially, electricity as modernizing force is centered on the aspiring engineer, an agent of the new regime. As the film unfolds, however, this topos of electricity as progress starts to break down when, for instance, we see it manifested in the straining roar of a British motorcycle left over from the Allied intervention during the Civil War: now the vehicle's motor, resourcefully appropriated by a local inventor, supplies electricity to a Bolshevik star hoisted upon a pole. Electricity is also linked to the body of an old villager who regularly ingests a brew made from defective grain in order to determine the brew's alcohol concentration and thus its viability as fuel for powering the motorcycle engine. Among electricity's other material guises is the rigged meshwork of lines that the engineer confronts and gingerly inspects. The crude network of power lines, seemingly everywhere, signals the decentralization of electricity, both as force and as the key point of the narrative. These physical manifestations not only question electricity as progress but cast doubt on the new government's rights to scientific knowledge and claims to social progress.

Electricity is often invisible to the human eye and so the film also stages it as a force that is not seen but is instead felt. As the story unfolds, electricity gradually becomes less of a contained entity and the narrative's purpose, and more of a multisensorial phenomenon. As such, it pervades the film's environment rather than being centralized in the plot of modernization, and potentially maps onto many surfaces and surroundings the outsider comes in contact with, most notably the villagers' features and their likeness in nature – the dry earth. Electricity is in the washed-out sky, the sound of the wind, and the shroud of the dust.

That the film's world is charged with electricity not only at the level of representation and narrative – the motorcycle, the red star, the wires, and the hero's objective – but also in ways that are sensed is due to the atmospheres emanating from the historical narrative environment of famine, privation and drought. Electricity is indissolubly part of the atmospheres that Shepitko's work creates. These atmospheres are immanent to the world of this story, whose raw material, though first fictionalized by Platonov, in the film is nonetheless rooted in the geographic specificity. The majority of the cast were non-professional actors from nearby villages in the southern Volga region. And so it is conceivable that some of them or their family members could have lived through the famines of 1921–22. The dusty steppe itself would have witnessed some of the action in this chapter of postrevolutionary history. The haunting quality of the images comes from the intersection of the geographic specificity and the photographic medium. This is also perhaps where the film's most urgent invitation to reach into the past is located. The visual recurring rhyme of the dry earth's texture and the, lined faces creates something akin to the concrete traces of what happened long ago. Felt history itself seems to be inscribed in these images.

The atmosphere of this sequence – and of much of the film – is constituted through the qualities most often associated with an electrical charge, metaphorically speaking, qualified by descriptions such as tense, excited, stimulating. The poverty-stricken inhabitants, whose melancholy portraits Shepitko makes us notice, stare at the engineer and force him to look back. Carefully framed by the camera and windows, they are suspended between the eras – past and future, pre and postrevolutionary, pre- and post-Stalin. The kinetic and sonic vibrations residing around the stillness of these images suggest a latent vitality, similar to the inert lines that inside carry an electric current. As humans, we emit electromagnetic radiation; our nerve cells produce electrical pulses. As an unseen but always present force, electricity moves between the villagers' bodies and the air in which they live, catching the protagonist in this crosscurrent.

But the electric atmosphere is not only a metaphor for a sense of tension, hidden energies, a heighted emotional state, or whatever else it communicates to the viewer from a narrative perspective. Nor is the atmosphere imbued with electricity merely the background in which the narrative is set. Instead, I suggest, the atmospheric is formative of the narrative. Through its affective, immersive qualities, the atmospheric connects the audience with the story's historical antecedent. Throughout the film and particularly in this sequence – with its energetic camerawork, mobile framing, straight cuts and rigorous compositions – electricity is understood as inextricable and ubiquitous. What might the implications be of staging electricity as atmosphere rather than an entity that connotes progress and future? What are the social and perhaps ethical consequences of such a move? To return to the question posed earlier: how might this treatment of history as environment change our perception of the past?

RAIN

Giving the environment and its atmospheres such a prominent place in a narrative film shifts the center in the established plotline of modernization from the character that represents modernity to an environment – the land, the people, their weather world – poised on the brink of a sea change. This plays out especially in the outsider's encounters with the locals, and in the merging of his knowledge acquired through education with the villagers' ingenuity that reclaims electricity as an enduring part of their existence. Authorized to deliver progress to the backwater, the protagonist instead is caught in its atmospheres that mediate his experience of the environment, reforming and retuning his body to the environment's specificities.

Staging the atmospheric as formative of the narrative introduces a new depth to the 1960s reappraisal of the romanticism of the revolutionary era. The putative objective of the anthology film *Beginning of an Unknown Century* was to celebrate the October Revolution and the inaugural years of the new state. In their initial proposal to the Film Commission at the Council of Ministers, the heads of the Experimental Film Studio, Grigory Chukhrai and Vladimir Pozner, avowed that the literary texts selected for the commemorative project 'most accurately and truthfully reproduce the authentic atmosphere, romanticism, and pathos of the era, revealing the widely humanistic sense of the revolution through the private destinies of people.'[32] If in the immediate post-Stalin period the revolution and the Civil War era were regarded as the golden moment unmarred by Stalinism, by the mid-1960s such an idealized view of the first Soviet decade did not stand up to scrutiny.[33] Formulating the proposal in a more critical manner would have jeopardized official endorsement. Years later, a senior associate who had worked at the Experimental Studio and taken part in the making of *Beginning of an Unknown Century*, said that the desire of those involved with the project was to show the revolution 'as a romantic, tragic phenomenon . . . that already in its embryonic phase [was] contradictory,' and to begin an 'honest conversation with the viewer.'[34] *The Homeland of Electricity* started the conversation by framing history as environment and its atmospheres, calling on us and the 1960s spectator to pay attention to the peripheral and the rarely noticed, to that which in traditionally conceived cinematic stories is either cut out, exists on the blurry edges of the screen, or is seen at a far distance.

The absorption of the narrative by the environment deemphasizes language. Shepitko's film, although using dialogue and other linguistic forms of communication, shunts words to a background position and has whole scenes with no or little dialogue. First-person narration, which comes from Platonov's text and is heard in the film's setup, disappears when the hero awakens near the village, and returns only in the very final shots. It is as though letting go of the verbal retelling of the hero's experience also lets go of the idea that the only valid path to history lies through the written or spoken word. During the 1960s, not only established historical narratives were thrown into doubt, but arguably language itself as the primary conveyor of truth was devalued, suspect, in need of decontamination and renewal. The falseness of words for decades had hidden the devastating truth about the atrocities carried out by Stalin and his government, which started to come to light in the 1950s. Cinema's role in communicating this knowledge to the public and making some sense of it was to reimagine the past in analytical, sensorial, affective, kinesthetic, and other ways afforded by the medium. I suggest that the great social importance of cinema at this time lies in its capacity to deconcentrate signification in verbal forms and instead scatter it across cinema's other expressive modes – lighting, framing, staging, duration, sound, figural and other movement. Meaning in the framework of history as environment and atmospheres need not be solely linguistic, disembodied, representational, and rely on the analysis of abstract semiotic signs but encompass a broad range of qualities. And Shepitko's film does precisely that.

To a significant extent, *The Homeland of Electricity* removes the center of gravity not only from narrative, but the human agent as well, who is typically the catalyst for a narrative's peripetia, propelling the movement of a plot. Instead, Shepitko ends the film with the explosion of the motorcycle whose spellbinding conflagration the villagers gather to watch, followed by the long-awaited rain – one of the very few divergences from the source material she allowed for in the screen adaptation.[35] As the peasants – their elongated faces as well as parts of faces in closeups and extreme closeups – watch the demise of the homegrown water pump, rainfall begins. It mingles with their tears, liquifying the atmosphere. The decision to conclude with rain can be read as the triumph of nature and the divine over reason and the revolutionary promise of progress – the prayer has been answered. The imagery of *Homeland*'s final shots recalls the famous montage of rain-soaked fruit at the end of Oleksandr Dovzhenko's *Earth* (1930), a poetic evocation of the cycles of nature. But the ending of Shepitko's short points to something else.

The continuity script indicated that the final shot was to be the closeup of an old peasant looking up at the sky and screwing up his eyes because 'it's hard to look at the rain with one's eyes open.'[36] The image was to be accompanied by the intensifying noise of rain. Emphasizing the multisensory interaction of humans with the weather world, the film concludes slightly differently – with a montage of the locals, standing still, looking out of the frame, some directly at the spectator, rain running down their bodies. If the electricity plot had the potential of containing the story at the start, the environment and its atmospheres absorbed it in the film's unfolding. By the end, the environment has taken over completely, which is visualized in the dramatic de-framing of faces and figures, as well as the mixing of rain and tears.

Two interlinked ideas are central to the realized ending: one is feeling the rain, which is a continuation of feeling the weather-world throughout the film; the other is the presence of the past. In contrast to the other sequences explored in the essay, where visual devices such as windows and balanced closeup composition restrain the faces similar to icons, and the convention of shot-reverse shot grounds them spatiotemporally, here the villagers' heads and figures are de-framed.[37] The shots feature entire faces alongside parts of their neighbors' bodies (see Fig. 5.4). A reverse shot does not impede the flow of these images, which introduces ambiguity in the looking relations. Partially seen, the figures extend into the offscreen surroundings and perhaps into other temporal modalities. Are they still watching the wrecked engine? Why are we asked to observe the trembling necks, doleful eyes, waterlogged beards? Are these melancholy figures grieving for their past or future? The blanket of rain separates the audience from the gaunt peasants and yet it liquifies the separation, making the normally imperceptible barrier of the screen visible, permeable, felt. The villagers seem to reach out directly to us – and especially the viewer of the 1960s who would have been reckoning with this piece of history. In the absence of the reverse shot, the audience takes the place between the villagers and the last image of the film – the earth whose crevasses begin to shimmer with water. This cinematic rain, then, is a medium that, through its affective, kinetic, sonic, and tactile qualities, allows the audience to connect with the film's world, people and ultimately the past.

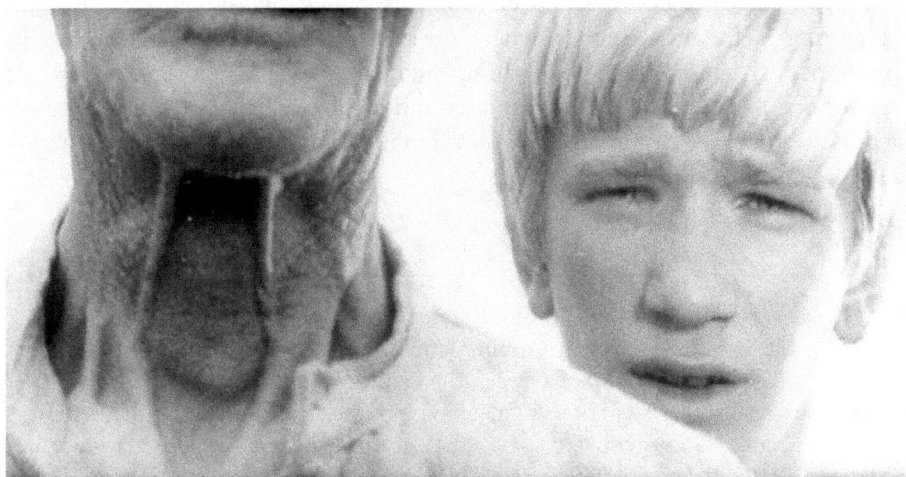

Figure 5.4 The rain commingles with the tears of the villagers.

Exploring our contact with such an immaterial yet potentially devastating weather phenomenon as wind, Ingold notes that to feel the wind is to experience 'a kind of interpenetration of the self and its surroundings.'[38] A commingling of the subject with the medium makes feeling possible. Though we cannot touch the wind, we touch *in* it.[39] To inhabit a fluctuating weather-world, writes Ingold, 'is to be immersed in the fluxes of the medium: in sunshine, rain, and wind. This immersion, in turn, underwrites our capacities – respectively – to see, hear, and touch.'[40] Although we can never be in the filmic environment the same way we can be in the wind, or in the weather, such tactile and visual perception is apt for considering the different ways we may relate to history, particularly when it is figured so atmospherically alive. The creators of *The Homeland of Electricity* painstakingly built the film's environment through the staging of the atmospheric, rendering a distant past resonant on many levels. It is as though the film wants us to feel history; to feel it through a weather-world that activates multisensory perception – the same way it activates the villagers, whose eyes, ears and skin we face in the final moments (**see Fig. 5.4**).

While we are able 'to touch our surroundings in the wind and see them in the sky, it is above all in the rain that we hear them,' Ingold says.[41] *The Homeland of Electricity* did not fare well with Soviet censorship. Its unconventional and critical reimagining of the country's formative period landed it, along with the rest of *Beginning of an Unknown Century*, in a twenty-year exile.[42] The rain that floods the screen in the end is silenced, although the script indicated that its sonic amplitude was to grow steadily. Whether it was Shepitko's decision to eliminate the sound of the rain or of those who were involved with the film's restoration in 1987 is unknown. In its place, the engineer's voiceover returns, overlaid by the musical score. But the power of multisensory film perception is such that even without the rain's audible presence we are still able to discern its sonorous aspect. Through the staging of the atmospheres, where the rain is the last element to make an appearance – what everyone was waiting and many were praying for – Shepitko's film seemed to ask Soviet audiences to try and inhabit a slice of the difficult past, or at the very least, to listen carefully for the sound of the distant rain.

NOTES

1. The Experimental Creative Studio (Eksperimental'naia tvorcheskaia kinostudiia, ETK) was founded in 1965 by Grigory Chukhrai, who served as the studio's artistic director, and Vladimir Pozner, the studio's administrative head. The company used the system of self-financing, produced films largely outside the centralized studio system, and survived until 1976. More about the creation and history of the studio see *Kinematograf Ottepeli: documenty i svidetel'stva*, ed. by Valerii Fomin (Moscow: Materik, 1998), 234–55.

2. The name for the omnibus film came from the title of the third part of Konstantin Paustovsky's autobiographical work *Story of a Life* (Povest' o zhinzi, 1946–1963, published 1967).
3. Vladimir Ognev, "Ne tol'ko vospominania." *Iskusstvo kino*, May 1987, 3–14.
4. Originally, there were 5 shorts in the project, but, largely due to reasons of censorship, only 3 were realized: *Angel* directed by Andrei Smirnov, based on a short story by Yuri Olesha; *Motria*, directed by Genrikh Gabai, based on the novella by Paustovsky; and *The Homeland of Electricity* by Shepitko. Smirnov's and Shepitko's films were restored and shown during perestroika together under the title of *Beginning of an Unknown Century*, while Gabai's contribution never saw the light of day. For more on the production and censorship of the omnibus project, see *Polka: Dokumenty. Svidetel'stva. Kommentarii.* Vyp. 3, ed. by Valerii Fomin (Moscow: Materik, 2006), 33–54.
5. Thomas Seifrid, *A Companion to Andrei Platonov's* The Foundation Pit (Boston: Academic Studies Press, 2009), 10–11.
6. On the history of "The Homeland of Electricity" and on the fact it might be a reworking of Platonov's *Technical Novel*, see A. Griaznova, "Tekhnicheskii roman i 'Rodina electrichesva' A. Platonova: tema preobrazovaniia mira," *Vestnik VGU*, No. 1, 2011, 20. For more on the relationship between the two works, see Bora Chung, "Andrei Platonov's *Technical Novel*: Revolution, Technology, and the Cost of Electrified Utopia," *Utopian Studies* 28.1 (2017): 148–67.
7. Denis Kozlov, "The Historical Turn in Late Soviet Culture: Retrospectivism, Factography, Doubt, 1953–1991," *Kritika: Explorations in Russian and Eurasian History*, 2.3 (Summer 2001, New Series): 577–600.
8. Kozlov, 578.
9. Ibid., 587.
10. Trouillot emphasizes that production of history outside of academia is key to understanding not abstract concerns for "the nature of history" but "how history works." Rolph-Michel Trouillot, *Silencing the Past: Power and the Production of History* (Boston: Beacon Press, 2018), 24–25.
11. Ibid., 3.
12. Steffen Hven, *Enacting the Worlds of Cinema* (New York: Oxford University Press, 2022), 17.
13. Ibid., 19.
14. My line of inquiry is adjacent to Alison Landsberg's concerns in *Engaging the Past: Mass Culture and the Production of Historical Knowledge* (Columbia University Press, 2015). Interested in how affect informs historical knowledge, Landsberg investigates the relationship between the past and the privileging in contemporary mediatized cultures of the experiential mode of engagement – be it a historical fiction film, TV historical dramas, or virtual exhibitions – and the role this relationship plays in acquisition of historical knowledge.
15. More on Platonov's play with language and the trouble the author got into because of it, see Nariman Skakov, "Introduction: Andrei Platonov, an Engineer of the Human Soul," *Slavic Review*, Vol. 73, No. 4 (Winter 2014): 719–26, and the whole issue of *Slavic Review*, "Platonov's Turkmenia."

16. Thomas Seifrid, *Andrei Platonov: Uncertainties of Spirit* (Cambridge: Cambridge University Press, 1992), 1 and 18.
17. Böhme develops a theory of atmospheres, noting that atmosphere "relates objective factors and constellations of the environment with my bodily feeling in that environment. This means: atmosphere is what is *in between* the two sides." Gernot Böhme, *The Aesthetics of Atmospheres* (Abingdon and New York: Taylor and Francis, 2016), 1–2.
18. For the articulation of the atmospheric not as an object of perception but its condition, see Hven who, in turn, references the French sociologist and urban planner Jean-Paul Thibaud. Hven, 44.
19. Böhme, *The Aesthetics of Atmospheres*, 3–8.
20. Tim Ingold, "Earth, Sky, Wind, and Weather," *The Journal of the Royal Anthropological Institute* 13 (2007), S25–26.
21. Tim Ingold, "The Atmosphere," *Chiasmi International* 14 (2012), 80.
22. For a history of the long association between electricity and sight, see Doron Galili, *Seeing by Electricity: The Emergence of Television, 1878–1939* (Durham: Duke University Press, 2020), Chapter 2.
23. Continuity script of *The Homeland of Electricity* published by the studio Mosfilm, 1967, f. 3234, op. 1, d. 24, 56, Rossiiskii Gosudarstvennyi Arkhiv Literatury i Iskusstva (RGALI), Moscow, Russia.
24. *Polka: Dokumenty. Svidetel'stva. Kommentarii*, ed. by Valerii Fomin, 39.
25. Vladimir Ognev, "Dvadtsat' let nazad," *Iskusstvo kino*, January 1988, 34.
26. More on this historical period, see, for example, Richard Stites, *Revolutionary Dreams: Utopian Vision and Experimental Life in the Russian Revolution* (New York: Oxford University Press, 1989).
27. Anindita Banerjee, "Electric Origins: From Modernist Myth to Bolshevik Utopia," in *L'Ère électrique - The Electric Age* (Ottawa: University of Ottawa Press, 2011), 289–304. For various attitudes toward electricity in the West, see Arthur Firstenberg, *The Invisible Rainbow: A History of Electricity and Life* (White River Junction, VT: Chelsea Green Publishing, 2020).
28. Banerjee focuses on the writings of the millenarian philosopher Nikolai Fedorov, in particular his conception of electricity as a force that could resurrect "common ancestors" and "reestablish the genealogical connections between all men and usher in an egalitarian worldwide 'Christian brotherhood'"; as well as the texts of the Symbolists Zinaida Hippius and Vladimir Shelonsky, and of the Futurist Velimir Khlebnikov. Banerjee, 295–300.
29. Ibid., 302.
30. Ibid., 300–302.
31. There are several instances in the film where the film stock is overexposed to create a washed-out, solarized effect.
32. *Polka: Dokumenty. Svidetel'stva. Kommentarii*, 34.
33. Kozlov, 587.
34. *Polka*, 34.
35. In Platonov's story, the young engineer builds the water pump and departs, satisfied that his goal has been achieved.

36. Continuity script of *The Homeland of Electricity*, f. 3234, op. 1, d. 24, 78, RGALI.
37. I thank Lilya Kaganovsky for raising the question of unframed/de-framed closeups in this scene during a Q&A at the Larisa Shepitko panel at ASEEES, October 2022.
38. Ingold, "Earth, Sky, Wind, and Weather," S29.
39. This phrase is Ingold's: "To feel the wind, then, is to experience this commingling. While we did not touch it, we touched *in* it," S30. And: ". . . it is not so much the wind that is embodied as the body, in breathing, that is *enwinded*," S32. Emphasis in the original.
40. Ibid., S30.
41. Ingold, "Earth, Sky, Wind, and Weather," S29.
42. More on the project's history and censorship, see *Polka*.

CHAPTER 6

The Senselessness of the Heroic Act and the Experience of War in *The Ascent*

Elizabeth A. Papazian

In the epilogue to his *Theory of Film* (1960), Siegfried Kracauer argues that modernity has changed "the relations between the inner universe and physical reality." We have become alienated from the material world through the fragmented nature of modern life and the "veil" of modernizing ideologies that relate physical reality (and our experience of that reality) "to some total aspect of the universe." Kracauer sees cinema as a way to break through the veil, to access inner life "through the experience of surface reality," in order to confront and question "our notions of the physical world."[1] This chapter proposes to examine Larisa Shepitko's harrowing war film, *The Ascent* (Voskhozhdenie, 1976), in an attempt to address the following question: what are the consequences, on the level of meaning, of the film's exploration of material experience?

The effect this "cruel" and "excruciatingly severe" film[2] produces on the viewer is attested in an anecdote about the reaction of a crucial early audience member, Pyotr Mironovich Masherov, the First Secretary of the Communist Party of Belorussia at the time. Masherov organized the first screening of the film for the Belorussian leadership; his positive assessment insured its acceptance by the Soviet ideological apparatus.[3] Shepitko's husband, the film director Elem Klimov, recalled sitting next to Masherov during the screening:

> He was in a good mood, offered me a cigarette, but within about ten minutes of the film he had forgotten about the world around him. Then he suddenly instinctively squeezed my arm, and I noticed that he was weeping. When the lights went up in the screening room, Masherov got up and, breaking with the Party etiquette that prescribes that one first listen to the opinions of subordinates and only later make a decisive

statement, he began to speak [. . .] very sincerely, profoundly, and with heartfelt anguish [. . .].[4]

Along similar lines, stories circulated about the experience of working on the film, and how the production affected its cast and crew, who endured extreme conditions of filming on location in winter, with crew members having their "hands frozen to the equipment" and extras sustaining frostbite.[5] As the actor Liudmila Polyakova explained in a recent interview: "We really felt like we had lived through it."[6]

The Ascent is an adaptation of a 1970 novella by the Belarusian writer Vasil' Bykov (Vasil' Bykaŭ) about two partisans in occupied Belarus in the winter of 1942 who are sent out on a mission to find food, but are caught by the Nazi police and sentenced to death alongside two villagers they encountered during their mission.[7] The story takes place over the course of two days, and follows the two soldiers closely: throughout the film, the viewer is denied the expected spatial and temporal contextual information of wide shots, parallel editing, or flashbacks.[8] Even character point-of-view shots and eyeline matches are used sparingly: the film generally rejects these conventional cinematic techniques for conveying character psychology and development.[9] Yet through its stylistic asceticism *The Ascent* conveys an intensity of feeling that seems to fulfil the ideal of cinema proposed by Andrei Tarkovsky in his 1967 essay, "Imprinted Time":

> I think that what a person normally goes to the cinema for is time: for time lost or spent or not yet had. He goes there for lived experience; for cinema, like no other art, widens, enhances and concentrates a person's experience [. . .].[10]

I wish to argue that in rejecting the psychological development of the two main characters and in focusing, particularly in the first half of the film, on the materiality of experience under the extreme conditions of the war, the film exceeds the boundaries of its ostensible central ideological conflict and its engagement with the Soviet mythology of the Second World War. Rather, the film poses broader, universal questions of moral life under extreme circumstances, and provides the audience with the conditions for engaging those questions through their own experiences—and their experience of the film.

The two main characters, Sotnikov and Rybak, represent a familiar ideological opposition in Soviet cinema of the "conscious" intellectual vs. the "spontaneous" man of the people—of *mind* vs. *body*—that became entrenched with the 1934 film *Chapaev*, an historical film about the Russian Civil War that helped establish the conventions of Stalin-era "socialist realist" cinema. Sotnikov is a math teacher from the city (Vitebsk), weakened by a cough that seems related to his terribly inadequate army uniform; Rybak, clad in a shearling coat and *ushanka*, is a healthy local man, familiar with the surrounding farms and geography.¹¹ But instead of coming together in the requisite symbolic synthesis firmly established in *Chapaev*, with the scrappy man of the people (the military leader Chapaev) becoming enlightened through the strict discipline of the Party represented by the Bolshevik intellectual (the commissar, Furmanov), here the two men remain resolutely separate, as two terms in a debate that cannot be resolved—a failure to merge into the ideal Soviet man that becomes profoundly evident at the moment of their arrest. Sotnikov adamantly refuses to give any information to the police interrogator, suddenly mastering his sickly body (with Bolshevik discipline): in a Dostoevskian verbal duel with his interrogator Portnov, he heroically endures torture.¹² But later, during the night in prison, as Sotnikov listens to the stories of the other prisoners who will be executed for helping the partisans, he decides he will give in to the interrogator in exchange for their freedom—an offer which is rejected the next day because he refuses to provide the required information (that is, he refuses to betray the partisan encampment in the forest). Rybak, on the other hand, avoids torture by appearing to reveal everything he knows, immediately, and the next day, as they are setting off to be executed, agrees to join the local police force in exchange for his life.¹³ At the scene of the execution of Sotnikov and three other captives, an onlooker calls Rybak "Judas."

The second half of the film, starting from the partisans' capture, shifts in tone, taking on a more symbolic and abstract character. The Christian allusions of Sotnikov's martyrdom and Rybak's betrayal are strikingly overt, including the *ascent* of the prisoners up the snowy Golgotha (reminiscent of Tarkovsky's imagined passion of Christ in *Andrei Rublev* [1966]), the composition of groups around Sotnikov, and the lighting of Sotnikov's ascetic face in the dark basement prison that lends his physical, human, kenotic suffering a saintly radiance—and, of course, the explicit association of the traitor with "Judas."

The association of the Bolshevik hero with the iconography of Christian martyrs has a long tradition in Soviet cinema.¹⁴ Dovzhenko's *Earth* (1930), a touchstone for Shepitko's film particularly on the visual level, features the village activist Vasyl as a static "positive hero"—that is, an already "conscious" hero—whose murder is framed as martyrdom: his father, Opanas, serves as the dynamic character whose conversion is sparked by the hero's sacrifice, and who moves from skepticism to acceptance of Bolshevik ideology. Sotnikov's proud confession of (Bolshevik) faith before he sets off to his execution fits perfectly into this tradition:

> No. Not Ivanov. My name's Sotnikov. Commander, Red Army. Born in 1917. Bolshevik. Party member since 1935. Teacher by profession. At the start of the war, I commanded a battery. It's a shame I didn't kill more of

you bastards. My name is Sotnikov—Boris Andreevich. I have a father, a mother, and a motherland.

But the iteration of the theme of Bolshevik martyr as kenotic Christ in *The Ascent* departs from Soviet cultural conventions in key ways. While Sotnikov's heroism is defined both by his extraordinary qualities and his faith in an ideal, aligning him with the socialist realist "positive hero" as a role model for Soviet citizens to aspire to, his heroic feat fails, both as a historical act *and* as a virtuous act to save his comrades. In *Chapaev*, in contrast, the eponymous hero sends for reinforcements, who are shown after his death riding forward to attack the enemy.[15] Sotnikov's act fails to move history forward in the way one expects of socialist realist sacrifice, even if that is simply a visual gesture towards the ultimate triumph of progress, as at the end of *Chapaev*. At the same time, on the local level, Sotnikov's belated realization that giving up information (or pretending to do so) could help *these* specific people in *this* specific situation comes too late—whether to save his fellow prisoners, who are executed alongside him, or the people hiding in the forest, who are still starving.

In an on-set interview, Shepitko called the film a "neo-parable," crediting the Belarusian writer Ales Adamovich (Ales' Adamovich), known for his "documentary" literary method, for the concept. As Shepitko explains, while the classic parable features the clash between good and evil, culminating in the triumph of good, accompanied by an openly stated moral, and narrated as laconically as possible, the "neo-parable" complicates both the initial moral dichotomy and the "clarity of the author's idea." Instead of clearly defined, morally opposed symbolic characters, the "neo-parable" offers a *chronicle*, replete with authentic details, of complex "living people whose characters are ambiguous [*neodnoznachny*], whose psychology changes depending on circumstances."[16] Shepitko asserted art's moral responsibility to pose the "eternal questions"— questions "about the meaning of life, about the inevitability of death, about fatal moments, and about the guarantees of immortality" [*o zalogakh bessmertiia*]— and to continue posing these questions, forcing the viewer to engage with them.[17] Each character in the film is compelled to define their position through a terrible, life-or-death choice. Sotnikov's stoic endurance and acceptance of death attain the coherence and clarity of a parable: Evil must be resisted, at all costs. But this victory is clouded, rendered ambiguous, by his failure as a Bolshevik hero, a standard he himself had enunciated. Along these lines, Valerii Golovskoi has articulated a central problem in the film: "Can a heroic act [*podvig*] be senseless?"[18]

The notion of the "senseless heroic act" leads us, on the one hand, back to the kenotic tradition, to suffering as imitation of Christ and as a supreme value (in contrast to Sotnikov's more pantocratic leanings towards judgement of the morally weak), and to the viewer's own "co-suffering" or empathy (*sostradanie*) in the process of watching the film: as Shepitko argued, "the style of *The Ascent* makes it uncomfortable to watch. But [. . .] It's not possible to wrap up a parable about the meaning of life and death, a story about a great feat, into a sweet pill. After all, art should 'explode' a person from within."[19] On the other hand, the senselessness of Sotnikov's heroism leads us to Shepitko's focus on the non-heroic, insignificant details—the "documentary expressiveness of the background" (*dokumental'naia vyrazitel'nost' fona*) that she associates with the film's "neo-parable" style.[20] In Shepitko's film, these two tendencies are inextricably intertwined: the viewer's engagement with the film as a kind of living through, even "co-suffering," depends on its documentary-like approach, leading us past the Soviet obsession with "heroic feats" to the actions of those who would not be considered heroes—whether in literature, cinema, or history. What about the ordinary acts of ordinary people?

In terms of plot, what is so unusual about the film—and its source text—is how it humanizes collaboration with the enemy, an act usually befitting only villainous characters in Soviet cinema. Although Rybak is portrayed as the morally weaker character who hesitates to risk his own life, at least twice in the film he makes moral choices that the viewer may well approve. First, when the two partisans encounter a village elder who appears to be a collaborator, Sotnikov wants to shoot the man immediately, while Rybak spares him (and takes a sheep). The village elder is arrested later, and executed; it turns out he was secretly working with the partisans. Second, although he knows it may cost him his life (and the failure of their original mission of bringing back food to the forest camp), Rybak refuses to abandon the wounded Sotnikov in the snow. That is, Rybak consistently chooses the *individual* over the broader, more abstract mission. Similarly, Demchikha, a mother of young children whose house the partisans find by chance, chooses, first, not to betray the partisans who have stumbled into her life, instead hiding them; and then, when she has been arrested and sentenced to death, leaving her children with no food or care, she chooses not to divulge the information that might save her—specifically, the name of the family who hid the Jewish child, Basya. The everyday ordinariness of such impossible choices is underlined by the "documentary expressiveness of the background"—for example, in the scene of their arrest at Demchikha's little house: when the two men sit inside as the police approach, Demchikha runs outside to meet them, and we see, through the window, on the sidelines of the scene of mortal danger, a snowman smiling in the corner of the frame, reminding us of the everyday existence of children who might still see the deadly, snowy expanse as a place to play (see Fig. 6.1).

The film's opening scene, too, serves to provide the broader expressive background that the rest of the film refuses to give us. It takes place behind the film's credits, functioning on the level of plot to establish the historical

Figure 6.1 A snowman in front of Demchikha's house, as seen through the window by Sotnikov and Rybak.

context, the partisans' dire living conditions, their physical exhaustion and nearly exhausted supplies, and to set in motion the journey of Rybak and Sotnikov. The scene follows a group of partisans and refugees as they cross a snow-covered open space to reach a forest. On the way, they encounter a German patrol, and they exchange fire. When they arrive in the forest, they rest and eat the scant remains of their food supply.[21]

The attention in this scene to "surface reality"—accomplished in particular through framing, camera movement, rhythm, and sound—far exceeds any ostensible descriptive purpose. Instead of merely adding an authentic feel to the background of the main storyline, the tiny details of the partisans' life in the forest establish the film's interest in the *materiality of experience* in the extreme conditions of the war, and the relationship of that material experience to inner life. It is tempting to suggest that the scene serves a function similar to what the Italian director Pier Paolo Pasolini called "free indirect subjective" discourse—that is, a technique of "immersion" into the mind of a character. Instead of indicating a character's perspective through point-of-view shots, the character's subjectivity suffuses the film: the atmosphere of the film reflects the character's subjectivity.[22] But in the opening sequence of *The Ascent*, the atmosphere does not correspond to any one character's subjective experience. Rather, the viewer feels the cold because it is objectively cold: the cold and hunger are experienced by *all* the people in the forest—and, as noted above, by the cast and crew themselves.

The eight-minute scene, made up of 43 shots, divides roughly into two halves: the first four minutes take place in the open, snowy expanse outside of the forest, while the second half takes place within the forest. The film opens with two seconds of a black screen accompanied by the sound of wind, which continues through the next four fairly short shots of the snowy location, taken with a static camera, interrupted first by the sound of machine-gun fire and then by voices. It is only in shot six, which begins with a motionless camera framing a few trees, that a human form emerges from behind what we understand is a hill, waves his arm, and the camera is set in motion, with a zoom-out that reveals more landscape, as many figures in black emerge slowly from behind the snowy hills, then, at their leader's gesture, move downhill, away from the camera, accompanied by a droning hum on Alfred Schnittke's musical soundtrack. As the members of the group move downhill, the first credit, the film's title, appears onscreen.

Shot seven continues with a handheld camera, framing the people in medium distance, as they head towards and past the camera diagonally, while the sounds of their movement are layered over the drone of the soundtrack (**see Fig. 6.2**).

Figure 6.2 Shot seven: Credit sequence and mobile camera.

SENSELESSNESS OF THE HEROIC ACT & EXPERIENCE OF WAR 123

The group includes armed men and unarmed civilians, carrying weapons and baggage, respectively, and supporting or carrying those too weak to walk. The camera changes direction, pausing to observe people passing laterally, then turning and following. The soundtrack includes sounds of people moving through snow, objects clanking, voices ("Hurry, hurry!"), and exerted breathing, with the droning sound dying down. Suddenly a panicked voice yells "Germans!" and the camera pauses as the leader pauses, looking towards and past the camera in distress. From here, the sequence from shots 8–25 presents the brief and frenetic exchange of gunfire, with a first glimpse of our two main characters, Rybak and Sotnikov, not yet introduced to us, holding off the German soldiers as the rest of the group flees into the forest.

Starting at shot 26, the group is located in the forest, again moving towards and past the camera diagonally (as in shot seven), accompanied by the sounds of their movement again: this time, the sounds of exhaustion are more prominent; there is no music; the credits have ended; the gunfire recedes into the background. One man leans against a tree and starts to slide downwards. The leader passes him and the camera follows him as he tries to help the fallen man up, and the other says "I can't," then the leader moves forward and pauses—the camera also pauses—and says "Let's halt!" and starts to sink towards the ground; the camera, along with everyone else within the frame, sinks towards the ground.

Up to this point one could describe the scene in terms of recognizable 1960s techniques, beautifully executed (with a dash of 1970s flavor provided by the zoom-out in shot six), in the self-conscious style that Lilya Kaganovsky has associated with "the possibility of a Soviet 'counter-cinema.'"[23] The opening shots frame the action with still-camera views of the landscape, three of which will reappear at the very end of the film, framing the film in the "poetic" manner of Dovzhenko's *Earth*.[24] On-location shooting in extremely cold winter conditions, emphasizing the sounds of that concrete time and place—the wind, the snow, the dragging of objects and tired people—complement camerawork that makes the viewer "feel" the camera as a palpable presence that, like a member of the group, follows the important information of danger (the cry of "Germans!") and the leader's commands (to get up; to flee to the forest; to rest). The "felt" camera provides the viewer with a material presence—a body—in the film. The reverse motion of the zoom out in shot six contrasts with the handheld camera: the optical effect of motion, as opposed to the physical motion of a camera in three-dimensional space, draws attention to the artifice.[25] The artificial, abrupt movement of the zoom after a series of static landscape shots introduces the mobile, "felt" camera, serving as another framing device, emphasizing spatial—and temporal—distance from the viewer, before we are suddenly plunged into the midst of the fleeing group of partisans and refugees, at medium distance.

During the action scene of confrontation between the partisans and the German soldiers (shots 8–25), there is a shift to a more recognizable narrative style. The camera cuts among the partisan leader, the German soldiers, the partisan shooters (as it turns out, Rybak and Sotnikov), and those who are shot, providing eyeline matches that allow us to follow the actions logically from a more objective position, without a body, before returning to the "felt" camera presence in the forest.

But then there is a change. The leader asks another member of the group to distribute what food he has left. A small bag is pulled out, and the sound of grains being poured into a metal pot connects to a close-up of the pot (shot 30), with an impossibly small amount of grain in it. From here, we see a series of close-ups of people of all ages, their clothing and faces dusted (or encrusted) with snow, receiving their ration: holding out their hands, receiving about a tablespoon of grains poured into it, eating it, and helping others to eat their portion, taking care not to lose a single grain. The camera sometimes moves to frame the process of distribution, getting closer and closer—to the point that we can see ice melting, saliva, and sweat—and eventually grows still, framing individual people for a few seconds each, coming extremely close, first to a woman's face, then a man's, frontally, looking directly into the camera (**see Figures 6.3–6.5**) The soundtrack includes breathing, coughing, people's movement in snow, and the disconcertingly *liquid* sound of the grains being chewed, now rejoined by the droning sound on the soundtrack (starting in shot 35).

On the one hand, the scene fits into the Biblical *and* socialist realist iconography of the whole film, creating a modern version of communion/commune, with the infirm helped by the relatively healthy, everyone receiving the same meager ration, and a churchlike silence punctuated by breathing and coughing. Even the upward gazes of people whose bodies are undergoing terrible suffering, which becomes a major visual theme of the second half of the film, first appears in this sequence. The clear sense of the hostile environment and the excitement of the escape from gunfire of the previous sequence are replaced by the reality of exhaustion, life-threatening cold, and the possibility of starvation.

The film as a whole, and the first half in particular, emphasizes what Lucía Nagib calls the "realist mode of production"—in particular, through on-location shooting in which the actors endured conditions similar to those experienced by their onscreen characters. As Nagib explains, in the realist mode of production, the cast and crew commit "to produce rather than just reproduce reality and to commit themselves to unpredictable events": "the illusionistic fictional thread (if it exists) interweaves with documentary footage and/or approach, as well as with crew and cast's direct interference with the historical world, aimed not only at highlighting the reality of the medium but also at producing, as well as reproducing, social and historical reality."[26]

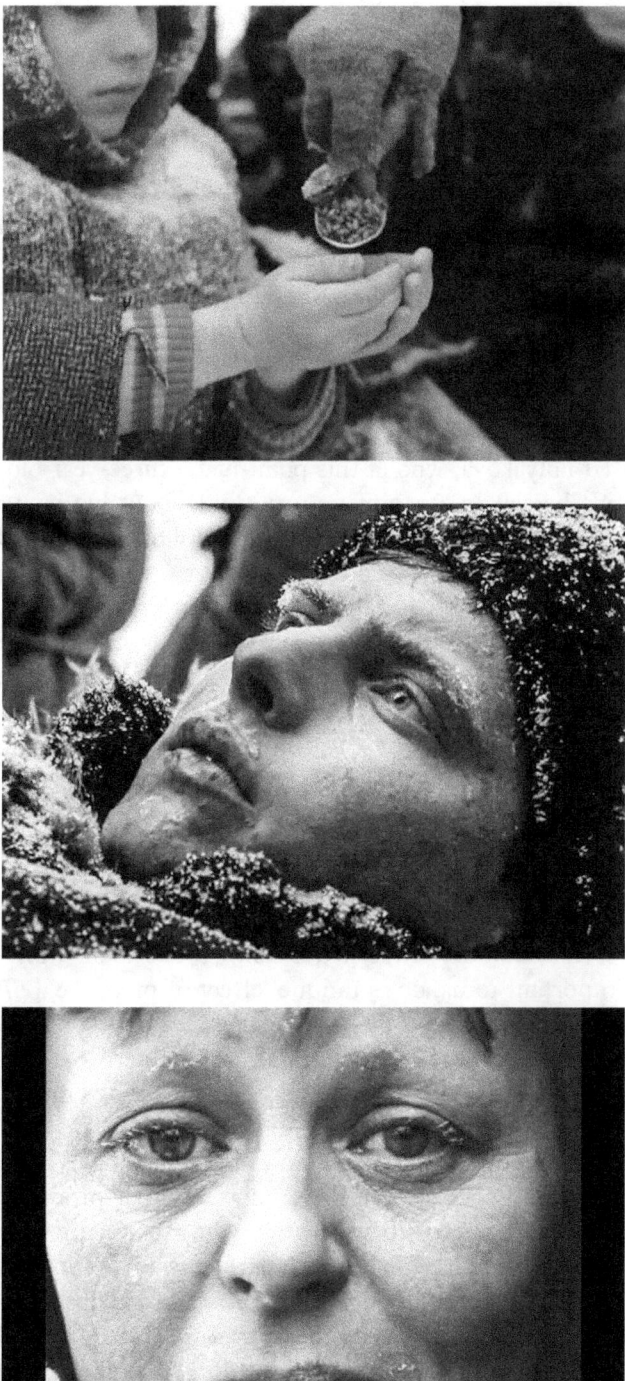

Figures 6.3–6.5 Close-ups of people in the forest receiving their portion of grain.

As noted above, the actor who played Demchikha, Liudmila Polyakova, attested to the powerful effect the filming had on the whole cast: "We really felt like we had lived through it." This coincided with Shepitko's insistence that actors not "play" their roles, but rather "inhabit [*prozhit'*] the role, in the full sense of the word 'inhabit.'"[27]

But the filming had a specific effect on Polyakova *personally*, based on her own connection to the *location*. As she explained, during the Second World War, when she was a small child, she and her mother were evacuated to the exact location of the filming, in Murom, Russia. The site of the execution scene was one that had particularly strong connotations for her, as her own mother had apparently collapsed from exhaustion and starvation and nearly frozen to death while walking up the very same hill that led to the execution site in the film. Polyakova had told Shepitko this story; on the day of shooting the execution scene, the director advised Polyakova, who at this point had a three-year-old child of her own, to imagine herself in this situation, to think about her own child. When she was standing on the stool in the role of Demchikha, waiting to be executed, Polyakova looked down the hill: "And so I remember, you know there, where the execution was, the execution . . . and there below—the ravine, the river . . . it was when they posed us with the nooses, so on those stools, and I look down. I look down. And I see, I see that river. I see that slope there. And my lips are whispering, and I . . . but something like that can't be, that just can't be."[28]

The shared sense among the cast and crew of experiencing, or "living through" the production process is referenced as well by director of photography Vladimir Chukhnov, who explained the camerawork in *The Ascent* in terms of a "documentary" style (*dokumental'nost' stil'ia*):

> It was necessary to crawl along with the actors in the snow, to run alongside them. It wasn't the strict structuring [*vystroennost'*] of the frame that was important to us, but a unique 'effect of presence' [*effekt prisutsviia*], a sense of belonging [*oshchushchenie soprichastnosti*] to what was happening. It was practically reportage: the camera operator had to demonstrate quick reactions and make artistic decisions on the fly.[29]

Chukhnov's description of filming emphasizes the crew's commitment to the "unpredictable events" of Nagib's "realist mode of production," a sense echoed in accounts of the frostbitten extras who participated in the opening sequence.[30] The "documentary" approach to the production of a historical film serves to recuperate a sense of *contingency*, in opposition to the teleological developmental narrative of Soviet history, a gesture that fits into the post-war, post-Stalin-era Soviet "counter-cinema" attempt to break with the entrenched norms of socialist realism.[31] To undertake this kind of resistance to history is particularly striking in a war film, the historical genre par excellence.

The realist mode of production is enhanced by the film's "mode of reception"—that is, "the focus on realism as a reality effect on the human body and senses"—the excruciatingly physical, even personal details of the soundtrack that emphasize the processes of the body.[32] We might speak here of a haptic visuality whereby the sensual qualities of surface take precedence over the perception of depth, shifting the relationship between viewer and image—and perhaps even a haptic use of sound.[33] But this haptic visuality is inextricable from Shepitko's use of the close-up. To return to the opening scene of the film, the shift over the course of eight minutes from wide, still shots of landscape, to a "felt" camera, to a brief action sequence, to a series of close-up shots, effects a change in narration and perception that is crucial to the film's exploration of material experience under extreme conditions—a style that hinges on the intense and repeated use of close-ups throughout the film.

As Mary Ann Doane has argued, the close-up—in its excess, even "monstrosity"—poses "a lurking danger, a potential semiotic threat to the unity and coherency of the filmic discourse."[34] Doane has noted the contradiction between two ways of understanding the close-up: on the one hand, it is an extracted fragment, a part of a whole, a detail; on the other, it is an abstracted and autonomous whole, a totality in its own right. In this latter understanding, the close-up abolishes offscreen space and so "cannot be defined as a detail, since it occupies the only space there is, constituting itself as its own whole or totality."[35] According to Doane, much of film theory has understood the close-up

> as stasis, as resistance to narrative linearity, as the vertical gateway to an almost irrecoverable depth behind the image. The discourse seems to exemplify a desire to stop the film, to grab hold of something that can be taken away, to transfer the relentless temporality of the narrative's unfolding to a more manageable temporality of contemplation.[36]

The close-up can be "domesticated" through the eyeline match, which reintegrates it into the spatial and temporal logic of narrative, where it serves the purpose of revealing "the interiority of a character through its magnification of detail and expression" but, nevertheless, retains its "excessive" quality that draws attention to the divide between the diegetic world (the world of the film) and the space of the viewer. "The close-up transforms whatever it films into a quasi-tangible thing, producing an intense phenomenological experience of presence, and yet, simultaneously, that deeply experienced entity becomes a sign, a text, a surface that demands to be read."[37]

In the close-up of a face, we confront both our desire to read (and know) the other and our recognition that we cannot know. Noa Steimatsky has recently examined the face in cinema as *dispositif,* or "a complex of figural functions and relations," and as "a way of seeing, a critical lens, a mode of thought."

Steimatsky emphasizes the "equivocal" visuality of the face, which we assume is "the most nuanced register of an inner life"; and so we "rush to embrace ineffable depths," but instead encounter opacity and illegibility.[38] This confrontation is crucial for understanding post-war cinema: "Questions of the face are concomitant with questions about the survival of art, about the possibility of aesthetic experience—the very possibility of expression, of inter-subjectivity as such after Auschwitz."[39]

In a reading of Carl Theodor Dreyer's *The Passion of Joan of Arc* (1928), a film that, like Dovzhenko's *Earth*, focuses intensely on close-ups of faces while thwarting spatial and temporal continuity by avoiding eyeline matches and establishing shots, Steimatsky argues that the emphasis on the human face "interfered with the ostensible narrative of transcendence and plunged the moving image back into the thick of life, the reality of the body's losing battle with death." Although

> we expect to be transported to some 'spiritual perspective,' or at least psychological depth, we sense at the same time a way in which the face is here both conduit and intrusion to such journey. In fact the face's physical being—by way of appearance, frequently marked by the haptic appeal of skin texture, wetness of cheeks, dryness of lips and so on—is often sensed as inordinately tangible.[40]

In this sense, through the mediation of the close-up that purports to offer us a character's inner life—in *The Passion of Joan of Arc*, the inner life of a saint—we come up against the impossibility of truly knowing any other person's experience: "The human face is where we encounter time and again, *in the visual*, what we cannot really know. The gap, or abyss, signaled here also means that Dreyer's audaciously foregrounded close-ups can in fact transpire *as distance*."[41]

In this sense we might read the series of close-ups in the opening sequence of *The Ascent* as a refusal of depth and a reinforcement of distance, with the inner life of characters—and actors, for that matter—remaining resolutely unknowable. But Shepitko goes even further through the use of direct, prolonged glances into the camera, a gesture that is established in the opening sequence and repeated throughout the film. The direct address creates a sense of *aperture*—on the one hand, a disruption of the illusion, marking the presence of the cinematic apparatus, of mediation, of the fact that this is a film and *not* reality—and, on the other hand, of inviting the audience into the reality of the film, to share in a communal *experience*. More specifically, it is a call to the audience, not only to consider the moral opposition between Rybak and Sotnikov, but to engage with the extreme situations of the minor characters, each of whom faces wrenching ethical dilemmas in everyday life that, in turn, affect all of the others.[42]

In a way, the heroic sacrifice of Sotnikov serves as a distraction that glosses over with Christian allusions the problem brought out by the film: the problem of ordinary people, of the people caught in between. As Franziska Exeler explains, "many choices that people in occupied territory made were 'choiceless choices'"—that is,

> when people were confronted with decisions, all options entailed a destructive effect on their personal lives, families, and local communities, as when a village head had to decide whether to hand over villagers as forced laborers to the Germans and fear reprisals from the partisans, or refuse to do so and fear German collective punishment.[43]

These "choiceless choices" are embodied in the people in the forest, Rybak, and most of all Demchikha.[44] While the rash, momentary decision of hiding two people who were fleeing from the Nazis in her attic led to her arrest, the decision not to betray the other family is one Demchikha hesitates over, at several different moments wavering. Perhaps she intuits that she won't just be "let go" and sent home to her children; that even if she survives and returns home, she will henceforth be known to all as a collaborator, like Rybak. As we look at the close-up of Demchikha's face as she waits on the gallows, mouthing words with her lips, we know only that she is experiencing *something*; the actor Polyakova's testimony about that moment and its connection to her own life tells us that the actual person being filmed was experiencing something at the point of production. We remain caught in the gap between experience and representation, transparency and opacity, self and other: in itself, the experience of lingering for a moment in this gap constitutes an experience of intersubjectivity.

Tzvetan Todorov distinguishes between two ways of classifying human activities, the *teleological*, which consists of "actions that can be defined by their purpose," that are judged "according to their end result," and the *intersubjective*, which consists of "actions whose distinguishing feature is that they establish a relationship between two or more individuals"—such as understanding, emulation, love, power, and "the constitution of self or other."[45] Demchikha consistently exemplifies the moral action Todorov names "caring." But she exchanges the ordinary virtuous action of caring for her own children for the heroic action of caring for strangers—the family that hid Basya; at the same time she embodies the (teleological) value of defeating the Nazis, first of all by refusing to collaborate with them, and second, by affirming another of the moral actions defined by Todorov, "dignity"—an action that transforms "a situation of constraint into one of freedom."[46] By making the impossible choice, Demchikha asserts her freedom to make a choice.

Here, again, as with the portrayal of Sotnikov's kenotic sacrifice, Shepitko's film aligns with what Exeler has called "the official narrative of the war as an 'all-people's war' (*vsenarodnaia voina*), according to which the population in occupied territory, with the exception of a few traitors, had wholeheartedly supported the fight for the Soviet motherland."[47] That is, Demchikha steadily remains on the right side of Soviet history. Rybak ultimately makes the wrong choice, and at the end of the film attempts and fails suicide; the film ends with a series of tormented close-ups of Rybak (looking almost, but not quite, directly into the camera), alternated with a slow tracking shot out the gates of the police compound—emphasizing how, in choosing to save his own life, Rybak has lost his freedom—before returning to the framing shots of landscape.

As Steimatsky shows us, the close-ups do not unveil the inner life of others, even as they lure us to confront that impossibility. Instead, the film calls us to experience, *ourselves*, the wrenching nature of everyday, life-and-death decisions; to experience the very materiality of these decisions. When Sotnikov cannot suppress his cough and betrays their location in Demchikha's attic as Rybak desperately holds his hand over his comrade's mouth, can we avoid thinking about stories, throughout history, of women in hiding inadvertently smothering their own infants in an effort to suppress their crying? When Rybak leaves Sotnikov to find shelter, can we avoid wondering whether he will return—or whether he has decided to cast off the burden of caring for his ailing comrade? Rybak's act of caring leads him to take the least logical, least instrumental action: returning for Sotnikov leads him to Demchikha's house, to the attic, to the cough, to the arrest. These are the cruel decisions, the "choiceless choices," that the Soviet state does not want the audience to linger on.

The alternation of these various cinematic gestures—of the fairly straightforward continuity editing of the combat sequence, of extreme long takes and mobile "felt" camera, and of mostly still close-ups—creates a rhythm that keeps the viewer engaged, allowing for an occasional respite from the intensity of experience, for example, in the suspense of a wartime drama of escape and capture. But ultimately the viewer is brought into the *experience* of the film—or, as some critics have written, "forced"—to engage with the ethical dilemmas it poses.[48]

As Shepitko said in an interview:

> [S]ince we got the chance to pose that same problem that arises over and over again for them (and for us), never leaving people alone, using contemporary material, with the details of living, still-warm conflicts—then to fulfil this task was our duty to the world and to ourselves.[49]

The point of the apparently senseless heroic act, then, is its effect on others, even if that effect is not to save their physical lives: the four fellow prisoners, first of all—especially Demchikha, who in the end makes the terrifying moral choice to protect the heroic act of the family that hid Basya over her own children's welfare; the internal audience of onlookers at the execution, especially the boy in the *budyonovka*, who seems to be a perfect amalgam of the lost hope of the "thaw" era for a return to something like the "true ideals of the Revolution" and an embodiment of Christian innocence; and, most important of all, the viewer, who lives through it.

NOTES

1. Siegfried Kracauer, *Theory of Film: The Redemption of Physical Reality* (1960). Princeton: Princeton University Press, 1997: 299; 287; 304.
2. In a review of the film, E. Bauman writes of its "severe, sometimes excruciatingly severe, manner." See "Voskhozdenie," *Vecherniaia Moskva*, 27 April, 1977. Online: https://chapaev.media/articles/8950 Viewed 1/19/2023. Shepitko noted in a post-screening discussion of the film published in *Sovetskii ekran*: "Many have spoken of [the film's] excessive cruelty . . ." See Shepitko, "Voskhozdenie k pravde. Stenogramma obsuzhdeniia posle prosmotra fil'ma 'Voskhozdenie'," *Sovetskii ekran* no. 1 (1978), 3.
3. Valentina Khovanskaia, who served as assistant director on several of Shepitko's films, recalled that Shepitko was concerned from the very beginning of the vetting process about her control over *The Ascent*. "'I will no longer allow the deformation of my cinema work [*kino*], I won't allow bureaucrats and pen pushers to spoil my . . . the end result of all that I have endured [*moe . . . moe, vystradannoe*]. Truth must prevail. But,' she held up her index finger, 'We have to fight them . . . I have already spoken with Masherov. He's the kind of guy we need. A partisan . . . and very smart . . . he's our guy. I'm certain he will help. [. . .]'" Valentina Khovanskaia, "Larisa. Vospominaniia o rabote s Larisoi Shepitko na kartinakh 'Ty i ia', 'Voskhozhdenie' i 'Matera'," in *Kinovedcheskie zapiski* no. 69 (2004): 117. Available online: http://www.kinozapiski.ru/ru/article/sendvalues/88/ Accessed January 19, 2023. See Valerii Fomin on the censorship of the screenplay in "Stsenarii napisan otlichno. Stavit' ni v koem sluchae nel'zia," in *Ekran i stsena* No. 20 (25 May 1995): 10.
4. Elem Klimov, interview with Irina Izvoilova, *Trud* 4 January 2003. https://www.trud.ru/article/04-01-2003/51289_vosxozhdenie.html Accessed 10/13/2022.
5. Shepitko, "Poslednee interv'iu," 1979 Interview with L. Rybak, in *Larisa: Kniga o Larise Shepitko*, ed. Elem Klimov (Moscow: Iskusstvo, 1987): 191.
6. «Вот было полное ощущение, что мы это пережили». "Vot bylo polnoe oshchushchenie, shto my eto perezhili." Interview with Liudmila Polyakova, *The Ascent*, DVD extras, Criterion Collection, 2021.
7. As Franziska Exeler has written, "Belorussia doubled its territory after the Soviet annexation of eastern Poland in 1939 and was then under Nazi occupation from 1941 to 1944. A main site of the German war of extermination in the East, this multilingual, multiethnic, and geopolitically crucial borderland was also at the center of Soviet partisan warfare. Of all the Soviet republics—indeed, of all the European countries—Belorussia suffered proportionally the highest human

losses." Exeler, "What Did You Do During the War? Personal Responses to the Aftermath of Nazi Occupation," *Kritika: Explorations in Russian and Eurasian History* vol. 17, no. 4 (Fall 2016): 805–835; 807. The police administration in German-occupied Belarus included a network of German police (*Gendarmerie*) who oversaw local police (*Schutzmannschaft*). See Martin Dean, *Collaboration in the Holocaust: Crimes of the Local Police in Belorussia and Ukraine, 1941–44* (New York: St. Martin's Press, in association with USHMM, 2000), Chapter 4, "Local Police Organization, 1941–44," 60–77. Dean notes that partisan warfare intensified in the autumn of 1942 (p. 69).
8. The notable exceptions are two brief fantasy sequences of escape from Rybak's point of view.
9. Eyeline matches are generally linked to Rybak rather than Sotnikov. We also get eyeline matches for minor characters—often in action sequences, discussed further later in the chapter. In the scene at Demchikha's house, Sotnikov looks out the window, but it is only when Rybak comes to look that we get a point-of-view shot through the window.
10. Tarkovsky, "Imprinted Time," in *Sculpting in Time*, trans. Kitty Hunter-Blair (London, 1986): 63. Translation modified slightly. (I am translating "*zhiznennyi opyt*" as "lived experience.") For the original see "Zapechatlennoe vremia," *Voprosy kinoiskusstva*, 1967, no. 10: 83. Tarkovsky briefly discusses *The Ascent* in a later chapter of *Sculpting in Time*, arguing that Shepitko's work with actors—and lighting—is "stilted and false," "more painful, more tortured, than in real life" (152). I will argue that, while the second half of the film becomes more stylized, throughout the film and particularly in the first half, Shepitko takes a documentary-like approach to her concept of empathic viewing.
11. *Chapaev* remained an important model for Soviet cinema in the 1970s. Khovanskaia recalls the discussion of the screen tests for *The Ascent* at Goskino, where the "pen pushers" (*chinushi*) from Mosfilm had sent them: "We need a hero that children will want to pretend to be when they play! We need a Chapaev, and you . . ." (121). Khovanskaia remembers that in order to get the film approved, they had Boris Plotnikov, the actor who played Sotnikov, made up as Chapaev, filmed him, brought the screen tests to Goskino, then destroyed the footage. See Khovanskaia, 121–122.
12. Shepitko, who frequently alluded to Dostoevsky in discussing the film and its source text, called the torture scene "the main conflict of ideas of the film [. . .] a duel between good and evil." See Lev Karakhan, "Krutoi put' 'Voskhozhdeniia,'" on-set interviews during the filming of *The Ascent*, in *Iskusstvo kino* No.10 (1976): 85–101, p. 92. Available online: https://chapaev.media/articles/8947 Accessed 1/19/2023.
13. The film elides the question of whether Rybak actually betrayed the location of the partisans in the forest. But would Portnov have spared him if he hadn't? Here the Dostoevskian moment of ideological dueling supersedes the historical realism of the plot: Portnov has won Rybak's soul from Sotnikov. Views of Portnov looking at Sotnikov at key moments indicate that his battle with Sotnikov extends to the souls of the other prisoners as well, particularly of Demchikha; for example, at the execution, we see Portnov looking at Sotnikov, conveyed via

camera movement rather than analytical editing, at the moment when Demchikha nearly surrenders. On the use of film form to convey character interiority see Karla Oeler's essay in the present volume. As in Dostoevsky, the little man who commits bad deeds seeks moral justification, or at least some indication that he is winning the duel.

14. On the traditional Russian "belief system that reveres endurance, powerlessness and sacrifice in this historical world as necessary, even holy, elements in life's anticipation of a future (and 'therefore' transhistorical) Utopia" (p. 26), see Nancy Condee, "No Glory, No Majesty, or Honour: The Russian Idea and Inverse Value," in *Russia on Reels: The Russian Idea in Post-Soviet Cinema*, ed. Birgit Beumers (London: I.B. Tauris, 1999): 25–33.

15. Moreover, by sending the woman machine-gunner Anka for reinforcements, Chapaev saves her, along with her implied future children, from the White Army encirclement.

16. The author of the "neo-parable" acts as a "conscientious chronicler [*letopisets*] of events." Lev Karakhan, "Krutoi put' 'Voskhozhdeniia,'" 87–88. Adamovich, whose "method of closing one's eyes to monument and listening to voices until the ruins underneath begin to move" inspired the writer Svetlana Alexievich, is best known for his Second World War novel *Khatyn* (1971), and for the screenplay it inspired, co-written with Elem Klimov, for *Come and See* (*Idi i smotri*, 1985). See Timothy Snyder, "Svetlana Alexievich: The Truth in Many Voices," *The New York Review of Books*, October 12, 2015. Online. https://www.nybooks.com/online/2015/10/12/svetlana-alexievich-truth-many-voices/ Accessed 2/3/2023.

17. Shepitko, "Obiazana pered soboi i pered liud'mi," TV interview (1977–78) with Felicitas von Nostitz at the Berlin Film Festival, transcribed in *Iskusstvo kino* No. 1 (1988): 94–95. Available online: https://www.liveinternet.ru/users/taris45/post414958286/ Viewed 10/8/2022. The viewer is drawn "into the cycle of events," which "makes us not just empathize [*soperezhivat'*], but mentally participate [*souchastvovat'*] in the action" onscreen. Lev Karakhan, "Krutoi put' 'Voskhozhdeniia,'" 89.

18. Valerii Golovskoi, *Mezhdu ottepel'iu i glasnost'iu. Kinomatograf 70-kh* (Moskva: Materik, 2004): 262.

19. Shepitko, Interview with S. Startsev, *Komsomol'skaia Pravda*, 24 April 1977. Available online: https://chapaev.media/articles/8949 Viewed 1/19/2023. Shepitko mentions the audience's co-suffering/empathy [*sostradanie*] in several interviews; for example: "[A]rt doesn't call us to suffer, but to empathize. Empathy—the capacity to feel another person's pain as one's own—elevates a person, raises him above his own self." Shepitko, "Obiazana pered soboi i pered liud'mi," TV interview (1977–78) with Felicitas von Nostitz at the Berlin Film Festival, transcribed in *Iskusstvo kino* No. 1 (1988): 96.

20. From Lev Karakhan, "Krutoi put' 'Voskhozhdeniia,'" 89.

21. The scene in the forest does not appear in Bykov's novella, though we learn that the group has run out of the steamed rye grains that they've been living on for a week. The moment in the novella that comes closest to the opening of the film appears towards the end of Chapter One, when Rybak offers some of his remaining rye ration to Sotnikov: "Without much eagerness, Sotnikov stretched

out his hand, which Rybak poured some into from his own handful. They both set to chewing the soft cold grains in silence."

22. Pier Paolo Pasolini, "The Cinema of Poetry," in *Movies and Methods* vol. 1, ed. Bill Nichols (Berkeley: University of California Press, 1976), 542–558.
23. That is, "a cinema marked primarily not by the strict codes of Socialist Realism, but by an idiosyncratic vision" (485). Kaganovsky, "Ways of Seeing: On Kira Muratova's *Brief Encounters* and Larisa Shepitko's *Wings*," *Russian Review* 71 (July 2012): 482–499.
24. *The Ascent* declares its debt to Shepitko's teacher Dovzhenko quite openly here, particularly in shot five, with its telephone poles in the snow marking the connection of this landscape at the periphery to centers of power.
25. See Doane, *Bigger than Life: The Close-Up and Scale in the Cinema* (Durham, NC: Duke University Press, 2021): 4. "There is always something uncanny or explicitly artificial about a zoom, which manufactures scale so blatantly and without shame, annihilating any physical space that the spectator might inhabit."
26. Nagib, *Realist Cinema as World Cinema* (Amsterdam: Amsterdam University Press, 2020): 23; 30. Open Source: https://www.aup.nl/en/book/9789462987517/realist-cinema-as-world-cinema Shepitko's use of non-professional, semi-professional, and theater actors who had never before acted for film fits into Nagib's concept as well.
27. Shepitko in Lev Karakhan, "Krutoi put' 'Voskhozhdeniia,'" 98. Shepitko repeated in later interviews that "the whole group experienced [*oshchushchala*] the film as a living organism. And we related to it as if it were alive. [. . .] And in our group, [. . .] everyone, starting from the worker who nailed nails, and, say, the lighting technician—experienced [*oshchushchali*] what they were doing as part of their lives." Shepitko, "Poslednee interv'iu," 191.
28. Transcribed from *The Ascent* DVD extras.
29. Lev Karakhan, "Krutoi put' 'Voskhozhdeniia,'" 90. Chukhnov also mentions needing to rely on his "habits of a newsreel filmmaker" ("*ot menia potrebovalis' dazhe navyki khronikera*," p. 90).
30. Elem Klimov recalled: "The exteriors for the film *The Ascent* were filmed in Murom. The winter was severe, minus 30 degrees. You can see actors in the scene with white spots on their faces—signs of frostbite. But while the performer goes into a heated bus after his scenes, the director isn't allowed to move away from the camera. On a short winter day, the sunlight disappears quickly. Often, after filming, she was carried to the hotel, half-frostbitten." In Izvoilova, "Voskhozhdenie," Interview with Elem Klimov.
31. See Kaganovsky, "Ways of Seeing," especially 482–486.
32. Nagib 2020: 28.
33. See Laura Marks, "Video Haptics and Erotics," *Screen* vol. 39, no. 4 (Winter 1998): 341–348.
34. Mary Ann Doane, "The Close-Up: Scale and Detail in the Cinema," *differences* (2003) 14 (3): 89–111; here, p. 90. Mary Ann Doane, *Bigger than Life: The Close-Up and Scale in the Cinema* (2021): 34.
35. Doane 2003: 107–108; Doane 2021: 48.
36. Doane 2003: 97.
37. Doane 2021: 19; 2; 38.

38. Steimatsky, *The Face on Film* (New York: Oxford University Press, 2017), 4; 13.
39. Steimatsky, 14.
40. Steimatsky, 23; 57.
41. Steimatsky, 63.
42. As Shepitko explained: "We are obliged to shake up those who have fallen asleep." In Lev Karakhan, "Krutoi put' 'Voskhozhdeniia,'" p. 87. On the use of aperture in socialist realist musicals, see Trudy Anderson, "Why Stalinist Musicals?" *Discourse* 17.3 (Spring 1995): 38–48.
43. Exeler, 810, "adapting a term coined by Lawrence L. Langer."
44. Dean writes that by the autumn of 1942, people conscripted into the local police force "could be in little doubt about the nature of the organization they were joining; but for most able-bodied men of military age the choice was one between paid service in the police, deportation to Germany or joining the partisans in the forest." Dean, 71. Or as Exeler puts it: "While all civilians found the space within which they could act circumscribed, that space was almost nonexistent for Jews and much larger for non-Jews." Exeler notes some examples: "volunteering to work in the German-overseen local police forces or giving shelter to Red Army soldiers, Jews, or partisans and risking their lives in the process. Yet wartime choices also included smaller, seemingly insignificant acts, such as taking furniture from a murdered Jewish neighbor's apartment or refraining from doing so." Exeler, 810–811.
45. Tzvetan Todorov, *Facing the Extreme: Moral Life in the Concentration Camps* (New York: Henry Holt, 1996): 286.
46. Todorov, 61.
47. Exeler, 832.
48. For example, Barbora Bartunkova makes this point in a recent essay: "Indeed, each shot in Shepitko's film forces the viewer to continue looking and experiencing the suffering of the protagonists." Bartunkova, "Facing Death, Confronting Human Nature: *The Ascent* (Larisa Shepitko, 1977)," in *Senses of Cinema*, issue 85 (December 2017). Available online: https://www.sensesofcinema.com/2017/soviet-cinema/1977-ascent-larisa-shepitko/ Accessed 1/19/2023.
49. Shepitko, "Obiazana pered soboi i pered liud'mi," 95.

PART IV

Time, Memory, Temporality

CHAPTER 7

White on White and *The Black Square*: Shepitko's *The Ascent*, Stan Brakhage, and Cinematic Abstraction

Anne Eakin Moss

After winning the top prize at the 1977 Berlin International Film Festival for *The Ascent* (*Voskhozhdenie*), her film about the fate of two Soviet partisans during World War II, Larisa Shepitko was invited to bring the film to the Fourth Telluride Film Festival in Colorado, USA. The Telluride organizers delighted in the provocative flaunting of political convention in the name of aesthetic principle: at the inaugural festival in 1974, Leni Riefenstahl was honored with a retrospective and Andrei Tarkovsky's *Solaris* (*Soliaris*, 1972) premiered alongside Dusan Makavejev's sexually transgressive *Sweet Movie* (1974). Introducing her film at Telluride in 1977, Sheptiko reportedly told the audience, "It is a miracle that I am here." Cold War animosity did not prevent the enthusiastic reception of her film, which received a standing ovation.[1]

Shepitko's admirers at the festival included the American experimental filmmaker Stan Brakhage, known for his fierce rejection of mainstream film conventions in favor of expressive, hand-held camera work and rapid montage, intensely personal subjects, as well as abstract experiments with directly scratching, painting, or printing plant and insect parts on celluloid. Brakhage was enchanted with Shepitko and her film, calling her "the greatest living story-teller of film."[2] He recounted how Jane Wodening, his first wife, distracted Shepitko's KGB handler so that the two directors could have an unsupervised conversation in a ticket booth, incidentally before a film program curated by his friend, the American artist Carolee Schneemann.[3] For reasons of her own, Schneemann decided to dispense with a conventional introduction and instead reprised for the occasion her 1975 "action" *The Interior Scroll*, during which, naked, she extracts a scroll containing a manifesto of feminist filmmaking from her vagina and reads it aloud. The manifesto begins:

> I met a happy man/ A structuralist filmmaker / – But don't call me that / it's something else I do – / He said we are fond of you / You are charming / but don't ask us to look / at your films / We cannot / there are certain films / we cannot look at . . .[4]

Tom Luddy, one of the festival organizers, recalled that Shepitko was "shocked speechless" by the performance, but Brakhage makes no mention of her reaction.[5] With Shepitko's KGB escort accompanying them to Schneemann's program, Brakhage wrote, "we only spoke of film." Though in a 1979 interview, Schneemann claimed somewhat counterintuitively that the manifesto was directed at American film critic Annette Michelson, who had slept through a screening of her films at an earlier festival,[6] one wonders if the performance could also be directed at her friend Brakhage, who was clearly enthralled by the stunning Soviet woman director who had made such a cold, male-dominated film with shots that verged on abstraction, in contrast to Schneemann's fleshy embodied performance art.

For her part, Shepitko seems to have appreciated Brakhage, complimenting his entry to the festival, a silent documentary titled *The Governor*. Aesthetically and thematically staid in comparison to his other works, it follows then-governor of Colorado Richard Lamm in *Man with a Movie Camera*-like fashion through the daily tasks of his office. Recalling Shepitko's interest in bringing his film to the Soviet Union. Brakhage later corresponded with Gosfil'mofond officials about sending instead a copy of his short film *Window Water Baby Moving* (1959), a highly intimate and expressionistic record of Wodening giving birth to their first child, as a gift for "the whole Russian People."[7] When Brakhage showed the film a few years later to Andrei Tarkovsky in a private screening at Telluride, he reported that the film incensed Shepitko's countryman, who called it "too scientific to be Art."[8]

In this essay, I offer an interpretation of Shepitko's *The Ascent* in the context of its American reception in the milieu of experimental art cinema embodied at Telluride. I ask how the terms of cinematic modernism as understood by Brakhage and his contemporaries might illuminate the film and the expectations for Soviet cinema in the international film circuit at the time. I also explore ways in which the film, in turn, may have had an impact on the aspirations and values of American modernism, engaged at the time in debates about formal experimentation, historical consciousness, and personal expression.

Brakhage's enthusiasm for Shepitko must have stemmed in part from the visual resonance of certain shots in *The Ascent* with his experimental short film series *Dog Star Man* (1961–64). In his film, flickering shots of a man struggling through a snow-covered forest are interspersed with shots of snow, sun, moon, flesh, frost, and branches that saturate the cinema screen and push the limits of legibility. The struggle of the two main characters in *The Ascent* – Sotnikov, the sickly weakling whose inner strength allows him to withstand torture and accept his death as a form of martyrdom, and Rybak, the indefatigable soldier who turns Judas to save his skin – is driven much more clearly by the film's narrative (adapted from a novella by Belarusian author Vasil' Bykaŭ). Yet closest to Brakhage's cinematography, as Jerry White observes, are shots in *The Ascent* captured via shaky handheld camera of Rybak dragging the injured Sotnikov through the snowy bushes, covering him with snow in the process, and at times obliterating the image with objects in extreme close-up.[9] In *The Ascent*, Sotnikov's view of celestial bodies – the pale daytime moon in the white sky as he prepares to shoot himself rather than be caught, and the whitened sun through snow-covered branches after Rybak rescues him – recall Brakhage's interspersed shots of solar flares, moon surface, and color filtered images of the setting sun through trees (**see Fig.** 7.1). Like the volatile camera in *Dog Star Man*, Shepitko's camera allows the snowy landscape to fill the screen with white and reduce legible information to almost zero. Both filmmakers imbue shots of near nothingness with heightened symbolic meaning, pointing toward the transcendent and existential.

Figure 7.1 Man in the snow, *Dog Star Man*, dir. Stan Brakhage, 1964.

While there was no direct influence of one on the other before 1977, the filmmakers shared an international vocabulary of modernist abstraction that hearkened back to the early Soviet and Russian Revolutionary avant-garde. Annette Michelson, the object of Schneemann's reproach in *Interior Scroll*, compared Brakhage to Sergei Eisenstein in her 1973 essay, "Camera Lucida/ Camera Obscura," isolating the formal properties of their film practice and arguing that whereas Eisenstein sees cinema as a means of making visible the very nature of thought, the result of Brakhage's filmmaking is "projecting the nature of sight itself as the subject of the cinema."[10] Michelson's celebration of the two filmmakers for what they reveal about the cinematic medium and its expressive possibilities elevated both according to the terms of Anglo-American high modernism, which valued the early Soviet avant-garde for its theorization of formal experimentation and rejection of the commodity value of art.[11] In positing Brakhage's inquiry into the nature of vision as a radicalization of Eisenstein's inquiry into the nature of thought, yielding in his films "a totally unmediated vision, eluding analytic grasp," Michelson helped to set the terms for his engagement with contemporary Soviet art moving forward.[12] Brakhage made sure the *Artforum* issue with Michelson's essay made it to Gosfilmofond as well.[13] Shepitko was clearly regarded at Telluride as a worthy representative of the Soviet tradition as understood in these modernist terms, all the more so for her perceived heroism for pursuing formal innovation in defiance of Soviet socialist realist norms.

With Brakhage's affinity for Shepitko in mind, and in the context of this moment in transnational cinematic modernism, we can see the shots that approach complete abstraction in *The Ascent* as creating a structuring symbolic logic for the film. In allowing light reflected from snow to saturate the lens and completely expose the filmstrip, both films could even be seen to operate in the tradition of Kazimir Malevich's aspirations to reduce art to the "zero of form," as the artist proclaimed about easel art in the 1915 manifesto "From Cubism and Futurism to Suprematism: The New Painterly Realism."[14] For Malevich, Suprematism aimed to obliterate figuration in easel art, and to generate a spiritual transformation in the viewer. In her introduction to Malevich's writings on film, Oksana Bulgakowa argues that the painter himself understood film to be "a continuation of Suprematist painting, in another medium."[15] Margarita Tupitsyn, also arguing for the cinematicity of the painter's Suprematist art practice, points to his 1918 painting *White on White* ("*Beloe na belom*") as an example of what Deleuze calls the rarefaction of the frame, "'the empty set [in image and cineme], when the screen becomes completely black or completely white.'"[16] Deleuze himself associates the practice of rarefaction with Brakhage and argues that these empty images render the outer frame of the cinema screen legible, generating "a dialectical relation between the image and its absence."[17] Malevich's *White on White* propels the bluish-white, off-kilter careening central

Figure 7.2 A composite of shots from the four opening shots of *The Ascent*.

square into that absence just as, at the very opening of *The Ascent*, Shepitko's viewers are confronted by four shots of whiteness in which the only movement is the blowing of snow across a barely visible landscape (see Fig. 7.2). Though these opening shots quickly resolve into comprehensibility – just as the cupola of a church becomes visible in the second shot, the sound of machine gun fire distinctly sets the historical time and place – nonetheless the church steeple, trees, and electricity poles etched black in the otherwise white image suggest a symbolic, rather than diegetic meaning.

Lilya Kaganovsky associates Deleuze's concept of the rarefaction of the frame with filmmakers Dziga Vertov and Andrei Tarkovsky, arguing that the 10 seconds of black screen that interrupt the Arctic ethnographic section of Vertov's *One Sixth Part of the World* (*Shestaia chast' mira*, 1926) establishes "a radically 'ethical' position, in that it forces the viewer into a different relationship to the film, to cinema, to the Arctic," one that prevents an objectifying or othering gaze.[18] Separately, Kaganovsky reads the whitened-out screen before the shot of the ocean surface on Solaris in Tarkovsky's film of the same name (*Soliaris*, 1972) as a confrontation with the atomic anxiety of the era, a fear of "that which is inassimilable and which cannot be placed within narrative or other symbolic structures."[19] Kaganovsky's reading of Deleuze's rarefaction bridges the difference between Michelson's Eisenstein and Brakhage, turning Brakhage's challenge to vision into a form of dialectical thinking through which the film becomes more than that which it represents. The screen filled to abstraction acknowledges the formal limits of the medium and thus brings the spectator into a new relationship with the work of art, beyond representation or diegesis.

The snow blindness out of which *The Ascent* emerges in its first four shots similarly asks the viewer to question the nature of seeing and its veridical powers. In the next, or fifth, shot, a partisan scout rises slowly from behind a snowbank captured in a long shot that puts the spectator in the uneasy position of machine-gunner or sniper. When he gives the all-clear, the camera zooms out as the rest of the partisans pop up from behind the snowbank to run away into the depth of the shot, and the film's title appears on screen. With this shot, the director seems to summon her narrative out of the whiteness of the image, making the characters secondary to the backdrop. Rather than establishing their relationship to one another with shot and reaction shot, they emerge out of the center of the image, easy targets on a backdrop of white. Similarly, later, when the main characters are imprisoned in a dark cellar, their faces emerge out of the blackness in patches of light thrown by door or window. The opening shots establish the existential import of the snowy coldness in the film as the characters' main antagonist both physically and spiritually. As much as the snow and cold pose a physical threat to the characters (as they did to the actors), the image of whiteness in the film signifies the certainty of death and the possibility of nothingness beyond it. In subjecting her cast and crew to the physical and cinematographic challenges of operating in a reported 40 degrees of frost, the director linked the process of filmmaking to a religious act of self-abnegation.[20]

The final three shots of *The Ascent* repeat almost identically from the opening – snowbank, electricity poles, church – and blowing snow obliterates the view of the church in the last shot before the word "KONETS" ("The End") appears in the whitened-out frame. Thus the film essentially consumes itself, producing the story out of whiteness, framing it with three images of whiteness, and returning the viewer to whiteness at the end. Just as rarefaction calls attention to the physical boundaries of the screen, here it also frames the temporal beginning and end of the film. What, asks this frame, has changed over the course of this film, and how are we to see differently now that it is done? Just as in the film the brave man turns out to be a coward, and the weakling proves himself a steadfast martyr, the viewer is asked to question their own moral balance sheet in the wake of war and Stalinism. The rarefaction of the screen seeks to displace the narrative story out of its historical moment into a transcendent space and time of sacrifice and judgement. The work Sheptiko demands of her viewers – to come to see the entire film frame as symbolic of the transcendent – has an analogue in Brakhage's filling the film frame with the intense and visceral image of the baby crowning as his wife gives birth in *Window Water Baby Moving*, as well as the existential ambitions of his later *Dante Quartet* (1981–87), the sections of which, "Hell Itself," "Hell Spit Flexion," "Purgation," and "'existence is song'" follow Dante's ascent from hell.

Jerry White compellingly extends the comparison Michelson made between Brakhage and Eisenstein to Shepitko as well as Andrei Tarkovsky and Sergei Parajanov, arguing that Brakhage's engagement with Soviet filmmakers indicated his investment in the concerns of world cinema and world history, contrary to the solipsistic, atemporal utopian formal experimentation with which Brakhage is sometimes associated. Indeed, the American's adulation for Shepitko certainly stemmed in part from the Cold War vision of Soviet artists martyred for the sake of art. Brakhage's praise – "the most important filmmaker I ever met through Telluride. Her films are feature length, story telling, in league with Murnau" – came after a screening of her husband Elim Klimov's tribute film, *Larisa*, at the Telluride festival in 1981, after Shepitko's untimely death in a car accident.[21] Paired with Jonas Mekas's elegiac film of return to Lithuania, *Paradise Not Yet Lost*, the film program suggested to Brakhage a tragically nostalgic vision of loss coupled with the suggestion of martyrdom to political oppression.[22] He called her "this famous but absolutely restricted woman narrative filmmaker from Russia," while also pointing out her Ukrainian roots and association with Oleksandr Dovzhenko, whose Ukrainian peasant origins he had celebrated in his film lectures published in 1977.[23] Whether or not this minoritarian position had much bearing on Shepitko's experience, for Brakhage and for other like-minded American artists and critics of the Cold War, it contributed to a vision of the dissident artist with special access to a certain kind of spiritual purity achieved through an art both above the society of spectacle because of socialist production economies and purified by having managed to escape from anti-religious, anti-individualist state oppression.

Since the 1960s, early Soviet avant-garde art had been making a major splash across Europe, climaxing with the celebrated 1979 Moscow-Paris exhibition, about which a German reporter enthused: "Some critics are sure to lose their heads in delight while standing before Malevich's *Black Square* ("Chiornyi kvadrat" 1913), the icon of Suprematism, as they now may identify the storehouses where Russia keeps its dangerous weapons—its "arsenal" of art—under lock and key."[24] We can sense that same delight in Brakhage's report of distracting Sheptiko's KGB handler in order to have an unsupervised conversation with her about art. Just as Soviet avant-garde art by Kazimir Malevich, Liubov Popova, El Lissitzky, and others emerged to a sense of almost breathless discovery outside the Iron Curtain in the 1960s, thanks to the 1962 publication of Camilla Grey's *The Great Experiment: Russian Art, 1863–1922* in the UK, and groundbreaking exhibits across Europe in the late 60s and 1970s, the films and theories of Dziga Vertov and Sergei Eisenstein became household names in modernist film circles thanks to the work of Jay Leyda and Annette Michelson, among others.[25]

All of these "discoveries" of the early Soviet avant-garde offered European modernists a new vocabulary for politically inflected forms of experimentation in art and cinema, from Godard's Dziga Vertov Group to leftist anti-colonial and anti-imperial art across the world in the 1960s and 70s. In the Soviet Union, however, while socialist realism remained the preferred mode of cultural production, and abstraction was still officially disapproved, the Soviet film industry allowed for a degree of continuity, as some of the most influential avant-garde filmmakers of the 1920s, like Shepitko's teacher, Dovzhenko, continued to teach in Soviet film schools into the post-war period and thus influence the next generation. As a form of international prestige and soft power during the Cold War, cinema offered a unique space for a certain amount of artistic autonomy and interchange with the West. The film festival circuit, as cultural Cold War battlefield, allowed for dialogue in an internationalist art cinema idiom. In Berlin to sit on the jury for the 1978 Berlin Film Festival, Shepitko was asked which foreign and Soviet directors made an impact on her. While disavowing any form of imitation, after a thoughtful pause, she answered that her films have a visual affinity and a "shared system of coordinates" with "first of all, of course, Bergman; Bresson; Buñuel, early Kurosawa," as well as Dovzhenko, Tarkovsky, and Klimov.[26]

Thus the formal resonance of shots in *The Ascent* with *Dog Star Man* can be seen as a product of an indirect conversation across borders over at least the previous two decades. Though the autobiographical themes and sustained rapid, abstract montage aesthetic of Brakhage diverged from the European directors with whom Shepitko claimed affinity, her dialogue with Brakhage suggests her openness to thinking about cinema's formal limits and its medium specificity. It is also telling that the directors she named were primarily representative of the pre-1968 phase of cinematic modernism, before the political demands of the moment in Europe drew cinema auteurs to focus on ideological critique rather than the ontology of cinema.[27] The fact that Brakhage found Shepitko's film to fit his own system of coordinates suggests that *The Ascent* seemed to him to still have something to say about the practice of cinematic modernism in the late 1970s.

In contrast to the filmmaking of Brakhage, or Ingmar Bergman, or Tarkovsky, for that matter, however, Shepitko's cinematography has a certain structural stability. The rarefaction of the image does not burn through the filmstrip as in the climax of Bergman's *Persona* (1966) and in Brakhage's *Art of Vision* (1965), nor does it approach the estrangement of the alien ocean in Tarkovsky's *Solaris*. Instead, the whitened-out frame remains a part of the snowy story world of the film. After the opening four shots and once the narrative of the film begins, the rarefaction of the screen by snow-bound whiteness comes to take on a stable semiotic meaning that is assigned to a character's point of view, unlike in Brakhage's films, where illegible frames persistently punctuate the rhythm of the film. When Sotnikov, separated from Rybak and injured in his flight, is sure he is about to be captured, he prepares to shoot himself, and the almost abstract shot of the pale moon in a cloudy sky is his point of view as he reconciles himself to death. But Rybak rescues him and drags the injured Sotnikov through the snow to temporary safety, completely covering his face and body in snow in the process, as if to express graphically his struggle with life and death. Sotnikov is almost submerged in the whiteness, and the handheld camera shots obscured by branches and snow directly transmit the men's desperation for escape. Answering a question from Werner Herzog about this scene at UC Berkeley's Wheeler Hall in 1977, Shepitko explained that she used the expressive tools of cinema "not to make a film that was simply educational or entertaining," but to force the viewer

> not to watch the film from the side. [. . .] We attempted to make the viewer into a participant in this two-dimensional representation, for them to pass through all the circles of hell together with the heroes, for them to undertake a voyage into themselves together with the heroes . . . we had to combine all the means that the cinematographer had at his disposal . . . montage, representation, and sound.[28]

Rather than estranging the viewer from image on screen by rarefaction, drawing attention to the limits of cinematic representation, or revealing its illusionism, Shepitko maximally used all of its affordances to pull the spectator into its action. Elsewhere, her cameraman, Vladimir Chukhnov, recalling crawling through the snow with the actors, compared the filming to that of documentary reportage wherein he was asked to give the viewer a "feeling of complicity with what was happening [*oshchushchenie soprichastnosti k proiskhodiashchemu*]."[29]

This scene is followed by one of the most visually memorable shots of the film, Sotnikov's face filmed through snow-covered branches, clearly symbolizing his entrapment and reconciliation to fate. It is as if he is caught between the photographic layers of the shot, and in fact we discover later that he is literally frozen to the tree, merging with the landscape and its whiteness (see Fig. 7.3). As he waits for Rybak to return, gazing directly into the camera, he lashes out at the branches that seem to trap him in the image, knocking off the snow and causing another white out of the screen. While critics have commented on the way in which this image reflects his existential trap, the agency of the landscape, or see the branches as Sotnikov's crown of thorns, I find a more direct semiotic referent.[30] The very branches overlaying his face suggest the form of a swastika, an impression that is reinforced by the appearance of

Figure 7.3 Branches suggesting a swastika in front of Sotnikov's face.

the swastika flag at the commandant's office just a few scenes later. Moreover, after Sotnikov disrupts the branches, the star on his Red Army hat, with its hammer and sickle in the center, comes more starkly into focus, as if to symbolize his resolve. Later he will be tortured with a branding iron in the shape of a five-pointed star. Also, the little boy in the town square at the end of the film wears a *budenovka* hat, the patch of the star itself removed presumably to satisfy the Nazi occupiers, but its outline clearly visible in the close up in which the boy meets Sotnikov's gaze before he is hung.

Thus, whether or not the branches in the earlier sequence intentionally suggest the form of a swastika, Sheptiko's cinematography operates on a directly symbolic register, relying heavily on familiar forms to convey their accustomed meanings. Just as the political iconography of the opposing sides is repeatedly foregrounded and made explicit, the images of snow, steeple, and cross are repeatedly framed so as to insist on their layered meaning as both referents to the diegetic world of the film and as symbols within ideological worlds of political and spiritual struggle. Many commentators note the way in which Sotnikov's face is lit to emphasize its similarity to a medieval icon in the cellar after he agrees to try to take the blame for the rest of the prisoners.[31] A similarly explicit sign might be seen in the strange dark blotch on the frame of the doorway of the village elder, where Rybak shoots a sheep (**see Fig. 7.4**). Is it the blood of the

THE ASCENT, STAN BRAKHAGE, AND CINEMATIC ABSTRACTION 149

Figure 7.4 Blood on the doorframe to fool the angel of death.

paschal lamb, smeared on the door frame to ask the angel of death to pass over their first-born son? If the biblical blotch is diegetic, that is, is meant to be part of the story world, perhaps so too is Sotnikov's halo, implying that his beatification actually transpires and is witnessed in the story world of the film.

If *The Ascent* indeed operates in this overtly symbolic register, then the white out of snow stably represents the enemy, a fatal obstacle to victory, and the certainty of death, both in the diegesis of the story and in its symbolic logic. Another shot of white on white is embedded in one of Rybak's fantasies of failed escape. After the two men are captured by a Nazi patrol and loaded onto a sleigh, Rybak contemplates escaping into a snowbank that is framed without horizon, completely white, and notably reminiscent of the snowbank in shot three of the opening sequence that reappears in the closing montage as well. In his mind's eye he imagines himself running to the snowbank, but finding no cover, he is shot, his body slumping into the snow. Therefore, he rejects the possibility of escape, out of fear of the nothingness of death, which he sees as symbolized by the white frame bordered only by the limits of the screen. If the snow represents death for both men, Sotnikov struggles through it with much difficulty, while Rybak shows determination to overcome and mark out his difference from it, striding confidently across the white fields and sensing the dangers below when he realizes that he is walking on the snow-covered surface of a thinly frozen lake. Yet in the end, his determination to overcome death leads Rybak to forfeit his immortal soul.

A directly symbolic interpretation of whiteness in the film invites symbolic interpretation of blackness as well. If the bright tonal quality of the first part of the film and moments of complete rarefaction to white symbolize the struggle against death, the darkness of the cellar in which the five condemned partisans spend their last night together also takes on symbolic meaning. There the five condemned prisoners weigh their fates on earth, their Dostoevskian conversation set in the underground with spiderwebs and shadows. After Rybak returns from the hanging, incontrovertibly having sold his soul to the devil in the form of the collaborator Portnov, he looks back on the cellar doors to the space where they made their last confessions and Sotnikov promised to take their sins on himself. This shot makes blackness legible in a uniquely stark way, one that is almost uncinematic (**see Fig.** 7.5). The square opening of the cellar is a completely black void, without shadow or any contours of depth, framed at the threshold with white snow and at the sides by wooden doors which recall a painting frame. In the context of this analysis, it immediately calls to mind Malevich's most famous painting, *Black Square* of 1915, which hung high in the corner of the first Suprematist exhibition in Petrograd, explicitly likening

Figure 7.5 Malevich's *Black Square* as framed in the cellar door.

itself to an orthodox icon. Just like in Malevich's painting, the shot of the cellar cants the black square slightly to the right, as if to set the viewer off balance and invite us to fall into the abyss. Despite the camera's zoom into the blackness of the cellar in the shot just before the gate is irrevocably barred on Rybak, the blackness remains bounded by the frame of the cellar door. There is no rarefaction of the screen image. Instead, the film maintains a tension between the doors framing the cellar and the frame of the screen. Nonetheless, in translating Malevich's *Black Square* into the language of cinema, whether intentionally or not, Shepitko's cinematic black square could be said to anticipate Deleuze's concept of the direct time-image, in which "people and things occupy a place in time which is incommensurable with the one they have in space."[32] Rybak may have been pardoned by the Nazis, but he has been condemned eternally by a higher judge. The black maw of the cellar contrasts his survival with the eternal nothingness of his soul.

Symbolic geometric forms proliferate in the film, reinforcing the association with Malevich's Suprematist compositions. For one, the black square of the cellar is prefigured in the square mouth of a heating stove, two of which appear at different moments in the film. The first is found in the ruins of the home where Rybak was hidden when wounded earlier in the war. Now burned down by the fascists, all that remains are snow-covered beams, a metal bed frame, frozen laundry on a clothesline, and the cold stove. Rybak reaches into one of the three blackened square holes and pulls out a round hand mirror that reflects his eye back directly at the camera, casting his disembodied gaze out of the round frame to confront the spectator. A second heating stove, this one a single square opening filled with hellish fire, is a notable fixture of the setting in the office of the inquisitor Portnov. A single shot that fills the camera frame almost entirely with a square of flame is matched to Sotnikov's gaze when he lies on the ground after having been beaten by the guard before the start of his interrogation. The square of fire and the strikingly square features of the office and its framing reinforce the sadistically curtailed horizon of Portov's worldview into which Rybak enters after agreeing to join the police.[33]

Similar geometric repetitions can be found in the gaping black circle of a gun muzzle, seen in Rybak's mind's eye when he again imagines the consequences of attempted escape towards the end of the film. He replicates that gaping circle with his mouth as he cries in horror over the fatal wrong choice he has made between being and nothingness after emerging from the outhouse where he unsuccessfully tried to hang himself. His suffering is linked visually with the black toilet hole over his shoulder, which is unambiguously metaphorical. Sotnikov had told Rybak in the cellar, "Rybak, we're soldiers. Don't crawl in shit, it won't wash off." Rybak answers: "So . . . into a hole [*v yamu*]? To feed the worms? Just so?" Thus, the film provides the viewer with a literal illustration of the verbal metaphor in this final scene. Rybak has descended into a circle of hell out of which there is no chance of escape. This shot of Rybak and the toilet hole, accompanied by the climatic moments of Alfred Schnittke's ominous score and Rybak's sobs, gives way to bells tolling and dissonant wind instruments fading to the whistling of the wind and the white out rarefaction of the final frame.

As we can see from the enthusiastic reception of the film in Berlin, Telluride, and Berkeley in 1977, Sheptiko's film was perfectly suited to an international audience of filmgoers saturated in symbolic language, even if the audience at the interview in Berkeley in 1977 seemed somewhat flummoxed by Shepitko's use of religious allegory in its narrative and symbolic registers. The questions at the Berkeley event suggested that a direct reading of the film as Christian allegory interested the American audience more as a sign of Shepitko's political independence and the autonomy of art in the context of a repressive state regime, than as the film's primary message in itself. The film appears to be made to order for the international film festival circuit, especially with its formal invocation of symbolic abstraction, and perhaps this hidden icon of Suprematism, whether it was consciously composed and consciously noticed or not. If the image of the cellar as black square is an explicit reference to Malevich's painting, then it constitutes a closed citational object, a yawning pit of existential despair for Rybak only, and not a breach in the film's illusionary world that opens out onto the spectator's own.

The Ascent so thoroughly fulfills the expectations of cinematic modernism – its reference back to the avant-garde, its themes of alienation and nothingness, its play with the rarefaction of the image, its sequences of estranging and non-continuous cinematography – that it consumes them, concluding with the same shots that begin the film, though they are given new meaning by the progress of the narrative. In fact, if we associate the snowbank in the very third shot of the film, which is identical to the third to last shot of the film, with the moment in which Rybak imagined escape from the sled and envisioned himself being shot, then this makes the opening and closing sequences, seemingly abstract, to be simply introducing and recalling crucial locations in the plot. Is the very first shot, of snow blowing across some flat surface, a shot of the frozen lake that crunches under Rybak's feet, warning him of the lack of escape route? If so, even these seemingly abstract shots do not escape the meaning-making of the film's narrative. The proliferation of geometric shapes in the film means that any one image of whiteness or blackness functions not as a symbol of the cinematic screen approaching the transcendent, but as mere metaphor, *reducing* the spectator's sense of implication in the narrative and responsibility to its images. The viewer is returned to the state of reader, rather than witness. Rather than opening the film's conflicts and visual images to the unknown, it forecloses on openness, leaving nothing to interpretation.

It is significant that this film appears at the end of the period Kovács defines as "late cinematic modernism," after the appearance of all the major works of the French new wave, Italian neo-realism, etc. He identifies Tarkovsky's *Mirror* (*Zerkalo*, 1974) as a pivot point from cinematic modernism to postmodernism insofar as it posits a "transcendental parallel universe" that would be a mark of postmodernism were that transcendence not contained within the auteur's autobiographical self-consciousness.[34] Similarly, in *The Ascent*, though moments of rarefaction to white or the near-rarefaction to black seem to open the film onto a transcendental world beyond the film frame, those moments of trial, judgement, and mortification remain in the story world of the film. As Shepitko answered to Werner Herzog in Berkeley, her goal was to "make the viewer into a participant in this two-dimensional representation." Thus the viewer, left with Rybak's point of view at the end of the film, has no choice but to live through the consequences of his collaboration with the fascists. The film renders the viewer complicit by the very fact of surviving the war unless they take upon themselves the spiritual fortitude of Sotnikov, passed on to them through the boy in the *budenovka* hat. As Shepitko also told the Berkeley audience, "this is not a historical film but a contemporary one." The American audience in 1977, highly receptive to what they perceived as a message of political dissidence, applauded her enthusiastically.[35]

Despite Kovács' timeline for the transition to postmodernism, the enthusiastic reception of *The Ascent* for its hermeticism, its enclosed mythological world and sign system, indicates the persistence of critical interest in the formal parameters of American modernism as defined by artists like Brakhage. One wonders if he would have acknowledged an influence of Shepitko's film, which she claimed was to lead viewers through the circles of hell, on the *Dante Quartet* that he began the year he saw Klimov's *Larisa*. His meticulous work on the 7-minute film over the course of six years reflects a persistent modernist sensibility of composition that produced what one critic aptly describes as "less an attempt to represent a subjectivity than a more inclusive, even universal subjective visual experience or encounter."[36] In 1989, Brakhage was able to see Shepitko's *Homeland of Electricity* (*Rodina elektrichestva*, 1967), and penned the following reflection on her filmmaking:

> Rather than juggle multiple levels of literate meaning, Shepitko envisions filmic story-telling as if the experience of 'tale' could be enclosed in a globe: her illuminations and shadows shift as if they were particles of 'snow' whirling around some central iconographic scene. Though the actors talk, and there is a narrative told through dramatic scenes, the film is so internally reflexive as to give an overall sense of singular metaphor in movement—i.e., in sparked transformation. She shows

herself to have been the inheritor of the great tradition of Alexander Dovzhenko, her teacher.[37]

This formulation of Shepitko's formal exactitude seems to apply just as much if not more so to *The Ascent* as it does to *Homeland of Electricity*. The snow globe metaphor captures not only the setting of *The Ascent*, but also the sense of autonomy prized by American modernism that resisted the onset of postmodernism. At the same time, Brakhage seeks to connect both Shepitko and himself to an historical art cinema lineage that starts with the Soviet avant-garde.

Thanks to restoration and film festival revival in the US, the film has popped up at other moments as a touchstone for this critical strand in American post-war modernism. In *Regarding the Pain of Others* (2003), Susan Sontag writes: "No photograph, or portfolio of photographs, can unfold, go further, and further still, as does *The Ascent* (1977), by the Ukrainian director Larisa Shepitko, the most affecting film about the horror of war I know." In 2010, the poet Fanny Howe published a poem titled "On Seeing Larisa Shepitko's *Ascent*" in which a figure burdened with the colonial traumas of the postwar world remembers "a single perfection / which was enough for him": "he remembered Larissa and her film. // It was called *The Ascent*. / And it showed her to be a saint."[38] Sontag's superlative and Howe's attribution of perfection recall a moment when Soviet art contained the possibility to transmit world-historical seriousness and moral purity, at least from the vantage point of the Rocky Mountains.

NOTES

The author wishes to thank Antonia Lant, Daniel Morgan, Paola Iovene, Kenneth Moss, and Lida Oukaderova for their generative comments on drafts of this essay, as well as the participants in the panel "The Cinema of Larisa Shepit'ko" at the ASEEES conference in 2022 for the productive discussion. Special thanks to Elena Razlogova, Andrew Vielkind, and the staff of the Brakhage Collection at University of Colorado Boulder for their help with archival sources.

1. Peter Lem, "The Telluride Film Festival: Part II," *The Straight Creek Journal* Vol. 6, issue 38 (September 22, 1977), 11–12.
2. Stan Brakhage, Letter to Bill and Stella Pence, September 7, 1977, Brakhage Collection, Box 47, Folder 16, Rare and Distinctive Collections, University of Colorado Boulder Libraries.
3. Jerry White, *Stan Brakhage in Rolling Stock, 1980–1990* (Waterloo, Ontario: Wilfrid Laurier University Press), 73–74, 156.
4. The text of the scroll and Schneeman's description of the circumstances of the performance can be found in Carolee Schneemann, "Interior Scroll" in

More Than Meat Joy: Complete Performance Works and Selected Writings, Bruce McPherson, ed. (New Paltz, NY: Documentext, 1979), 234–239.
5. Tom Luddy, "Remembering Larisa," *Film Watch* (Telluride Festival Program Guide, 2008), 104.
6. "Carolee Schneemann," in Scott MacDonald, ed., *A Critical Cinema: Interviews with Independent Filmmakers*, vol. 1 (Berkeley, LA and London: University of California Press, 1988), 134–151, 143–144.
7. Letter to Vladimir Dmitriev, January 19, 1978, Brakhage Collection, Box 29, Folder 3: Larissa Shepkito (1978), Rare and Distinctive Collections, University of Colorado Boulder Libraries. Brakhage, troubled with finances, could not afford to send a print of the longer film Shepitko had admired. His use of "Russian" likely was intended as an anti-Soviet dig. Americans who encountered Shepitko at this time referred to her interchangeably as a Soviet, Ukrainian, or Russian director.
8. White, *Stan Brakhage*, 120.
9. White, *Stan Brakhage*, 299–300.
10. Annette Michelson, "Camera Lucida/Camera Obscura (1973)" in *On the Wings of Hypothesis: Collected Writings on Soviet Cinema*, ed. Rachel Churner (Cambridge, MA and London: The MIT Press, 2020), 27–58, 54. She described the trajectory from the Soviet avant-garde to American independent cinema on a broader scale in her landmark lecture and essay, "Film and the Radical Aspiration," *Film Culture* Vol. 47 (Fall 1966): 34–42 and 136.
11. For a helpful overview of the many ways in which critics have defined cinematic modernism: as a practice of reference back the early 20th century avant-garde, as a community of interlocutors on the international film festival circuit, and as a practice that departs from classical Hollywood film style and insists on cinema's ability – in fact its obligation – to express the problem of human alienation and point the viewer toward the transcendent, see András Bálint Kovács, *Screening Modernism: European Art Cinema, 1950–1980* (Chicago and London: University of Chicago Press, 2007).
12. Michelson, "Camera Lucida/Camera Obscura," 55. The two carried on a mutually appreciative correspondence about this article among other things. See the Brakhage Collection, Box 47, Folder 16, Rare and Distinctive Collections, University of Colorado Boulder Libraries
13. Letter to Vladimir Dmitriev.
14. Kazimir Malevich, "From Cubism and Futurism to Suprematism: The New Painterly Realism" (1915), in *Russian Art of the Avant-Garde: Theory and Criticism*, John Bowlt, ed. (New York: Thames and Hudson, 1991), 116–135, 118.
15. Oksana Bulgakowa, "Malevich in the Movies: Rubbery Kisses and Dynamic Sensations," trans. by Elif Batuman and Lyubov Golburt, in Kazimir Malevich, *The White Rectangle: Writings on Film*, ed. Oksana Bulgakowa (Berlin and San Francisco: Potemkin Press, 2002), 9–29, 28.
16. Margarita Tupitsyn, *Malevich and Film* (New Haven: Yale University Press, 2002), 22. Bracket in original.
17. Giles Deleuze, *Cinema 2: The Time-Image*, trans. Hugh Tomlinson and Robert Galeta (Minneapolis: University of Minnesota Press, 1989), 200. See also Giles

Deleuze, *Cinema 1: The Movement-Image,* trans. Hugh Tomlinson and Barbara Habberjam (Minneapolis: University of Minnesota Press, 1986), 12.

18. Lilya Kaganovsky, "'The Threshold of the Visible World': Dziga Vertov's *A Sixth Part of the World* (1926)" in *Arctic Cinemas and the Documentary Ethos,* Lilya Kaganovsky, Scott MacKenzie, and Anna Westerstahl Stenport, eds. (Bloomington, IN: Indiana University Press, 2019), 46–67, 64.

19. Lilya Kaganovsky, "*Solaris* and the White, White Screen" in *Picturing Russia: Explorations in Visual Culture,* Valerie A. Kivelson and Joan Neuberger, eds. (New Haven: Yale University Press, 2008), 230–232, 232.

20. On the filming process, see L. Karakhan, "Krutoi put' Voskhozhdeniia" *Iskusstvo Kino* No. 10 (October 31, 1976): 85–101 and excerpts from a 1978 interview in Larisa Shepitko, "Obiazana pered soboi i pered liud'mi" *Iskusstvo Kino* No. 1 (January 31, 1988): 93–98.

21. Jerry White, *Stan Brakhage,* 73. At least this was his estimation in 1981, two years before a notorious encounter with Tarkovsky. The disjunctive, laconic style is characteristic of Brakhage's writing. The association with Murnau may have to do with the German director's black and white expressionist style, but it too may have been with his death in a car accident, graphically described in Brakhage's film lectures. Stan Brakhage, *Film Biographies* (Berkeley: Turtle Island, 1977), 270.

22. White, *Stan Brakhage,* 79.

23. Cited in White, *Stan Brakhage,* 74. Brakhage, *Film Biographies,* 273–89.

24. Cited in Oksana Bulagkowa, "'Moskva-Berlin, Berlin-Moskau, 1900–1950': Memory and Forgetting" *The Russian Review* 80 (October 2021): 581–602, 583.

25. The first edition of Jay Leyda's *Kino: A History of the Russian and Soviet Film* came out in 1960 from George Allen & Unwin Press, and his edited volumes of Eisenstein's essays came out in the 1960s. Leyda, *Kino,* 3rd edition (Princeton: Princeton University Press, 1983). Sergei Eisenstein, *Film Form: Essays in Film Theory,* Jay Leyda, ed. and trans. (London: Denis Dobson, 1963). See Michelson's collected essays on Soviet cinema from the 70s–90s in *On the Wings of Hypothesis.* On the reception of Vertov in 60s, see John Mackay, "The 'Spinning Top' Takes Another Turn: Vertov Today" *KinoKultura* No. 8 (April 2005) http://www.kinokultura.com/articles/apr05-mackay.html.

26. *Razgovor s Larisoi* [*Talks with Larisa*], directed by Elim Klimov, (1999; Moscow: Kul'tura), The Criterion Collection. Although this feature includes the same 1978 interview transcribed in Shepitko, "Obiazana," this section was omitted from the 1988 *Iskusstvo Kino* piece.

27. Kovács argues that after 1968, "art and film history provided no more inspiration for further renewal of modern cinema" in Europe. *Screening Modernism,* 350.

28. Tom Luddy with Larissa Shepitko, "Winner of the Grand Prize at the 1977 Berlin Film Festival; West Coast Premiere!" (University of California, Berkeley Art Museum and Pacific Film Archive; September 9, 1977, digitized 2020), Internet Archive. https://archive.org/details/bampfa-audio_03557.

29. Karakhan, "Krutoi put'," 90. Brakhage similarly attributes to the handheld camera a kind of complicity, taken to the extreme in *Window Water Baby Moving,* in which he holds the camera intimately recording his pregnant wife's body.

30. Merrill offers a convincing critical review of these readings. Jason Merrill, "Religion, Politics, and Literature in Larisa Shepit'ko's *The Ascent*" *Slovo* 18, No. 2 (Autumn 2006): 147–162, 152.
31. See Merrill, "Religion, Politics," 150.
32. Deleuze, *Cinema 2*, 39.
33. One wonders if Shepitko's shot was influenced by the shot of Rosebud burning in the furnace in Orson Welles's *Citizen Kane* (1941). On possible interpretations of this image, see Deleuze, *Cinema 2*, 117.
34. Kovács, *Screening Modernism*, 394.
35. For an article that evaluates the degree of Shepitko's nonconformity in Cold War terms, see Karen Rosenberg, "Shepitko," *Sight & Sound* 56, No. 2 (Spring 1987): 119–22.
36. Adrian Danks, "Across the Universe: Stan Brakhage's *The Dante Quartet*" CTEQ Annotations on Film, Senses of Cinema (July 2004), http://www.sensesofcinema.com/2004/cteq/dante_quartet/.
37. White, *Stan Brakhage*, 265.
38. Fanny Howe, "After Seeing *The Ascent* by Larisa Shepitko," *Black Renaissance* 10, 2/3 (Summer 2012), 54.

CHAPTER 8

Liquid Time: *The Homeland of Electricity* as Unprocessed Trauma

Lilya Kaganovsky

Larisa Shepitko's third film, the 1967 *The Homeland of Electricity* (Rodina elektrichestva, based on a 1926 Andrei Platonov short story by the same title) is the story of the coming of electricity to a remote village, and the utopian dream of the transformation of the world by Soviet power. Filmed at the Experimental Creative Studio named after Oleksandr Dovzhenko, *The Homeland of Electricity* was part of a trilogy of films—a film almanac, titled *The Beginnings of an Unknown Age* (Nachalo nevedomogo veka) – that included Andrei Smirnov's *Angel* and Genrikh Gabai's *Motria*, and was meant to celebrate the 1917 Revolution and the 50th anniversary of the USSR State Committee for Cinematography (Goskino). Instead, two of the novellas (Shepitko's and Smirnov's) experienced a fate similar to that of Aleksander Askoldov's *Commissar* (Komisar, 1967): banned by Goskino, with instructions given for their immediate destruction, the two films were preserved by the cameraman Pavel Lebeshev who was able to have a positive print struck from the negatives, and the editor Valeria Belova who hid the prints on the shelves of Mosfilm.[1] As such, these became practically the first "shelved" films of the post-War period, marking the cultural turn from the Khrushchev Thaw to Brezhnev-era Stagnation.[2]

Coiled around other films, *The Homeland of Electricity* and *Angel* remained hidden on the shelves of Mosfilm until 1987 (and after Shepitko's tragic death in a car accident in 1979), when Shepitko's husband, the director Elem Klimov, asked for them to be located and restored. And while we do not have the fully finished product as Shepitko might have conceived of it, what we can clearly see in this work is Shepitko's return not only to the narrative time of the story—the year 1921—but to the visual language of avant-garde filmmaking: to Oleksandr Dovzhenko's *Earth* (Zemlia, 1930), Sergei Eisenstein's *General Line*

(General'naia liniia / Staroe i novoe, 1929), and even, to Eisenstein's unfinished (banned and destroyed) *Bezhin Meadow* (Bezhin lug, 1936). Taking Platonov's original narrative of parched earth, a generator that runs on moonshine, and a village of Old Believers, Shepitko transforms the story of communist future (symbolized by the youthful protagonist) into a story of the nation's traumatic and unworked-through past. The choice of Bulat Okudzahva's "Sentimental March" (Sentimental'nyi march, 1957) to conclude the film echoes the turn from the past as a repository for futurity (as Marianna Hirsch and Leo Spitzer have recently imagined it in their 2019 book *School Photos in Liquid Time*), to the past as unprocessed trauma.[3] Shepitko's *Homeland of Electricity* thus becomes part of the larger "crisis of memory" at the heart of Soviet sixties' cinema that we also find in her earlier *Wings* (Kryl'ia, 1966), but also in Mikhail Romm's *Nine Days of One Year* (Deviat' dnei odnogo goda, 1962), Marlen Khutsiev's *Lenin's Guard* (Zastava Il'icha, 1961/1965), Askoldov's *Commissar*, and others.[4] In this chapter, I look at the difference between the original Platonov short story and Shepitko's reimagining of it forty years later through the lens of unprocessed trauma and the shift between the optimism of the twenties and their belief in the transformative power of the Soviet state to the loss of that belief in the 1960s.

THE HOMELAND OF ELECTRICITY, 1926 | 1939

Andrei Platonov's remarkable short story (first published in 1939 in the journal *Industriia sotsializma*, but likely written in 1926[5]) tells the story of an impoverished and starving village in the middle of a drought and its single source of pride: a power generator that brings electricity to its starving residents. The unnamed narrator of the story resembles other Platonov protagonists from the 1920s who yearn for a rational and scientific transformation of the world by scientific and technological means. For many of these characters, electrification is the goal of their existence, representing the victory of consciousness over matter.[6] In this way, the protagonists also resemble Platonov himself, who in the 1920s worked for GOERLO to electrify the village of Rogachevka, near Voronezh, and posited electricity as a force that would transform the world.[7] "Electrification is the realization of communism in matter" (*Elektrifikatsiia est' osushchestvlenie kommunizma v materii*), writes Platonov in one of his essays, echoing Lenin's famous formulation: "Communism equals Soviet power, plus the electrification of the entire country."

In typical Platonov fashion that erases distinctions between the natural world, man-made technology, and the body, the story links electricity generated by a turbine engine with the light and energy of the human body, positing that the machine must be treated with the "tenderness" (*nezhnost'*),

Figure 8.1 The village of Rogachevka in the 1920s.

and comparing the deep ravines formed in the parched soil to the ribs of a human skeleton. The story, narrated by a young, unnamed protagonist, is set during the 1921 drought, and opens with a series of conflations of the human and the machine, the animate and inanimate. The opening of the story consistently references death, from the ashes and dust (*prakh*, as in the expression "from dust to dust") that cover the dry earth, to the flowers that that year have "no more smell than metal shavings," to the deep cracks formed "in the body of the earth" that look like "gaps between the ribs of a lean skeleton."[8] Working at a power plant in town, the narrator spends "all the energy of his life" caring for the turbine generator "precisely, tenderly, and carefully." Despite his youth, he returns home so exhausted that he barely has time to remove his clothes before falling deeply asleep; as if "all of the light inside" of him had gone out forever.

Woken from this death-like sleep by the president of the town council (*gubispolkom*), the narrator is sent on a semi-mythical quest. A letter from the deputy chairman of the village of Verchovka, written in verse, informs them that while the village is already equipped with a working electric dynamo, the machine's psychology prevents it from being fully useful to the villagers: it originally belonged to the Whites, Stepan Zharenov explains, and thus was born a foreign agent (*chuzhaia interventka*).[9] Help is needed to turn this semi-hostile machine, thundering and producing electricity, into something practical.

While the letter is full of poetical flourishes, the narrator and the president of the *gubispolkom* Ivan Chunyaev, being "practical men and not poets," can immediately see the "truth and the reality" (*pravdu i deistvitel'nost'*) of the state of the village. In the counterrevolutionary turbine uselessly pumping out electricity they see the bright, electrified future of communism:

> We saw light in the bleak darkness of a poor, barren space – the light of a human being on a suffocated, dead earth – we saw wires hung on old wattles, and our hope for the future world of communism, the hope we needed for our daily hard existence, the hope that alone makes us human, this hope of ours turned into electric power, even if for now it was bringing light only to distant straw huts. (237)[10]

This is a very cinematic image; indeed, we have seen it multiple times. The power lines stretched across the sky, electrical wires leading from tall poles to ramshackle houses, the single lightbulb burning inside the peasant hut— these are symbols of (communist) modernity so beloved by the Soviets and repeatedly captured on film by the likes of Dziga Vertov, Esfir Shub, and others at around the same time as Platonov was composing this story. Soviet films promoting new electric (and by extension, Bolshevik) power typically showed electrical wires connecting an electrical tower to a house in a village, on the one hand; and a peasant family inside their home, working by electric light, on the other.[11] We see this in Shub's 1927 *The Great Road* (Velikii put') in the episode titled "Let's Electrify the Soviet Village!" where, as Emma Widdis has noted, the process of electrification is charted in a representative succession of images: "from a panorama of the village (illuminated at night, as in many images of the period), the camera moved successively closer, to street lamps, and then followed a cable running into an individual home and moved through a lighted window into the home itself." And in Vertov's 1926 *Stride, Soviet!* (Shagai, Sovet!) we see a similar visual metaphor at work: the electrical grid spreads out from the center to periphery, from Moscow to small towns to country villages; and finally, inside the peasant hut, illuminating a portrait of Lenin, the "Father of Electrification," hanging on the wall.[12]

Moreover, the "truth and reality" of the village so visible to the narrator through the lines of the poetic text is not the truth and reality of the current situation (where electricity is simply being wasted), but of the future: like socialist realist writers to come, the narrator can see not just reality, but "reality in its revolutionary development," not life as it is but "as it should be."[13] Like his protagonist anticipating the bright future of communism, Platonov anticipates or channels the socialist realist future of Soviet literature.[14] At the same time, there is also something of the fairytale quest here; Chunayev tells the narrator, "*stupai tuda*" (go there), echoing the Russian fairytale formula: "Go I know not whither and fetch I know not what" ("Stupai tuda, nevedomo kuda, prinesi to, nevedomo chto"), and generally refers, with irony, to a poorly defined or impossible task.[15] And, as in a typical fairytale structure, the narrator's path is guided by the number three: it takes the protagonist three days to reach the correct village by foot, because there are three villages by the same name: Upper Verchovka, Lower Verchovka, and Poor Verchovka ("a Verchovok okazalos' tri—Verkhniaia, Staraia, i Malobednaiai Verchovka" [238]).

Poor Verchovka's power generator turns out to be a two-cylinder British motorcycle bearing the company name "Indian," half-buried in the sand and powering a motor that generates electricity for a single lightbulb placed on a high pole, burning during the day. The motorcycle is surrounded by onlookers from nearby villages who take an active interest in this miracle of the production of electricity, smiling proudly and petting the engine as if it were something dear to them:

> An English two-cylinder "Indian" motorcycle, with half of its wheel buried in the ground was revolving a small dynamo with roaring force. The machine, placed on two short logs, was shaking with the rush of its work. An elderly man sat in a sidecar smoking a hand-rolled cigarette; an electric lightbulb burning on a high pole was illuminating the day; and all around were carts with unhitched horses, eating fodder, and on the carts sat peasants, who watched with pleasure the action of the fast-moving machine. Some of them, thin in appearance, expressed open joy: they came up to the machine and stroked it like a sweet creature, smiling with such pride, as if they had taken part in the enterprise, though they themselves were from out of town. (240)

The mechanic in the motorcycle sidecar, listens to the engine as if it were music, daydreaming about the internal combustion engine:

> The power plant mechanic, seated in his motorcycle sidecar, paid no attention to the reality around him: he thoughtfully and heartily imagined the element of fire raging in the machine's cylinders, and listened with a passionate gaze, like a musician, to the melody of the gas vortex bursting into the atmosphere. (240)

When asked why they are wasting energy powering an electric lightbulb during the day, the mechanic explains that he is testing the machine by letting the different parts of the engine "get used to each other" (*prigartovalis'*), while "agitating" the masses of passers-by who come through the village to gaze in wonderment at this miraculous by-product of Soviet power.

The power generator is indeed an agent of British colonialism now put in the service of the Revolution: the narrator reads out the number of the engine under the seat of the motorcycle, as well as the note that this military unit belongs to the 77th British Colonial Division. The underground cables lead back to the village, and at night light up the houses in order to make it possible for people to read, thereby "preserving the revolution from darkness" ("i vecherom, dolzhno byt', torzhestvenno siiali okna derevenskikh izbushek, okhraniaia ot t'my revoliutsiiu" [241]). In a memorable Platonovian trope, the power generator is fueled by moonshine (*khlebnym spirtom*), made from bread collected by the villagers. The bread used to make the alcohol to power the machine was hidden by the rich landowner who fled with the Whites and buried the grain in a field, where it has spoiled. But that is only the literal explanation. Much more powerful is the metaphoric Soviet connection of "electricity" with "enlightenment": according to the mechanic, the villagers value reading more than food, and thus, despite the hunger that awaits them after this summer's drought, last year's bread is going to feed the machine and produce electric light for reading ("Poka drugoi radosti u naroda netu, pust' budet u nego svet i chtenie" [242]). As A. Griaznova notes, the generator assembled by the residents of Verchovka transforms the bread necessary for the physical existence of the body into electricity, understood as the "substance of science" necessary to create socialism—"that 'kindred' world where death, hunger and orphanhood will be defeated."[16]

Both nature and machines in this story (as is typical for Platonov) are animated and anthropomorphized, where machines and plants have human feelings while men and women are turned into mechanisms. Flowers that have no more smell than metal shavings begin to resemble people griped by madness: "patiently, in place of the crops, there grew chervil, burdock, the pale flowers of the 'goldenrod' that look like the face of a man with an expression of madness, and other ryegrasses, which always cover the earth during the dry spells" (244).[17] The embodied machine becomes vulnerable and humanized:

> I groped the whole body of the machine – it was hot and tormented, the strong moonshine exploding in the cylinders with a hard fury, but the bad lubricating oil was not holding in the rubbing parts nor enveloping them in a relieving gentle film. The engine fluttered in its frame, and a vague, thin voice from within its mechanism sounded like a warning of mortal danger. (245)[18]

An old man's stomach also serves as the digestion mechanism for ensuring the proper strength of the moonshine ("sobstvennyi zheludok i kishki starika-degustatora byli priborom dlia ispytaniia goriuchego" [242]).

Platonov's short story ends with victory: the narrator figures out a way to water the communal fields by constructing a water pump powered by the motorcycle engine, and even though the distillery making moonshine explodes, the old man who oversees it is thrown clear and will recover. This way, the fields will have water and in the fall the starving village will have a harvest, and the protagonist returns home to his mother, feeling like the "first task of his life" has been accomplished (248).[19]

HOMELAND OF ELECTRICITY, 1967 | 1987

Shepitko's film, however, takes an entirely different turn. A film closely concerned with ecology and the environment, *The Homeland of Electricity* can be placed somewhere between Shepitko's debut feature, *Heat* (Znoi, 1963) in which Soviet power brings water to the desert, and her final film, *Farewell to Matyora* (Proshchanie s Materoi; completed by her husband, Elem Klimov and released in 1981 as *Farewell*), in which a village is flooded to make a dam for a hydroelectric power plant.

Shepitko's *Homeland of Electricity* opens with archival photographs from *Pravda* reporting on the 1921 drought, and a voice-over narrating Platonov's introductory text word for word. A cut to a young man (Grinya, played by Sergei Gorbatiuk, but voiced by Sergei Nikonenko), framed against a white wall as we continue hearing him read the letter-in-verse (still in a kind of voice-off, as the image and sound do not match), introduces us to our protagonist, who will be sent to the village to help with the power generator. The next

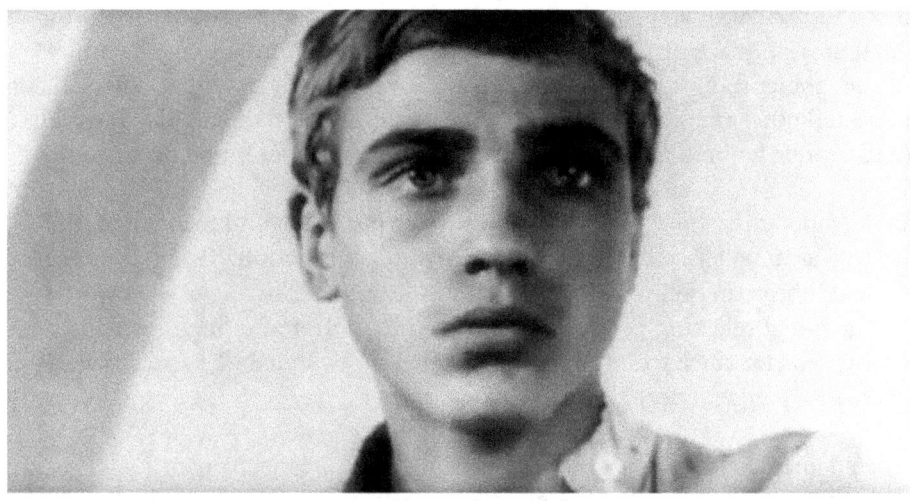

Figure 8.2 Grinya (Sergei Gorbatiuk).

sequence of shots are tight close-ups of the protagonist's face, asleep in the field with a May bug crawling across his brow, and the sound of wind blowing across the dry steppe. Startled from sleep, the protagonist witnesses a religious procession (*krestnyi khod*) in the distance and hears the sounds of singing – the prayer (*moleben'*) sung by the priest and the women following him praying for rain – mixed with the continued howling of the wind. We see the *krestnyi khod* in long shot before Shepitko changes perspective and cuts to medium and close-up shots of the villagers, captured by the camera in a moment of praying. The boy and girl mentioned by Platonov in his story enter the frame as the camera moves through the procession and pause in a two-shot in the foreground to laugh at the priest wearing pants underneath his robes.

In other words, aside from the unexpected cut to the sleeping protagonist, Shepitko is staying very close to the original literary material, including taking all of the dialogue from Platonov's text. We see this also in the sequence that follows, in which the protagonist talks with the old woman about the absence of God and then carries her home in his arms. The sequence begins with the villagers placing an icon of the Virgin Mary (Mother of God / *Bogoroditsa*)— but "without her God," a detail insisted on by Platonov – against the desiccated wall of a ravine. In the icon shown in the film, Mary holds her hands in a such a way as if cradling a baby that is not there. Likewise, Shepitko draws a visual parallel between the old woman's bald head and the dry soil (which Platonov describes in similarly anthropomorphic terms), panning the camera slowly back over the dusty and desolate landscape to the icon, now, recalling the old woman herself: "At the sight of the village, I stopped because I noticed a large quantity of dust off the side of the road and saw a procession of people slowly marching on the dry, bald earth" (238).[20] The visual parallels echo Platonov's conflation of bodies and earth and of the animate with the inanimate. The old woman's bald head is like the dry earth, her pain and sacrifice like that of the Virgin. Carrying the old woman home "like an eight-year-old child" suggests that time is running backwards rather than forward, while Mary's missing child underscores that the future promised by the coming of the Messiah no longer exists. The son now carries the mother in his arms, rather than the other way around.

The first important change that Shepitko introduces into the film is to replace the single electric lightbulb being illuminated by the motorcycle engine (for the purposes of "agitation and propaganda") in Platonov's text with a five-pointed star resembling the Kremlin stars, installed in the 1930s on five towers of the Moscow Kremlin. The original Kremlin stars replaced the gilded eagles that had symbolized Imperial Russia, and were themselves replaced in 1937 with new ones made of ruby glass in time for the 20th anniversary of the October Revolution.[21] While for a viewer in the 1960s, a single lightbulb might not have evoked the kinds of associations that would have been obvious to readers in the 1920s, the five-pointed star is almost "too much": a synecdoche for Soviet power, its purely decorative function—unlike the highly utilitarian lightbulb – speaks more clearly to the useless energy generated by the motorcycle engine. Gone also is the explanation that the generator allows the villagers to read at night, though later, we are shown a small stack of books that the villagers have already read and the much, much larger stack of books that they have yet to read. Similarly, the old man responsible for testing the alcohol strength of the moonshine now appears not as a well-functioning machine, but as a relic of a time before: the mechanic even wonders if in the future, an instrument could be invented that would do the same job once the old man dies.

As Grinya walks around the village checking the power lines that connect the ramshackle huts to the power generator, he is aware of everyone looking at him, a panoptical gaze of visual surveillance.[22] There is something carceral about the placement of the villagers here, each at their own window, isolated and locked away inside their houses, and inside their frames. Camera movement, editing, and Roman Ledeniov's score feel even more modern in this context—indeed, this is the most French New Wave-inspired sequence in the film – and is directly at odds with the visual images of the ramshackle houses and the old villagers peering through the windows.[23] The Picasso painting (but not the bidet) mentioned in Platonov's story appears briefly in the frame as another useless and incomprehensible relic of the past, as the villagers gather materials to make the water pump. The sound of sheet metal being beaten becomes the sound of the village church bells, an amazing sonic montage where the old world and the new world intersect. Finally, in a sequence that visually echoes the famous milk separator sequence in Sergei Eisenstein's *General Line*, the villagers—assembled together, with faces selected for "type" (*tipazh*) and shot in medium and close up from below—anxiously watch a water pump in anticipation of the coming liquid that will arrogate the dry fields.

With a few exceptions, Shepitko's film follows the original text faithfully until the end, when it abruptly deviates from the optimistic conclusion of Platonov's short story. Instead of the explosion of the distillery which can be fixed, the motorcycle engine itself blows up, leaving the villagers without any electrical power at all. The long-awaited rain that falls on the bereft faces, shot in close up and frequently de-framed, looks like tears, and the voice-over—again quoting Platonov, but from a much earlier moment in the story—tells us that the villagers did not even notice this rain, or the fact that their hope, the only thing that made them human, had been fulfilled. Indeed, if we look again at the original text, we will see that "hope" there referred to electricity and communism, not rain:

> We saw light in the bleak darkness of a poor, barren space – the light of a human being on a suffocated, dead earth – we saw wires hung on

old wattles, and our hope for the future world of communism, the hope we needed for our daily hard existence, the hope that alone makes us human, this hope of ours turned into electric power, even if for now it was bringing light only to distant straw huts. (237)

In other words, where Platonov and his protagonists continue to believe in Soviet power and the bright future that they can see through the bleak and desolate reality, it is clear that Sheptiko and her protagonists no longer do. The film ends with the image of the dry cracked soil absorbing the rain until there is nothing left. If there is hope here—hope that makes us human, hope for a communist future transformed by electricity, if there is a light that illuminates the ramshackle hut, the light inside each person on this stifled, dead earth—it is not visible in Shepitko's film. This is a turn away from the past as a repository for futurity (as it appears in Platonov's text), to the past as unprocessed trauma.

LIQUID TIME

Building on their notion of *postmemory*,[24] Marianna Hirsch and Leo Spitzer have recently articulated the idea of "liquid time": images (school photographs, for example) that show us "not only the past in which they were taken but the present and the futures contained in that past, futures that their diverse subjects may have been envisioning." Photographs, they argue, "keep developing in unforeseen directions when they are viewed and re-viewed by different people in different presents. In 'liquid time' they are not fixed into static permanence; rather, they remain dynamic, unfixed, as they acquire new meanings, in new circumstances."[25] It is precisely this liquid, unfixed, dynamic temporality that is at the heart of Platonov's story that tries to see through the bleak present to the bright future to come. But it is also at work in Shepitko's traumatic reimagining of it forty years later, in which the past shown on the screen speaks so clearly to the unrealized future. There is liquid temporality not only to Platonov's short story (set in 1921, written in 1926, rewritten in 1933, published in 1939), but also to the futures contained within it, futures that Platonov or his characters may have been envisioning but that have now failed to come to pass.

In 1921, when the story was set, and even in 1926 when it was (most likely) written, the village's lack of able bodies and the broken-down houses spoke of the Revolution and Civil War and the continuing struggle for Soviet power, not yet fully established, and of the bright future yet to come. But in 1967, for the 50th anniversary of the Bolshevik Revolution, Goskino wanted to know "where Shepitko found such a place and such people." According to Valeria Belova, the film's editor, the film was shot on location in Astrakhan with the local villagers used as actors.[26] For the role of the unnamed protagonist, Shepitko chose a non-professional actor, whose youth and inexperience made him perfect for the role. Like directors in the 1920s, she was working with the idea of *"tipazh"* that also extended to the villagers: "The main actor's lack of life experience, special knowledge, or skills did not hinder the director: according to film critics, the most important thing in this case was 'type'"—a teenage protagonist with "a pure and youthful face" (*geroi s "chistym litsom otroka"*). The roles of peasants from the drought-stricken village were played by local villagers who "did not need to act": they simply "lived within the frame" (*oni prosto zhili v kadre*).[27]

According to Valery Fomin, Shepitko, in undertaking a film adaptation of Platonov's prose, faced perhaps the most difficult task of the three filmmakers: how, by what means, to convey on the screen such an unusual style of the writer? The young cameraman D. Korzhikhin suggested the use of a special anamorphic lens that would lightly deform the image by compressing it horizontally. The figures thus became slightly elongated and "iconic," very much in keeping, notes Fomin, with the nature of the narrative that had been conceived: "not as a life-like everyday story, but as a gospel parable about a young messiah who had come to a hopeless world to give people light. Not just an electric light – the light of truth . . ."[28]

In February 1968, deputy chairman of Goskino Vladimir Baskakov explained to the representatives of the Experimental Creative Film Studio, under the aegis of which *The Beginnings of an Unknown Age* was made, that it was impossible to release the almanac because it contained a "number of incorrect positions in the interpretation of our history."[29] According to critics, the finale was one of the reasons for banning *The Homeland of Electricity*. As Leonid Gurevich recalls,

> the film was shot in the lower reaches of the Volga, in a village with the affectionate name of Seroglazka [Grey Eyes]. The name had nothing to do with reality: the bare sandy steppe of the Kalmyk, muddy yellow streams and drying furrows, old ramshackle huts made of logs salvaged from the river. Extreme heat, water from dirty wells, poor food supplies, tomatoes and watermelons from fields covered in pesticides, indigestion for all, hard life without any modern conveniences . . . Larisa deliberately chose this location [*natura*] – it was truly Platonovian. Drought, dust, poverty, emaciated people in canvas shirts and breeches (only two professional actors, the rest – peasants from the village) . . . An ascetic hungry world – all skin and bones! – sheep droppings and, in a pile of dust, iron-clad goods piled up in courtyards. And next to it – a dream: to make a pump out of this stuff and give water to the parched earth.[30]

But whereas Platonov's short story ended with the successful completion of the mythological quest and the "young, poor, and calm" protagonist starting on his homeward journey knowing that one of his "life's goals had already been achieved," Shepitko's film ended with fire and rain. As Vladimir Ognev recalls,

> In the rain provided by nature, [authorities] saw a hint – it was God who watered the earth, not the Bolsheviks who invented a cunning engine from a trophy motorcycle. After all, the pump ruptured! So the revolution failed . . .? I have added that question mark. The people on whom the fate of cinema once depended, put a period. Both to the sentence and to the film as a whole.[31]

It was not enough for the film to be banned: along with the second cine-novella, Smirnov's *Angel*, Goskino ordered all copies of the film including the original negatives erased. And while we can only speculate on the different fates of the many unmade Soviet films (as Evgenii Margolit does[32]), we might note the degree to which Shepitko's *Homeland of Electricity* visually resembles another destroyed film that survives only in fragments, in single frames lovingly cut out and preserved by its editor, Esfir Tobak: Sergei Eisenstein's 1936 *Bezhin Meadow*.[33] A similar visual style, a white-on-white color palette, a central episode of a raging fire, and an ambiguous subtext of religion and religious symbols unite these two banned films, made thirty years apart. And while there is no possible way that Shepitko could have seen *Bezhin Meadow* as a student at VGIK, her *Homeland of Electricity* owes as much to Platonov's text as to Eisenstein's film.

In the 1930s, when Platonov was writing his own "arrested" text, the novella, *Technical Romance* (Tekhnicheskii romans), based in part on "The Homeland of Electricity," the hope that "makes us human" was already beginning to fade.[34] *Technical Romance* ends on a completely different note than "The Homeland of Electricity," much closer in tone to Shepitko's ending and the ambiguity of its relationship to the world-building project of communism. "But where is freedom?" wonders the engineer Sheglov, as he walks past the graves of his parents, his brothers and sisters, "dead forever, and forgotten by all of humanity," "it is far in the future, beyond the mountains of labor, beyond the new graves of the dead."[35]

"What happened to the idea of [Platonov's] story seven years later," asks Vitaly Shentalinsky in his introduction to the 1991 publication of *Technical Romance*, "when it was being transformed into a novel? A metamorphosis: the flight of a butterfly from its cocoon, the artist's emergence from a misty, beautifully spiritual dream into the sober, tragic light of truth."[36] Or, As O. Kovalov wrote in *Soviet Screen* (Sovetskii ekran) in 1987:

> We have no other writer who more strongly and relentlessly exposed the destructiveness of the idea of self-appointed construction of the welfare of the people and its apologists – satraps, bureaucrats, slaves to dogma,

petty kings, fools, leaders, crooks in mustard jackets, all voracious locusts, causing hunger, terror, desolation and destruction of all life.[37]

By the time Shepitko's novella was finally shown on the big screen at the Central House of Cinema (Tsentral'nyi dom kino) in 1987, the dream of communist utopia was over and audiences could see what Shepitko's camera and directorial eye had already "fixed" twenty years earlier, and arguably, what Platonov had already described thirty years before that: the parched, emaciated, destroyed nation not as the homeland or "birthplace" (*rodina*) of electricity but as its graveyard.

CODA: THE HOMELAND OF ELECTRICITY, 1981 | 2017

In 1981, the composer Gleb Sedel'nikov (1944–2012) completed an opera based on several Platonov stories, titled *The Homeland of Electricity*, which was never staged during his lifetime. The world premiere took place on June 2, 2017, at the Voronezh State Opera and Ballet Theater. *The Homeland of Electricity* is the first and, so far, the only opera based on the works of Platonov, and it is symbolic that its world premiere took place in Voronezh, the city where Platonov was born and lived, and which holds an annual festival of arts in his honor. Sedelnikov wrote not only the music but also the libretto for this work, based on Platonov's autobiographical texts from the 1920s: the stories, "About the Extinguished Lamp of Ilyich," "The Homeland of Electricity," "Aphrodite," and "Sampo," as well as poetry and excerpts from his short book, *Electrification*.

The one-act opera consisting of four scenes (introduction, prologue, epilogue, and conclusion) was conducted by the Voronezh State Theater conductor Yury Anisichkin, who had had the idea of showing the opera on the Voronezh stage ever since he received the score from Sedelnikov in 2012. The performance was staged by the drama director Mikhail Bychkov, artistic director of the Platonov Festival of Arts and the Voronezh Chamber Theater. The set design—with visual references to the Soviet avant-garde art of the 1920s, including Tatlin's *prouns* and Malevich's Suprematist paintings—was created by Bychkov's permanent co-author, Nikolay Simonov. The critic Natalya Gaag notes that Sedelnikov's music makes a strong impression: it is unusual, vivid, sharply characterized. It has the traditional harmony and revolutionary audacity of sounds: from an almost intimate prayer, where the chorus of people asks nature for blessed rain, to an almost revolutionary rap with placard appeals: "Electric light will give the village a useful hobby" and "Electrification is as much a revolution in technology as October 1917. Its introduction will change the character and very essence of people."[38] With

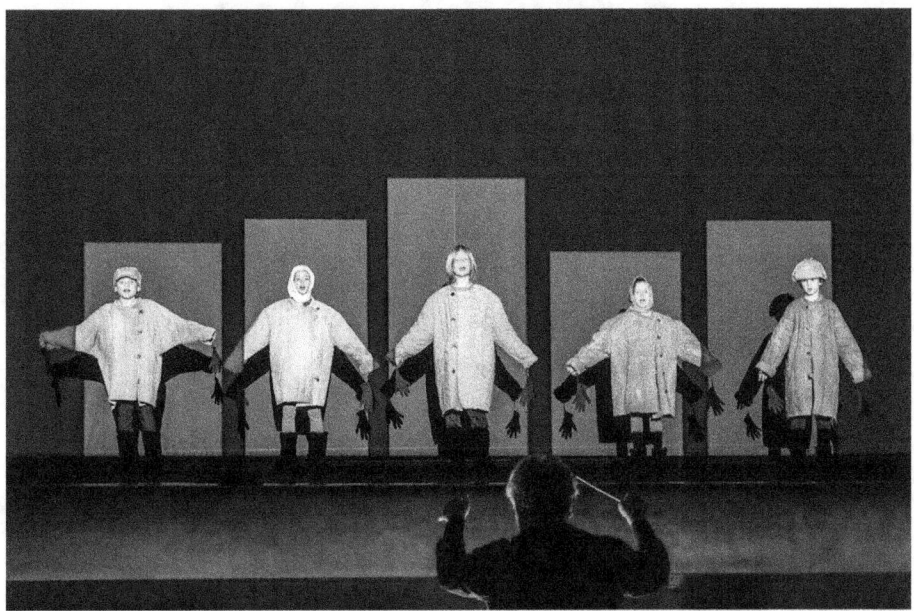

Figure 8.3 The Opera, *The Homeland of Electricity*, Voronezh, 2017.

three casts and around 130 people, Bychkov emphasizes the folk nature of the difficult Platonov language with many voices, where the chorus becomes the main character of the performance.

The prologue uses the authentic texts of some of the prayers included in the procession for rain and, like Shepitko, the libretto makes use of Platonov's own language, taken directly from his works. But the result, when seen from the distance of nearly 100 years, is radically different. Platonov's early prose, imbued with the revolutionary spirit of expectation and transformation of life, of the future-to-come, is reinterpreted first by the composer in 1981, and then by the authors of the performance in 2017. The result, "is a story of Russia, of the difficult lives of ordinary people, of their aspirations for the new world, of their gains and losses." And despite the fact that in the finale the power plant, which brought the light of new life to dark Rogachevka, burns up in a fire set by the class enemies, "hope and faith in their own strength, in the good that will forever triumph over evil, remain the main protagonists of the opera."[39]

Reviewing the opera for the Moscow festival, The Golden Mask, music critic Tatyana Davydova notes that the opera opens and ends cinematically with a voice-over narration "from the author," affirming the hope for a brighter future and the belief in a communist paradise, where people will learn not only to build power plants at every step, but also to "grind up the evils of life." Many of the naive and ingenuous remarks of the characters, who believe that soon they, the builders of socialism, "will eat cake and not suffer from a shortage of chicken eggs" (text taken directly from Platonov), might today be received ironically, but the libretto raises "serious timeless themes, including the desire to make the world a better place, loyalty to the common cause, perseverance, and hard work." Electrification, she writes, does not only imply a literal illumination of Rogachevka, which has not seen light "since the creation of the world," but becomes "a virtually religious symbol of people's access to light."[40]

"What is this one-act play about?" asks the music and art critic Anna Shalagina, about the construction of the power plant in the village of Rogachevka, in which Andrei Platonov participated together with his brother and other like-minded people? About how the power plant was built and how it burned down? The simpler the plot, the more complicated the implication. Time. People. Revolution. These are the main 'protagonists' in the opera, while the questions of history remain open.[41]

And yet, if we look closely at the choice of costuming and set design[42]—at the dull grey and bright red quilted jackets of the actors reminding us of prisoners returning from the Gulag, at the minimal sets reminding us of the barren wasteland of rural Russia, the agit-prop slogans churning out empty rhetoric, and the Foucauldian placement of performers, each isolated in their own frame or grouped together as undifferentiated masses, we might understand what the production is hinting at (or openly speaking about): not the bright future of communist utopia as it was imagined by Platonov in the 1920s, but its bleak past as recorded in Shepitko's film and today's liquid, uncertain present.

NOTES

1. Valerii Fomin, "Izmena: Neskol'ko nozhei v spinu revoliutsii," *Ekran i stsena* no. 45 (1997), 46. See: https://chapaev.media/articles/10329 and https://www.bbc.com/russian/features-39222478. After refusing to make changes to *The Commissar*, Askoldov lost his job, was expelled from the Communist Party, charged with social parasitism, exiled from Moscow, and banned from working on feature films for life. He was told that the single copy of the film had been destroyed, but all of the materials (negatives, positives, phonograms, cuttings of negatives and positives, etc.) were transferred to the national film archive, Gosfilmofond. The film was shelved by Goskino for twenty years and restored and released in 1987.
2. Alexander Prokhorov, "The Unknown New Wave: Soviet Cinema of the 1960s" in *Springtime for Soviet Cinema: Re/Viewing the 1960s*, Alexander Prokhorov, ed. (Pittsburgh: Russian Film Symposium, 2001).

3. Okudzhava's "Sentimental March" was written in 1957 and dedicated to the poet Evgeny Evtushenko. Marlen Khutsiev included Okudzhava's performance of this march in his film, *Zastva Il'icha* (Lenin's Guard), in the poetry evening episode shot at the Polytechnical Museum. This is the end-credit song of the restored two-film almanac, *Nachalo nevedomogo veka* (1987) and probably would not have appeared in the original.
4. See: Kaganovsky, "Soviet 1960s Cinema and the Nuclear Catastrophe: Mikhail Romm's *Ordinary Fascism* and *Nine Days of One Year*," in *Critical Memory Studies: New Approaches*, ed. Brett Kaplan (London: Bloomsbury Press, 2023), 236–280.
5. Platonov reworks parts of the unpublished 1926 "Birthplace of Electricity" into his novella, *Tekhnicheskii roman*, one of three manuscripts seized during an NKVD house search in 1933. See: Vitaly Shentalinsky's introduction, "The Arrested Word," to Andrei Platonov, *Tekhnicheskii roman* (Moscow: Ogonek, 1991).
6. A. Griaznova, "'Tekhnicheskii roman' i 'Rodina elektrichestva' A. Platonova: Tema preobrazovaniia mira" (Voronezhskii gosudarstvennyi universitet, 2011).
7. Platonov participated in the building of the electrical power plant in the village of Rogachevka, and described his experiences in another short story, "O potukhshei lampe Il'icha" (The Extinguished Lamp of Ilych).
8. Andrei Platonov, "Rodina elektrichestva," in *Sobranie Sochinenii v piati tomakh*, vol. 1 (Moscow: Informpechat', 1998), 236–248; here: 236. All translations are mine, unless otherwise noted.
9. «У нас машина уж гремит — свет электричества от ней горит; но надо нам помочь, чтоб еще лучше было у нас в деревне на Верчовке, а то машина ведь была у белых раньше, она чужою интервенткой родилась, ей псих мешает пользу нам давать.» (Our machine is already rattling – its electric light is on; but we need help to make it even better in our village in Verchovka, for the machine was with the Whites before, it was born as a foreign interventionist, its psyche prevents it from giving us benefit [237]).
10. «Мы увидели свет в унылой тьме нищего, бесплодного пространства, — свет человека на задохнувшейся, умершей земле, — мы увидели провода, повешенные на старые плетни, и наша надежда на будущий мир коммунизма, надежда, необходимая нам для ежедневного трудного существования, надежда, единственно делающая нас людьми, эта наша надежда превратилась в электрическую силу, пусть пока что зажегшую свет лишь в дальних соломенных избушках.»
11. Emma Widdis, *Visions of a New Land: Soviet Film from the Revolution to the Second World War* (New Haven: Yale University Press, 2003), 27.
12. Widdis, *Visions of a New Land*, 27.
13. *Pervyi vsesoiuznyi s"ezd sovetskikh pisatelei: Stenograficheskii otchet* (Moscow: Khudozhestvennaia literatura, 1934).
14. See Petre Petrov, *Automatic for the Masses: The Death of the Author and the Birth of Socialist Realism* (Toronto: University of Toronto Press, 2015).
15. "Go I Know Not Whither and Fetch I Know Not What" is a Russian fairy tale collected by Alexander Afanasyev in *Russian Fairytales* (*Narodnye russkie skazki*, 1855–1863); it has variants in many cultures and languages.

16. Griaznova, 22.
17. «В этих же посевах с терпеньем росли купыри, репей, бледные цветы «златоуста», похожие на лицо человека с выражением сумасшествия, и прочие плевелы, которыми всегда зарастает земля во время действия сухих стихий.»
18. «Я ощупал все тело машины—оно сильно грелось и мучилось, крепкий самогон взрывался в цилиндрах с жесткой яростью, но плохое смазочное масло не держалось в трущихся частях и не обволакивало их облегчающей нежной пленкой. Мотор трепетал в раме, и неясный тонкий голос изнутри его механизма звучал как предупреждение о смертельной опасности.»
19. «Я шёл один в тёмном поле, молодой, бедный и спокойный. Одна моя жизненная задача была выполнена»
20. «На виду деревни я остановился, потому что заметил большую пыль в стороне от дороги и рассмотрел там толпу народа, шествующую по сухой, лысой земле.»
21. As Julia Chadaga has argued, "In the 1930s, the official discourse around the Kremlin stars strove to transfer religious meaning to the Soviet state's own creations. The Kremlin stars were raised in the very period when cathedrals were being demolished on official orders, including major churches in the Kremlin itself. The man-made stars would take their place; they would become the new beneficiaries of the people's devotion." See: Julia Bekman Chadaga, *Optical Play: Glass, Vision, and Spectacle in Russian Culture* (Evanston: Northwestern University Press, 2014), 173.
22. See, Viktoria Paranyuk in this volume.
23. Different directors and different cameramen, but Smirnov at least was definitely looking at the French *nouvelle vague* as inspiration. See: https://ru.wikipedia.org/wiki/Начало_неведомого_века.
24. *Postmemory*, as Hirsch and others have defined it, it describes the relationship of the second generation to powerful, often traumatic, experiences that preceded their births but that were nevertheless transmitted to them so deeply as to seem to constitute memories in their own right. It describes the relationship that subsequent generations bear to the personal, collective, and cultural trauma or transformation of those who came before and that "characterizes the experience of those who grow up dominated by narratives that preceded their birth, whose own belated stories are evacuated by the stories of the previous generation shaped by traumatic events that can be neither understood nor recreated" (Marianna Hirsch, *Family Frames: Photography, Narrative, and Postmemory* [Cambridge, Mass: Harvard University Press, 1997]; 22).
25. Marianna Hirsch and Leo Spitzer, *School Photos in Liquid Time: Reframing Difference* (Seattle: University of Washington Press, 2020), 13.
26. «Где вы нашли таких людей? – возмущенно и грозно вопрошали в Госкино. А в фильме большинство ролей исполняли самые простые реальные жители одной из астраханских деревень.» ["Where did you find such people?" they asked the Goskino indignantly and menacingly. But in fact, most of the roles in the film were simply played by the real-life inhabitants of an Astrakhan

village]. See interview with Valeria Belova, https://irinakiu.livejournal.com/673726.html
27. https://ru.wikipedia.org/wiki/Начало_неведомого_века
28. Fomin, Izmena (https://chapaev.media/articles/10329).
29. Fomin, Izmena (https://chapaev.media/articles/10329).
30. Leonid Gurevich, "Cherez vsiu zhizn'," *Kinostsenarii* n. 2 (1996): https://chapaev.media/articles/8927
31. Fomin, Izmena (https://chapaev.media/articles/10329).
32. Evgenii Margolit, *Iz"iatoe kino. 1924–1953* (Moscow: Dubl'-D, 1995).
33. See: Esfir' Tobak, "Moi gigant," *Kinostsenarii: al'manakh* 6 (1997): 126–144.
34. Andrei Platonov, *Tekhnicheskii romans* (Moscow: Ogonek, 1991).
35. Platonov, *Tekhnicheskii romans*, 34.
36. Platonov, *Tekhnicheskii romans*, 4.
37. «И нет у нас другого писателя, столь сильно и неотвязно разоблачавшего гибельность идеи самозваного устроительства народного блага и ее апологетов — самодуров, бюрократов, рабов догмы, мелких царьков, дураков, вождей-горлопанов в горчичных галифе, всей этой прожорливой саранчи, несущей голод, ужас, запустение и гибель всему живому.» (Oleg Kovalov, "Iz smiren'ia ne pishutsia stikhotvoren'ia," Sovetskii ekran, n. 23 [1987]): https://chapaev.media/articles/8925
38. https://proteatr.info/platonov-terra-incognita-v-zhanre-opery/
39. https://www.theatre-vrn.ru/repertoire/opera/rodina-elektrichestva/
40. https://www.intermedia.ru/news/321071
41. https://www.theatre-vrn.ru/repertoire/opera/rodina-elektrichestva/
42. Costume by Yulia Vetrova; lighting design by Ivan Vinogradov; and multimedia design by Bychkov.

PART V

Landscape and Environment

CHAPTER 9

Methods of Conquest: Larisa Shepitko's *Heat*, Soviet Russian Colonialism, and the Representation of the Virgin Lands Campaign in Soviet Cinema of the 1950s–60s

Zdenko Mandušić

After Larisa Shepitko and Irina Povolotskaia spent a year attempting to make a film based on their script *Tebia zhdut* / *Waiting For You* at the Dovzhenko Film Studio in Kyiv, the VGIK classmates departed for Kyrgyzfil'm Studio in Frunze (now Bishkek) to film an adaptation of Chingiz Aitmatov's short story "The Camel's Eye."[1] Set during the Virgin Lands project of the 1950s and 1960s, Larisa Shepitko's VGIK diploma film *Znoi* / *Heat* (1962) features a young male engineer arriving to a peripheral, rural community in the Kazakh-Kyrgyz steppe to join a work brigade tasked with taming and cultivating this landscape. *Heat*'s complicated production indicates a range of connections to developments in the post-Stalinist Soviet film industry, including the history of films about collective farms and the mobilization of cinema to glorify the government's monumental programs. This essay reframes existing understandings of *Heat* and Soviet cinema of the 1960s by locating the film's narrative, visual style, and the treatment of voice within broader patterns of stylistic continuity and change, specifically in connection with other cinematic representations of Nikita Khrushchev's massive agricultural campaign.[2]

As is well-known, conditions during the production of *Heat* in Anarkhai, the arid steppe between Kazakhstan and Kyrgyzstan, were particularly harsh, with temperatures reaching 40 degrees Celsius. Additionally, Shepitko and other members of the crew became infected with Hepatitis A, which almost prompted Kyrgyzfil'm to cancel the production and to write off the sunk cost as a "creative failure" (*tvorcheskaia neudacha*).[3] Another difficulty was that the production did not have a studio-approved literary script. Kyrgyzfil'm did not accept the initial variant, submitted by veteran scriptwriter Iosif Ol'shanskii, and gave Shepitko and Povolotskaia a month to revise the text. Due to a tight production schedule, there was not enough time to completely revise the literary script. Instead, Shepitko and Povolotskaia wrote scenes during the production, a day or two before they were scheduled to be filmed. The first-time director again revised the film's dialogue with Semen Lungin and Il'ia Nusinov after a three-month pause in production due to the virus outbreak among the crew; Povolotskaia left the production due to the viral infection.[4] Shepitko claimed that the need to write and practice these scenes did not leave time and energy during the production to develop the "ideal compositions of conceived scenes" ("ideal'noe voploshchenie zadumannogo risunka"), prompting the director to consider the eleven-month production of *Heat* as a continuation of her training as opposed to a thoroughly refined application of her ideas.[5] In subsequent films, especially *Kryl'ia / Wings* (Mosfil'm, 1966) and *Voskhozhdenie / The Ascent* (Mosfil'm, 1977), Shepitko developed a distinct film style, both visually and thematically, which Lilya Kaganovsky associates with the concept of women's "counter cinema."[6] Nevertheless, despite its flaws and production problems, Shepitko's first feature importantly indicates the development of narrative and visual strategies of Soviet colonial practices, both aural and visual.

When compared to other films representing the Virgin Lands project, *Heat*'s narrative and audiovisual strategies indicate a process of stylistic development and change from the first feature films produced in 1954 to the early 1960s. Richard Stites identifies the normative elements of the dominant epic plot in Virgin Lands films in the following way: "Out on the steppe, modernity springs forth from a semi-desert under the hands and brains of the hero, his wise and kindly mentor, and a crew of young, idealistic, ethnically varied Komsomols."[7] These epic elements are intercut with representations of the Soviet idyll on collective farms structured around the "theory of conflict-ness." These films focused on competitive agricultural production development, presenting examples of model workers as well as their foils—settlers with poor discipline and cynical attitudes. As Peter Rollberg points out, films about the conquest of the *tselina* (Virgin Land) featured a range of standard elements, including scenes that show large numbers of Komsomol members arriving to an uninhabited landscape, which established the notion of frontier settlement; the ceremonial naming of new settlements on signposts planted into the ground, representing agricultural and cultural claims of dominion over nature; and the eventual triumphant survey of new homes and the cultivated landscape in the finale of many films.[8] Following earlier large-scale Soviet projects, the 1950s Virgin Lands films presented Khrushchev's agricultural campaign in monumental terms. In his discussion of the early Virgin Lands film *Pervyi eshelon /*

*The First Echelon (*Mosfil'm, Mikhail Kalatozov, 1955), Sergei Kapterev identifies this film as an example of the post-Stalinist "new-monumentalism."[9] Along with its classic socialist realist narrative, namely the conquest of nature into a cultivated Soviet garden, director Mikhail Kalatozov and his cinematographer Sergei Urusevskii implemented a visual monumentality through strategies that include the mobile wide-angle camera, mass scenes, and the presentation of the steppe landscape in dynamic tracking shots.

As a Virgin Lands film, *Heat* moves away from the monumental plot of conquering uncultivated space agriculturally and ideologically toward what Evgenii Margolit has described as the Thaw-era revision of man's relationship to nature.[10] In Shepitko's film, the windswept, arid steppe resists cultivation. Along with the geographic imaginary of the Virgin Lands, one of the central issues is the representation of settlers and other inhabitants of those lands or, in some films, their problematic absence. Instead of earlier narratives featuring large casts of Komsomol settlers, *Heat* focuses on a smaller group of characters. As opposed to the arrival of hundreds of young men and women, only one Komsomol member arrives and joins a brigade consisting of five other people. Shepitko also filmed *Heat* with a cast of Kyrgyz actors and a crew, which included many Kyrgyz film technicians, a significant departure from previous films in this subgenre. However, the dubbing of *Heat* by ethnic Russian speakers in the version of the film released throughout the Soviet Union and abroad produced a dissonance between image and sound. Although the Kyrgyzfil'm Studio later dubbed *Heat* into Kyrgyz, international film festivals such as Karlovy Vary and the Frankfurt Asian Film Week presented it as an "Asian" film with a Russian soundtrack.[11]

Indexical references mainly do not acknowledge the complete dubbing of *Heat*. Bibliographical sources from the 1960s, including *Iskusstvo kino / Film Art*, the main industry journal for Soviet cinema, and the all-encompassing, encyclopedic catalog *Sovetskie khudozhestvennye fil'my / Soviet Artistic Films*, do not identify the film as dubbed into Russian nor do they include information about the ethnic Russian actors who voiced the Kyrgyz characters in the widely-distributed, author's version of the film.[12] Information regarding dubbing and voice actors is also absent from the current website of Kyrgyzfil'm Studio.[13] Additionally, the studio's YouTube channel presents *Heat* in the Russian authorial version and does not include the names of the voice-over actors in the credits.[14] As these sources indicate, historical and contemporary records of Shepitko's diploma film obscure a fundamental aspect of audiovisual representation, indicating the consequences of Soviet colonial practices. *Heat* presents a tension between the visual representation of Kyrgyz characters within conventions of Virgin Lands films and the substitute disembodied voices, which represent the erasure and displacement of the local, non-Russian voices as markers of a regional, historically determined linguistic specificity.

THE VIRGIN LANDS CAMPAIGN AS CULTURE

Launched in 1954, the Virgin Lands campaign or *Osvoenie tseliny* was Nikita Khrushchev's plan to open uncultivated and fallow lands in Siberia, the steppes of Kazakhstan, the Volga Region, and the Urals for farming and settlement as part of a bid to increase agricultural production. Denis Kozlov writes, "this initiative was propagated as a specifically socialist endeavor of voluntary, enthusiastic labor: thousands of young people were mobilized for the task."[15] Soviet planners counted on the enthusiasm of young settlers, and the government had to mobilize 300,000 students and Komsomol members for each harvest.[16] Soviet youth were instrumental for the Virgin Lands campaign and as part of Khrushchev's wholesale plan to revitalize communist ideals and regenerate social and political practices.[17] In this regard, the Virgin Lands films functioned as audiovisual means for recruiting the Soviet youth needed for Khrushchev's agricultural campaign. Vladislav Zubok characterizes the campaign in terms of the young participants: "From 1954 to 1960, entire classes of university students and high school students from Moscow, Leningrad, and other major cities were sent to work in the Virgin Lands."[18] Khrushchev's agricultural campaign produced appellations that closely identified participants with the large-scale undertaking and the frontier land. The discourse around the Virgin Lands project defined the people who came to Kazakhstan and Siberia initially as "settlers" (*novosely*) and "newcomers" (*pribyvshye, priezzhie*), and later, during the height of the public veneration of the project in the 1960s, as *tselinniki* (Virgin Landers).[19] However, as Michaela Pohl has argued, the Virgin Lands legend and its transmedia presentation obscure the presence of local Kazakhs and millions of people, the so-called special settlers whom the state deported and relocated to Kazakhstan under Stalin.[20]

Historians describe the Virgin Lands campaign variously as a successful endeavor and a failure. With impressive but not record-breaking harvests, which increased between 1954 and 1964, Martin McCauley considers Khrushchev's Virgin Lands Project positively.[21] Nevertheless, Michaela Pohl points out that Western authors continually repeat three stereotypes about the Virgin Lands: "that those so-called volunteers were enlisted by 'semi-compulsory methods,' that the project was a colonial policy that ran counter to the interests of the Kazakhs, and that it failed to produce grain and led to disastrous dust storms."[22] For example, in their book, *An Environmental History of Russia*, Paul Josephson et al., describe this project as Khrushchev's most environmentally devastating and costly program to agriculture, leading to erosion and despoliation.[23] Focusing on the human element in her research, most notably the dynamics of arriving settlers and the population already in the not-so-Virgin Lands, Pohl asserts that through this monumental project, Khrushchev made "enormously successful investments in Kazakhstan's people and the country's future."²⁴ These investments resulted in the "rehabilitation through jobs and apartments of hundreds of thousands of deportees and former inmates of the Gulag," as well as the development of a regional workforce and the training of administrators and managers.²⁵ Russian language scholars acknowledge the benefits and flaws of Khrushchev's agriculture program and the system, asserting that the Virgin Lands campaign had social and economic benefits as well as costly mistakes stemming from the lack of agricultural and ecological research.²⁶

Along with its impact on Soviet agriculture and demographics, an expansive propaganda campaign defined the Virgin Lands for Soviet citizens. Writers, poets, painters, poster artists, and filmmakers represented the project through texts and images. In this regard, films about the Virgin Lands project figure into a transmedial audiovisual campaign, which included fictional and non-fictional narratives, poems, songs, paintings, posters, newsreels, and feature-length documentary and fiction films.²⁷ Guided by the directives of the Party, producers of Soviet culture wrote and made images about the project defining the undertaking "as the great heroic project of the age."²⁸ The cultural campaign presented the settlers as "pioneers on a frontier with patriotic overtones and references to the great construction adventures of the 1930s and to cult figures such as Pavlik Morozov and Pavel Korchagin."²⁹ As Mieka Erley asserts, writers drew keywords regarding the Virgin Lands from Khrushchev's declarations about the project.³⁰ Literary critics such as V. Kardin encouraged writers to "show the high romanticism of the heroic battle for grain."³¹ Nikita Khrushchev directly urged writers, artists, and filmmakers to produce "a great number of good books, films, plays, and musical compositions about the working people of the Virgin Lands—the remarkable heroes of our times."³² Posters, paintings, and films dedicated to the Virgin Lands themes draw on the iconography of Stalin-era campaigns.³³ Film reviewers asserted this connection in their discussion of the cinematic representation of the project. In his review of Aleksandr Medvedkin's *Pervaia Vesna / The First Spring* (1954), K. Slavin compares the representation of Komsomol members in this first feature-length documentary about the Virgin Lands project with earlier undertakings such as the construction of Magnitogorsk and the industrialization of the Dnipropetrovsk, known today as Dnipro.³⁴

In this manner, Shepitko's *Heat* follows the stylistic development of the Virgin Lands films, which Soviet studios produced as part of the transmedial campaign to promote Khrushchev's agricultural project.³⁵ As the appearance of Virgin Lands films from 1954–1956 indicates, the cinematic representation of the campaign was part of the Soviet film industry's thematic plan for these years. In the coordinated production of these films, Gor'kii Central Studio of Children's and Youth Films in Moscow and the Alma-Ata Film Studio (later renamed Kazakhfil'm Studio) led with three films each. As a production house specifically focused on young viewers, the core audience for the Virgin Lands media campaign, Gor'kii Studio produced films that blended moralist and socialist values.[36] Since Alma-Ata was Kazakhstan's central film studio, regional connections motivated its production of Virgin Lands films. The two Mosfil'm productions, *The First Echelon* and *Alenka* (Boris Barnet, 1961), are significant because of their directors, Mikhail Kalatozov and Boris Barnet, both of whom had extensive experience making films prior to their Virgin Lands projects. Other well-established film directors such as Sergei Gerasimov, Aleksandr Medvedkin, and Iosif Kheifits also made films in this subgenre. In addition to his fictional representation in the form of the comedy-musical film *Restless Spring*, Medvedkin also directed the previously mentioned documentary *The First Spring*. For young filmmakers, such as Lev Kulidzhanov, Iakov Segel', Larisa Shepitko, and Boris Stepanov, thematic planning for films about the Virgin Lands campaign allowed them to make their first feature-length films.

CONTINUITY AND CHANGE

As productions made in response to political direction from the Central Committee and Khrushchev, the Virgin Lands films indicate a need to narrativize and give audiovisual form to the monumental agricultural project. For example, filmmakers utilized extreme, wide shots with low horizon lines prevalently in Virgin Lands films (Fig. 9.1). Such low-angle, low horizon shots are included in *The First Echelon*, *My zdes' zhivem / We Live Here* (Alma-Ata Film Studio/ Kazakhfilm Studio, Shaken Aimanov, 1956), *Bespokoinaia vesna / Restless Spring* (Alma-Ata Film Studio/Kazakhfilm Studio, Aleksandr Medvedkin, 1956), and *Alenka*. Iosif Kheifits's *Gorizont / Horizon* (1961) utilizes long-angle, handheld shots prevalently throughout the film, including several that heavily feature the low horizon line and the vast sky of the Kazakh steppe. *Heat* also includes low-angle landscape shots with low horizons (see Fig. 9.1). These shots show the silhouette of the film's young and earnest protagonist Kemel', underneath the sweeping expanse of the sky. In two separate scenes, Kemel' walks into the receding landscape frustrated with the oppressive behavior of Abakir, the disillusioned former Stakhanovite tractor driver, who treats the youthful Komsomol member harshly and menaces Kalipa, his romantic partner.

Such shots in *Heat* are reminiscent of similar ones in *Zemlia / Earth* (VUKFU, Oleksandr Dovzhenko, 1930), especially considering that Dovzhenko was Shepitko's VGIK mentor. Peter Rollberg writes, "Shepitko's teachers in many ways defined her artistic approach: Dovzhenko informed it with a sense of lofty poetic pathos, whereas (Mikhail) Romm imbued it with an interest in the cinematic reflection of contemporary societal conflicts."[37] However, to only associate the low-angle, low-horizon shots in *Heat* with Dovzhenko and *Earth*

Figure 9.1 Low-angle, low-horizon silhouette shots, clockwise from the top: *The First Echelon, Restless Spring, Heat*, and *Alenka*.

would reflect the tendency of associating stylistic developments in Soviet films from the post-Stalinist 1950s–60s to the avant-garde films of the 1920s. At the same time, the prevalence of this specific type of shot in Virgin Lands films indicates that this was a common formal element of the subgenre, which highlighted the enormous expanse of the landscape by juxtaposing lone human figures against the broad elemental sky.

Heat includes several other prominent formal and thematic elements common to Virgin Lands films, especially in the composition of the *mise-en-scène* and the definition of character types. These shared features include extreme wide shots of tractors and plows tilling the soil, full shots foregrounding tractors, plows, and their operators, obligatory scenes in field kitchens and dining under makeshift, wood and cloth shelters, and depictions of the hardworking, committed Komsomol members along with negative examples of workers. Scenes in Virgin Lands films of communal meals outside allow directors to develop connections between characters and landscapes, primarily through the persistent wind that blows against the makeshift structures, indicating the contact between the Komsomol members and nature. Radios are another reoccurring feature of Virgin Lands films, including *Heat*. They appear almost always in communal settings, including the collective listening of radio broadcasts and transmissions, as well as the sending and receiving of messages over the airwaves. As their transmissions overcome vast expanses of space, radios link the periphery to the center.

The First Echelon, *Restless Spring*, *Eto nachinalos' tak / It Began Like This* (Gor'kii Studio, Lev Kulidzhanov and Iakov Segel', 1956), and *Heat* all feature negative examples of behavior in workers who display a range of anti-communal attitudes and behaviors. In *The First Echelon*, Eduard Bredun plays Genka Monetkin, whose lack of discipline leads him to drink too much alcohol; eventually he ignites a wildfire that threatens the state farm. In *It Began Like This*, a young Rolan Bykov, before he went on to play the jester in Andrei Tarkovskii's *Andrei Rublev* (1966/1971/1988), plays Vasiia Lapshin, whose drinking leads to the death of the Komsomol brigade leader Vasilii Petrovich Skvortsov (Valentin Zubkov). Skvortsov dies when he tries to save the drunk Lapshin from a plot of land mined with explosives for land clearance. The negative example in Aleksandr Medvedkin, Zhenia Omega (Sergei Gurzo), is not an alcoholic but is lazy and unfocused. In *Heat*, Abakir is an oppressive presence to both Kemel' and Kalipa. Abakir doesn't drink in the film and is a skilled worker, continuing, at least nominally, to fulfill his task. Nevertheless, Abakir tells Kemel' that the youthful and earnest Komsomol member is misguided in thinking that the sovkhoz (a state-owned farm in the former Soviet Union) will ever succeed. Abakir further urges Kemel' to only trust himself, implying that he cannot rely on the Soviet community.

Virgin Lands films frequently feature romantic subplots involving Komsomol settlers. Medvedkin's *Restless Spring* and Aimanov's *We Live Here* include ethnically mixed romantic couples. As with earlier kolkhoz films depicting life and labor in the country, love stories in Virgin Lands films are, in Oksana Bulgakowa's words, "insignificant detour(s) from the main plot of the socialist competition."[38] Beyond these subplots, Virgin Lands films draw on sexual symbolism. As Mieka Erley writes, in literary and visual representations of the Virgin Lands campaign, "The discourse of virginity is inescapable in the cultural production surrounding the Virgin Lands campaign. Erotic energy powers the myth of the Virgin Lands, with the fertility of the land and the nation its implicit goal."[39] For example, in Kulidzhanov's *It Began Like This* (1956), tensions rise between Lesha Antonon (Nikolai Dovzhenko) and Tania Gromova (Liliana Aleshkina), overtly about their work in the fields but suggesting romantic and sexual attraction. These tensions come to a head when the Komsomol couple reveals their shared interest in one another. The film subsequently presents them lying in a field at night, having consummated their relationship presumably. The satisfaction of sexual desire in Kulidzhanov's film triggers a rainstorm, ending the drought threatening the agricultural undertaking in *It Began Like This*. In this regard, the film exemplifies Erley's claims regarding the representation of the Virgin Lands campaign as a "space of sexual freedom and exploration away from the scrutiny of family and neighbors and the claustrophobic dormitories, communal apartments, and villages of postwar European Russia."[40] According to Erley, Shepitko's *Heat* "is relatively loyal" to the plot of Chingiz Aitamotiv's original plot, representing the conquest of the Virgin Lands as a sublimated sexual conquest and includes scenes of sexual and Oedipal violence.[41]

In terms of narrative and audiovisual strategies, filmmakers made Virgin Lands films within broader patterns of continuity and changes in Soviet cinema. This chapter is particularly interested in patterns of continuity and changes that define film style, specifically which motifs and devices filmmakers mobilize in their renditions of the *tselina* narrative of taming the frontier for agriculture and building new communities. Virgin Lands films include elements of "kolkhoz films," or films set on collective farms, one of the dominant film genres of the Stalinist period. Bulgakowa writes that the "kolkhoz film" did not align with the established system of film genres, "detective stories, melodramas, comedy, slapstick – all of which were acknowledged to be cinematic because of their well-developed and clearly defined patterns to represent motion (the chase scene in detective stories, the gags, and stunts in slapstick; the dramatic tension of a last-minute rescue in a melodrama)."[42] According to Bulgakowa the "nebulous" definition of kolkhoz film produced hybrids of established genres. In this regard, the name "kolkhoz film," refers to the milieu and the subject, the representation of labor.[43]

Cinematic representations of the campaign to cultivate fallow land in Siberia and Kazakhstan from the 1950s and 1960s include important elements of kolkhoz films, especially Stalinist kolkhoz musicals. Early films about the conquest of the *tselina* such as *The First Echelon*, *Restless Spring*, *It Began Like This*, and *Ivan Brovkin na tseline / Ivan Brovkin in the Virgin Lands* (Gor'kii Studio, Ivan Lukinskii, 1958), include scenes in which Komsomol members sing songs on their way to or already at work on the Virgin soil. In this manner, these films echo the kolkhoz musicals of Ivan Pyr'ev, most notably *Kubanskie kazaki / Cossacks of the Kuban* (Mosfil'm, 1948).

Although *Heat* does not include scenes of cheerful singing by Komsomol settlers, Shepitko's film belongs to the Soviet cinematic history of representing tractors from the late films of the 1920s avant-garde, famously in *Staroe i novoe / The General Line* (Sovkino, Sergei Eisenstein and Grogorii Aleksandrov, 1929), and *Earth*, to the celebration of tractors in *Traktoristy / The Tractor Drivers* (Mosfil'm and VUKFU, Ivan Pyr'ev, 1939) and *Kliatva / The Vow* (Tbilisi Film Studio, Mikheil Chiaureli, 1946).[44] Following Bulgakowa's claim that genres can be differentiated according to distinct patterns for representing motion, the geometric movement of tractors and plows across vast terrain presents a type of motion specific to the kolkhoz film genre and, by extension, the Virgin Lands films. Films such as *The First Echelon*, *It Began Like This*, and *Restless Spring* feature tractors prominently in the depictions of the campaign. In this regard,

Shepitko utilizes some standard compositions of tractors plowing the earth. At the same time, *Heat* also features Shepitko's and her crew's attempts to innovate preceding aesthetic choices of Virgin Lands films by accentuating the volume, mass, and texture of the tractor.

Along with the influence of her mentors and the lineage of tractors in kolkhoz productions, the representation of the tractor in Shepitko's film indicates patterns of stylistic continuation and change within the Virgin Lands films. This approach includes the condition of these mechanized vehicles and their representation on the screen. In her discussion of *Heat*, Jane Costlow argues that the two tractors in *Heat* appear as "rusty, water-guzzling behemoths controlled by a bully."[45] But when compared to the depiction of tractors in other Virgin Lands films, which young and experienced filmmakers consistently represent as engaged in the struggle with the elements and the uncultivated nature of the *tselina*, the tractors in *Heat* don't appear to be in any worse condition. Moreover, the two tractors in Shepit'ko's film perpetuate a fascination with mechanized vehicles as representatives of modernity and dominion over nature. A common narrative element of Virgin Lands films, including *Heat*, is the desire of aspiring Komsomol members like Kemel' to learn how to operate tractors. Filmmakers also drew sharp contrasts between the tractors and other types of farming vehicles. In Shepit'ko's film, the brigade leader initially assigns Kemel' to drive a horse-drawn cart to the young man's great disappointment. In Medvedkin's *Restless Spring*, the fumbling Zhenya Omega tries to drive a tractor without adequate training and crashes into the outdoor brick stove of the temporary field kitchen. As punishment, he must drive a horse-drawn cart with a water barrel like the one Khmyr' (Petr Zinov'ev) drives in Medvedkin's *Schast'e / Happiness* (Moskinokombinat, 1935). The water cart in *Heat* recalls those in Medvedkin's films. Together, these water carts foreground a distinction between the mechanized, modern tractors and the rickety horse-drawn cart that appears as a vestige of the pre-industrial period.

In *Heat*, the mechanized vehicle is contested territory for the earnest believer in communist ideals and the cynical former model worker. Abakir restricts Kemel''s access to the tractor and turns the machine initially against him. In an early scene, when Abakir challenges Kemel' to find the water release valve of an overheated tractor, the handheld camera follows Kemel' as he squats down and looks under the vehicle. In the next shot, the camera shows the eager Komsomol member crawling underneath the tractor in close-up (Fig. 9.2). While the Komsomol enthusiast is underneath, Abakir releases the tractor's water on him. In this sequence, camera movement, shot scale, and *mise-en-scène* combine to create the impression that Kemel' had entered the machine. The underside of the mechanized vehicle and its internal build present new ways of considering the Soviet tractor, which is presented in Virgin Lands films frequently frontally, in perspective, or behind and heading away from the camera (**see Fig.** 9.2).

METHODS OF CONQUEST 189

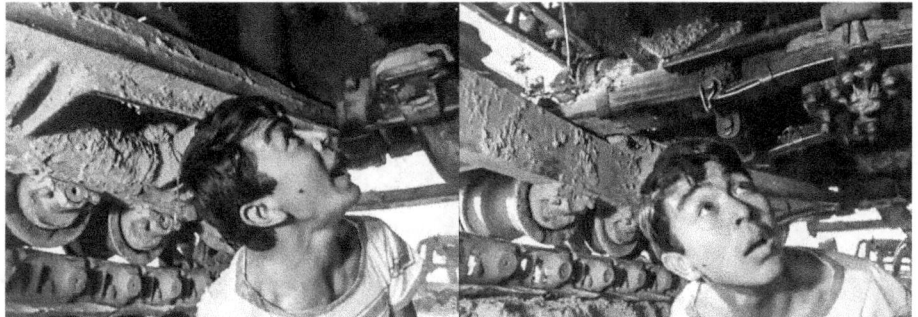

Figure 9.2 Kemel' underneath the tractor in *Heat*.

The struggle of wills between Kemel' and Abakir again visually foregrounds the mechanized vehicle when the young enthusiast declares that he will no longer operate the water cart and insists that the brigade leader assign him to one of the plow-trailers attached behind the tractors. Shepitko utilized handheld camerawork, acute angles, and close-up shots to emphasize the exacting long hours of plowing the arid steppe while foregrounding the tractor's size, mass, and plodding movement. The conflict between *Heat*'s protagonist and his adversary comes to a head when Kemel', at Kalipa's urging, starts up and begins to drive one of the tractors. When the enraged Abakir runs after him and stands in the tractor's path, the two characters have a tense stand-off, at the height of which a rapid montage sequence presents close-ups of the tractor, Kemel', and his antagonist. In this manner, Shepitko's *Heat* expands the reoccurring subplot of Virgin Lands films and the mastery of the tractor by developing a visual strategy reliant upon handheld camerawork, and close-up shots, both of which were popular stylistic devices of Thaw cinema initially mobilized in Mikhail Kalatozov and Sergei Urusevskii's *The First Echelon* and then further developed in *Letiat zhuravli / The Cranes are Flying* (Mosfil'm, 1957) and *Neotpravlennoe pis'mo / The Unsent Letter* (Mosfil'm, 1959).

DUBBING, AUDIOVISUAL COLONIALISM, AND THE ERASURE OF KYRGYZ VOICES

Up until Shepitko's *Heat*, many Virgin Lands films featured mainly ethnic Russian Komsomol settlers arriving to the Kazakhstan steppe. In 1965, Kazakh director Shaken Aimanov criticized films such as *It Began Like This*, *The First Echelon*, and *Horizon* for suggesting that the Virgin Lands were uninhabited. "And if a representative of the indigenous population suddenly appears in the frame, then he looks in these films like an 'exotic' pendant."[46] As Peter Rollberg asserts, Aimanov did not want Kazakhstan depicted as a "denationalized territory."[47] In this regard, the Kazakh actor and film director indicates the colonial implications of the Virgin Lands campaign, specifically in the cinematic depictions of the Soviet empire's borderlands and the people who live there.[48] Aimanov's film *We Live Here* presents one of the most heterogeneous casts in the Virgin Lands subgenre. Alongside ethnically Russian actors, the cast features Kazakh actors in prominent roles, including the regional and collective farm administrators, workers cultivating the land, a Kazakh family, and an ethnically mixed marriage.[49] As Michaela Pohl shows, "the Virgin Lands were not exactly virgin . . . they were populated by present and former Gulag inmates, Chechen, Ingush, and German exiles, as well as indigenous Kazakhs."[50] Virgin Lands films that show interactions between settlers and the local populations present these encounters positively and foreground cooperation, but historians suggest otherwise. The various groups newly arrived or previously residing in Kazakhstan in the 1950s interacted with each other frequently in tense and hostile ways, leading to hundreds of violent episodes and ethnic clashes.[51]

In Lev Kulidzhanov and Iakov Segel"s *It Began Like This*, the Komsomol members arrive in what appears to be an uninhabited part of the Kazakh steppe. The film doesn't include any characters or cast members from Kazakhstan. Mikhail Kalatozov's *The First Echelon* represents native Kazakhs in a few shots visiting the site of the sovkhoz. Aleksandr Medvedkin's *Restless Spring* features more scenes, which prominently include Kazakhs actors, including a Kazakh member of the Komsomol brigade Idris (Idris Nogabaev), who is in a relationship with Olga Kosharov (Rimma Shorokhva), a brigade leader named Khabash Atabaev (Kenebai Kozhabekov), and in one scene, the female chairman of a nearby state-farm, Khafiza Beisenova (Rakhiia Koichuaeva). Consequently, it is significant that Medvedkin made *Restless Spring* at the Alma-Ata Film Studio, which had regional interests in the theme of the Virgin Lands project.

Kyrgyz actors play all the major roles in Shepitko's film *Heat*. The director asserts that she was instructed to only use Kyrgyz performers and not to look for actors from other Soviet republics. Volotbek Shamshiev plays the film's main protagonist, the Komsomol member Kemel'. Khurmukhan Zhanturin plays Abakir Dzhurave, and Klara Iusupzhanova plays the role of Kalipa. Kyrgyz actors also played the roles of the film's secondary characters, such as the worker Sheishen (Kumbolot Dosumbaev), who desperately wants to leave the project, Sadabek (K. Esenov), the brigade leader, and his wife Al'dei (Darkul' Kuiukova). Non-Kyrgyz actors only appear in one scene, playing truck drivers from the nearby hydropower plant construction site. In this regard, the mostly Kyrgyz cast in *Heat* is a stark departure from the primary focus on ethnically Russian Komsomol members in the Virgin Lands film. However, in the official version of the film, the representation of Kyrgyz characters in *Heat* is restricted to the visual image since the dialogue in the film was dubbed by Russian voice actors, a common practice for films produced at the Kyrgyzfil'm Studio. This type of dubbing was part of broader dynamics related to the language spoken in cinema. James Steffan writes:

> Films in non-Russian languages were dubbed into Russian or given even more intrusive Russian voice-over summaries for distribution outside the republic of origin. On the surface, this was nothing unusual since in the Soviet film industry, much like in Italy, dialogue was generally post-synchronized from the start in domestic productions and imported films were also dubbed as a matter of routine. But given the significant role that nationality occupied in Soviet political discourse, dubbing could also be seen as a literal homogenization, even suppression, one might say, of the voice of non-Russian peoples.[52]

Shepitko was unsatisfied with the dubbing of *Heat*, considering it to be a total defeat ("I tut ia poterpela polnoe porazhenie") and asserting that the film is "badly voiced by wonderful actors" ("Fil'm preskverno ozvuchen prekrasnym akterami"). The film was dubbed at Gor'kii Film Studio in Moscow. According to Tolomush Okeev, *Heat*'s sound engineer, Shepitko was still experiencing symptoms of the viral infection during post-production work on the film. The theoretical portion of her diploma project reveals that afterward, she considered the film's soundtrack a significant failure. Initially, Shepitko states that *Heat* was post-synchronized by Russian actors ("Kartina tonirovalas' russkim akterami"). As James Steffan indicates, this was not unusual. However, Shepitko states that the actress Valentina Karaeva was not a good match for the visual image of Kalipa. The dissonance between voice and image is particularly noticeable in a scene near the middle of the film, in which the older Al'dei badgers an already distressed Kalipa, blaming the young woman for the abuse Abakir inflicts upon her. Klara Iusupzhnova's physical performance as Kalipa and Valentina Karaeva's voice are not synchronized, drawing attention to the film's dubbed soundtrack.

Continuing, Shepitko asserts that there was a much bigger problem with the sound. She reframes the post-production sound work on *Heat*, stating: "Essentially, the film was not post-synchronized, but dubbed" ("Po sushchestvy, proiskhodila ne tonirovka, a dubliazh"). This shift in the description of the soundtrack indicates a more profound intervention, which brings into question the film's audiovisual representation of Kyrgyz characters. As Shepitko states in her discussion of the film, Iosif Ol'shanksii wrote the literary scrip for *Heat* "without leaving Moscow," which implies that even though the film was based on the story of a prominent non-Russian writer, the literary treatment of the film was still developed in the colonizing center.[53] Shepitko rehearsed and shot the film in Russian, which was made difficult, according to the director, by the actors' "poor command" of the language.[54] She subsequently condemned this decision, claiming that it was a "major mistake" to make actors perform in a language foreign to them as it led to inhibition and artificiality.[55] Thus, the post-production dubbing erased and replaced the accented Russian of native voices and homogenized the visual representation of Kyrgyz characters, indicating mistreatment of non-Russian languages and accented Russian in Soviet cinema.

A similar situation occurred with Andrei Konchalovskii's adaptation of Chingiz Aitmatov's short story "The First Teacher" in a film with the same title.[56] After the production of *The First Teacher*, Konchalovskii lamented dubbing the Kyrgyz actors in his film using native Moscow-Russian voice actors. His original conception had been for the film to be in Kyrgyz. "The images would sound much more truthful, and authentic accompanied by the temperamental and staccato Kyrgyz speech with subtitles or, let's say, the translation of a voice-over narrator."[57] After the production, however, he was left without a rough-cut of the audio track ("chernovye fonogrammy") since the actors spoke interchangeably in Russian and Kyrgyz. Fearing that some semantic inflections from the script would be lost on viewers if the film was dubbed in Kyrgyz, Konchalovskii decided on Russian. Afterward, he regretted not at least having Kyrgyz speakers dub the film in Russian so that their accents would have preserved some of the color, intonational richness, and originality of the Turkic language. Discussing this issue in *Iskusstvo kino*, he calls the decision to dub the film in Russian a mistake, proclaiming that it was about time film crews were equipped with portable, noiseless sound recording equipment, which could record the authentic breath and intonation of actors in each step and movement.[58]

Unlike the dubbing in *The First Teacher* and *Heat*, there were contrasting developments in other Soviet non-Russian Republics. In Kazakhstan during the 1950s, there was a movement toward producing films in the native Kazakh language. "At a meeting of the Communist Party members of the Alma Alta film studio in 1958, a majority voted in favor of shooting all feature films in Kazakh, beginning in 1959."[59] Kazakh critics took strong positions in the debates regarding which language should be used in Alma Alta films. "Critic and film historian Kabysh Siranov was a strong proponent of shooting Kazakhstani pictures in Kazakh and only then dubbing them into Russian, or, alternatively, shooting a Russian version simultaneously alongside the primary Kazakh one."[60] In contrast to dubbing *Heat* with ethnic Russian voice actors, dubbing films into the majority language of the Central Asian Soviet Republics presents a different dynamic. Kyrgyzfil'm Studio began to dub feature films into Kyrgyz in 1953. By 1962, the studio had dubbed 200 of the best Soviet and foreign films. Gulbara Tolomushova, a specialist on Kyrgyz cinema, recently confirmed that *Heat* was subsequently dubbed into Kyrgyz for circulation in the republic.[61] However, dubbing was not extensive; by 1991, of the 5,577 films in the inventory of the Central State Archive of Film and Photography of the Kyrgyz Republic, only nine percent were dubbed into Kyrgyz.[62] Other republican studios dubbed films in non-Russian languages at higher numbers. In Kazakhstan in 1941, the State Film Committee issued an order to begin the systematic dubbing of feature films into the Kazakh language.[63] Kazakhfil'm Studio reportedly had the capacity to dub 70 films from Russian and other languages annually.[64] Tadjikfil'm studio dubbed 30–40 full-length feature films into Tadjik per year in addition to a number of documentaries.[65] By the 1970s, Uzbekfil'm Studio dubbed more than 60 films into Uzbek every year.[66] Turkmenfil'm dubbed about 50 Russian and foreign films per year into Turkmen.[67] According to Elena Razloga, Soviet republican studios selected films for dubbing based on their political importance; propaganda-themed documentaries and revolution-themed films were considered high priorities in this regard; and dubbing also considered the film's potential to attract a large audience.[68]

The post-production dubbing for *Heat* and *The First Teacher* should be considered in relation to broader developments in Soviet cinema of the Thaw and earlier periods. As Kristin Roth-Ey writes, "The USSR was a multilingual, multiethnic state; Soviet cinema as a market (as opposed to an art form) was not."[69] Roth-Ey continues, "Success on the all-Union screen spoke Russian, but more than that, it was channeled through Russia and *marked* Russian."[70] The systematic development of sound cinema technology in the 1920s revealed what Nataša Ďurovičova calls "the problem of language."[71] This problem was solved differently by various national cinemas. In the Soviet Union, subtitles as an option for translating films were limited initially due to illiteracy. Later, this avoidance of textual transcription persisted out of concern for the viewer's pleasure and the split attention that subtitles require. Eleonory Gilburd writes: "Dubbing and subtitling coexisted for much of the Soviet cinematic engagement with both sound and foreignness, but from the 1950s on, commercial release relied primarily on dubbing."[72]

Dubbing non-ethnic Russians into Russian by using actors with standard pronunciation raises questions about the relationship and the unity of the visual and audio tracks in *Heat* and *The First Teacher*. Gilburd explains: "During the global transition to sound in the late 1920s . . . the ventriloquism of the dub had disconcerted audiences across Europe. Dubbing erased original voices in an operation that felt eerie to spectators then and that some scholars have described as violent."[73] The increasing appearance of foreign films on Soviet screens in the 1950s was contingent upon dubbing these films into Russian. In this context, the Ministry of Culture and Goskino (The State Committee for Cinematography) utilized subtitles to limit access to foreign films, guided by the belief that few people would enjoy textual translations of films.[74] At the same time, as Gilburd points out: "Dubbing often has implied dissimulation . . . Dubbing hides its operation behind synchrony and so opens the door to trickery: different intonations, imperceptible shifts in connotation, or significant excisions. And it is a small step from dissimulation to censorship."[75] Shepitko's and Konchalovskii's post-production laments about the soundtrack of their debut films suggests their awareness that dubbing *Heat* and *First Teacher* into standard Russian brings about dissimulation and the whitewashing of both accented Russian and non-Russian Soviet languages. In this manner, *Heat* adjusts the genre formula as a Virgin Lands film by casting Kyrgyz actors for all major roles, but dubbing the film's soundtrack perpetuates the type of omissions in Virgin Lands, which Shaken Aimanov criticized.

CONCLUSION

All the films Kyrgyzfil'm Studio produced up to and including *Heat*, between 1953–1962, were dubbed into Russian, which means that this was the standard practice from 1953 when the studio began making fiction films. As it indicates an administrative and film industry bias toward the standard Russian dialect, the justification for dubbing Kyrgyzfil'm productions into the dominant language was to make them distributable throughout the Soviet Union. The film garnered positive critical attention at film festivals. *Heat* won the prize for best debut at the 14th Karlovy Vary IFF in 1963 and prizes for best film at the Frankfurt International Film Festival and the All-State Film Festival in Leningrad. At the International Film Festival of Central Asia and Kazakhstan in Dushban in 1964, *Heat* won awards for best film, and both Bolotbek Shamshiev and Klara Iusupzhanova received awards for their performances.

Since international and Soviet film festivals screened *Heat* with a Russian soundtrack, the awards given to Shamshiev and Iusupzhanova emphasize the relationship between the voice and the image, casting in relief the audiovisual methods of cultivating the Virgin Lands and their local inhabitants. Post-synchronization of the audio tracks and film images generates an illusion of reality that functions in Shepitko's *Heat* hand-in-hand with the cultivation of the supposedly empty steppe. In this regard, Shepitko's and Konchalovskii's comments indicate that overwriting the native language eliminated a sense of aural authenticity. This artificiality is even more glaring in the context of cultural developments during the post-Stalinist Thaw that emphasized authenticity and sincerity as cultural values. In the context of the Virgin Lands films, *Heat* represents the synergy of linguistic and visual colonial strategies of the Soviet center toward the borderlands of the empire.

NOTES

1. Shepitko, Larisa. "Znoi: Teoreticheskaia chast' diplomnoi raboty L. Shepitko," in *Larisa: Kniga o Larise Shepitko* edited by Elem Klimov (Moscow: Iskusstvo, 1987), 153.
2. Scholars such as Jane Costlow, Liudmila Mazur, and Mieka Erley have previously discussed Sheptiko's *Heat* in the context of Khrushchev's major agricultural campaign and films about Soviet collective farms. My essay builds upon these studies by examining patterns of continuity and change in film style. See Mazur, Liudmila "Zabytaia legenda: Khudozhestvennye *fil'my* ob osvoenii tseliny 1950–1970–kh gg.," *Dokument. Arkhiv. Istoriia. Sovremennost': Materialy VI Mezhdunardonoi nauchno-prakticheskoi konferentsii*, Ekaterinburg. 2–3 December, 2016, 477–484; Costlow, Jane "Parched: Water and its absence in the films of Larisa Shepit'ko," in *Meaning and Values of Water in Russian Culture*, edited by Jane Costlow and Arja Rosenholm (New York: Routledge, 2017), 207–221; Erley, Mieka. *On Russian Soil: Myth and Materiality* (DeKalb: Northern Illinois University Press, 2021), 113–129.

    My discussion draws on previous writing about the depiction of landscape and space in Soviet culture and film. Specifically, Shepitko's representation of the arid steppe can be contrasted to the acculturated, pastoral landscapes in Stalinist films and the Thaw-era re-engagement with nature on a human scale. See Margolit, Evgenii. "Peizazh s geroem," *Kinematograf ottepeli. Kniga pervaia.* edited by Vitalii Troianovskii. Materik, 1996, 99–117; Oukaderova, Lida. *The Cinema of The Soviet Thaw: Space, Materiality, Movement* (Bloomington: Indiana University Press, 2017); Widdis, Emma. *Visions of a New Land: Soviet Film from the Revolution to the Second World War* (New Haven: Yale University Press, 2003); Dobrenko, Evgenii, and Eric Naiman, Eds. *The Landscape of Stalinism: The Art and Ideology of Soviet Space* (Seattle: University of Washington Press, 2003).

    My research and thinking about Shepitko's *Heat* also benefited from my supervision of a Master's Thesis on the development of Kyrgyz cinema, which discussed *Heat* as an opportunity for native film-workers to gain training and work experience as part of Shepitko's film crew. Tureski, Andrew. "Kyrgyzfil'm and the Onscreen Development of Kyrgyz Culture and National Identity," 2022, University of Toronto, Master's Thesis.

    This project also benefited from suggestion and comments by colleagues in the Department Slavic Languages and Literature at the University of Toronto, where an early version of this text was presented on October 26, 2022.
3. Okeev, Tolomush. "Kak molody my byli . . .," *Larisa: Kniga o Larise Shepitko* edited by Elem Klimov (Moscow: Iskusstvo, 1987), 113.
4. Shepiko, "Znoi," 154.
5. Ibid.
6. Kaganovsky, Lilya. "Ways of Seeing: On Kira Muratova's *Brief Encounters* and Larisa Shepit'ko's *Wings*," *The Russian Review*, Vol. 71, No. 3, 2012, 482–499.
7. Stites, Richard. "To the Virgin Lands: The Epic and the Idyll in the Cinematic Representation of Khrushchev's Great Adventure," in *Passion and Perception:*

Essays on Russian Culture by Richard Stites, edited by David Goldfrank (Washington D.C.: New Academia Publishing, 2010), 309.
8. Rollberg, Peter. *The Cinema of Soviet Kazakhstan, 1925–1991* (Lanham: Lexington Books, 2021), 87.
9. Kapterev, Sergei. Post-Stalinist Cinema and the Russian Intelligentsia, 1953–1960: Strategies of Self-Representation, De-Stalinization, and the National Cultural Tradition. PhD diss., (New York University, 2005), 162–164.
10. Margolit, Evgenii. "Peizazh s geroem," *Kinematograf ottepeli. Kniga pervaia.* edited by Vitalii Troianovskii. (Moscow: Materik, 1996), 99–117.
11. Gulbara Tolomushova, email message to author. October 25, 2022.
12. See "Znoi" in Antropov, V. N. and E. M. Barykin, Eds. *Sovetskie khudozhestvennye fil'my. Annotirovanny katalog.* vol. 4 (1958–1963), (Moscow: Iskusstvo, 1968), 470; "Fil'mografiia," *Iskusstvo kino*, no. 6, 1963, 150.
13. Kinostudiia Kyrgyzfil'm. http://kirgizfilm.ru/. Accessed 10 October, 2022.
14. Shepitko, Larisa. "Znoi," *YouTube*, uploaded by Kinostudiia Kyrgyzfil'm, 12 December, 2019, https://www.youtube.com/watch?v=3L7miNEFWpo.
15. Kozlov, Denis. Introduction. *The Thaw: Soviet Society and Culture during the 1950s and 1960s*, edited by Denis Kozlov and Eleonory Gilburd (Toronto: University of Toronto Press, 2013), 10.
16. Michaela Pohl, "From White Grave to Teslinograd to Astana: The Virgin Lands Opening, Khurshchev's Fogotten First Reforms," in *The Thaw: Soviet Society and Culture during the 1950s and 1960s*, edited by Denis Kozlov and Eleonory Gilburd (Toronto: University of Toronto Press, 2013), 276.
17. Kelly, Catriona. *Soviet Art House: Lenfilm Studio under Brezhnev* (New York: Oxford University, Press, 2021), 13.
18. Zubok, Vladislav. *Zhivago's Children: The Last Russian Intelligentsia* (Cambridge: Belknap Press of Harvard UP, 2009), 125.
19. Pohl, *The Virgin Lands Between Memory and Forgetting: People and Transformation in the Soviet Union, 1954–1960*, Phd diss. (Indiana University, 1999), 145.
20. Pohl, "From White Grave to Tselinograd to Astana," 272.
21. See McCauley, Martin. *Krushchev and the Development of Soviet Agriculture* (London: Macmillan Press, 1976), 216.
22. Pohl, "From White Grave to Tselinograd to Astana," 271.
23. Paul Josephson et al., *An Environmental History of Russia* (Cambridge: Cambridge University Press, 2013), 145.
24. Pohl, "From White Grave to Tselinograd to Astana," 301.
25. Ibid., 300.
26. See Uvarkina M. A. and O. Iu, Uvarkina, "'Tselinnaia epopeia': Istoriko-politologicheskii analiz," *Nauka o cheloveke: gumanitarnye issledovaniia*, No. 1, Vol. 11, 2013. 180–189. https://cyberleninka.ru/article/n/tselinnaya-epopeya-istoriko-politologicheskiy-analiz/viewer. Accessed December 8, 2022. Ardak Serikbaevna Abdiraiymova, Roza Seidalievna Zharkynbaeva, and Akylbek Bedelkhanovich Carsenbaev, "Sotsial'no-ekonomicheskie i politicheskie aspekty osvoeniia tselinnykh I zalezhnykh zemel' v Kazakhstane," *Oriental Studies*, No. 2, Vol. 15, 2022, 214–227. https://cyberleninka.ru/article/n/sotsialno-

ekonomicheskie-i-politicheskie-aspekty-osvoeniya-tselinnyh-i-zalezhnyh-zemel-v-kazahstane/viewer. Accessed December 8, 2022.
27. Literary texts about Khrushchev's program include the collection *Na zemliakh tselinnykh / In the Virgin Lands* (1955), which included lyric poems and short stories. Poems and short texts were also published in Soviet newspapers and magazines. See Erley, *On Russian Soil*, 115–116. For documentary films about the Virgin Lands campaign see Sidenova, Raisa. "The Topographical Aesthetics in Late Stalinist Soviet Documentary Film," *A Companion to Documentary Film History*, edited by Joshua Malitsky (Hoboken, NJ: Wiley Blackwell, 2021), 71-94.
28. McCallum, Claire E., *The Fate of the New Man: Representing & Reconstructing Masculinity in Soviet Visual Culture, 1945–1965* (DeKalb: Northern Illinois University Press, 2018), 47.
29. Stites, Richard. *Russian Popular Culture: Entertainment and Society since 1900* (Cambridge: Cambridge University Press, 1992), 144.
30. Erley, *On Russian Soil*, 115.
31. Ibid., 116.
32. Khrushchev, Nikita. "Osvoenie tseliny–bol'shaia pobeda Leninskoi politiki partii," *Pravda*, 19 March, 1961, 4.
33. In their previously cited studies, Mieka Erley and Claire McCollum discuss the paintings of the Virgin Lands. Additionally, L. G. Apen'sheva discusses paintings and posters produced about the agricultural projects in "Tema tseliny v otechestvennoi zhivopisi," in *Agrarnaia nauka – sel'skomu khoziaistvu: sbornik materialov: XIII Mezhdunarodnaia nauchno-prakticheskaia konferencuia* (Conference Proceedings), February 15–16, 2018, 116–119, Barnaul, Russian Federation: Altai State University. For a discussion of Virgin Lands posters, see Ioffe, Mark, "Agitatsionnye plakaty na sel'skokhoziaistvennye temy," *Iskusstvo*, No. 4, 1955.
34. Slavin, K. "Geroi pervoi vesny," *Sovetskaia kul'tura*, July 13, 1954, 1.
35. Liudmila Mazur includes Shepitko's film in the group of films connected to the "Virgin Lands" campaign. Her list consists of fiction films directly related to the Virgin Lands campaign: *Nadezhda / Hope* (Gor'kii Studio, dir./scen. Sergei Gerasimov, 1954), *Pervyi eshelon / The First Echelon /* (Mosfi'm, Mikhail Kalatozov, 1955), *Eto hachinalos' tak / It Began Like This* (Gor'kii Studio, Lev Kulidzhanov and Iakov Segel', 1956), *Berezy v stepi / Birch Trees in the Steppe* (Alma-Ata Film Studio/Kazakhfilm Studio, Georgii Pobedonostsev, 1956), *Ivan Brovkin na Tseline / Ivan Brovkin in the Virgin Lands* (Gor'kii Studio, Ivan Lukinskii, 1958), *Alenka* (Mosfi'm, Boris Barnet, 1961), *Znoi / Heat* (Kyrgyzfil'm Studio, Larisa Shepitko, 1963), *Poseldnii khleb / The Last Bread* (Belarus'fil'm, Boris Stepanov, 1963). "Zabytaia legenda: Khudozhestvennye *fil'my* ob osvoenii tseliny 1950–1970–kh gg.," *Dokument. Arkhiv. Istoriia. Sovremennost': Materialy VI Mezhdunardonoi nauchno-prakticheskoi konferentsii*, Ekaterinburg. 2–3 December, 2016. Ural Federal University, 2016, 479. I would also add: *Mat' i syn / Mother and Sun* (Alma-Ata Film Studio/Kazakhfilm Studio, Sultan-Akhmet Khodzhikov, 1955), *Bespokoinaia vesna / Restless Spring* (Alma-Ata Film Studio/Kazakhfilm Studio, Aleksandr Medvedkin, 1956), *My zdes' zhivem /*

We Live Here (Alma-Ata Film Studio/Kazakhfilm Studio, Shaken Aimanov, 1956), *Gorizont / The Horizon* (Lenfilm, Iosif Kheifits, 1961), *Odnazhdy noch'iu / One Night* (Alma-Ata Film Studio/Kazakhfilm Studio, Aleksandra Gintsburga & Emira Faika, 1959); as well as documentary films: *Pervaia vesna / The First Spring*, (CSDF, Aleksandr Medvedkin, 1954), *Novosti dnia No. 17 / News of the Day No. 17* (CSDF, A. Rybakova, 1954), *My byli na tseline / We were in the Virgin Lands* (CSDF, V. Troshkin & V. Khodiakov, 1956).

36. Stites, "To the Virgin Lands," 315.
37. Rollberg, Peter, "Shepitko, Larisa Efremova," *Historical Dictionary of Russian and Soviet Cinema* (Lanham: The Scarecrow Press, 2009), 622.
38. Bulgakowa, Oksana. "The Socialist Hybrids," in *Genre Hybridisation: Global Cinema Flows*, edited by Ivo Ritzer and Peter W. Shulze (Marburg: Schüren, 2013), 338.
39. Erley, *One Russian Soil*, 117.
40. Ibid., 113.
41. Ibid., 121–123.
42. Bulgakowa, "The Socialist Hybrids," 337.
43. Ibid.
44. Costlow connects *Heat* to the depiction of tractors in Dovzhenko's *Earth* and Eisenstein's *The General Line* as well as the *Tractor Drivers* and *The Vow*, See Costlow, "Parched: Water and its absence in the films of Larisa Shepit'ko," 213–214.
45. Ibid, 214.
46. Aimanov, Shaken. "Obrashchaias' k druz'iam," *Iskusstvo kino*, No. 10, 1965, 19.
47. Rollberg, *The Cinema of Soviet Kazakhstan, 1925–1991*, 91.
48. In this regard, this essay draws on previous work in Russian studies examining the Soviet bloc through postcolonialism and the representation of the ethnic, Oriental Other in Russian and Soviet Cinema. For examples, see Honarpisheh, Farbod. "The Oriental 'Other' in Soviet Cinema, 1924–34," *Critique: Critical Middle Eastern Studies*, Vol. 14, No. 2, 2005, 185–201.
49. An interethnic romance is also featured in Aleksandr Medvedkin's film *Restless Spring* (1956).
50. Kozlov, Denis. "Introduction," *The Thaw*, edited by Denis Kozlov and Eleonory Gilburd (Toronto: University of Toronto Press, 2013), 10. Pohl, "From White Grave to Teslinograd to Astana," 10–11.
51. Ibid.
52. Steffan, James. *The Cinema of Sergei Parajanov* (Madison: University of Wisconsin Press, 2013), 79.
53. Shepitko, *Larisa: Kniga o Larise Shepitko*, 163.
54. "Vse oslozhnialos' pokhim znaniem russkogo iazyka." Ibid., 159.
55. "Ibo eto velo k neizbezhnomy zazhimu i naigryshu." Ibid.
56. Filmmakers, critics, and scholars tend to relate *Heat* to Andrey Konchalovskii's *Pervyi uchitel' / The First Teacher* (Mosfilm and Kyrgyzfil'm, 1965), also his first films; both are adaptations of literary texts by Chingiz Aitmatov, both were filmed in Kyrgyzstan, and feature Kyrgyz actors almost exclusively. Doraiswamy, Rashmi. "The Encounter of Modernities: Cinematic Adaptations of Two Stories by Aitmatov," *Cultural Histories of Central Asia*, edited by Rashmi Doraiswamy,

Routledge, 2022, 132–152. See also Bazarov, Gennadi. "A Culture to Share with the Young," and Tolomush Okeev, "Searching for a Lost identity," *Cinemas of the Other: A Personal Journey with Film-Makers from the Middle East and Central Asia*, edited by Gonul Donmez-Colin (Intellect, 2006), 191–197, 197–203; Stishova, Elena. "Re-visions of *The Sky of Our Childhood*," *Cinema in Central Asia Rewriting Cultural Histories*, edited by Michael Rouland, Gulnara Abikeyeva, and Birgit Beumers (I. B.Tauris, 2013), 137–146.

57. ". . . gorazdo pravdivee i dostovernee budut zvuchat' eti kadry, soprovozhdaemye kirgizskoi temperamentnoi i otryvistoi rech'iu s subtitrami, skazhem, ili s perevodom." Mikhalkov-Konchalovskii, Andrei. "Nekotorye soobrazheniia po postanovke 'Pervogo uchitelia'", *Iskusstvo kino*. No. 1 (January 1967), 42.
58. Ibid.
59. Rollberg, *The Cinema of Soviet Kazakhstan, 1925–1991*, 111.
60. Ibid.
61. Gulbara Tolomushova, email message to author, October 25, 2022.
62. Rollberg, Peter, "Kyrgyzfilm Studio," *Historical Dictionary of Russian and Soviet Cinema* (Lanham: The Scarecrow Press, 2009), 391; Eugene Huskey, "Kyrgyzstan: The Politics of Demographic and Economic Frustration," *New States, New Politics Building the Post-Soviet Nations*, edited by Ian Bremmer and Ray Taras (Cambridge University Press, 1997), 26.
63. Rollberg, Peter. *The Cinema of Soviet Kazakhstan 1925–1991*, 39.
64. Ibid., 188.
65. Rollberg, Peter. "Tadjikfilm Studio," *Historical Dictionary of Russian and Soviet Cinema* (Lanham: The Scarecrow Press, 2009), 679.
66. Rollberg, Peter. "Uzbekfilm Studio," *Historical Dictionary of Russian and Soviet Cinema* (Lanham: The Scarecrow Press, 2009), 721.
67. Rollberg, Peter. "Turkmenfilm Studio," *Historical Dictionary of Russian and Soviet Cinema* (Lanham: The Scarecrow Press, 2009), 708.
68. Elena Razloga, email message to author. October 30, 2022.
69. Roth-Ey, Kristin. *Moscow Prime Time: How the Soviet Union Built the Media Empire That Lost the Cultural Cold War* (Ithaca: Cornell University Press, 2011), 86.
70. Ibid., 87.
71. Ďurovičova, Nataša. "Translating America: The Hollywood Multilinguals 1929–1933." In *Sound Theory/Sound Practice*, edited by Rick Altman, (New York: Routledge, 1992), 139.
72. Eleonory Gilburd, *To See Paris and Die: The Soviet Lives of Western Culture* (Cambridge: The Belknap Press of Harvard University Press, 2018), 178.
73. Ibid.
74. Ibid., 180.
75. Ibid.

CHAPTER 10

Larisa Shepitko's Ecologies

Lida Oukaderova

Larisa Shepitko's directorial career is bracketed by two films, *Heat* (Znoi,1963) and *Farewell* (Proshchanie, 1981), that directly engage Soviet environmental practices by looking at specific episodes of the Soviet "conquest" of nature and its effects on human life.[1] In *Heat*, it is the effort to develop the virgin deserts of Kyrgyzstan into fertile agricultural fields that comes under the camera's close scrutiny. And in *Farewell*—a work that was mostly filmed by Shepitko's husband Elem Klimov after she died in a car accident just at the start of the shoot—it is the life and death of Matiora, a small island shown in its last days of existence, just before it would be flooded as part of a hydroelectric station's construction. Based on these two films, it is safe to say that the natural consequences of Soviet industrial developments were central to Shepitko's cinematic thinking. This is not at all surprising, given that ecological criticism began to permeate Soviet public and scientific debates with increasing urgency in the 1960s and especially 1970s, just at the height of Shepitko's career. It was, indeed, becoming a pervasive matter that was impossible to ignore. Shepitko's environmental filmmaking, furthermore, is not to be restricted to works explicitly about the Soviet industrialization of nature. Although her most acclaimed production, *The Ascent* (Voskhozhdenie, 1977), is far removed from such a focus, turning instead to partisan fighting in rural Belorussia during World War II, nature remains crucial to the film. More than half its running time pictures Belorussia's open, freezing, snow-covered landscapes that are endlessly traversed by its protagonists—with the spaces' overwhelming, strange whiteness providing a lasting image of the environment within which human struggles transpire.[2] While the film's intense narrative drama revolves around the partisans' moral resilience and betrayal, its visual form instantiates a restless exploration of how to shoot and represent the natural setting in which this story unfolds. It is in such explorations—in Shepitko's diverse representational forms—that I want to locate her ecological preoccupations, as her practices of filming nature raise questions of what it means to look at the world in an environmentally just way, and who might be a subject capable of enacting such a vision.

After a brief discussion of the 1950s and 60s Soviet "conquest" of nature and the environmental criticism this generated—addressing, in particular, the apparent shift in this ecological criticism's conception of the human subject vis-à-vis the natural world—this chapter will turn to Shepitko's three films *Heat*, *The Ascent*, and *Farewell*, although I will limit my analysis of the last film to only a few observations, since it is primarily a product of Klimov rather than Shepitko. I argue that Shepitko's ecological visuality unfolds through a persistent discord between her landscapes and the humanist values, rooted in longstanding historical and moral imperatives, that her characters' actions and thoughts exemplify. Pervasive, excessively material, and often hostile, Shepitko's landscapes fail to align with the rightfulness of her unquestionably virtuous protagonists. It appears, in this discord, that her life-long scrutiny of the depth of human morality stands at odds with her ardent commitment to cinema's material realism—to the kind of exposition of physical reality through the recording camera that Siegfried Kracauer advocated in his writings on film. Her narrative exploration of looking "up," toward the heights of human capacity, is expressed nowhere more forcefully than in the literal and metaphorical language of upwards movement in *The Ascent*; but in the same film, this rising view is persistently counteracted by her camera's look *downwards*, by its "descent" towards the earthly ground, the inhuman, the non-moral. In this contrast, Shepitko suggests it is not the moral and historically progressive human subject through whom natural reality—or more precisely stated, nature as a subject of ecological vision and consciousness—can be made present on screen, but rather the material workings of film itself.

In such confrontation between nature's material documentation and its perception through a historically and morally progressive subjective lens, Shepitko's work offers a productive case study for ecological film theory. Jennifer Fay's *Inhospitable World: Cinema in the Time of the Anthropocene* is of a particular interest to this chapter, and especially Fay's impactful rereading of Kracauer's writings on film and photography in light of more recent ecological discussions. As is well known, Kracauer described our relationship to the world as a process of ever-increasing "receding": ideology, religion and, eventually, science have dominated the ways of our environmental understanding and, in the process, impaired our ability to experience reality in all its flows, contingencies, and material particularities. Cinema, rooted in a mechanical recording of the world and thus freed of predetermined human perception, "renders visible what we did not, or perhaps even could not, see before its advent . . . and we are free to experience it because we are fragmentized."³ Writing this after World War II, Kracauer imagines the subject's "fragmentation" as a form of release from all master narratives, faith in which could not but shatter in the wake of wartime atrocities that had been previously unthinkable—a release that makes viewers more attuned to film images marked "by a fringe of indeterminate visible meanings."⁴

Recorded nature is the embodiment of indeterminacy *par excellence*. It is, Fay asserts, "what history does not account for and what challenges ideological claims to coherence or totality. A 'natural' image may appear to the onlooker as almost incomprehensible matter."⁵ A cinematically reproduced nature challenges any conceptually totalizing framework, evacuating its meanings, depriving viewing subjects of any stable epistemological position.⁶ This liberation from conceptual frameworks, be they grounded in ideology, religion or science, cannot be thought of as simply a "progressive" emancipation in any conventional way—to be subject to such release is to lose one's sense of wholeness, and with that, a stable position of mastery in the world. Via Kracauer and his interpreter Gerhard Richter, Fay describes this loss of position as an experience of "extraterritoriality"—a condition in which our place of habitation is forever estranged and cannot be felt anymore as home. In contrast to the typical canonization of Kracauer's exile writing as that of a humanist, Fay stresses that he is "among the more prominent postwar intellectuals to promote alienation, dejection, and experiences of desubjectification ... as foundations for critical thought."⁷ He also promotes these as foundations for cinematic experience, in which film technology might help us "to imagine an estranged and selfless relationship to an inhospitable or even posthospitable earth that may not accommodate us."⁸ Freed from the burden of knowledge, consented to a dejected position, the viewer might reconsider, through film, how to relate to the world anew, to tune into its indeterminate and meaningless contingencies, all while aware that neither a harmonic unity with this world nor mastery of it is possible.

All this said, Kracauer's writings cannot be blindly imposed on Soviet cultural production. Most significantly, his consideration of WWII atrocities as a turning point of human release from any totalizing faith cannot be easily justified for Soviet culture: after all, the latter reaffirmed, through the war suffering and victories, the superiority of Soviet subjectivity, continuing to exploit war experiences for the celebration of Soviet, and later Russian, conceptions of selfhood and state.⁹ But the final two decades of Soviet socialist culture—that is, the 1970s and 80s, nearly the entirety of Shepitko's film-making career— were marked by a steadily declining faith in the socialist project. An ecological turn that took place in Soviet thinking about nature during these same decades contributed, at least partially, to this decline: first, it made painfully obvious the *global* nature of the environmental crisis, disregarding nations' ideological foundations and historical aspirations; and second, it brought home the profound errancy of humans' belief in their supremacy within/over systems of the natural world, as both scientists and philosophers began to stress humans' necessary imbrication into the network of all-existing material and atmospheric phenomena. Shepitko's cinema is part of this ecological turn: it repeatedly questions the validity of Soviet history and subjectivity in the face of the inhospitable surrounding world, just as it persistently situates "alienation, dejection and experiences of desubjectification" as a mental place from within which to perceive, inhabit, and relate to the earth. Every film discussed in this chapter closes with an "extraterritorial"—or more simply stated, homeless—view onto the world. If faith, alternately in Soviet history or Christian narrative, exists in *Heat* and *The Ascent* as a (however feeble) counter to such displacement, extraterritoriality, in *Farewell*, is a final, all-encompassing condition: it is positioned as the ultimate reality to be reached at socialism's end road.

SOVIET ENVIRONMENTALISM

In the decade before Shepitko finished her studies at VGIK in 1963, the USSR staged multiple exuberant celebrations over the country's continuing "conquests" of nature, which were then followed by rapidly intensifying public debates over the environmental catastrophes these conquests produced. The Soviet leader Nikita Khrushchev's "Virgin Lands" campaign of the 1950s is well known. Fearful of food shortages in a shrinking economy immediately after Stalin's death, Khrushchev implemented a policy of massive development of agricultural lands that had been deemed infertile, especially in Western Siberia and Kazakhstan, often to the dismay of local authorities who worried of a Russian takeover of their territories.[10] After a highly successful mobilization campaign in the mid-1950s, cemented in romantic images of young people arriving on trains to remote and unwelcoming terrain, Khrushchev relished his program's apparent initial success: Soviet grain output increased by 70 percent toward the end of the 1950s in comparison to the last five years of Stalin's regime. But by the early 1960s, the Virgin Lands' harvests peaked and began to diminish, failing to meet governmental and popular expectations. In 1963, drought hit many of the newly developed areas, unleashing a new cycle of food shortages, necessitating a grain acquisition from abroad, and drawing renewed scrutiny to just how ill-suited these lands were for industrial-scale agriculture.[11] In the meantime, the Central Asian Aral Sea—in the past the world's fourth-largest lake, now nearly completely dried up—started to shrink, as water from the feeding rivers was diverted toward irrigation systems for the neighboring cultivation of cotton fields. By the time the USSR collapsed, many of the formerly Virgin Lands had returned to their unproductive state, only now abused by industrialization and chemicals that had been used unchecked in the previous decades.[12]

Postwar environmental disasters were not limited to the development of Virgin Lands but encompassed the industrial air and water pollution throughout Soviet territories, stretching from Lake Baikal in Siberia to the Kola peninsula in the Arctic North. Concerned primarily with economic development and modernization, Khrushchev's policies significantly accelerated the degradation of eco-systems.[13] But precisely because of that, the country began to experience a rise in public environmental criticism, which eventually grew into a significant ecological movement, supported by scientific institutions and popular activism. In the late 1950s, a number of Soviet republics passed a series of environmental laws, including the 1960s Law on Nature Protection in the Russian Federation.[14] Although these laws, according to historical assessments, did little to effect consequential change, they provided a framework for discussions and for the emergence of non-governmental activist groups throughout Soviet territories, paralleling the process taking place in much of the industrialized world. As the historian Julia Obertreis puts it in reference specifically to Central Asian environmental developments, if the debate on the misuse of natural resources was already well in place by the early 1960s, by 1975 the issue of *ecology* as such entered the public realm, with a demand for an "ecological style of thinking" and an "ecological ethics of scientific and technical cadres."[15] Such thinking implied not only a consideration of the ecological repercussions of new engineering projects but also a broader, philosophical discussion about "mankind's responsibility to future generations and . . . the need to harmonize technology and nature."[16]

The shift from environmental to ecological thinking entailed a broader acknowledgement of the all-encompassing and often irreversible effects of human life on the environment. Evoking the proper meaning of "ecology," it also entailed recognition of the perpetual interactions between all organic and inorganic elements and systems, within which the human was only one—however highly effectual—participant. This latter fact could not have remained inconsequential for Soviet conceptions of history and mankind. Although Soviet scientists and philosophers generally continued to insist that a socialist state and its planned economy was much better equipped to provide solutions to ecological crises while still serving *the interests of men*, they also understood the extreme complexity of ecological considerations, within which the "interests of men" was a rather dubious category. In a discussion of knowledge acquisition in ecological studies, a certain Yurii Trusov stressed specifically the groundlessness of placing any subject at the center of any particular environment: "the ecological approach can be represented as research into the interaction of a certain, arbitrary, 'central,' 'principal' object X with its environment . . . within an ecosphere's system."[17] The central, principal object in Trusov's discussion is explicitly not fixed (in other words, it does not have to be human, and when it is, it is only so accidentally), and his use of quotation marks indicates clearly the randomness of who, or what, might occupy this role. Any element, any "sub-system" or "medium"—such as air currents, an insect, a soil sample, or molecular particles—might take central stage within ecological studies, thus providing a new angle from which to consider a system's whole operation and significance.

Thus, if an "ecological style of thinking" were to become dominant in Soviet discourse, Marxist historical teleology could hardly be maintained. Accordingly, the scientist Moisei Markov wrote in his aptly titled 1977 article "Are We Learning to Think Anew?" that "it has become a recognized fact that civilized society is still intensively 'working' on transforming our planet, where nature herself once created the conditions for the origins of life, into a desert, annihilating life."[18] Without dividing the world into socialist and capitalist camps, and appealing to people primarily as earthly inhabitants rather than ideological subjects, he pivots ecology against global human history, considering the latter as an accelerated process towards death rather than toward an improved life. Similar ideas, which the environmental historian John Bellamy Foster designated as "global humanism," were articulated by the Soviet philosopher Ivan Frolov, who argued for "moving away from the illusion of anthropocentrism and rejecting the traditional hegemonic relationship to nature."[19] Much Soviet ecological writing, to be sure, maintained that socialist planning would allow for a responsible use of natural resources to prevent environmental catastrophe; at the same time, the very premise of ecological science as manifested in these Soviet writings articulated a conflict between human history and natural development, one that demoted the human subject from a position of dominance to one of equivalence with any other terrestrial organism.

HEAT

As part of her final project for the studies at VKIG, Shepitko travelled to Kyrgyzstan in 1962 to work on a film adaptation of Chingiz Aitmatov's just-published 1961 story "The Camel's Eye." After a prolonged filming that was interrupted by Shepitko's and others' serious cases of hepatitis, the film was released to significant critical acclaim, earning the young director Soviet and international film prizes and helping to launch her career. The film's subject could not be more fitting for the times: it is set in the wide-open Anarkhai steppes, where a unit of just six people, living in a yurt, plows daily the expansive surrounding fields with the charge of transforming them into fruitful agrarian terrain. Shepitko described her interest in Aitmatov's story as a way to explore the young, post-Stalinist generation and to understand the parameters of the new Soviet "positive hero": "Who is he, the young person (*chelovek*) of the 60s? What is his inner world, his ideals? What does he rebel against and what does he support? And, most importantly, is he aware of the full responsibility laid on him by the time and the people?"[20] The film establishes such a "hero" in the figure of Kemel'—an idealistic young man who is fully committed to Soviet industrial and agricultural goals and is deeply infected with the romanticism of such pursuits. His idealism, however, quickly crashes against the cynicism of Abakir, a highly skillful, exemplary socialist worker whose attitude and character are however far from properly "socialist." Abakir is presented as an objectionable despot of the Stalinist generation, whose vileness becomes especially obvious in his treatment of the young female brigade member Kalipa, whom he abuses physically and exploits emotionally. Throughout the film, he also takes as his task to mistreat Kemel', constantly undermining his beliefs and work dedication.

One of the major confrontations between these two male figures concerns precisely the Virgin Lands of the Anarkhai steppes. At one point, Abakir sarcastically questions Kemel': "Do you still believe in this nonsense [of a better life on Earth]? You should believe only your own eyes and hands. Look around, look at this dead soil. Do you know why we need to plow this dust? To prove to our descendants that nothing can grow here." Kemel', fully in tune with Soviet politics of land cultivation, reacts to this statement with horror. We, too, are meant to sympathize with the film's positive hero, to take *his* point of view, not Abakir's. And yet the camera seems to do the opposite throughout the film, readily accepting Abakir's advice to look with "one's own eyes" at the surrounding fields in order to make a judgement of how things really are on this Kyrgyz terrain. What we witness is not far from Abakir's truth. The film is filled with shots of the steppe's "dead soil," which surrounds and dwarfs the protagonists, and on which nothing but thorny, parched bushes grow. The only "product" of their plowed fields appears to be the dry, dirty dust that sweeps up and covers the workers during their exhausting labor. If in most Soviet films on the development of Virgin Lands, the results of harsh work are evident in the ultimate appearance of lush fields, the landscape of *Heat* remains bare and arid until the film's last image. The only tangible difference between developed and undeveloped grounds are the plowed rows of black soil that, however, display even less vegetation than the uncultivated surface. Things are also not helped when Kemel' runs into another group of workers in the area, who are supposedly building an irrigation system for the desert. Although Kemel' seems to easily accept their work will bring much-needed water to the area, these men are portrayed as a brutish bunch, manically driving through the fields with no clear purpose and never shown realizing any kind of agrarian transformation.

Where *Heat*'s landscape *does* exhibit life that is visually more agreeable with human values is in a side story focusing on Kemel's encounters with a young, native shepherdess: the two strike up a romantic relationship that develops entirely in the open nature. In an overtly symbolic act, their first encounter takes place at a water spring surrounded by a tiny oasis of lush vegetation—the only natural water source in the immediate surroundings. In later sequences of their encounters, the images of "dead soil" yield to shots of the landscape's attractive, curvy hills where the couple rides horses and which the shepherdess in particular traverses effortlessly. It is, indeed, through the figure of this young woman that Shepitko reimagines landscape as an inhabitable and metaphorically "fertile" place, able to accommodate harmoniously both people and animals. The Shepherdess herself is shown as an exotic animal of sorts: nameless, never saying a word, and communicating through gestures, grimaces, horse riding and occasional laughter. She is one with nature and animals, moving through the fields with fluid ease—all in stark contrast to the obsolete, taxing labor of the agricultural unit.

On the one hand, such images insist that no matter how grim and lifeless the landscape is, it becomes graceful and alive when freed from the human insistence to treat it as a means to economic and ideological ends. On the other hand, the projection of a Soviet colonial imaginary onto the landscape cannot be overlooked. These images preach a return to the past, to a kind of preindustrial, and even preverbal, culture. It is striking that the shepherdess is never shown in any social environment of her own, appearing out of—and disappearing into—nowhere every time she is active in a scene. If the film wants to suggest there is a chance of harmonious oneness between human and non-human life, it does so by speaking through another historical frame of reference. The landscape, through the young woman's figure, is exoticized and presented as infinitely "other." It is the one aspect of the film in which Shepitko's visuality succumbs to a colonial fetishization, replacing one register of sexualized imagery of agricultural development (embedded in the "virginity" of the land) with another (the land's "fertility" when considered together with the shepherdess's figure).[21]

Besides this exotically inflected harmony between the shepherdess, Kemel', and the landscape, Shepitko's footage of the steppe's unwelcoming nature remains, to the end, immune to Kemel's moral superiority, and to the historical aspirations his figure represents. This soil does not yield to the manipulation of the photographic lens—or, rather, Shepitko decides to leave the grounds largely untouched by the aesthetic possibilities of cinematic technology. This is particularly discernable in the difference between her landscape images and the often overly dramatized presentations of main figures, filmed in extreme close-ups and slanted angles that impose on them an external affectivity and signification. The lack of such overt cinematic imposition onto the landscape makes the latter endure as a material reality, marked—to repeat Kracauer— "by a fringe of indeterminate visible meanings."[22]

Heat ends without any clear resolution. After the conflict between Abakir and Kemel' reaches its peak, Abakir decides to quit, leaving the unit and Kemel' in their moral triumph. But Kemel's victory—presented as a *historic* victory of the young, progressive generation over the despotic, Stalinist, and old—remains fully at odds with the film's final shots of the same dead landscape that we saw in its earlier parts. Shepitko's question of the new "positive hero"—of his awareness of the demands of the time—is answered positively: Kemel' is fully aware of the demands he is charged with and marches towards the future, in just the way the Soviet state imagines it. However, the film raises yet another question: of whether he is aware of the demands of space, of nature and the environment, which are articulated in the film as a matter of simply recognizing visual, material facts. He does not seem to be. The figure who is—Abakir—is a decisively regressive historical subject, someone who has fallen out of history and is either unable or unwilling to advance with the "demands of the time." While he is ejected from the film in the concluding moments, made both "extra-historical" *and* "extra-territorial" to the film's space, his view on the environmental state of things remains present after his departure, aligning his and the camera's perception of the material reality of the steppe.

The Ascent

Let me first outline, briefly, the story. Two WWII partisans—the boisterous, confident Rybak and the sickly, quieter Sotnikov—depart from their group in the rural areas of Belorussia in search of food. Their journey involves leaving a relatively shielded woody area to traverse wide-open fields, scavenging for provisions from scattered and impoverished households. Inevitably, they run into German soldiers passing through the same fields, and while both partisans manage to escape, Sotnikov gets injured and nearly immobilized. After more wandering (with Rybak dragging Sotnikov through the snow), they end up in the house of Demchikha, who, despite her hesitation and fear of persecution, offers help. German occupiers and their local collaborators, however, ultimately find the protagonists and, after an extended ride on a sleigh through the snow-covered fields, deliver them to the occupation authorities of a nearby village. An intense drama unfolds in the film's last part, as Sotnikov, injured and emaciated, remains strong in the face of adversity and accepts his death, even gaining some physical strength in the process; while Rybak, terrified of torture and dying, decides to collaborate with the fascists, with the justification that he would be more helpful to the partisans in this position. After Sotnikov, along with Demchikha and other civilians, including a child, is executed by hanging in a series of heart-wrenching shots, Rybak has to confront living with an all-consuming guilt. Immediately following the execution, he unsuccessfully attempts suicide. *The Ascent* ends with his primal cry while facing the landscape, followed by the film's final shots empty of figures, dominated by the whiteness of the surrounding terrain that repeats, in reverse, the film's opening sequence.

There is no narrative thread of conquering, industrializing, or cultivating landscape in this film. In contrast, it is dominated by pristine and mostly uninhabited nature that is only occasionally marked by human traces. Absolute whiteness prevails, its look frequently tending towards abstraction. If the impossibly raw, wintry conditions realistically exacerbate the soldiers' already extreme deprivations, the otherworldliness of the white fields also communicates metaphorically an experience of fundamental alterity created by partisan warfare, to which we cannot have any real access. Yet more explicitly, the landscape begins to denote a generally religious space with the appearance of a Christian allegory in the film's second half, as Sotnikov emerges as a Christlike figure. With this allegorical imposition, *The Ascent* transforms the specific story of Soviet partisans' struggles into a universal narrative of redemption.

And yet neither a metaphorical reading nor allegorical imposition do full justice to the film's natural spaces, as it is precisely the physical tangibility of the film's landscapes that renders them both excessively present and incomprehensively abstract. This emphasis on materiality and its abstraction begins in the film's very first shot, which shows a nearly undifferentiated surface: a wavy pattern of what appears to be nothing more than a projected film stock, taking up the screen before it is succeeded by a legible shot of landscape. The film's natural setting, and the story that takes place within it, emerges out of—and then disappears into—this material nothingness, as if the photographic process itself mimics a natural history of birth and death. If, as Kracauer aptly noted, photography acts like nature, burying history "as if under a layer of snow," Shepitko partially removes this layer for the duration of the film, only to fully place it back at the film's closure. Nature and cinematography impinge here on history, "obliterating significance" alongside each other.[23] The ecological view of *The Ascent* comes forth in such a constant push-and-pull between meaning and its erasure; it begins, one could say, where allegory fails—in the material remains that resist accommodation within any and all allegorical structures.

A complex relation between legibility and abstraction organizes much of *The Ascent* already from its start. One of the most striking sequences in this regard appears mid-way through the film, as Rybak drags the injured Sotnikov through the woods to their edge. Rybak decides to test if they should leave the relative safety of the trees and enter into the wide-open fields before them. Leaving his companion behind, he enters the open space as if it were a great unknown—a space of nearly undifferentiated whiteness, with barely detectable boundaries between ground and sky and no objects to offer any framework for a human-centric orientation. Rybak moves gingerly, fearful of his own steps, quickly realizing that he is walking over a frozen lake and

Figure 10.1 Rybak in the landscape's all-consuming whiteness.

turning back. While this shot remains grounded in a narrative-motivated space (we *are* led to know he has tread onto a lake), the camera engages here the light and snow so as to transcend the environment's purely material dimensions and present it as an extraordinary space: one that is foreign, inaccessible, and terrifying in its abstraction, which seems about to swallow the protagonist (**see Figure 10.1**). What Rybak is about to be swallowed by is, of course, the water under the layer of snow and ice on which he treads—as we distinctly hear the sound of the cracking surface. The all-consuming whiteness *is* the landscape's material reality that remains fully indifferent to, and unaffected, by human and narrative deeds.

Or we can take a different sequence, earlier in the film: it starts with a high-angled pan, as the camera gazes at the ground from a birds-eye view, showing initially nothing but a monotonously textured surface. Without any distinct figures or objects on this surface, the shot is impenetrable, offering no indication of scale and refusing the viewer a clear position from which to ascertain the filmed space[24] (**see Figure 10.2**). Only when Rybak and Sotnikov reappear within the frame—two small figures moving through the sea of white—can we reestablish coherent perspectival relations. This odd shot seems to have no other motivation than to present the environment in estranging ways, to refuse us any mastery over the emerging image. The estrangement of this shot has little to do with, for instance, the famously defamiliarizing birds-eye-view of Alexander Rodchenko's 1930s constructivist photography, which, in the art

Figure 10.2 Landscape without any coordinates or scale.

historian's Aglaya Glebova's interpretation, served to provide audiences with an all-encompassing view of a territory as a means to constructing their knowledge of what is taking place around the country.[25] Shepitko's strategy works in the opposite way—to confuse and disorient, depriving the viewer of any knowledge whatsoever. We see here not a part of a whole, but a slice of land that appears as if a non-terrestrial terrain.

However, a shift in representational register takes place midway through the film, with the emergence of Sotnikov's transformation into a Christ-like figure and the introduction of explicitly Christological allegory. This transformation is overt and has been discussed in the critical literature on *The Ascent* more than any other aspect.[26] Shepitko directly pointed to an interest in Christian narrative in searching for an actor reminiscent of Christ to play Sotnikov (and Boris Plotnikov apparently fit the bill)—or, even more blatantly, by evoking Christ's ascension in her film's title.[27] The integration of Christian narrative into the film offers an interpretative refuge: once activated, every image can be placed within its already-established order. Sotnikov leads as a figure of salvation around whom humble mortals assemble; Rybak explicitly turns into Judas (he is called so by one of the observing villagers); and the snowy hill onto which the captives ascend to be executed is understood thus as Golgotha.

This allegorical presence becomes fully evident first in the scenes of Sotnikov's torture and subsequent night in the cellar; once it appears, however, its hermeneutical force can be stretched retrospectively to include much earlier sequences. Most significant here is the moment after Sotnikov is shot and made unable to move, lying on his back in the snow and looking pensively into the sky, as he faces the real possibility of immediate death. In the following shot-reverse shot sequence, we see him and the moon "communicating" with each other (see Figure 11.3). It is the first time in the film where nature appears not as an arduous setting but as an element with which to commune. This is also the first moment in the film where we observe the explicit generation of an allegorical form—something else is visibly passing through Sotnikov's mind and sensations, something outside the strict narrative of partisan war. And as the allegorical structure insinuates retrospectively, the communion is not so much with nature, but with the divine; or the insinuation is that these two, nature and the divine, are becoming intertwined, one speaking through the appearance of the other. (An image of communion with the sky is repeated later, when Sotnikov is shown laying on a carriage, now as a captive, and an elaborate play of shadows transpires on his face—as if nature/God were caressing the emaciated soldier. This is particularly notable, as the view of the sky betrays no sun and clouds to produce such a play of shadows: we see only a monotonous grey above—the color that has been present throughout the film.) Sotnikov emerges from this encounter with a sense of purpose. If up to that point he was a rather useless character—his physical weaknesses, after all, had earlier gotten both protagonists in trouble—now he becomes integrated into a larger order, finding a spiritual home despite the devastating material conditions of war and the freezing surroundings in which he lies.

Considering the entirety of Shepitko's work, her recourse to an allegorical form in *The Ascent* is rather surprising.[28] There is nothing of the sort in her previous films, which are marked by a preoccupation with the here-and-now of Soviet reality without any need for a secondary (much less transcendental) order to be imposed on it. Neither is there any inevitable need for allegory in *The Ascent*: the moral struggles that dominate the film's last section could easily be introduced without a turn to Christian iconography by simply presenting the resilience and strength of Soviet soldiers and their occasional failure to withstand adversity. As I've suggested, the resort to allegory establishes an interpretative framework, helping to assemble diverse elements of the film, including its spatial abstraction (whiteness, for instance, pointing towards a religious transcendence), into an overarching story of redemption. But such a pronounced imposition of allegorical meaning also achieves the opposite, exposing the arbitrariness of such an assemblage: we are invited to interpret Sotnikov's communion with the moon, for instance, as one with God, but why does it have to be this way? The same could be asked of the sequence on the frozen lake: we could read it, retrospectively, as Rybak's fearful entrance into—and retreat from—the world's transcendental otherness, but again, there is absolutely nothing that obliges us to read it that way. Even more, such allegory serves to fragment, and raise doubts about, the Soviet iconography of war and suffering. If a religious symbolization is needed to assert meaning, then the Soviet order, on its own, is not enough to assert meaning.[29] Once we begin to question the interpretative necessity of the Christian narrative throughout the film, the arbitrary and fragmented natures of both Soviet history *and* the natural environment come into focus.

It is this kind of interpretative conundrum—allegory's desire to assert an absolute meaning and its simultaneous inability to do so—that became the focus of Walter Benjamin's 1928 book *The Origin of German Tragic Drama*, written just as Kracauer was beginning to write on photography and bearing notable parallels to Kracauer's film criticism. Benjamin resuscitates here the seemingly archaic allegorical form and places it at the center of modernist aesthetics. His initial focus is 17th-century baroque German dramas, whose repetitive use of allegory he identifies as a way to lay claim to language in a manner in which material presentation and transcendental meaning would fully, absolutely fuse with one another. Yet what he also finds in these dramas is a realization that such an operation of language is impossible, and that allegory fails, again and again, to assert the intrinsic necessity of precisely what it proposes. In the words of Benjamin's interpreters, "the allegorical gaze looks out for the enigmatic knowledge that would grant possession of the world but ends up as a disenchantment of the universe: it promises meaning but hits in the face with contingency."[30] For Benjamin, the cause of such an allegorical compulsion resides in the world's gradual secularization, and more concretely in the political upheavals during the 30 Years War, during and after which German writers could not perceive history any more as a history of salvation; instead, they came increasingly to see history's unfolding as a series of disconnected events, a repetitive piling up of crises and catastrophes.

For the purposes of this essay, what is particularly interesting in Benjamin's discussion is the place nature occupies within his allegorical conception. He writes, "In allegory, the observer is confronted with the *facies hippocratica* of history as a petrified, primordial landscape. Everything about history that, from the very beginning, had been untimely, sorrowful, unsuccessful, is expressed in a face—or rather in a death's head."[31] *Facies hippocratica*—the appearance of the face immediately before death—is referred to describe history: it is the face of history, a dying face of history, a dying belief in history as progress or salvation. The materialization of this dying face occurs through a "petrified, primordial landscape." Not only does nature itself lose any transcendental meaning in these German dramas (it does not reveal anything from within, eternally and automatically moving through its cyclical repetition), but history becomes like nature, without any divine plans for its order. History turns into *natural history*, the direction of which is necessarily towards death and decay. Nature in allegory for Benjamin is like cinematically recorded reality in Kracauer: both express the contingencies of the world, acting against the profusion of totalized meaning and historical teleology.

Shepitko's own "petrified, primordial landscape" in *The Ascent* takes on a role that is parallel to Benjamin's discussion: suggesting the signification of a religious, spiritual space within the film's allegorical construction, it asserts itself as a petrifyingly material, here-and-now place that appears, to use Fay's words, as "an almost incomprehensible matter." With this, the film figures not only an abdication of progressive history—"history as salvation," be it in the form of Christianity or Marxism—but also a fragmentation/absolution of the self, which takes two distinct, and opposite, forms. One relates to Sotnikov: in a communion with the divine universe, he abandons himself to an order that already exists, to which he responds, and which envelops and absorbs him. The other relates to Rybak: in the film's post-allegorical remains, in the concluding sequence in particular, the fallen hero also commutes with the landscape but without any interference of the divine, offering a much more somber image of his place within that environment.

After Rybak's unsuccessful attempt at suicide in the outhouse of the German administrative office, we see him walking out into the courtyard, grieving his moral failure in a dramatic performance (**see Figure 10.3**). Wanting now to die but condemned to live, he looks out towards the gate that opens onto the snow-covered fields stretching towards the horizon. The

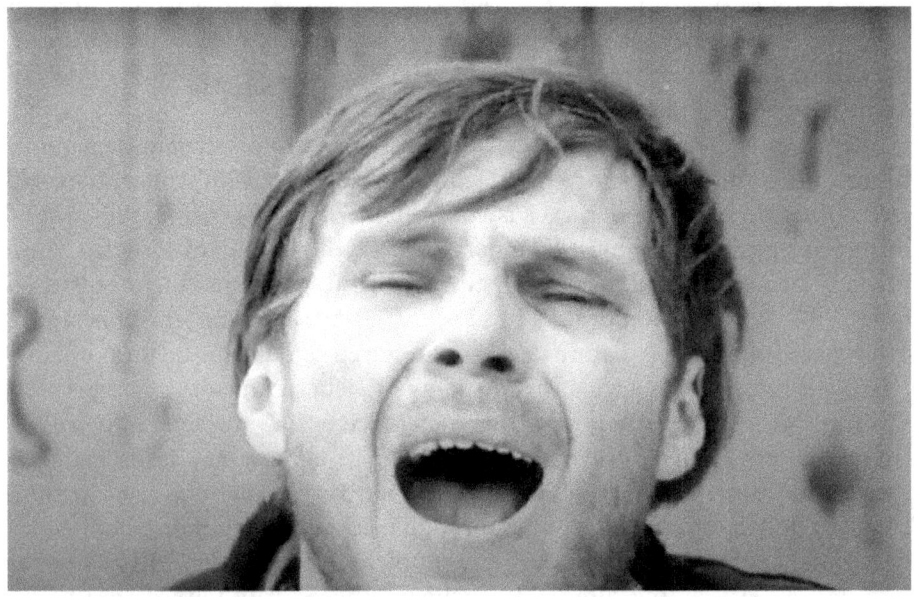

Figure 10.3 Rybak in a state of psychic collapse.

camera's behavior here is striking: it moves as if helping him to escape into the space beyond the gate in a strangely ghostly, embodied motion, while Rybak's body remains positioned in place. This ghostly gaze stops right outside the gate, as if suspended in air while looking onto the landscape. After a brief return to Rybak, who continues to be in a state of psychic collapse, we are back to the same suspended landscape image, which is then followed by a series of static shots looking like isolated snapshots, including the exact three images with which the film started. Finally, the film ends with its screen being covered by whiteness, with all legible traces disappearing into nothing.

These final images are of a familiar kind: we have seen all these spaces before, and they are conventionally realistic rather than frighteningly abstract. But they are now uncanny and strange at the same time, their familiarity taken away as soon as it is established. Their strangeness emerges and persists for two main reasons. First, because of the unresponsiveness of this landscape to Rybak's being: mostly static, repetitive, and indifferent, the landscape remains incommensurate with his psychic state, and his demolished condition is not projected into the image. Second, because the landscape is seen as if by him, at least partially, as the camera makes an effort to align its own "objective" gaze with his disturbed vision. Intertwined, the mechanical gaze of the camera and the gaze of a dejected man who has fallen out of history (and is comparable in this to Abakir from *Heat*, though Rybak's fall is more profound) determine the landscape's final view—manifesting, as in Shepitko's first film, its extra-territorial *and* extra-historical dimension.

It might cut against common sense to associate Shepitko's profoundly failed figure with something critically "good"—with a productive image that offers more than a condemning spectacle of Rybak's overpowering collapse. Her numerous discussions of the film, to be sure, leave no doubt about her embrace of Sotnikov, of the moral and spiritual strength for which he stands, and of cinema's ability to explore and articulate the core of humanist ethics. But in the extended final sequence, Shepitko grants Rybak time to grieve and look, just as she grants *us* time to face the depth of his destruction while facing, *with* him, the landscape. The sequence registers an interest in what is left after morality—especially after an allegorically established morality—has been evacuated. What is left is a simultaneously familiar and terrifying view onto the terrain which will never be perceived or experienced as home. Discussing Kracauer's preoccupation with cinema's non-moral, "downward" orientation, Fay argues that we might understand it as a way to extend "to the spectator an outright desubjectivized view of existence, a vision that models a selfless history of the future and promotes estrangement as the basis for postapocalyptic environmental thought." Shepitko's camera—even if its exploration of allegory and ascension looks up rather than down—ultimately assumes just such a desubjectivized view of existence as Fay describes, leaving us with an estranged, fragmented, and utterly material environment as the world's lasting view. In direct contradiction to Sotnikov's spiritual selflessness, we are left with Rybak's postapocalyptic shudders, his "lesser than self"—and with a question of what kind of future this still surviving figure might offer.

Farewell

Shepitko's final project, *Farewell*, initially titled *Farewell to Matiora*, is an adaptation of Valentin Rasputin's 1976 novel of the same title. "Matiora" refers to a fictional island and village, supposedly located in the midst of the Angara River—the only river flowing out of Lake Baikal in Eastern Siberia. The place, featuring a tight community of overwhelmingly older women who have resided on the island their entire lives, is about to be flooded as part of a hydroelectric station construction in Bratsk, which was one of the most ambitious Soviet industrial projects of the 1960s.[32] The film's drama begins to unfold when the population is ordered to depart Matiora and take residence on the mainland; while some islanders seem to be content with the relocation, others are severely distressed, especially the older Daria, who emerges as the film's central figure. In agony, she takes her time to properly "prepare" her house for death and funeral, washing it as if it were a human body, and decorating it with flowers before allowing it to be burned down before the flood. Much of the film consists of sorrowful scenes as local authorities burn houses, level the cemetery, and bulldoze mature, age-old trees while the population observes, with terror, the tearing down of their existence. In contrast with the previous two films, *Farewell* does not exhibit much ambiguity with regards to ethical, progressive history and environmental development. The film—along with Rasputin's novel—has little sympathy for the "forward-thinking" authority figures who erase the island and enforce relocation. Their destructive appetites are presented as ungrounded in any necessity (despite Shepitko's assertion to the contrary[33]), and we are offered little contextual justification that would allow positive reasoning about their actions. Progressive history leads to nothing but catastrophe, establishing a lucid finale to Shepitko's—and now also Klimov's—ecological cinema.

Yet the film remains committed to simple *human* history, which is recast here as natural history, an organic cycle of birth and death, evident especially in Daria's attempt to save her predecessors' graves. If the island's flooding erases the past without traces, seeking to put a completely different "future" in its place, Daria is devoted to enabling the ruins of the past to be absorbed "naturally" into nature. The ethical gaze here, furthermore, is aligned not with the camera's looking up and forward, towards the bright horizons of a better world, but rather with its obstinate view downwards, towards the elemental materials of the Earth. One of the most prominent sequences in this regard is Daria's visit to the woods, soon after the villagers are directed to vacate the island. The sequence begins with the camera's angled descent towards the ground, where we see at first only a bundle of sick vegetation before discerning Daria's figure hidden within the greenery, appearing as if that of a hermit, or better, a human animal in its element within the woods. In the following shots, Daria walks through the thicket of brush, kneels down in an extensive period of contact with the ground, and pats the grass in a state of nearly religious devotion. We see extreme close-ups of an anthill, with thousands of bugs filling almost the entire screen as they move aimlessly around; a natural water spring, with intensely bubbling water coming from underground; and thick vegetation, over and over (see Fig. 10.4). Sometimes views are subjective, explicitly from Daria's perspective. Other times, they are from the camera's perspective and include Daria within the frame. But the interchange establishes them to be of the same kind—characterized by a gaze that observes life taking place on or near the ground. If Daria's view betrays a deeply spiritual veneration of this plant and animal world, it is not suggested to be of a transcendental kind: it is a veneration of the material multiplicity of life, the meaning of which does not extend beyond the facts of its own existence.

In discussions of Rasputin's novel immediately upon its publication, critics emphasized the root correlation of "Matiora" and "*mat'*"—the island's name and the Russian for "mother"—that he undoubtedly exploits in his writing.[34] Matiora's etymological kinship extends, however, not only to "mother" but also

Figure 10.4 The camera looking closely at the natural world.

to "matter" (*materia*), to which the islanders have to bid farewell. Shepitko/Klimov's film is keen on exploring the break-up of a previously symbiotic relationship between humans and environmental matter, as we see most specifically in Daria's interactions with trees and soil. One of Rasputin's critics, Yuri Seleznev, in an essay titled "Earth or Territory" (or "Soil or Territory"—"*Zemlia ili territoriia*"), argued that the island is treated in the novel as either earth/soil or territory—just as our planet can be treated both ways.[35] When we consider the environment as earth or soil, he writes, we understand it as belonging to "everyone," and assume responsibility for passing it on to future generations. While Seleznev calls the human in this relation an "owner" or "propriator" (*khoziain*), this ownership—as we see in Daria's actions in *Farewell*—does not involve a subject/object dichotomy, or a possessive mastery associated with exploitation, but presents itself as a dialogical relation, in which humans are organically subordinated to, and respectful of, the earth's cycles.

To treat the earth as *territory*, by contrast, is to consider it only as a medium for human goals, who inhabit the planet as "tourists" in an "estranged" relation to it. While Seleznev's discussion does not directly align with Kracauer's notions of territory and extraterritoriality, it nevertheless resonates with his terms, as Seleznev examines earth as both a possible home and as estranged matter. Interpreting Kracauer, Gerhard Richter understands "territory" as both a place that is "settled, circumscribed, defined, articulated and distinguished" *and*, in an etymological relationship with "terror," as an area "from which people are turned off."[36] Or in Fay's words, "Territory at once marks the earth—terra—as a settling place we may call home and designates as terrifying an area that will not be settled."[37] In *Farewell*'s concluding sequences, territory loses all sense of home; it also does not appear as Seleznev's touristy place. Rather, it expands as terror in the final, overwhelming images of fog and water. As a group of men, sailing on a boat in the early morning hours, tries to reach Matiora to collect the last remaining residents, it becomes surrounded by dense fog. The group loses its way and assumes that Matiora was flooded overnight. Although this is not entirely true—the camera switches to Daria and others to show them still in the house awaiting their voluntarily accepted fate—the film leaves us with the men disoriented and practically blind in the fog, and screaming in despair for Matiora—or mother, or matter. The film ends with images of nature—the island's plants, fog, river. Realistically shot while partially disappearing into abstraction (the encroaching fog comparable here to *The Ascent*'s whiteness), it is a world that will never be "settled," and that the surviving protagonists (all believers in the socialist future) will have to inhabit in a permanent exile (see **Fig. 10.5**).

Shepitko's *Heat*, *The Ascent*, and *Farewell*, while different in their particular contexts, all end as a variation of the same—with images that are realistic but uncanny, full of specific detail yet tending towards abstraction, with natural

Figure 10.5 The estranged land at the end of *Farewell*.

elements literally taking over the screen, especially in the last two films. The camera, throughout these three films, overwhelms viewers with its presentation of nature's materiality—through bluntly factual shots of snow, soil, dust, water, plants, fog, bugs and more—such that it blankets the screen and obliterates narrative space and meaning. No historical teleology and no progressive historical subject are linked to the gaze established in this process. The subjects who are receptive to this kind of vision, and to the camera's mechanical, unassuming gaze, are "fragmented"—that is, expelled from progress, shattered by catastrophes both historical and personal. With this, Shepitko's visual ecology demands not only an evacuation of grand historical narrative but a destabilization of consciousness itself. It is through this destabilization, finally, that a new environmental thinking can emerge.

NOTES

1. I wish to thank Raymond De Luca for his productive feedback on this chapter.
2. Most of the film was shot in the provincial city of Murom, because of "the lack of real winter" in Belorussia. For a detailed account of the shooting, see Lev Karakhan, "Krutoj put' Voskhozhdeniia," *Iskusstvo kino* 10 (1976): 85–101.
3. Sigfried Kracauer, *Theory of Film: The Redemption of Physical Reality* (Princeton: Princeton UP, 1997), 300.

4. Kracauer, 303.
5. Jennifer Fay, *Inhospitable World: Cinema in the Time of the Anthropocene* (Oxford: Oxford UP, 2018), 173.
6. It is notable that science in Kracauer's philosophy occupies an analogous place to religion or ideology, as far as the perception of physical reality is concerned. He writes, "The truly decisive reason for the elusiveness of physical reality is the habit of abstract thinking we have acquired under the reign of science and technology. No sooner do we emancipate ourselves from the 'ancient beliefs' than we are led to eliminate the quality of things." Kracauer, 299–300.
7. Fay, 181.
8. Fay, 20.
9. On the emergence of Soviet war narratives and "the cult of victory" see Jeremy Hicks, *Victory Banner over the Reichstag: Film, Document, and Ritual in Russia's Contested Memory of World War II* (Pittsburg: University of Pittsburg Press, 2020).
10. In his expansive biography of Khrushchev, William Taubman writes that "Kazakh party leaders he consulted were against the idea: they feared traditionally Kazakh lands would end in the hands of Russian and Ukrainian farmers." William Taubman, *Khrushchev: The Man and His Era* (New York, London: W. W. Norton, 2003), 262.
11. Taubman, 606–608.
12. On this history, see D. J. Peterson, *Troubled Lands: The Legacy of Soviet Environmental Destruction* (Boulder: Westview Press, 1993); and Nicholas Breyfogle, *Eurasian Environments: Nature and Ecology in Imperial Russian and Soviet History* (Pittsburgh: University of Pittsburgh Press, 2018).
13. For a detailed survey of Russian and Soviet environmental history see Paul Josephson, Nicolai Dronin, Ruben Mnatsakanian, Aleh Cherp, Dmitry Efremenko, and Vladislav Larin, *An Environmental History of Russia* (New York: Cambridge University Press, 2013).
14. Laurent Coumel, "A Failed Environmental Turn? Khrushchev's Thaw and Nature Protection in Soviet Russia," *The Soviet and Post-Soviet Review* 40, no. 2 (2013): 167–189.
15. Julia Obertreis, "Soviet Irrigation Policies under Fire: Ecological Criticism in Central Asia, 1970s–1991, in *Eurasian Environments: Nature and Ecology in Imperial Russian and Soviet History*, ed. Brefogle, 119.
16. Obertreis, 119.
17. Yuri Trusov, "The Ecological Approach and Problems of Moulding the Noosphere," in *Philosophy and the Ecological Problems of Civilisation*, ed. A. D. Ursul, trans. H. Campbell and M. A. Greighton (Progress Publishes: Moscow, 1983), 60.
18. Moisei Markov, « Nauchilis'- li my myslit' po-novomu ? » *Voprosy filisofii*, 2 (1977) : 30–35, 2.
19. Ivan Frolov and Viktor Los', "Filosofskie osnovaniia sovremennoi ekologii," in *Ekologicheskaia propaganda v SSSR*, ed. D. M. Gvishiani (Moscow: Nauka, 1984): 5–26. 15. Foster considers Frolov's work as "an important first step in the creation of a new ethic of global ecological humanism. John Bellamy Foster, "Late Soviet Ecology and the Planetary Crisis," *Monthly Review*, 67.2 (2015): 1–20, 13.

20. Larisa Shepitko, "Znoi: Teoreticheskaia chast' diplomnoi raboty" in *Larisa. Kniga o Larise Shepitko*, ed. Elem Klimov (Moscow: Iskusstvo, 1987), 57–63, 57.
21. This aspect of *Heat* asks for further analysis, especially in the transnational context of cinema's colonial imaginary. Ella Shohat's "Gender and the Culture of Empire" offers a particularly rich discussion of Western cinema's vocabulary in presenting discoveries and conquests of "primitive" lands. Gendered Western colonial gaze is at its center, "seeing" the foreign territories in feminine terms, with evocation of fertility, virginity, but also wildness and exoticism that need to be tamed and explained. Ella Shohat, "Gender and the Culture of Empire: Towards a Feminist Ethnography of the Cinema," in *Taboo Memories, Diasporic Voices*, ed. Ella Shohat (New York: Duke University Press, 2006), 17–69.
22. The kind of tension between material reality and purposeful narrative that runs through Shepitko's film might be seen through Kracauer's lens—his description of a film artist as "a man who sets out to tell a story but, in shooting it, is so overwhelmed by his innate desire to cover all of physical reality—and also by a feeling that he must cover it in order to tell the story, any story, in cinematic terms—that he ventures ever deeper into the jungle of material phenomena in which he risks becoming irretrievably lost if he does not, by virtue of great efforts, get back to the highways he left." Kracauer, 255.
23. Sigfried Kracauer. "Photography," in *The Mass Ornament: Weimar Essays*, ed. and trans. Thomas Levin (Cambridge: Harvard University Press, 1995), 47–63, 47.
24. These kind of shots in *The Ascent* are reminiscent of Mikhail Kalatozov's *The Unsent Letter* (Neotrpravlennoe pis'mo, 1960), a film that also challenges viewers' visual mastery over the images by presenting white spaces devoid of any clear perspective.
25. Aglaya Glebova, "Elements of Photography: Avant-Garde Aesthetics and the Reforging of Nature," *Representations*, Vol. 142.1 (2018): 56–90.
26 For the discussion of the biblical presence in *The Ascent*, see Barbara Quart, "Between Materialism and Mysticism: The Films of Larissa Shepitko," *Cineaste*, 16.3 (1988): 4–11; F. Beardow, "Soviet Cinema — War Revisited. Part 3," *Rusistika*, 17 (1998): 11–24; Karen Rosenberg, "Shepitko," *Sight & Sound*, 56.2 (1987): 119–122; and Jason Merrill, "Religion, Politics and Literature in Larisa Shepitko *The Ascent*," *Slovo*, vol. 18.2 (2006): 147–162.
27. On Shepitko's planning of the film, and her search for a Christ-like looking actor, see the documentary *Larisa Shepitko's Golgotha* (Golgofa Larisy Shepitko, dir. Konstantin Golenchik, 2017), available at https://www.youtube.com/watch?v=Tg2UfCWpCa8&t=1907s&ab_channel=%D0%A1%D1%82%D1%83%D0%B4%D0%B8%D1%8F%D0%9D%D0%B5%D0%BE%D1%84%D0%B8%D1%82.
28. In Soviet discussions of *The Ascent*, *pritcha* is the category used to describe the film's imposition of the Christian narrative; *pritcha* is understood and translated as both parable and allegory. According to Yuri Klepikov, who worked with Shepitko on the script, the allegorical infusion was central to her conception from start. He writes, "we were concerned with a creation of such an imagery which

would allow to shoot the film in a stern, ascetic, form of a *pritcha*. [. . .] The film's reality should appear not as a flat, everyday imitation of life but as a reflection of certain meanings, which would lead to lucid, moral formula of a *pritcha*." Klepikov, "Gipoteticheskaia rezhissura," *Iskusstvo kino* 8 (1986): 66–75, 73.

29. In post-Soviet discussions, Andrei Shpagin published an insightful analysis on the place of religion in Soviet war films of the 1960s and 1970s, as a way to confirm or depart from the conventional Soviet war mythology. Shpagin argues that *The Ascent* cannot "sustain the metaphysical weight" of the Christian allegory, that the absolute meaning on which such an allegory insists, remains unconvincing. Shpagin, "Religiia voiny," *Iskussto kino* 6 (2005): 73–89, 87. In an earlier criticism, Andrei Tarkovksii also takes apart Shepitko's need for *mnogoznachitel'nost'*, which Tarkovskii describes as an excessively obvious imposition of deep significance onto her characters, which he considers to be a failure. He does not talk about the allegorical form or Christianity, but his criticism implies the kind of overlaying of external meaning over a set of figures or events that is inherent to allegory. Andrei Tarkovskii, *Zapechatlennoe vremia: archivy, dokumenty, vospominania* (Moscow: Podkova, 2002), 73.

30. Stéphane Symons, *Benjamin: The Presence of Mind, Failure to Comprehend* (Leiden: Brill, 2013), 91.

31. Walter Benjamin, *The Origin of German Tragic Drama*, trans. John Osborne (London: NLB, 1977), 666.

32. Rasputin's novel is based in the author's personal experiences of growing up in a village on the Angara River that was flooded during the construction of Bratsk hydro-electric station. As Breyfogle notes, the station was the largest in the world at the time of its completion in 1967 and was heralded "as one of the great triumphs of Soviet socialism." Breyfogle, 4.

33. Though Shepitko herself suggested that the absolute need to build the station needs to be made obvious, thus staging a kind of irresolvable conflict. This "absolute need" is not made visible in the film.

34. While the novel and film present a historically accurate fact of Soviet administrations intentionally flooding territories during the hydroelectric station's construction, Matiora itself is a fictional place. Naming it as such allows Rasputin for a rich symbolic play through the words' etymological connections.

35. Yuri Seleznev, "Zemlia ili territoriia," *Voprosy literatury* 2 (1977): 49–63.

36. Gerhard Richter, "Homeless Images: Kracauer's Extraterritoriality, Derrida's Monolinguialism of the Other," in Maayan Amir and Ruti Sela, eds., *Extraterritorialities in Occupied Worlds* (Goleta: Punctum Books, 2016), 377–422, 384.

37. Fay, 197.

CHAPTER 11

The Shepitko Sky: Larisa Shepitko's Meteorological Cinema of Immersion, Wonder, and Openness

Raymond De Luca

In a 1969 interview at the Moscow Film Festival—the only one he offered a foreign magazine, the French monthly *Positif*—about his resounding, yet controversial, new film *Andrei Rublev* (1966), the legendary Russian filmmaker Andrei Tarkovsky was asked about the sky.[1] "Is the absence of sky in your film intentional?", a reporter inquired, "We never see the sky, only the earth."[2] Tarkovsky concurred: "I am captivated by the process of growth of everything that comes from [. . .] the earth: the trees, the grass [. . .] the sky only figures as the space towards all that is born and grows on earth rises up. [. . .] For me, the sky is empty [. . .] I only give any importance to its reflections on earth, in the river, in the puddles."[3] Implicitly citing his cinematic muse Aleksandr Dovzhenko, namely his Stalin-era masterwork *Earth* (*Zemlia*, 1930), Tarkovsky elaborated his interest in the terrestrial, characterizing the sky as a mere backdrop to the world's unfolding. The Earth figures only in phenomenal form in and of itself, as soil; earthlings simply dwell under a sky, as if stranded on the Earth's outer surface. For Tarkovsky, to better apprehend the world—and ourselves in it—we must look *down*. The sky is empty, devoid of substance: a stark rebuke of the Soviet space race that located human destiny upward in the cosmos. The Apollo 11 moon landing had, after all, coincided with the 1969 Moscow Film Festival.[4]

For Larisa Shepitko, however, the sky signified something different. Shepitko had been one of Tarkovsky's creative interlocutors who, in 1963, had graduated from his *alma mater*, Moscow's All-Union State Institute of Cinematography (VGIK) as part of a new generation of Soviet filmmakers.[5] After Joseph Stalin died in 1953, Soviet society, boosted by Nikita Khrushchev's renunciation of Stalinism in 1956, underwent a cultural liberalization popularly known as the Thaw. This period allowed artists and filmmakers an unprecedented degree of freedom to reflect on Soviet life and society not only more truthfully and subjectively, but also in more aesthetically striking ways.[6]

Across all her films, Shepitko presents the sky as something that people and things are not outside of or under but *in*, that is, as an enveloping, ever-changing site of contact between the Earth and its inhabitants. Through zero-gravity aerial shots, dizzying upside-down perspectives, panoramic landscapes that subsume the world's things into the sky's vastness, and weather motifs (clouds, wind, mist), Shepitko blurs the otherwise fixed coordinates between ground and air, solids and vapors. In her three major films *Heat* (*Znoi*, 1963), *Wings* (*Kryl'ia*, 1966), and *The Ascent* (*Voskhozhdenie*, 1977), the Earth's substances and its atmosphere are bound together in their growth and movement. Shepitko's protagonists, landscapes, and even narrative structures comingle with the sky. The ambiguous endings accompanying almost all Shepitko's films draw inspiration from the sky's open-endedness. Shepitko studies what it means to be caught up in the fluctuation of atmospheric currents.

This chapter, drawing on the theories of atmosphere and perception advanced by the French phenomenologist Maurice Merleau-Ponty and, more recently, Elaine Scarry and Tim Ingold, argues that Shepitko's cinema presents a world without enclosure, a place of ever-changing horizons, viewed only by Earth's inhabitants as they embark on their various paths. People do not traverse the ground's pre-formed surface in Shepitko's work; rather, they move through a world that is always in formation in a perpetual state of flux, immersed in the medium. They walk through sky. The inconstancy and indeterminacy of Shepitko's work, conveyed by her insistent overhead views, stages not only a political critique against the myopic ideology of the Soviet state, which viewed land and sky as inert material to be dominated and reconfigured, but also contests popular ideas about the environment's binary composition, the sky-earth dualism. Shepitko shows us that we dwell in a world of comings and goings, subject to changes in atmosphere.

OBDURATE ETHEREALITY, *HEAT*

The opening shot of Larisa Shepitko's diploma featurette *Heat*, based on a story by the Kyrgyz novelist Chinghiz Aitmatov, "The Camel's Eye" (*Verbliuzhii glaz*, 1960), begins with an image of several automobile passengers as they traverse the Kazakh steppe, an immense grassland in Central Asia.[7] A young boy falls asleep on a man's shoulder, and the driver comments: "He had been looking out the window since we left Frunze," the Soviet-era name for the present-day capital city of Kyrgyzstan, Bishkek.[8] The boy is fatigued, the driver explains, because "it's so boring outside—nothing but steppe and stones." The monotonous sight of uninterrupted wheatlands for countless miles has a soporific effect on Shepitko's seventeen-year-old protagonist, Kemel (played by Bolotbek Shamshiev). The image of a teenager sleeping as a vehicle traverses the savannah-like plains of Central Asia recalls the boy in Anton Chekhov's 1888 novella *The Steppe* (*Step'*), who finds himself in a daze while drifting through the steppe aboard a horse chaise.

> Meanwhile, before the eyes of the travelers there now spread a wide, endless plain cut across by a chain of hills. Crowding and peeking from behind each other, these hills merge into an elevation that stretches to the right from the road all the way to the horizon and disappears in the purple distance [. . .] He was worn out from the jolting ride [. . .] was tired and wanted to sleep. His head was heavy, his eyes kept closing, and his thoughts were tangled like threads.[9]

Outside, there is nothing *but* earth, and these yawning vistas, scorched by the sun, sedate the viewer. Invoking Chekhov, *Heat*'s opening image suggests that little has appreciably changed on these lands since the nineteenth century. The steppe is (still) fallow ground for as far as the eye can see.

It is no wonder, then, that we learn Kemel is being transported to Anarkhai, a vast region between Kazakhstan and Kyrgyzstan, as part of the Soviets' Virgin Lands campaign (*Osvoenie tseliny*, 1953–1964). Spearheaded by Khrushchev, the Virgin Lands Campaign was, at its most basic, an effort to cultivate thousands of hectares of untilled land in Siberia and Kazakhstan to address the USSR's chronic shortages of grain. On a deeper level, though, the Virgin Lands Campaign was the centerpiece of a broader ideological and cultural rejuvenation of society as envisioned by mid-century Soviet officials after Stalin's death. The Virgin Lands Campaign was intended to remobilize society on behalf of an optimistic, self-sufficient vision of state socialism. As the future Soviet leader Leonid Brezhnev wrote (whom Khrushchev commissioned to Kazakhstan), "It was the great idea of the Communist Party to turn the lifeless, remote but fertile eastern steppes of the country into a land with a developed economy and a high level of culture."[10] The Soviets would, at long last, transform the steppe into a fertile region that belied Chekhov's (and Shepitko's) portrayal of turgid barrenness. Communist planning and industry were to enrich—impregnate—these virginal lands and (re-)enchant society with the promise of Soviet productivity.

Like Aitmatov's story "The Camel's Eye," however, Shepitko challenges the discourse of mastery pervading the Virgin Lands Campaign, which Soviet propaganda conveyed in expressly libidinal terms.[11] Kemel is an ardent believer in the transformation of the steppe, but his ambitions are continually foiled: he is belittled by his superiors, assigned the unglamorous job of a water carrier (as opposed to a tractor driver), and he nearly kills a man out of frustration.

The reality of life on the steppe inhibits Kemel. He also has a dream of marrying a nomadic shepherdess whom he meets surrounded by lambs, a symbol of her, and the earth's, virginity. Yet Kemel fails to recognize that the industrial push of the Virgin Lands Campaign is obliterating her traditional ways of life. Desecrating the steppe, Kemel cannot consummate his relations, betraying the counterproductive nature of the Soviets' Oedipal struggle against the steppe. The more Kemel tries to prove himself, the more distant his conquest. *Heat* exposes the Thaw's more quixotic elements.

As Mieka Erley writes, Shepitko also aesthetically undercuts the Soviets' "high modernist dreams" to transform the Kazakh steppe into an oasis vis-á-vis *Heat*'s insistent focus on dust.[12] Throughout the film, "dust cannot be ignored: it fills the frame, it obstructs our vision, it insists upon its stubborn materiality. At moments, dust makes the diegesis of the film illegible [. . .] Materiality does not always conform to the 'cultural scripts' that we use to master it."[13] The land itself becomes a site of resistance to Soviet utopianism.[14] The earth's recalcitrance in *Heat* is an example of what has been called the "obdurate materiality" of late Soviet culture, that is, the motley objects, things, and textures whose sheer presence obstructs the channels of Soviet power and ideology.[15] In *Heat*, the triumphalist rhetoric of the Virgin Lands Campaign is asphyxiated by dust.

But what *is* dust? Substantively, dust is comprised of fine particles of solid matter, which, on Earth, churn through the atmosphere and amass on surfaces. In especially arid regions like the Kazakh steppe, though, dust is less sedentary. High velocity winds can relocate dust to nearby areas, often to calamitous effect because it can destabilize topography and overwhelm farmland. This sort of wind-borne dust is known as "fugitive dust," whose ruinous consequences become even more pronounced when human behavior, such as ploughing or grazing, haphazardly loosens topsoil. The impact of fugitive dust on the Virgin Lands Campaign was immense. In 1965 alone, dust storms destroyed over five million hectares of the steppe and fueled agricultural conditions akin to those in the 1930s American Midwest during the Dust Bowl.[16] One scene in *Heat*, for instance, shows two men quarreling as they are buffeted by fierce winds. The howling wind overwhelms their spat about the best strategies for grain collection and tractor speed. This episode acknowledges the devastating effect wind erosion had on the steppe, suggesting that the Soviets' slapdash campaign to cultivate Central Asia was not only reckless, but self-defeating.

Thus, the dust clouds Shepitko calls attention to in *Heat* are not just the consequence of the ground, but of the ground's *interaction* with the atmosphere. The British anthropologist Tim Ingold has theorized the synergistic relation between air and earth.[17] Most often, people perceive the atmosphere as a kind of "ceiling" under which human beings dwell. The sky is understood as something external, as a layer on top of the Earth, making us the ex-habitants on the world's surface. As Ingold reveals, however, whenever we are on solid ground, we are always "touching" the atmosphere. To feel wind or sun or rain is to experience a co-mingling with the atmospheric forces acting on Earth. Outside, we are always immersed in the fluxes of the medium. We do not live on congealed terrain; rather, we live on land undergoing change, in a perpetual state of becoming.

In *Heat*, Shepitko acknowledges how the Kazakh steppe, contra Soviet ideology, does not exist in the open as inert, untouched land, what Brezhnev called "lifeless." It exists *in* wind. It is engulfed by its medium. Frequent shots in *Heat*, indeed, erase the border between sky and earth. Many of Shepitko's landscape shots have no vanishing point; sky and land seemingly stretch out until their convergence. We also see characters backdropped by nothing but sky, as if they are standing on clouds (**see Figure 11.1**). The sky, Shepitko suggests, intermingles with the earth, not as its backdrop, but as a participant. The Virgin Lands Campaign was so preoccupied with the materiality of the world's sedimented surfaces—land, dirt, grass—and less so with the ethereality of its media: air, wind, clouds, and weather in which substances take shape and dissolve. The Earth and sky are not separate but, rather, in permanent exchange. The sky makes itself *felt* on Earth. The windstorms Shepitko portrays in *Heat* intimate how the sky is agential. It is not an empty encasing, but, through its own pulses and fluctuations, a contributor to the making of our

Figure 11.1 Characters backdropped by nothing but sky.

world. Despite its immateriality and fleetingness, wind is a form of sky power. As Ingold writes, the wind does not "have agency; rather [it] *is* agency. The wind [. . .] is its blowing, not a thing that blows."[18]

The experience of filming *Heat*, indeed, reiterated how otherwise immaterial atmospheric pressures impinged themselves on the lived realities of the earth and its inhabitants. Under the open sky, temperatures on the Kazakh steppe soared to over 120 degrees Fahrenheit. The excruciating heat melted film stock and incapacitated several members of the film crew, including Shepitko.[19] The difficulty of filming *Heat* documents how human beings dwell in the medium of the world, susceptible to the invisible forces immersing us. That Shepitko titled her debut *Heat* concedes how terrestrial experience is not wholly determined, as Soviet-Marxist ideologues would claim, by the materiality of substances and surfaces. Our engagement with the physical world, even on the desiccated steppe, has as much to do with the ungraspable and ephemeral energies shaping life on earth, whether wind or heat. The immateriality of matter, for Shepitko, matters.

Furthermore, Shepitko's sky in *Heat* not only makes it felt through dust clouds or sweltering temperatures. Several shots reveal how the sky arranges itself more menacingly, as if taunting benighted Soviet planners. One sequence follows Kemel as he makes a trip to collect water. He realizes that, somewhere along the way, he lost a bucket. A long shot then shows Kemel running around the steppe backdropped by the vast sky. This shot presents a solitary figure whose tiny stature (a boy of only seventeen on the cusp of sexual maturity) is dwarfed by the enormity of the horizon. Kemel is engulfed by sky, becoming an almost unnoticeable presence futilely toiling on the world below, a figurative speck of dust. When Kemel returns, he learns that his co-workers secretly had a spare bucket. Narratively, Kemel's trip is pointless, a fact Shepitko throws into sharp relief by juxtaposing him against the sky. The sky reduces Kemel, like all Soviet planners, into a nullity. The vastness of the sky mocks the outsized ambitions of the Virgin Lands Campaign.

The sky's looming presence is also captured in a scene that depicts a flock of crows soaring above Kemel, and he averts his gaze to avoid being attacked. The flock (re: murder) of crows adds a touch of the Gothic to *Heat*. Its obvious cinematic referent is Alfred Hitchcock's *The Birds* (1963), a horror film that follows a flock of birds terrorizing a small California town. Like Kemel, that film's heroine (Tippy Hedren) repeatedly also avoids eye contact with the birds, who loom in the background and surveil Hitchcock's characters. In the American context, *The Birds* tapped into the nascent ecological concerns catalyzed by the publication of Rachel Carson's *Silent Spring* (1962).[20] Though it is unlikely that Shepitko saw *The Birds*, which was released in the same year as *Heat*, she would have been familiar with Hitchcock.[21] The ominous crows in *Heat*, like Hitchcock's, allude to the environmental catastrophe hastened by the Virgin Lands Campaign, which devastated the steppe and only redoubled the USSR's pre-existing grain shortages.[22] It is as though these birds are emissaries of the sky, airborne harbingers of ecological apocalypse that—like fugitive dust—suggest how communist dreams beget colossal destruction.

Yet, at other moments in *Heat*, the sky is far less indifferent or portentous. It frequently appears in sublimely delicate and wispy configurations, as if Shepitko re-creates on celluloid an Impressionist painting full of intricately patterned clouds and sun beams. The insistent presence of a dreamy, ever-changing horizon in *Heat* suffuses this gritty, telluric film with an otherworldly quality, elevating its distinctly "earthly" content into the realm of the metaphysical. Thus, the texture of Shepitko's sky in *Heat* is less an instance of "obdurate materiality" than of obdurate *ethereality*. That is, the sky is not a "thing" to be managed or overcome, but, rather, an ever-present site of activity that takes shape in striking ways in the form of wind, weather, clouds, heat, and birds.[23] Shepitko's sky is stubbornly enigmatic as it confounds the world below. In *Heat*, Shepitko reveals that, as earthlings, we are always *in* sky, ever vulnerable to its elusive variations.

HEAD IN THE CLOUDS, *WINGS*

The ethereal quality of the sky in *Heat* becomes even more pronounced in Shepitko's follow-up film *Wings*, a movie that centers on a former Red Army fighter pilot, Nadia Petrukhina (superbly acted by Maya Bulgakova), as she navigates her disappointingly ordinary life as a school principal. Though World War II had been a horrifically tragic experience for the Soviet people, it also afforded Soviet culture a degree of personal freedom that was proscribed during the 1930s under Stalin.[24] Wartime nonconformity was especially true for Soviet women who were legally allowed to leave the home and serve in the Red Army.[25] After Germany's surrender, however, Soviet authorities demobilized women and began promoting a return to traditional gender roles, with a focus on natalist policies to help society recover from the war's demographic catastrophe.[26]

Though revered by those who lived through World War II, Nadia struggles to connect with the postwar generation in the liberalized cultural atmosphere of the Thaw. She dresses androgynously and appears overly manneredly in all her interactions. The *mise-en-scène* of *Wings* underscores the stiltedness of Nadia's behavior by confining her within the frame: "as a motionless body measured by male hands; as a mute, framed face on a local television channel; as an inhibited figure standing in a café, stared at by a group of men; and in a photograph nailed to a wall in a local museum."[27] The tight, enclosing camerawork, manipulated by Igor' Slabnevich, contributes to Nadia's portrayal as a kind of sentient mannequin. It is not a coincidence that *Wings* begins with a dressmaker delineating the coordinates of Nadia's body, as if affixing her for a display window.

The only relief for Nadia comes in the dreamy images of the sky that unexpectedly recur throughout *Wings*. Nadia's experiences as a pilot during World War II enter the diegesis vis-à-vis shots of a fluidly moving sky that counterpose her present life's inflexibility. These elastic images corroborate that Nadia's "framed and stultifying relation to space is not the only one" she knows.[28] Thus, we are given access to the sky in *Wings* vis-à-vis Nadia's interiority. The sky is visualized through Nadia's daydreams, reveries, and memories. In *Wings*, the sky is a mental landscape that equates the overhead expanse of blue with the mind, specifically a woman's. For much of *Wings*, Nadia has her head in the clouds, as it were. She is physically present but psychically elsewhere.

The connection Shepitko posits between thought and the sky is a long-standing one in human culture. The mind, it is said, is catalyzed by skygazing, which begins with the act of looking up. Since antiquity, philosophers have characterized the sky as "the condition and origin of imagination."[29] Its open-endedness, "furnished" by ever-changing clouds, engenders both what we think and *how* we think: expansively, subtly, profoundly, and volatilely. The sky, in other words, absorbs the perceiver in its own swells and currents. For the French philosopher Maurice Merleau-Ponty, the open sky is not an object of contemplation, but the very "homeland of our thoughts."[30]

The first aerial intermezzo in *Wings* begins when Nadia, after an uninspiring date, rests her head in her hand—assuming *the* classic pose for contemplation *à la* Auguste Rodin's *The Thinker* (1904)—and looks up. Though Nadia is indoors, Shepitko cuts to an image of a plane gliding through the sky. It performs several aerobatic maneuvers, suggesting Nadia's dexterity as a pilot. Mentally, Nadia casts herself out of her cramped apartment. She leaves her home for Merleau-Ponty's "homeland," the very source of wonder and imagination: the sky. In *Wings*, Shepitko uses the sky to affirm the vastness of a woman's inner world, despite the limitations of her social order.

It is as if, then, the sky comes out of Nadia herself. In *Wings*, we are not watching the sky as we had in *Heat*, but watching how Nadia's thoughts lift us into the sky. The free-floating point-of-view shots used in each of Shepitko's aerial interludes perceptually replicate the free-flowing quality of Nadia's mind (**see Figure 11.2**). Thus, these zero-gravity images cannot be easily categorized into what the French film theorist Gilles Deleuze, in his ambitious survey of film history, described as "time-images"—durational shots from a character's vantage point of the world as it unfolds in real time—or as "movement-images," which focus on a character's actions through space.[31] Rather, the sky in *Wings* is a "neuro-image" that creates an impression

Figure 11.2 Neuro-images of the sky.

of Nadia's interior landscape, which need not adhere to the ordinary rules of time and space.[32] These "neuro-images" confound cinematic taxonomies through their alternative synthesis of visual material. Through the sky, Shepitko tests the parameters of cinematic aesthetics as envisioned by male theorists and filmmakers, just as Nadia challenges the gendered strictures of postwar culture, as exemplified by the dressmaker, exactingly measuring Nadia's body, with whom *Wings* begins.

That this image of the sky appears after Nadia (politely) rebuffs a male suitor is also not incidental. The blueness of the sky—blue, Goethe says, "yields our gaze"—induces affective complexity.[33] "Feeling [. . .] lies not just in what we *do* but in what we *are*," that is, in the ever-changing atmosphere as embodied subjects who are (even on solid ground) susceptible to the sky's variations in ways that can evoke emotional responses concerning wistfulness, desire, nostalgia, and pleasure.[34] In *Wings*, Nadia recalls the sky after a failed romantic encounter because it (the sky) was where Nadia met the only man she ever loved, Mitya, another Red Army pilot. We learn, however, that a German aircraft gunned down Mitya, and Nadia bore witness to his crash. The wistfulness conveyed by Nadia's vision of the sky is, most basically, a longing for her lost lover. Yet it also betrays Nadia's more capacious desire to escape the patriarchal expectations of postwar society, personified by her lackluster suitor, that assume a middle-aged woman is in need of a man.

The following episode shows Nadia babysitting her neighbors' children. Nadia perfunctorily looks after them (covering her face with an aviation magazine to avoid their chatter), and she takes them to an airfield so that *she* can admire the planes. Dressed in a kerchief and a billowy blouse like a maternal Russian peasant woman—a far cry from her typically dour and androgynous appearance—Nadia is paid several compliments by her former male co-pilots, as if their old comrade-in-arms had been a mother-in-waiting all along. As viewers, we intuit Nadia's discomfort in adapting to the natalist regime of postwar society. The subsequent scene then shows Nadia in a kitchen mindlessly peeling potatoes, the domestic chore *par excellence*. The camera slowly tracks the coiling potato skin downward, visually re-enacting the tedium of Nadia's labor.

This long take of a woman peeling potatoes, which depicts the unglamorous and thankless work of women at the heart of the male-dominated world, looks ahead to an identical scene in what has been called "the first masterpiece" of feminist cinema: Chantal Akerman's *Jeanne Dielman, 23, quai du Commerce, 1080 Bruxelles* (1975).[35] As Lilya Kaganovsky argues, Akerman pioneered a kind of "counter cinema" that disrupted the aesthetic and topical conventions of mainstream cinema by accentuating alternative ways of looking at and occupying the world, often from a woman's point of view.[36] In *Jeanne Dielman* and *Wings*, both Akerman and Shepitko observe women peeling potatoes in long takes that make apparent the invisible labor of women "condemned" to their kitchens. These films dislodge the prevailing standards of cinematic eventhood, which coalesce around spectacle and drama, by portraying tiresome household chores. The hidden lives of women become "cinematic," and, in *Wings*, so, too, do their patterns of thought.

The camera tracks up from the potato peels to reveal Nadia's absentminded gaze. She is looking off-screen somewhere beyond the domiciliary confines of the kitchen, an illusory space that, though immaterial, is far "realer" than the vegetables she is holding in her hands. The matter of Nadia's mind overtakes the frame, and the screen is again filled by sky. The camera glides through the air, and our gaze is positioned from the perspective of a pilot, Nadia's during the war.

Yet this daydream is interrupted when Nadia's neighbor interjects, inquiring about the children. The sound of the woman's maternal concern causes reality to crash back into view, which the camera captures through a blurry close-up of a window that sharply comes into focus, reiterating the juddering fact that Nadia is "here" in the monotony of everyday life and not "there," somewhere up in the air. Irritated, Nadia asks: "Why should anyone be peeling potatoes on a Sunday afternoon?" She then storms out of the kitchen, saying:

"I'm going to a restaurant." Rebuffing the "un-cinematic" chores of cleaning and cooking—someone will now peel potatoes for *her*—Nadia protests the culture of postwar domesticity and, by turn, motherhood.[37] Inspired by her vision of the sky, Nadia abandons the kitchen and "extends herself into the street" by heading into Sevastopol's city center, where she will explore the spaces of postwar urbanism on her own, ideally uninterrupted.[38] Daydreams about the sky motivate Nadia's passage through real space. Wondering, for Shepitko, is a precondition for wandering. The culturally transgressive form of female *flânerie* configured by *Wings* is both earthbound and airborne, physical and psychical.

Additionally, in Soviet film history, the sky had fraught political connotations. The bird's-eye-view was a mainstay of cinema under Stalin, which celebrated pilots as conqueror figures capable of mapping and, therefore, extending state control and surveillance over the USSR's vast territory.[39] In Oleksandr Dovzhenko's *Aerograd* (1934), Iuli Raizman's *Pilots* (*Letchiki*, 1935), and Mikhail Kalatozov's *Valerii Chaklov* (1941), a film named after the pilot who made the first flight from Russia to the United States over the North Pole, aerial shots betray a Foucauldian, "controlling gaze" that "aligned with the totalizing" and "heroic vision" of Socialist Realism.[40]

By contrast, in *Wings*, Shepitko presents images of the sky in which the (female) pilot does not aspire for power, but sinuosity and spontaneity. Shepitko's sky is an *anti*-Soviet sky that rejects Soviet culture's drive toward mastery, reminding us again of Merleau-Ponty's aphoristic theory of the sky: "I am not *set over against* it as an acosmic subject; [. . .] I abandon myself in it and plunge into its mystery [. . .] I am the sky itself as it is drawn together and unified, my consciousness is saturated in its limitless blue." The sky, Shepitko recognizes, is experienced as a fusion between the perceiver and the world. It is not something "out there" to be overcome. The sky, if we open ourselves to it, can facilitate experiences of self-dissolution that integrates us into the world and the world into us. If Shepitko in *Heat* revealed that we exist in sky—subject to its meteorological fluctuations on earth—then Shepitko in *Wings* shows how sky also exists in *us*. The sky dwells in Nadia not only as memories, but as literal vapor: air. "Saturated in its limitless blue," Nadia carries traces of the sky with her into the cramped, indoor spaces of postwar urbanism.

It is telling, then, that Nadia's "acute presence of her own sensory experience" culminates when she is caught in a thunderstorm.[41] She stretches her hands toward the falling rain and lets it wash over her. The rain, like the winds of *Heat*, is a consequence of the sky's atmospheric shifts. The steadily falling rain draws out the contours of Nadia's material surroundings as it blankets the world in the sound of its own reverberations. Immersing herself in the haptic sensations of the rain, Nadia immerses herself in sky and is, in turn, submerged by it. While the people around her brandish umbrellas, Nadia chooses to mingle with the atmosphere, giving herself over to an experience of heightened presence that has escaped her for most of the film. The sky, as Merleau-Ponty puts it, "invades" all beings, and it is up to us to "meet this invasion," that is, to turn ourselves over to the sky's currents and recognize our interconnectedness with the world.[42] As David Macauley writes, "with our heads immersed in the thickness of the atmosphere or our lungs and limbs engaged with the swirling winds, we repeatedly breathe, think, and dream in the regions of the air."[43] Breathing in and out in the rain, Nadia takes in her medium; her inhalations are air becoming breath, and her expirations are breath becoming air. Life itself, *Wings* reveals, is born on the currents of the sky.

THE SKY AND JUSTICE, *THE ASCENT*

Shepitko's final film *The Ascent*, based on the 1970 Russian war novel *Sotnikov* by Vasil Bykov, takes place somewhere in Nazi-occupied Belarus during World War II. It follows a Soviet partisan (played by Boris Plotnikov) who is captured, tortured, and eventually executed by German soldiers. Critics celebrated *The Ascent* as one of the most significant works of Russian cinema for its unflinching portrayal of life on the Eastern Front.[44] Shepitko here rejected any hint of Socialist Realist propaganda that glorified life during the war in favor of exploring the conflict's brutalizing impact on ordinary citizens, and the sensitive topics of prisoners of war and Russian collaborators.

At first glance, *The Ascent* has little to do with the sky—much of the film unfolds indoors in the cramped spaces of attics, barns, holding pens, and interrogation chambers, while the portions of the film that do take place outside are focused on the earth: the punishingly cold landscape of a Belarusian winter. The continual upward glances of the film's protagonist, Sotnikov, have been interpreted not as literal skyward ones, but as looks to the numinous, appeals toward the divine. Drawing inspiration from traditional Russian icon painting and Fyodor Dostoevsky's *The Brothers Karamazov* (*Brat'ia karamzovy*, 1880), Shepitko has Sotnikov look up to convey his pleas to God like Christ on the cross.[45] The ascendant gaze in *The Ascent*, it is said, yearns for spiritual ascension.

Sotnikov, however, finds himself hopelessly earthbound, in the inexorable reality of being held prisoner by Nazi soldiers and Russian turncoats. Whereas all Shepitko's other films entertain moments of otherworldliness vis-à-vis the sky, *The Ascent* is too earthly, too blighted by the vicissitudes of terrestrial drama. It struggles, in a word, to ascend. Hence, the camera, maneuvered by Pavel Lebeshev, enacts the *d*escent of Sotnikov's ascendent pleas through downward tracking shots onto the snow-covered land. The vision of hell in *The Ascent* is not of fire and brimstone, but of permafrost: an infernal tundra.

The torrid winds of *Heat* have been replaced by gales of snow and ice, whose howls obstruct the soundtrack. In *The Ascent*, Shepitko reminds us that the arctic is also, meteorologically, a desert, not unlike the Kazakh steppe. Both *Heat* and *The Ascent* share a topographical interest in weather regions that overwhelm human beings' sensory capacities. The final sequence of *The Ascent* is nothing but images of snow drifts and frozen ground. The dreamy sky of *Heat*, it seems, no longer has a place in *The Ascent's* frostbitten diegesis. If anything, the grey sky in *The Ascent* replicates the endless tracts of snow on earth, fueling an impression that the whole world is a claustrophobic ball of ice. Shepitko's characters have lost access to sky.

The absence of the sky in *The Ascent*, I argue, relates to the questions of justice raised by the film more broadly. The sky, Elaine Scarry notes, is consistently distributed around the globe. Everyone is a "beneficiary of the sky" in that its "manifestations—its habit of alternating between blue and black, the phases of the moon, the sunrise and sunset—are present everywhere."[46] Everyone can claim "each piece of the sky" as uniquely "theirs."[47] The sky, in this sense, is "fair." It does not privilege any individual at anyone else's expense; it is equally capacious. Thus, Scarry argues, building on John Rawls's theory of fairness, the sky's symmetry is essential to our conceptions of justice, which likewise strive for a symmetry in human relations.[48] Justice hinges on a commitment to equality, a state of balance concerning peoples' rights. Though human society fails to evenhandedly administer justice, the sky is an example of something fundamentally just. It is everywhere regardless of "the specific ground on which fate has placed" us.[49] The sky is a model of ethical fairness and equanimity, a vision of what a utopian realm of absolute equality looks like in plain view right above our heads. Justice, as it were, reaches for the sky. Sotnikov's upturned gaze in *The Ascent* is not only beseeching for deliverance, but it is also crying out for *fairness*, an entreaty to alleviate the injustices endured by prisoners of war. In *The Ascent*, Shepitko allies our solidarities with those who are unjustly denied sky. The unfairness that often entails forms of imprisonment is redoubled by the absence of sky. Sotnikov's gazes futilely attempt to reconnect with the horizons that stretch out equidistantly in all directions, for all people.

Yet *The Ascent* demonstrates how the sky, notwithstanding its natural state of equilibrium, can be maldistributed based on the actions of humanity on Earth. Gagged and captured, Sotnikov loses contact with the sky. Whether camouflaging himself in brush, hiding in an attic, or being tortured in a detainment facility, Sotnikov is stripped of opportunities for skygazing like the kind enjoyed by Kemel in *Heat* and Nadia in *Wings*. The carceral world of a prisoner of war is one in which the sky has been "stolen" from them. The sky, Shepitko reveals, is not ever-present to all those who wish for it. Rather, it is a resource that is obstructed or enabled by human actions. The sky can be *made* unfair; it can be distributed differently for different people, which offsets its egalitarian dispersal. Like other forms of justice, the sky can be selectively and prejudicially apportioned.

Shepitko's sky in *The Ascent*, then, does not attend to an idea of justice as a static concept of equality, but to the more fluid matter of distributive justice as a function of equity: how inequalities are arranged and administered. The contextual specificity of any situation can result in lop-sided allocations of justice that regard some as "more equal" than others, that is, as more deserving of moral consideration, which inhibits genuine equality. In *The Ascent*, the symmetry of the sky is made asymmetrically unobtainable for Sotnikov because he is a Russian partisan in 1940s Belarus. The details of Sotnikov's biography constrain his access to justice and, in turn, sky. Everyone is not automatically a "beneficiary of the sky." Skygazing is socially and historically contingent. *The Ascent* concedes how justice is as fickle and fleeting as the ever-changing sky.

In this way, Shepitko presciently foresees how modern-day environmental justice also relates to matters of the sky. The forces of industrialization, climate change, air pollution, and urban sprawl—all of which started to garner worldwide attention in the 1970s through the early environmentalist movement in the final years of Shepitko's life—drastically erode the sky's accessibility in human culture, whether through smog, light pollution, or architecture.[50] These issues became particularly apparent in the late Soviet period as enormous chemical factories, often built next to residential complexes, belched pollutants into the air on an unprecedented scale with zero government oversight.[51] The smoggy conditions in some cities like Dneprodzerzhinsk became so dire that thousands of people needed to be evacuated from hazardous sites in 1976.[52]

Accordingly, environmental decay became a hallmark of late Soviet cinema, a "green" form of cultural dissidence, in films like Andrei Konchalovsky's *Siberiade* (*Siberiada*, 1978), Tarkovsky's *Stalker* (1979), and Elem Klimov's *Farewell* (*Proshchanie*, 1983), an "ecological fable" that Shepitko herself conceived of.[53] With their focus on wildlife, alienated characters, decrepit urban environments, and natural degradation (garbage, smog, deforestation, etc.), these films exemplify the environmental anxieties and injustices of late Soviet culture. The absence of the sky in *The Ascent* can thus be extrapolated as part of the "green turn" among Soviet filmmakers.

The sky above Sotnikov always appears grey and blurred, conjuring to mind not only snow, but also the toxic curtain of haze blanketing the cities of late socialism. In *The Ascent*, Shepitko's sky is shrouded by intersecting forms of injustice: political, carceral, and ecological. If Shepitko demonstrates how human beings are subject to the pulses of the sky above, then, so, too, does she show how the condition of the sky is determined by humanity below; the two exist in reciprocity.

The "fairness" of the sky, though, does not only raise questions about equality and justice. As Scarry argues, "A single word, 'fairness,' is used both" in reference "to the ethical requirement for 'being fair'" and "in referring to the loveliness of countenance."[54] Etymologically, the word "fair" is linked "to the verbs *vegen* (Dutch) and *fegen* (German) meaning 'to adorn,' 'to decorate,' and 'to sweep' [. . .] But *fegen* is in turn connected to the verb 'fay,' the transitive and intransitive verb meaning 'to join,' 'to unite,' 'to pact' [. . .] the making of a covenant or treaty or agreement."[55] Our notions of justice and ethical fairness tangle with ideas of beauty: aesthetic fairness.

The sky, then, is fair in that it is, on its own, equally distributed across the world, while it is also visually fair: enthralling, pleasing, striking. The injustice Sotnikov endures in *The Ascent*—and the spectatorial sympathy he evokes on his and, by turn, on all prisoners' of war behalf—entails not only a scarcity of ethical consideration, but also a loss of beauty. The beautiful, Scarry teaches us, facilitates an experience of "un-selfing," that is, beauty allies our concerns with our own self-preservation in service of the beautiful object before us.[56] To behold something as "fair," then, is to affirm a desire for the continuation of, what Scarry calls "the ongoingness of," beauty's presence that exists outside of us.[57] "People seem to wish there to be beauty even when their own self-interest is not served by it; or perhaps more accurately, people seem to intuit their own self-interest is served by distant peoples having the benefit of beauty."[58] Without beauty (fairness) some of our capacity to think capaciously (fairly) about others and the world beyond ourselves, to "give up our imaginary position at the center of the universe," is sorely diminished. "The absence of beauty is a profound form of deprivation."[59] The injustices of wars and jails evacuate the beautiful out of everyday life.

Indeed, the absence of the sky in *The Ascent* is even visually unjust. Having viewers dwell in the windswept, grey backdrop of war-torn Belarus, Shepitko makes us, like Sotnikov, long for the dreamy overhead vistas in *Heat* and *Wings* as an ethical and aesthetical source of fairness. The unfairness of *The Ascent* intensifies our desire for a just outcome to the war and, by turn, a recovery of beauty in the world, which, in *The Ascent*, struggles to emerge—just as it often does in real life. Nevertheless, moments of beauty do peer through *The Ascent*'s otherwise darkened diegesis. There are a few moments when, looking up, Sotnikov (and the camera, assuming his point of view) catches a glimpse of the night sky. In each instance, he sees a full moon shining in the distance (see **Figure 11.3**). The image of the moon in *The Ascent*, at first blush, again relays Shepitko's critical commentary on the folly of the Cold War space race: on the hidebound ambition to conquer the skies while people needlessly suffer on earth. The Apollo moon landing, mentioned above, occurred only a few years before *The Ascent*'s premier. In a deeper sense, the moon in *The Ascent* adds a lyrical flourish, a hint of beauty, to this punishing film that, at times, seems bereft of hope.

Enchantment with the moon dates to the earliest manifestations of human culture.[60] The Paleolithic sketches of animals scrawled on the limestone

Figure 11.3 Sotnikov looking at the moon.

interiors of the Lascaux caves in France, among the oldest artefacts in human history, feature a lunar calendar chronicling the moon's activity in the sky.[61] Of all the sky's motley "furnishings," the moon has been perhaps *the* catalyst of human imagination, and it is no wonder that it has been a vital element to cultural production: Vincent van Gogh's *Starry Night* (1889); Georges Méliès's *Le Voyage dans la Lune* (1902); and Laurie Anderson's *To the Moon* (2020), to cite but a few entries from myriad examples. For many cultures, the moon is a symbol of transience and transformation, having to do with everything from werewolves to the tides to romance, biology, and passion to premonitory thinking. In *The Ascent*, Sotnikov's glances at the moon suggest the possibility of alteration, a figurative sea change on land, that belies the interminable realities of war and imprisonment. The moonlight faintly promises a return of fairness—beauty and, therefore, justice—to the world beneath the sky. "Beauty is pacific," Scarry concludes, "its reciprocal salute to the continued existence, its pact, is indistinguishable from the word peace."[62] The exquisite image of the moon in *The Ascent* makes us hunger for tranquility, a desire for freedom and weightlessness out from under the burden of terrestrial injustice, much like the sort wished for by Nadia in *Wings* and Kemel in *Heat*.

To conclude, Shepitko's sky functions as a site of atmospheric knowledge conducive to desire, wonder, and fantasy—not unlike a movie screen. The sky, in all Shepitko's films, is an *aesthetic screen* by which to read and experience the world, always wishing for it to be otherwise.[63]

THE OPEN END

Each film discussed in this chapter—*Heat*, *Wings*, *The Ascent*—does not end in a traditional narratological sense. Any narrative is the result of an act of storytelling, which must stop somewhere. Conventionally, a story rarely simply stops. Rather, it will offer a sense of closure, a "phenomenological feeling of finality that is generated when all the questions saliently posed by the narrative are answered."[64] Closure facilitates a sensation of resolution. It is an impression of completeness that helps the audience exit from a story-world, "the degree to which the complicating event has been resolved and, consequently, how its emotionality has decreased."[65] Ever elusive, Shepitko disfavors this sort of pat ending, another gesture of resistance to the self-assuredness of Soviet ideology that claimed to have resolved all of history's quandaries.

The ending of *Heat* consists of Kemel's primary antagonist abandoning the Virgin Lands Campaign to the dismay of his wife, who blames Kemel for ruining their marriage. The final shot of the film shows Shepitko's characters with their backs turned to the camera watching the man fade into the distance. They share with Shepitko's viewers the uncertainty of what is in store for the steppe. At the end of *Wings*, Nadia finally re-enters the cockpit of a plane and—to the surprise of a throng of male pilots—unexpectedly takes off into the sky. It is unclear whether Nadia, a kind of Soviet Amelia Earhart, impulsively sets off on a joyride, departs for a new location, or commits suicide. Perhaps the freedom afforded by death is Nadia's only escape out of the rigidly patriarchal culture of the postwar order? Nadia's fate is, literally, left up in the air. Finally, *The Ascent* concludes after the execution of Sotnikov with his comrade Rybak (Vladimir Gostyukhin) undergoing an out-of-body vision of himself escaping the German prison only to be gunned down. Rybak then attempts to hang himself, whereafter he stares at an open gate before collapsing. The camera "exits" the gate and presents us with a series of de-populated wintry landscape shots to close the film. The fate of Rybak, or that of any other Russian collaborator, is unknown. We can only infer what happens to them based on the actual events of World War II. None of Shepitko's endings generate "a phenomenological feeling of finality." They are kept open, exposed to chance. These non-endings reject closure, replicating the fickleness and open-endedness of the sky.

The sky, in fact, has no limit. Its vastness stretches for miles overhead, when at a certain point of elevation, the air becomes so thin that sky turns into space, which extends out to infinity. There is no "closure" to the sky, only mystery, randomness, and irresolution—three descriptors that aptly characterize

Shepitko's cinematic project. The sky, for Shepitko, presents an ever-changing view of the world just as her films offer open-ended, alternative views onto Soviet culture. It is hauntingly coincidental, then, that Shepitko, this lover of skies perished in a freak automobile accident. Just as Shepitko's films lack definitive endings, there was no closure to her life or career. Shepitko became a thing of the sky, a vaporous memory, while her films linger with us on earth.

NOTES

1. Andrei Tarkovsky, "The Artist in Ancient Russia and in the new USSR," interview with Michel Ciment, Luda Schnitzer, and Jean Schnitzer (1969), trans. Susanna Rosenberg in *Andrei Tarkovsky Interviews*, ed. John Gianvito (Jackson: University of Mississippi Press, 2006), 16–31.
2. Ibid., 25.
3. Ibid., 25–26.
4. The 1969 Moscow Film Festival took place between July 7 and July 22, 1969, while the Apollo 11 moon landing occurred between July 16 and July 20, 1969.
5. Tarkovsky makes a note of Shepitko's untimely death, a result of a high-speed car accident, in his diary in July 1979. Andrei Tarkovsky, *Andrey Tarkovsky: Time Within Time, The Diaries 1970–1986*, trans. Kitty Hunter-Blair (London: Faber and Faber, 1994), 186.
6. For the Thaw's impact on cinema, see Josephine Woll, *Real Images: Soviet Cinema and the Thaw* (London: I.B. Tauris, 1999).
7. Born into a Kyrgyz and Tatar family, Aitmatov, considered to be one of the best-known figures in Kyrgyz literature, began publishing during the Thaw. For a reading of "The Camel's Eye," see Mieka Erley, *On Russian Soil: Myth and Materiality* (Ithaca: Cornell University Press, 2021), 81–84.
8. Since the early nineteenth century, Bishkek had been known as Pishpek, but Soviet authorities renamed it "Frunze" after the Red Army leader Mikhail Frunze.
9. Anton Chekhov, "The Steppe," *The Complete Short Novels*, trans. Richard Peavear and Larissa Volokhonsky (New York: Vintage Classics, 2005), 6, 31.
10. Leonid Brezhnev, *Tselina* (Moscow: Izd. Politicheskoi literatury, 1980), 2.
11. "By the Thaw period, writers had abundant resources for euphemizing and sublimating sexual content. Readers of the 1950s and 1960s were shocked by direct reference to sex, but they were quite used to its sublimation in earthly folkloric tropes of plowing, sowing, and harvesting. In Virgin Lands cultural production, the plowing of the 'first furrow' was the most important recurring sexual motif." Erley, 79.
12. Ibid., 83.
13. Ibid., 82–83.
14. Lida Oukaderova discusses how another film, Mikhail Kalatozov's film *The Unsent Letter* (*Neotpravlennoe pis'mo*, 1960), which follows the adventures of three Soviet geologists in central Siberia, also presents the earth in a way that

"appear[s] disorienting, defying the control and mastery of a centralized locus of power." Lida Oukaderova, *The Cinema of the Soviet Thaw: Space, Materiality, and Movement* (Bloomington: Indiana University Press, 2017), 51.
15. Ibid., 151–179.
16. Paul Josephson et al., *An Environmental History of Russia* (Cambridge: Cambridge University Press, 2013), 151.
17. Tim Ingold, "Earth, Sky, Wind, and Weather," *The Journal of the Royal Anthropological Institute* 13 (2007): S19–S25.
18. Ibid., S31.
19. "'Znoi.' Kak khrupkaia devushka Larisa Shepitko snimala fil'm o sil'nykh liudiakh," *Limon* (June 2015): https://limon.kg/ru/news:66179.
20. Carter Soles, "'And No Birds Sing': Discourses of Environmental Apocalypse in 'The Birds' and 'Night of the Living Dead,'" *Interdisciplinary Studies in Literature and Environment* 21.3 (2014): 528.
21. For the openness of Thaw-era film culture, see Lilya Kaganovsky, "Postmemory, Countermemory: Soviet Cinema of the 1960s," *The Socialist Sixties: Crossing Borders in the Second World*, eds. Anne E. Gorsuch and Diana P. Koenker (Bloomington: Indiana University Press, 2013), 235–321. Knowledge about foreign films also came through discussions and reviews in popular Soviet film magazines. See, for example, a negative review of Hitchcock's *Pyscho* (1960) published in a 1963 edition of *Iskusstvo kino*. *KinoArt* (June 16, 2020): https://kinoart.ru/reviews/yad-ubivayuschiy-zritelya-sovetskaya-otritsatelnaya-retsenziya-na-film-psiho-hichkoka.
22. Josephson et al., 146–152.
23. The Virgin Lands Campaign coincided with the height of the Soviet space race, another effort to conquer the skies. With its barren expanses of land, the Kazakh steppe became a kind of moonscape, the epicenter of the Soviets' dreams of conquest that hailed not only the spreading of communism on earth but throughout the galaxy. *Heat* resists the discourse of (extra-)terrestrial conquest during the Virgin Lands.
24. For the "loosening of the screws" of Stalinism during the war, see Peter Kenez, *A History of the Soviet Union from the Beginning to the End*, 2nd ed. (Cambridge: Cambridge University Press, 2006).
25. Unlike other combatant countries, the Soviet Union mobilized women *en masse* after the outbreak of hostilities—over 800,000 women during the war, and over half of them were in front-line duty. See D'Ann Campbell, "Women in Combat: The World War II Experience in the United States, Great Britain, Germany, and the Soviet Union," *The Journal of Military History* 57.2 (1993): 318. Stanislav Rostotsky's iconic film *The Dawns Here are Quiet* (*A zori zdes' tikhie*, 1972) thematizes the newfound freedoms of and challenges faced by Red Army women soldiers.
26. Irene Sánchez Cózar, "The Invisible Combatants of World War II: Soviet Female Soldiers in the Socialist State," *Global Strategy* (May 2022): https://global-strategy.org/the-invisible-combatants-of-world-war-ii-soviet-female-soldiers-in-the-socialist-state/
27. Oukaderova, 117.

28. Ibid., 126.
29. Jeffrey N. Peters and Katharina N. Piechocki, "Early Modern Clouds and the Poetics of Meteorology: An Introduction," *Romance Quarterly* 68.2: 66.
30. Maurice Merleau-Ponty, *Phenomenology of Perception*, trans. Colin Smith (London: Routledge & Kegan Paul, 1962), 24.
31. See Gilles Deleuze, *Cinema 1: The Movement-Image*, trans. Hugh Tomlinson and Barbara Habberjam (Minneapolis: University of Minnesota Press, 1986); Deleuze, *Cinema 2: The Time-Image*, trans. Robert Galeta (Minneapolis: University of Minnesota Press, 1989).
32. Patricia Pisters, *The Neuro-Image: A Deleuzian Film-Philosophy of Digital Screen Culture* (Stanford: Stanford University Press, 2012).
33. Quoted in Merleau-Ponty, 244.
34. Ingold, S29.
35. Lilya Kaganovsky, "Ways of Seeing: On Kira Muratova's *Brief Encounters* and Larisa Shepitko's *Wings*," *The Russian Review* 71 (2012): 482.
36. Ibid., 483.
37. In *Wings*, Nadia has an adopted daughter with whom she has a somewhat strained relationship. Nadia conceals the fact of her daughter's adoption to maintain her traditionally "feminine" image as a woman who has given birth.
38. This interrupted vision anticipates a later scene when Nadia, impulsively breaking into dance, sees a gaggle of men leering at her. She immediately stops and awkwardly waves, "projecting her sense of reification under the gaze of men." Oukaderova, 126.
39. For pilots in Stalin-era film, see Emma Widdis, *Visions of a New Land: Soviet Film from the Revolution to the Second World War* (New Haven: Yale University Press, 2003), 128–135.
40. Ibid., 135.
41. Oukaderova, 132.
42. Merleau-Ponty, 317.
43. David Macauley, "The Flowering of Environmental Roots and the Four Elements in Presocratic Philosophy: From Empedocles to Deleuze and Gauttari," *Worldviews: Environment, Culture, Religion* 9 (2005): 307.
44. For *The Ascent*'s release history, see Anastasia Sorokina, "*The Lady Vanishes*: Soviet Censorship, Socialist Realism, and the Disappearance of Larisa Shepitko," *Film Matters* (Winter 2017): 21–27.
45. For the religious overtones of *The Ascent*, see Jason Merrill, "Religion, Politics, and Literature in Larisa Shepitko's *The Ascent*," *Slovo* 18.2 (2006): 147–162; Jane Costlow, "Icons, Landscape, and the Boundaries of Good and Evil: Larisa Shepitko's *The Ascent* (1977)," *Border Visions: Identity and Diaspora in Film*, eds. Jane Kazecki et al. (Lanham: Scarecrow Press, 2013).
46. Elaine Scarry, *On Beauty and Being Just* (Princeton: Princeton University Press, 1999), 119–120.
47. Ibid., 20.
48. Ibid., 93–101.
49. Ibid., 121.

50. The United Nations, for example, held its first conference on environmental protection in 1972, in which Soviet representatives reluctantly participated after initially backing out. Yet Soviet authorities banned the publication of Carson's *Silent Spring*, which in the United States catalyzed the creation of the Environmental Protection Agency (EPA), out of fear that it would spark a similar civic movement for greater environmental stewardship. Josephson, et al., 191.
51. Throughout the late 1970s and early 1980s, Soviet emissions of sulfur dioxide into the air topped over 25 million tons annually, far more than that of any other European country. Ibid., 221.
52. Ibid., 217.
53. Shepitko and Klimov had been romantically involved since the 1960s, but the two had worked separately. In the late 1970s, Shepitko planned to adapt Valentin Rasputin's 1976 novel *Farewell to Matyora* (*Proshchanie s Materoi*) about the deleterious impact of Soviet industry and urbanization on the Russian peasantry. Shepitko, however, died in a car accident in 1979 after the first day of shooting. The film was completed by Klimov, now a widower, in 1981.
54. Scarry, 91.
55. Ibid., 91–92.
56. Ibid., 113.
57. Ibid., 111.
58. Ibid., 123.
59. Ibid., 118.
60. For a cultural history of the moon, see Bernd Brunner, *Moon: A Brief History* (New Haven: Yale University Press, 2011).
61. For a thrilling exploration of these caves, see Werner Herzog's 2013 documentary *Cave of Forgotten Dreams*.
62. Scarry, 107.
63. For a sustained theorization of "the-sky-as-screen" metaphor, see Kristi McKim, *Cinema as Weather: Stylistic Screens and Atmospheric Changes* (Oxfordshire: Routledge, 2013).
64. Noël Carroll, "Narrative Closure," *Philosophical Studies* 135 (2007): 1.
65. Tilmann Habermas and Nadine Berger, "Retelling Everyday Emotional Events: Condensation, Distancing, and Closure," *Cognition and Emotion* 25 (2011): 208.

PART VI

Shepitko in Post-Soviet Cinema

CHAPTER 12

The White, the Black, and the Gray: The Problem of Choice in Larisa Shepitko's *The Ascent* and Sergei Loznitsa's *In the Fog*

Sergey Toymentsev

INTRODUCTION

After the release of Sergei Loznitsa's war drama *In the Fog* [*V tumane*] (2012), both domestic and international film critics were quick to notice how much it overlaps with Larisa Shepitko's *The Ascent* [*Voskhozhdenie*] (1977). In his interviews Loznitsa admits her influence as well as unavoidable similarities with *The Ascent*, since both films are literary adaptations of Vasil' Bykov's stories, yet he rejects the pathos it elicits. As he elaborates,

> *The Ascent* is also based on Vasil' Bykov's story, which is *Sotnikov* [or *The Ordeal* in English translation]. He wrote *In the Fog* later, already in the eighties, and the subject matter of this story is a variation of *Sotnikov*'s one. Hence the similarities and differences. I begin my film with the hanging scene, which is the culmination and one of the final sequences in Shepitko's film. There is no such scene in the original, yet I had to add it, because it is very important and sets the tone of the film. The scene, just like the entire movie, is restrained and devoid, as far as possible, of any pressure, accentuation, and pathos. That pathos does figure in Shepitko's film. In this sense, it is a stylistic disagreement as well as a different take on the subject matter.[1]

Loznitsa is thus fully aware that his adaptation of Bykov's novella stylistically and ideologically departs from Shepitko's by offering a new interpretation of the partisan resistance movement in Nazi-occupied Belarus, devoid of patriotic sentiments. Vasil' Bykov's war stories are usually viewed as the dramatization of the liminal situation in which a protagonist must make a choice between good and evil, in which the latter stands invariably for deserting or collaborating with the Nazis and the former is reduced to nothing but death. Whereas almost all Soviet adaptations of Bykov's stories celebrate the protagonist's freedom of choice made in favor of self-sacrifice, Loznitsa is skeptical about the possibility of existentialist autonomy and moral agency in the context of life-and-death situations and argues instead for the primacy of deterministic conditions in one's decision-making. As he likes to reiterate in his interviews, "There is an amazing phrase at the end of Bykov's story: 'A person can't do everything. Sometimes it's not possible to do anything at all.' This is exactly what bothers me. The situation has developed like this – and you are its hostage . . ."[2]

In this chapter I would like to examine how Shepitko's *The Ascent* and Loznitsa's *In the Fog* diverge in their treatment of the problem of choice faced by Bykov's protagonist by placing them in their respective historical and ideological contexts as well as look at how both films nonetheless complement rather than contradict each other in their interpretation of the writer's existentialist ethic and ideas which evolved over time. I will also discuss both films in the context of Gilles Deleuze's taxonomy of cinematic images by viewing *The Ascent* as example of the affection-image that celebrates spiritual choice and *In the Fog* as that of the impulse-image which, on the contrary, problematizes the subject's free agency.

VASIL' BYKOV'S *THE ORDEAL* AND *IN THE FOG* IN CONTEXT

In his 1973 essay "How *Sotnikov* Was Written," Vasil' Bykov delves into the reasons that motivated him to write the novella and begins with the following disclosure:

> First and foremost, I was interested in two moral questions, which can be simplified as follows: what is a person in the face of the crushing force of inhuman circumstances? What is he or she capable of when the possibilities to defend his or her life are exhausted to the end, and it is impossible to prevent death?[3]

This oft-quoted statement succinctly captures the philosophical essence of *The Ordeal*, yet it can equally be applied to any other story written by Bykov from the late 1950s to the 1990s, since almost all of them focus on how war transforms a person and how one could remain human in the face of inhuman circumstances. Even though Bykov was preoccupied with one and the same subject throughout his long and prolific career, his answers to these moral questions differed over time, depending on the changing ideological climate of the Soviet regime as well as the evolution of his own literary method. Whereas in his early and mid-career writings Bykov diligently explores the psychological motives of the soldiers' courage and readiness for self-sacrifice, thereby affirming their freedom and responsibility for their decisions and actions, since the 1980s his protagonists' act of suicide is no longer viewed as a heroic deed but rather as that of destiny or one's inevitable surrender to overpowering circumstances. Both *The Ordeal* and *In the Fog* perfectly illustrate the writer's uneasy and lifelong transition from romantic existentialism to gloomy determinism. Yet before we look into the details of these novellas, a few more examples from Bykov's oeuvre would clarify the logic of this development.

In his early war stories, such as *The Crane's Cry* (*Zhuravliny krik*, 1959) and *The Third Flare* (*Tret'ia raketa*, 1961), Bykov explores the sources of courage and treachery by having his characters assigned an impossible task to defend a certain territory against the Nazis, in which almost all of them perish, albeit heroically. By delineating their psychological portraits, he demonstrates how each of them are acutely aware of the impossibility of their mission and that each of them nevertheless must make a commitment to carry out their patriotic duty to the very end. It is hard not to notice how Bykov's economy of sacrifice increasingly loses its pragmatic value throughout the years, thus prioritizing its metaphysical essence. Whereas in his earlier works the soldiers' heroism is rewarded with the Red Army's regaining its position, his later characters in the 1970s often sacrifice themselves for nothing, without being able to change anything with their deaths. For example, in *Monument* (*Obelisk*, 1971) a group of reckless schoolchildren in the occupied Belarusian village attack one of the local Nazi collaborators and are captured instead. After the police promise to release them if their schoolteacher Moroz surrenders, the latter turns himself in while knowing he'd still be executed together with his students. In *To Live Until the Dawn* (*Dozhit' do rassveta*, 1972), the lieutenant Ivanovsky fails his mission to locate the German ammunition dump, yet, instead of getting back to the regular army with his remaining group, he blows himself up with a German soldier. As Zina J. Gimpelevich points out, for many "the lieutenant is obviously a fanatic" or "kamikaze figure." Yet, she continues, "this type of fanaticism . . . was typical of the time, and it brought victory, however bloody and bitter, to the Soviets . . . The secret of this victory against vastly better-equipped armies lies in these unprecedented human losses, in which Soviet soldiers often willingly sacrificed their lives."[4]

Sotnikov is therefore one of Bykov's typical "kamikaze" characters, "depressed by the weight of guilt"[5] and willing to sacrifice themselves. During the night before execution, Sotnikov decides to take the blame upon himself, hoping to save others; and with this decision he experiences an existentialist epiphany:

> Now everything was clear and categorical. So as not to console himself with empty hopes, he shook off one after another all the illusions he had had in life, and knew that ahead there lay nothing. In a way this was a

relief, because it gave him the opportunity to limit severely his choice of action. If anything now remained in life to concern him, it was only his final responsibilities towards the people around him . . . Once he had come to terms with his own death, for a few hours he achieved a strange, almost absolute independence from the strength of his enemies. Now that he had abandoned all hope of preserving his own life he felt able to indulge other more altruistic ideas. He felt that he had gained a new *opportunity*, which could not be suppressed by the enemy, nor by circumstances, nor by anyone in the world. Since he was afraid of nothing, he had a clear advantage over the others, and over his former self as well. Of course this was the advantage of a dead man, but at the same time it seemed the main, and perhaps the only real value in his essentially insignificant life (emphasis added).[6]

This passage showcases how Sotnikov, being the burdensome weakling throughout the entire journey and whose sickness has compromised his competence for the assigned mission and thus becomes the cause of its failure, finds in death an *opportunity* to shine and affirm himself as a dead man in resolute clarity and absolute freedom. Even though his self-sacrifice does not save others from hanging, the very thought of it empowers him as autonomous subject transcending fear, circumstances, and his former self. Many readers would find his change of character unexpected or illogical, since "at first [he] seemed to be rather spineless."[7] Yet his discovery of an inner spiritual core beyond the everyday self seems to derive from the impractical or immaterial nature of his personality. As Vasil' Bykov appears to suggest, for those who prioritize moral values over practical matters and who selflessly consider their life "essentially insignificant" the choice between life and death "in the face of the crushing force of inhuman circumstances" is relatively easy. That is, the spiritual choice in favor of death appears to be somewhat consistent with one's inability to succeed in life.

As is known, the original title of the novella was intended to be *Liquidation*, yet it was changed into *Sotnikov* by Aleksandr Tvardovsky's suggestion to pacify the censors. For Bykov, however, the "main dramatic conflict of the plot is shared equally between two people: Rybak and Sotnikov."[8] Furthermore, in his essay "How *Sotnikov* Was Written" he elaborates how Rybak's character is based on the real story of his acquaintance whom he met among German prisoners towards the end of the war. Presumed to have been killed on the battlefield, Bykov's acquaintance was captured by the Germans and offered to collaborate with them, which he accepted while hoping to escape later. But since he failed to escape, afterwards he became one of the Nazis himself. In his essay, therefore, Bykov formulates the main question that his novella attempts to address: how does one who used to be a good and reliable person become a traitor in the face of death? For Bykov, it is the survival instinct that is responsible for one's treachery. Yet in his novella he complicates this argument: Rybak who is more prone to survive is also more capable of completing a mission, whereas Sotnikov, uninterested in survival, is, however, incapable of completing a mission. The "kamikaze figure" of Sotnikov who fails the mission yet is ready to die for the cause reframes the question of choice as that of one's inner predisposition. The main question that the novella seems to posit is thus: who would be a better fit for the military mission, a weaker soldier but loyal in the face of death or a stronger one but potentially treacherous? The choice between these options would be that between idealism and pragmatism. And in Bykov's ethical system (as well as for his Soviet commentators), it is of course one's idealist commitment to moral principles and patriotism that prevails over the pragmatism of the survival instinct.

Throughout his career Bykov keeps coming back to the problem of this alternative – between the idealism of death and the pragmatism of life – as if he seemed unsatisfied with the choices made in *The Ordeal*. For example, in his 1978 novella *To Go and Not Return* (*Poiti i ne vernut'sia*) he restages the same dramatic conflict between two partisans – Zosia and Anton Golubin – who personify the opposite sides of the dilemma. In the 1980s, however, he is no longer interested in exploring one's idealist opting for death in terms of choice. As Gimpelevich observes, "by the middle of the 1980s, or as soon as perestroika started, Bykau's familiar 'optimistic tragedy' gave way to stronger existentialist tendencies."[9] In his later writings, Bykov's protagonists sacrifice their lives not because of their choice but because death is viewed as inevitable, as the only viable option left for them. For example, in *Sign of Misfortune* (*Znak bedy*, 1982) the peasant woman Stepanida commits suicide by self-immolation because she is no longer capable of enduring sufferings from the Nazis. In *The Raid* (*Oblava*, 1988) focused on the horrors of collectivization, the gulag fugitive Chviodar returns to his native village; yet, instead of being welcomed by his neighbors, he is chased down by them to the swamps where he decides to drown. In *The Quarry* (*Kar'ier*, 1986), Bykov "continues his lifetime literary investigation of moral choice,"[10] and once again he arrives at the same conclusion he came to earlier: that one's self-sacrifice is but the only decision that one must make in order to remain human. In this novel the wounded lieutenant Ageyev, hiding in the Nazi-occupied Belarusian village, sends a young woman he loves on a dangerous mission, who is then caught and probably executed; fifty years after the war he is still tormented by guilt and can't find peace with himself. It is in this context of Bykov's literary evolution that we should read his "gloomiest"[11] novella *In the Fog* (*V tumane*, 1988) focused on the railroad worker Sushenya who is accused of treason he never committed and whose suicide is viewed as the only option left for him.

Both Sotnikov and Sushenya are, therefore, typical protagonists in Bykov's speculative fiction and personify different stages in his writing career. Whereas in his earlier writings one's self-sacrifice is celebrated as the moral choice between alternatives, later it is mourned as an inescapable inevitability. The difference of these two approaches to the problem of choice is similarly reflected in Shepitko's and Loznitsa's adaptations: whereas the former views it in terms of existentialist melodrama, the latter demystifies it through cinematic naturalism.

THE ASCENT AND THE AFFECTION-IMAGE

In an interview to the question about why she decided to make *The Ascent*, Shepitko responds that this decision came to her almost by accident after she went to the cinema to see a war drama *The Living and the Dead* [*Zhivye i miortvye*] (Aleksandr Stolper, 1964). While being deeply moved by a dramatic scene in which an unarmed Soviet soldier throws a stone at a German tank and dies, she all of a sudden noticed how other viewers sitting next to her were discussing who would go for ice cream during the break. As she exclaims,

> This tragic scene did not touch them at all! As if something got dull or fell asleep in them. How so? How is it that we, filmmakers, managed to "lull" viewers to such an extent that they became so indifferent . . . It is then that a firm intention to adapt Vasil' Bykov's *Sotnikov* first came to me . . . The film that we are shooting I would like to address first of all to such "dormant" people, such as my cinema neighbors. We must shake those who have fallen asleep.[12]

In her interviews Shepitko repeatedly emphasized how important it was for her as the filmmaker to affect the viewer emotionally: "My goal is to address emotions directly, and only then the upper layers of consciousness."[13] In this regard, Susan Sontag described *The Ascent* as "the most affecting film about the sadness of war."[14] It is precisely because of its intensely affective nature that Shepitko's film falls out of the Soviet war film canon by subverting its aesthetic and ideology of heroic action with her intentionally passionate take on the subject as well as uncharacteristic metaphysical and moral questions. To put the film's difference in terms of Deleuze's taxonomy of cinematic images, in contrast to a typical war movie based on the sensory-motor schema of the action-image, *The Ascent* foregrounds the spiritual affect via the affection-image which unmoors the narrative from its normal anchorage in the world.

For Deleuze, the affection-image is abstracted from the spatio-temporal coordinates and, unlike the action-image that relies on the concrete tension between forces such as in exertion-resistance, action-reaction, and excitation-response, deals with the possible or potentiality without actualizing it. Expressed primarily by the close-ups of characters' faces, affection-images deindividuate and depersonalize them by isolating their affects from any empirical context and thus suspending the action-oriented narrative. Such suspension is effectively accomplished in Dreyer's *Passion of Joan of Arc* (1928) which, for Deleuze, is "the affective film *par excellence*" that develops simultaneously in two directions or temporalities that "ceaselessly intersect, one of which is endlessly arriving and the other is already established . . . one goes the whole length of the historical event, but that one ascends inside the other event."[15] On the one hand, the film documents Joan's trial and historical characters involved in it: the bishop, the judges, the people, etc. On the other, through a series of short close-ups it extracts from the trial the passion or martyrdom of Joan, which "enters into a virtual conjunction with that of Christ."[16] The film's historical temporality is presented in the actual state of things, whereas inside it there is another temporality which is affective and suprahistorical (or virtual) and which "goes beyond its own actualisation" and "only refers to the faces which express it."[17]

In another interview Shepitko tries to compare *The Ascent* to other religious films:

> I couldn't name a single film "similar" to the one we were about to make. Buñuel's "Nazarine"? Bergman's "Seventh Seal"? Pasolini's "The Gospel According to St. Matthew"? All these films seemed close to the direction of our work. And yet they didn't suit us at all. These are smart, philosophically deep, and brilliantly done pictures. But you watch them as if completely from aside, too rationally and abstractly. The point here is that they are based on the genre of a "pure" and quite traditional parable, which, for all its intellectualism and depth, cannot engage and shock emotionally.[18]

By dismissing famous religious films as being too abstract and rational, Shepitko does not mention Dreyer's *Passion of Joan of Arc* as an example to follow, yet the latter does align with her striving for the viewer's emotional engagement. Many critics have noticed the excessive and meticulous use of close-ups in *The Ascent*. As William Guynn points out, "It is difficult to recall any film since Dreyer's *Passion of Joan of Arc* that is so intensely focused on the human face as a terrain to be explored."[19] Indeed, *The Ascent* is probably the only war movie in the history of cinema consisting of so many close-ups and could equally be called the Soviet "documentary of faces."[20] Furthermore, just as *Passion of Joan of Arc* inscribes an eternal Christological narrative of Joan's martyrdom into her historically documented trial, so does *The Ascent* with a typical wartime story by emphasizing its timeless dimension. This is how Shepitko elaborates the difference of her film from the original:

> The plot of the novella is simple and might seem familiar at first glance . . . But, as is often the case, the depth of its artistic insight

made it only an occasion for a detailed and unvarnished study of a person, his consciousness and subconscious, at the moment of the most difficult choice – between life and death.[21]

[Sotnikov] deals with the question of immortality on a different, spiritual level. Here he comes into conflict with Portnov, who believes that if there is nothing up there, then everything is permitted. In Bykov's novella everything is decided on the level of Rybak and Sotnikov. We decided to deepen Portnov's character because both Portnov and Sotnikov understand each other and deal with such questions at the highest level.[22]

In Shepitko's suprahistorical drama, therefore, the problem of choice between life and death is played out between Sotnikov, Rybak, and Portnov, each of whom, according to the film critic Elena Stishova, represent moral, pre-moral, and amoral ethics respectively.[23] What is most interesting about *The Ascent* is that the characters' ethical perspectives are expressed primarily through the affection-images of their faces. It is through a succession of close-ups accompanied by Alfred Schnittke's multilayered score that Sotnikov is torn away from real space and time and elevated to Christ-figure status. For example, when he is wounded in the snowy field, he decides to shoot himself with a rifle, while staring up into the sky. As Jane Costlow observes, "The face we see as he attempts and fails to commit suicide, or weeps in anguish, is an icon of absolute suffering."[24] Costlow goes as far as to describe all the faces in *The Ascent* as being "reminiscent of icons, religious images fundamental to Orthodoxy," among which Sotnikov is "the film's most obvious icon."[25] This is most evident in the cellar sequence, when he awaits execution with others and his gaunt, icon-like face is illuminated against the dark, ominous background, or in his "transfigured face" during the scene of the hanging (see Fig. 12.1).

As Shepitko points out, Rybak does not have that spiritual core that Sotnikov has: "When he tragically realized that he howled like a dog."[26] Whereas beatific Sotnikov spiritually transcends his human nature, Rybak does so from the other end of the spectrum – animality. In contrast to Sotnikov's transfigured face, Rybak's face is disfigured through violent affects such as fear, terror, confusion, distress, desperation, and anguish. For example, in the end, tormented by guilt, he attempts to hang himself in the outhouse by squeezing his head into the noose of his belt, thus signaling a complete obliteration of his personality (see Fig. 12.2), or when he falls on his knees afterwards and weeps in despair.

Portnov's close-ups complete Shepitko's triangle of ethical choices by offering a consciously anti-humanist perspective that cynically downgrades human beings as scum. Despite his character's explicitly siding with evil and darkness

Figure 12.1 Sotnikov's close-up during the execution.

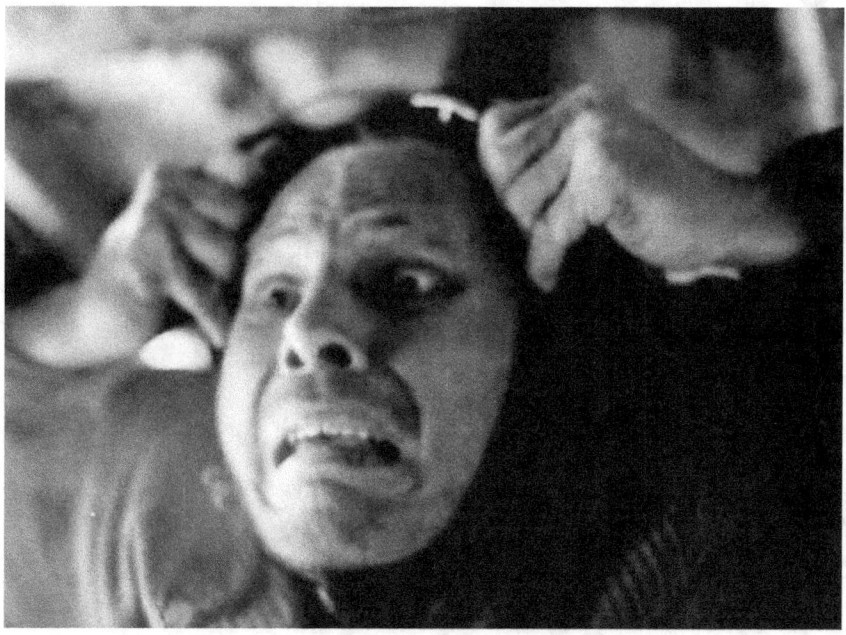

Figure 12.2 Rybak's close-up during his suicide attempt.

in the film, there's nothing terrifying in his facial expressions displayed by his smugness, penetrative gaze, quiet attentiveness, inquisitive observation, and restrained bewilderment. Unlike Rybak's betrayal, Portnov's decision to collaborate with the Nazis is driven by knowledge and argumentative logic rather than survival instincts, as he claims that he knows "what a person really is." Nevertheless, his amoral certitude is challenged every time he is confronted with Sotnikov's subliminal courage. In the scene of interrogation and torture, for example, he averts his gaze from Sotnikov by failing to endure his unsurpassable spiritual superiority (**see Fig.** 12.3). In the hanging scene, after all the condemned are executed, a medium close-up lingers on Portnov's distant face for about forty seconds, revealing signs of his slight stupefaction, which are confirmed in the following full shot when we see him standing still while everybody is moving around.

For Deleuze, the close-up is not the only agent of affects in the affection-image. More subtle affects are expressed by space or "any-space-whatever" abstracted "from a determinate space"[27] as well as light and color. Discussing early black-and-white cinema in terms of the dynamics of light, Deleuze contrasts Expressionist cinema (e.g., F. W. Murnau), predicated on visual opposition between light and shadow, and cinema of lyrical abstraction (e.g.,

Figure 12.3 Portnov's close-up when he confronts Sotnikov's gaze.

Josef von Sternberg) in which "light no longer has to do with darkness, but with the transparent, the translucent or the white."[28] Whereas the former dramatizes the struggle between light and darkness as independent entities, the latter, by imposing white on white, foregrounds "light's adventure with white" and presents shadow as its own consequence, as "the place where the light stops."[29] Depending on their different lighting techniques, each cinema produces its own kind of space: an Expressionist gothic space with its shadows and depth as "the location of the struggle, which sometimes draws space into the bottomlessness of a black hole,"[30] or a white space of lyrical abstraction where "the white . . . circumscribes a space corresponding to the luminous," in which "is inserted a close-up face which reflects the light."[31]

It's not that the cinema of lyrical abstraction, "defined by the relationship of light with white,"[32] downplays the significance of shadows and darkness; rather, it assigns them a different role. As Deleuze writes,

> The point is that Expressionism develops a principle of opposition, of conflict or of struggle: struggle of the spirit with darkness. While for the adherents of lyrical abstraction, the act of the spirit is not a struggle but an alternative, a fundamental 'Either . . . or'. Shadow is therefore no longer an extension to infinity, or a reversal to the limit. It no longer extends a state of things to infinity, it will, rather, express an alternative between the state of things itself and the possibility, the virtuality, which goes beyond it.[33]

As Deleuze points out, there are very diverse adherents of lyrical abstraction (e.g., Tourneur, Dreyer, Bresson), yet their films are characterized by the same principle of white-black alternation, "established between one image and the next, or in the same image," which "seems to correspond to the alternation of terms, good, evil and uncertainty or indifference." According to the characters' choice, they could be differentiated into different moral types: such as the white men of good and virtue in Dreyer, "the grey men of uncertainty" and "the creatures of evil"[34] in Bresson. Yet for Deleuze the true matter in choice is not between the terms of an alternative, such as good or evil, but "between the modes of existence of the one who chooses." Just as for Blaise Pascal and Søren Kierkegaard, he argues, the authentic choice consists in "the consciousness of choice as steadfast spiritual determination,"[35] in one's choosing choice itself in conditions that seem to deny the very possibility of choice, which often "implies the sacrifice of the person."[36] Those who make a choice between the terms of an alternative or are unable to choose between them in given circumstances are stuck in the actual state of things, while "the character who makes true choice raises the affect to its pure power or potentiality" and thus transcends the actual world towards the virtual. As he writes,

> The character of true choice is discovered in sacrifice or rediscovered beyond the sacrifice which constantly begins over again in Bresson; it is Joan of Arc, it is the person condemned to death, the parish priest. In Dreyer, it is Joan of Arc again, but it is also the great trilogy, Anne of *Day of Wrath*, Inger of *Ordet*, finally Gertrud ... Why have these themes so much philosophical and cinematographic importance? ... It is because, in philosophy as in the cinema, in Pascal as in Bresson, in Kierkegaard as in Dreyer, the true choice, that which consists in choosing choice, is supposed to restore everything to us. It will enable us to rediscover everything, in the spirit of sacrifice, at the moment of the sacrifice or even before the sacrifice is performed.[37]

Deleuze's existentialist typology of characters in the cinema of lyrical abstraction, which apparently foregrounds one's self-sacrifice in favor of the virtual as an authentic choice, strongly resonates with Shepitko's ethical priorities in *The Ascent*. As is known, she came across Bykov's novella while being hospitalized after a fall that critically damaged her spine. Because of her own life-and-death situation in the early 1970s, she took this story rather personally:

> For the first time I found myself in the face of death and, like any other person in such situation, I was looking for my own formula of immortality ... It is then that I read Vasil' Bykov's story *Sotnikov*, while being in that new state of mind. And I thought that it was this state of mind that I could express in *Sotnikov*'s adaptation. As I was telling myself, this story is about me, about my ideas of what life is, what death is, and what immortality is. I decided that this story could only be transferred to the screen as a story about myself. About a person who, by the will of fate, could have been born thirty years earlier and ended up in a tragic situation ... passed all the ordeals ... calculated the formula of immortality for himself ... By the way, for many it turned out to be unacceptable that this film took its stylistic form close to biblical motifs. But this is my Bible, for the first time in my life I fully subscribe to this picture.[38]

By turning Sotnikov into a Christ figure whose self-sacrifice would be viewed as the ascent towards God or *theosis*, Shepitko was undertaking her own quest for immortality and thus following the spiritual tradition in European art cinema (especially Bresson) while utilizing stylistic techniques of lyrical abstraction discussed above. Many critics have noticed how lighting and color are crucial for *The Ascent*. As Stishova points out, the film's stark black-and-white color reproduces its radical division of cinematic space into spiritual opposites, between which no third option is available for a person: "either you die with honor or live in shame."[39] Guynn also notes Shepitko's "frequent use of chiaroscuro—the strong contrast between light and dark areas of the image."[40] Nevertheless, despite *The Ascent*'s expressionist emphasis on the contrast between light and darkness, it is not about the spirit's struggle between the two, but rather about an alternative presented by them, precisely because of the film's abundant use of white.

The film opens with a series of extreme long shots of winter landscape which Costlow describes as "a minimalist study in white on white, with skeletal traceries of black and gray."[41] For nearly one-fourth of the film the white continuously dominates the screen as we follow the protagonists wandering in the forest and fields, running, crawling and rolling "through the blindingly white snow."[42] As the film production designer Yuri Raksha elaborates, "nature . . . is the film's third protagonist . . . it is reticent, monotonous, and stern, like hopelessness. This is why we needed the ascetic plasticity of the black-and-white spectrum. Restrained coloring: clear sky, white snow."[43] Furthermore, in Bykov's story, part of the duo's journey takes place at night, yet Shepitko's night is unexpectedly white, as we see the white moon on a gray cloudy sky when wounded Sotkinov is about to commit suicide. Even Sotnikov's hair appears whiter in the end, which, as Mercedes Camino points out, confirms "his transformation into a martyr."[44] Furthermore, the film concludes with a series of panoramic shots of snowy landscape and blizzard, some of which are identical to the opening shots: they carry no narrative significance and can hardly suggest the film's chiastic structure, yet they do enclose the entire film in a luminous whiteness that points towards metaphysical transcendence.

Shepitko's use of black is similarly consistent with its symbolic role in the cinema of lyrical abstraction, which is that of a spiritual alternative or choice. It is in the darkness of the cellar that both Sotnikov and especially Rybak make their choices: the former decides to sacrifice himself for others, while the latter hopes to survive at all costs. During the execution the Nazi collaborator Portnov wears all black. And in the hanging scene Sotnikov's last close-up is followed by a cut to black, as if he plunges into the dark abyss. Also, after his betrayal and having joined the Nazis, Rybak stares at the empty dark cellar where the prisoners spent the night, with the camera's zooming in on it as if it were a bottomless black hole sucking him in. This scene was suggested to Shepitko by Yuri Raksha. As he comments, "Do you remember that image of the cellar's black hole which Rybak sees when he comes back to the yard of the police precinct. This is where his crisis begins. This black hole – I saw it as in a dream with Rybak's eyes, and I shuddered. Larisa got it immediately."[45]

Yet in the alternation between black and white, whiteness still prevails in key moments of the film, and the actors, according to Shepitko's guidelines, had to express this transition through their acting. This is how, for example, she instructs them to react to the light after the long scene in the dark cellar:

> Here the viewer too must get used to the light. The previous scene in the cellar . . . will run in semi-darkness. But now the prisoners are taken out of the cellar into the yard where there are the sun, snow, and air. You need to demarcate this boundary. Not too much, but noticeably enough. You need to be surprised by the light as if you didn't expect it.[46]

In another scene, after Rybak is terrified by the darkness of the cellar he has metaphorically fallen into, he decides to escape it by hanging himself with his belt. Yet unable to do so, he desperately stares back into the white vastness of rural scenery through the gate of the yard and experiences a breakdown because of his tremendous alienation from that nature. Again, Raksha's comments are helpful here: "In our plain, seemingly monotonous and inexpressive nature we were looking for one image which is central in the film, even though it is not spelled out: that of Motherland . . . It is this Motherland that does not accept Rybak [in the end] when he can't get out to it through the open gate."[47] Also, in the sequence of Sotnikov's hanging, the cut to black that swallows up his swinging head on a rope is nevertheless followed by the white image of a sky filling up the entire frame.

By closely following the logic of the affection-image, *The Ascent* dramatizes a spiritual alternative between the actual (physical survival) and the virtual (self-sacrifice), visually coded as black and white respectively, and affirms the moral priority of the latter via iconic close-ups, excessive whiteness, and the emotional soundtrack. By adapting a wartime story to a metaphysical parable, Shepitko was thus pursuing her own agenda to express her personal commitment to moral perfectionism and eternal values (or immortality), which also testifies to the dominant discourse of transcendence among the Soviet intelligentsia in the 1970s. Being truly a product of its own time, *The Ascent* could hardly appear at any other period of Soviet or post-Soviet cinema. Loznitsa's adaptation, which came after perestroika, the post-Soviet 1990s, and during an authoritarian comeback in Putin's Russia, offers a contrasting perspective on Bykov's work.

IN THE FOG AND THE IMPULSE-IMAGE

Unlike *The Ascent*, Sergei Loznitsa's *In the Fog* is shot in a dark palette of grays, browns, and dark greens that often obscures the details of the forest landscape and sets the gloomy tone for the entire film. The effect of visual indiscernibility is further intensified towards the end of the film when the dense fog rolls in and covers the screen, thus emphasizing the atmosphere of uncertainty and disorientation during the war and occupation. It would be tempting to view Loznitsa's film as another variation of the affection-image focused on "the grey men of uncertainty"[48] in situations of doubt or non-choice, following Deleuze's symbolic differentiation of color: "the white marks our duty, or our power, the black our impotence, or our thirst for evil, and the grey our uncertainty, our seeking or our indifference."[49] And yet, even though many critics defined its genre as an existentialist or philosophical parable, *In the Fog* exemplifies a completely different type of image in Deleuze's taxonomy, that of the impulse-image which eschews the notion of free agency altogether and foregrounds instead the determinism of natural and social conditions.

By placing the impulse-image between the "realism of the action-image" and "the idealism of the affection-image," Deleuze nevertheless insists on its "perfect consistency and autonomy"[50] due to its essentially naturalist characteristics that other images are powerless to represent. First, the impulse-image is set in the so-called "originary world" outside civilization "which rumbles in the depths of all the milieux and runs along beneath them;"[51] it "is a beginning of the world, but also an end of the world, and the irresistible slope from one to the other."[52] Second, such a world is populated not by humans but by human animals engaged in perverse modes of behavior – "cannibalistic, sado-masochistic, necrophiliac, etc." – and fighting with each other in "a constant predator-prey relationship."[53] Third, the impulse-image, as its name suggests, primarily deals with impulses "*extracted* from the real modes of behaviour current in a determinate milieu, from the passions, feelings and emotions which real men experience in this milieu."[54] Similarly, the actions of such human animals are not actions *per se* motivated by a rational choice or commitment but rather "primordial acts"[55] or energies propelled by "raw and primordial impulses"[56] and expressed in perpetual cruelty and violence. Finally, the impulse-image "could only grasp the negative effects of time; attrition, degradation, wastage, destruction, loss, or simply oblivion."[57] Subjected to the logic of the death-drive, its temporality is "inseparable from an entropy."[58] For Deleuze, the filmmakers of the impulse-image along with "naturalist authors deserve the Nietzschean name 'physicians of civilisation'. They diagnose civilisation."[59] By uncovering base instincts beneath human actions, they offer a relentless deconstruction of social and cultural phenomena.

Characteristically enough, all of Loznitsa's fiction films, from *My Joy* (2010) to *Donbass* (2018), heavily rely on the aesthetic of the impulse-image which is usually described by his commentators as *chernukha* or *neo-chernukha*.[60] Even though *In the Fog* is far less radical than his other features, it still meets the criteria of cinematic naturalism which manifests itself already in the opening sequence. As Loznitsa himself points out in an interview, the film begins with the scene of public execution which is one of the last in *The Ascent*. Whereas

Shepitko scrutinizes the faces of the condemned and their sympathizers with a dramatic soundtrack, in Loznitsa's film the prisoners marching to the gallows are seen from the back and no non-diegetic music is added to the scene. In fact, their execution occurs off-screen as the camera pans around the market square peering into the everyday activities of local community and compellingly demonstrating its regular course of life under occupation. Behind the curious bystanders observing the spectacle, we see farmers selling their products, children eating or playing around, a girl flirting with a German soldier, a butcher serving his customers at the cookhouse, people arriving by train and those carrying suitcases in the far background. We also see the Germans mingling with the locals and engaged in various interactions with them: carrying a helmet full of white eggs, showing a rifle to a one-armed youth, having boots polished by a shoe-shiner, riding a horse across the market square, having lunch outdoors. As this intricately choreographed sequence pointedly suggests, the distinction between inhabitants and occupants is blurred and life goes on as usual, while we hear the death sentence read out in Russian (probably by one of the collaborators) and the sound of suffocation along with the creaking of the gallows rope. By extracting the true motives underlying the local people's behavior, Loznitsa finds no signs of their heroism or patriotism but only evidence of their adaptability and moral flexibility driven by their survival instinct.

Whereas Shepitko dispenses entirely with the flashbacks present in Bykov's original by following the Aristotelian unities of time, place, and action, Loznitsa, on the contrary, effectively implements recourse to the characters' pasts to shed further light on their backgrounds. According to the flashbacks in *In the Fog*, neither Burov nor Voitik, dispatched to execute Sushenya for his alleged treason, are the exemplary partisans motivated by patriotic feelings. Burov joins the partisans because he has nowhere else to go after he sets his own truck on fire, the one that he built with his bare hands prior to the war and that was then confiscated by the Nazi police. Voitik turns out to be a self-serving and opportunistic coward who previously betrayed the villagers supplying food for partisans and now, while being on watch in the woods, runs away after discovering an ambush in which Burov is fatally wounded. From Sushenya's flashback, besides the proof of his innocence, we learn how his coworkers decide to sabotage a Nazi-operated railway only to piss off their hated boss. Despite Sushenya's attempts to dissuade them, by telling them that this is a foolish and reckless idea and that the Germans would certainly identify them as responsible for the sabotage and retaliate, they nevertheless persist in undoing a joint bolt on a railroad track and are caught immediately after the train crash.

Neither Burov's nor the railroad workers' rebellious deeds have rational and intelligible ends; they are rather driven by a personal vendetta that has nothing to do with patriotism. In fact, their impulsive outbursts result in more harm than benefit to the cause of the resistance: the railroad workers are hanged for their pointless sabotage that could also unleash a purge in the village, while Burov's mother and sister are killed after he flees to the forest. And now, fooled by the Nazis, Burov and Voitik are on a mission to kill one of their own whom they suspect of treason only because his comrades were hanged, while his life was spared. In Loznitsa's film, therefore, we do not see the war between the Nazis and the locals defending their homeland, a theme often exploited in Soviet war movies as well as post-Soviet blockbusters. What we see is the disruption of communal ties and dehumanization among locals themselves, in which neighbors and childhood friends turn against each other and become enemies. As Sushenya wonders himself in his last conversation with Voitik,

> So you say it's war and everything can happen. But has everything changed in just a year and a half? Does a person change so quickly, so that before the war you see one person but during the war another? I have lived here for 37 years. Everyone knows me. I have always been respected. Never quarreled with anyone. So why don't you believe me now? It turns out all of you believe the Germans, but not one of your own. Nobody trusts me: neither neighbors, nor you. Even my wife has doubts. Have I changed? How will I change if I was born like this?

Towards the end of the film, after Burov dies from his wound, Voitik also gets ambushed and shot to death, which leaves Sushenya alone with the corpses of his fellow executioners. Yet again he is not killed by the Germans but by two local *polizei*, one of whom turns out to be Voitik's old acquaintance Drobina whom he met on some occasion before the war. Although we learn this detail from Bykov's story which Loznitsa does not clarify in the film, it is apparent that both Nazi collaborators are local since they speak Russian. Being locals, they are nevertheless inconceivably cruel towards the one who used to be their neighbor by robbing him and finishing him off once he is seen still alive.

In Loznitsa's amoral world Sushenya is presented as "the moral center of the film,"[61] even though he makes everyone feel uncomfortable because of his excessive righteousness. He refuses to collaborate with the Nazis, he selflessly cares about his family, he doesn't run away after Burov is wounded in the ambush, and he carries him on his back like his cross when he dies, refusing to leave him to scavenger crows. Finally, seeing no other options left for him, he commits suicide as the only way to save his family. Some critics even describe him as "saintly."[62] Tim Cawkwell, for example, is particularly generous with religious metaphors, for whom Sushenya

> recalls no one so much as Dostoevsky's Myshkin in 'The Idiot', whose innocence counter to reason attracts scorn. Yet it also attracts fascination,

and the film's power derives from the way Sushenya's role as the almost-mute witness to the suffering around him makes it a compelling story of martyrdom. Is it a religious martyrdom? . . . After his heroic exertions to save his would-be executioners, Sushenya sits exhausted between the bodies of Burov and Voitik like Christ on the cross between the two thieves, so that the story in effect has been the tracing of his *via crucis*, his Calvary and Golgotha. This final image is a closure, but it is also a picture of an atonement, that Sushenya like Sotnikov is martyred on behalf of the Belarussian people allowing some redemption to be drawn from these terrible events.[63]

Cawkwell's reading of Sushenya's character along Christological lines, which brings Sotnikov up in comparison, is somewhat predictable, given that in the opening sequence, as Masha Cerovic and Irina Tcherneva rightly point out, Loznitsa himself draws our attention to the name of the village Bogovizna – literally "God's point of view" – and a lamb that will be sacrificed.[64] And yet, Loznitsa's religious connotations may seem misleading and should not be taken for granted. Just like the eponymous heroine in his later feature *The Gentle Creature* (2017), Sushenya is not a saint worthy of fascination, but a helpless victim or prey hunted down by predators and human animals. By no means should his Christ-like passivity and self-sacrifice be mistaken for exemplary martyrdom or model behavior, since he hopes to escape his dire fate till the very last moment. Unlike Sotnikov's, Sushenya's self-sacrifice is not chosen but forced upon him by inhuman circumstances. In the naturalist universe of the impulse-image, to which *In the Fog* fully subscribes, the notion of free will is but an illusion or beatific fantasy which must be abandoned or revised (or "traversed," psychoanalytically speaking) before the true reality can be

Figure 12.4 Sushenya sits between the bodies of Burov and Voitik.

accepted. This message is powerfully pronounced in the film's symbolic ending, which is not, however, the image of Sushenya sitting with a gun between two corpses, as Cawkwell argues. The film ends with a blanket of white fog covering the entire screen through which we hear a gunshot suggesting Sushenya's suicide. The impenetrable whiteness of the fog, standing for the triumph of the originary world of forest over people, absorbs the protagonist into its own indiscernibility and thus emphasizes the literal absence of the subject in the action we hear. This is where that *The Ascent* and *In the Fog* diverge most starkly in their treatment of self-sacrifice: whereas the former dramatizes the event through the close-ups of Sotnikov and the boy, highlighting their emotional bonding in shot-reverse shot fashion, the latter obliterates the protagonist's visual presence in the last scene and thus deprives him of agency in his final act of self-sacrifice. Unlike Shepitko, Loznitsa allows no empathy or compassion for his characters by consistently avoiding close-ups and non-diegetic music. Rather, through exceedingly long takes and silence he evokes the viewer's more sober and analytical perspective on how humans cease being humans. Unlike Shepitko who seeks immortality or transcendence of humanity through heroic self-sacrifice, Loznitsa demands our rational understanding of the historic conditions of dehumanization and moral degradation. For this purpose, the aesthetic resources provided by the impulse-image turn out to be more effective than those of the affection-image.

CONCLUSION

Vasil' Bykov is one of the most adapted writers in Soviet and Russian cinema. There exist over twenty Russian-language films based on his war stories, which symptomatizes the national film industry's insatiable demand for WWII narratives. Shepitko's and Loznitsa's adaptations, however, are highly exceptional in this trend, as they turn Bykov's wartime story into an existential parable about moral choice, albeit from diametrically opposite ideological and aesthetic perspectives. Whereas Shepitko ecstatically affirms the freedom of choice through the expressive powers of the affection-image, such as close-ups, subjective camera, luminous whiteness, and music, Loznitsa offers a dispassionate deterministic analysis of human motives through the naturalist aesthetic of the impulse-image that ruthlessly exposes the full extent of moral degradation and irrationality of violence as well as muddles the distinctions between enemy and ally. Whereas the affection-image comes from the ideology of moral idealism and its optimistic belief in human nature, the impulse-image is emphatically post-humanist and post-ideological in its reduction of humanity to animality. As is known, Deleuze was never fond of the impulse-image because of its intrinsic inability to get to the virtual and "time as pure form" due to "its obligation to keep time subordinate to naturalistic co-ordinates, to make it dependent on impulse."[65] Even though the naturalists are the "physicians of civilization" by diagnosing its symptoms and ills, their brutal cynicism and uncompromising deconstruction of human endeavors could hardly evoke in the audience transcendent aspirations. In this regard, both films, besides testifying to the different periods in Bykov's lifetime preoccupation with the ethic of self-sacrifice, should also be viewed as complementary to each other: just as *In the Fog* completes *The Ascent* with a more sober, down-to-earth look at the conditions of moral choice, so does the affective power of the latter make up for the dismal nihilism of the former.

NOTES

1. Oleg Sul'kin, "Rezhisser Sergei Loznitsa: "Ia ne ishchu, ia nakhozhu,"" *Golos Ameriki*, 15 June 2013. https://www.golosameriki.com/a/loznitsa-interview/1682247.html
2. Nikolai Karaev, "Sergei Loznitsa, atomy i pustota," *Postimees*, 5 June 2012. https://rus.postimees.ee/864722/sergey-loznica-atomy-i-pustota
3. Vasil' Bykov, "Kak byla napisana povest' "Sotnikov,"" *Vasil' Bykov. Sobranie sochinenii v chetyrekh tomakh. Tom 4* (Molodaya gvardiya: Moskva, 1986), 334–341, 335.
4. Zina J. Gimpelevich, *Vasil Bykau: His Life and Works* (Kingston: McGill-Queen's University Press, 2005), 66.
5. Vasil' Bykov, *The Ordeal* (London: The Bodley Head Ltd, 1972), 97.
6. Ibid., 143–144.
7. Gimpelevich, *Vasil Bykau*, 70.
8. Ibid., 67.
9. Ibid., 133.
10. Ibid., 122.
11. Ibid., 133.
12. Lev Karakhan, "Krutoi put' "Voskhozhdeniya,"" *Iskusstvo kino*, Issue 10 (1976), 85–101, 86.
13. Larisa Shepitko, "Poslednee interv'iu" in Elem Klimov, *Larisa. Vospominaniya, vystupleniya, interv'iu, kinostsenarii, stat'i.. Kniga o Larise Shepitko* (Moskva: Iskusstvo, 1987), 179–196, 189.
14. Susan Sontag, *Regarding the Pain of Others* (London: Picador, 2004), 122.
15. Gilles Deleuze, *Cinema I: The Movement-Image*. Translated to English by Hugh Tomlinson and Barbara Habberjam (Minneapolis: University of Minnesota Press, 1986), 106.
16. Ibid., 108.
17. Ibid., 106.
18. Lev Rybak, "Poslednii razgovor," *Kinopanorama: sovetskoe kino segodnia*. Vypusk 3 (Moskva: Iskusstvo, 1981), 133.

19. William Guynn, *Unspeakable Histories: Film and the Experience of Catastrophe* (New York: Columbia University Press, 2016), 124–125.
20. Andre Bazin, *What Is Cinema? Vol. 1*. Translated to English by Hugh Gray (University of California Press, 2004), 109.
21. Karakhan, "Krutoi put' 'Voskhozhdeniya'," 86.
22. Shepitko, "Poslednee interv'iu," 173.
23. Elena Stishova, "Khronika i legenda" in Elem Klimov, *Larisa. Vospominaniya, vystupleniya, interv'iu, kinostsenarii, stat'i.. Kniga o Larise Shepitko* (Moskva: Iskusstvo, 1987), 276–289, 285.
24. Jane T. Costlow, "Icons, Landscape and the Boundaries of Good and Evil: Larisa Shepitko's *The Ascent* (1977)" in Jakub Kazecki, Karen A. Ritzenhoff, and Cynthia J. Miller, eds. *Border Visions: Identity and Diaspora in Film* (Lanham: Scarecrow Press, 2013), 75–90, 84.
25. Ibid., 80.
26. Shepitko, "Poslednee interv'iu," 173.
27. Deleuze, *Cinema I*, 111.
28. Ibid., 93.
29. Ibid., 94.
30. Ibid., 111.
31. Ibid., 93.
32. Ibid., 112.
33. Ibid.
34. Ibid., 113.
35. Ibid., 114.
36. Ibid., 115.
37. Ibid., 115–116.
38. Shepitko, "Poslednee interv'iu," 190.
39. Stishova, "Khronika i legenda," 277.
40. Guynn, *Unspeakable Histories*, 126.
41. Costlow, "Icons, Landscape and the Boundaries of Good and Evil," 76.
42. Thomas Puhr, "'We need extreme situations'. Brutal poetry in Larisa Shepitko's *The Ascent*," *Film International* 19.2 (2021), 189–193, 189.
43. Yuri Raksha, "Moio proizvedenie – nash fil'm" in Elem Klimov, *Larisa. Vospominaniya, vystupleniya, interv'iu, kinostsenarii, stat'i.. Kniga o Larise Shepitko* (Moskva: Iskusstvo, 1987), 129–137, 133.
44. Mercedes Camino, *Memories of Resistance and the Holocaust on Film* (London and New York: Palgrave Macmillan, 2018), 95.
45. Raksha, "Moio proizvedenie – nash fil'm," 136.
46. Karakhan, "Krutoi put' 'Voskhozhdeniya,'" 95.
47. Raksha, "Moio proizvedenie – nash fil'm," 134.
48. Deleuze, *Cinema I*, 114.
49. Ibid., 117.
50. Ibid., 123.
51. Ibid., 125.
52. Ibid., 126.

53. Ibid., 128.
54. Ibid., 124.
55. Ibid., 125.
56. Ibid., 133.
57. Ibid., 127.
58. Ibid., 126.
59. Ibid., 125.
60. The term *chernukha*, derived from the word *chernyi* (black) and denoting *ochernenie* (blackening or muckraking), refers to a tendency toward negativity and pessimism in the arts and mass media that took place in the late Soviet 1980s and the post-Soviet 1990s due to glasnost and perestroika. In Russian film studies *chernukha* is used to describe films of this period focused exclusively on the naturalist exposure and critique of social ills in Soviet and post-Soviet society. For more details see Sergey Toymentsev, "The Birth of Naturalist Violence in the Russian *Chernukha* Film" in *The Palgrave Handbook of Violence in Film and Media* (Cham: Springer International Publishing, 2022), 275–295. Contemporary Russian films using the genre features of *chernukha* are often described as *neo-chernukha*. See, for example, Dusty Wilmes, "National identity(de)construction in recent independent cinema: Kirill Serebrennikov's *Yuri's Day* and Sergei Loznitsa's *My Joy*." *Studies in Russian and Soviet Cinema* 8, no. 3 (2014): 218–232.
61. Denise J. Youngblood, "Sergei Loznitsa: *In the Fog* (V tumane, 2012)," *KinoKultura*, Issue 39 (2013). http://www.kinokultura.com/2013/39r-vtumane.shtml
62. See, for example, Leslie Felperin, "In the Fog," *Chicago Tribune*, 25 May 2012. https://www.chicagotribune.com/entertainment/ct-xpm-2012-05-25-sns-201205251219reedbusivarietynve1117947639-20120525-story.html
63. Tim Cawkwell, *The New Filmgoer's Guide to God: From the Passion of Joan of Arc to Philomena* (Market Harborough: Troubador Publishing Ltd, 2014), 127.
64. Masha Cerovic and Irina Tcherneva, "*Dans la brume*: strates du regard sur l'occupation nazie," in Céline Gailleurd, Damien Marguet, and Eugénie Zvonkine, eds. *Sergueï Loznitsa: Un cinéma à l'épreuve du monde* (Lille: Presses universitaires du Septentrion, 2022), 139–151, 141.
65. Deleuze, *Cinema I*, 127.

Index

Note: The index is arranged in word-by-word order. Page numbers in italics refer to figures. The letter n following a page number refers to a note.

abstraction
   in *Ascent, The*, 142–3, 152, 209–11, 212, 218–19
   legibility and, 209–11
   lyrical, 257–8
   modernist, 142
   Soviet Union's disapproval of, 146
action-images, 252–3, 261
Adamovich, Ales', 30, 119
affection-images, 248, 252–3, 261
Aimanov, Shaken
   on Virgin Lands films, 189
   We Live Here (*My zdes' zhivem*), 184, 186, 190
Aitmatov, Chingiz, 28, 240n
   "The Camel's Eye" (*Verbliuzhii glaz*), 179, 224
Akerman, Chantal, 9
   Jeanne Dielman, 23, quai du Commerce, 1080 Bruxelles, 232
Akhmadulina, Bella, 28–9
Aleksandrov, Grogorii *see* Eisenstein, Sergei and Aleksandrov, Grogorii
Alma-Ata Film Studio (later Kazakhfil'm Studio), 183–4, 190, 192
Anarkhai, 179, 205, 206, 225
Andreev, Nikolai, 30
Anisichkin, Yury, 170
Annensky, Lev, 30
Antonioni, Michelangelo: *La Notte*, 10
Antonova, Clemena, 94n
Aral Sea, 203

Artiomovsk (Ukraine), 1–2
Ascent, The (Voskhozhdenie), 24–7, 86, 89, 91, 116–31, *121*, *143*, *148*, *149*, *150*, 208–16, *210*, *211*, *214*, 265
   and the affection-image, 252–60
   allegory, 90, 152, 209, 211–13, 215
   American reception of, 139
   American rights and distribution, 25
   Berkeley screening (1977), 25, 152, *153*
   and Brakhage's *Dog Star Man*, 140–1, 146
   and Bykov's *The Ordeal*, 44, 77–8, 81, 117, 253–4, 258
   characterisation, 117–18, 120
   choice, 119, 120, 129, 130
   close-ups, 49–50, 82, 84, 85, 88, 89, 124, *125*, 127–8, 130, 141, 253, 254, *255*, *256*, *256*, 265
   credit sequence, *122*
   ending, 239
   environment, 200–1
   filming conditions, 117
   framing techniques, 85–7
   free indirect discourse, 77, 78, 82–3, 86, 87, 88, 93–4, 121
   and German's *Trial on the Road*, 39, 49–50, 53
   historic context, 120–1
   House of Cinema Veterans showing, 30
   Howe's poem on, 154
   inspiration for, 252
   interiority, 127
   landscape, 209, 215, 259
   legibility and abstraction, 209–11

Ascent, The (Voskhozhdenie) (*cont.*)
    light and darkness, 259–60
    locations, 3, 126
    and Loznitsa's *In The Fog*, 261–2, 265
    modernism, 152
    moon, 237, 238, *238*
    movement, 201
    nature, 218–19, 259, 260
    as a neo-parable, 119–20
    Orlov on, 31
    Pasolini on, 78
    plot, 120, 208–9
    production process, 126–7, 144, 147
    rarefaction, 143, 146–7, 150, 152, 153
    recognition for, 4, 8, 152, 234
    and religious films, 253
    religious motifs, 50–2, *51*, 87–8, 89–90, 118–20, 124, 148–9, 209, 211, 212–13, 234, 254, 258
    sky, 234–9
    sleigh ride, 82–7
    socialist realism, 119, 124
    Sontag on, 154
    soundtrack, 84, 122, 124, 127, 152, 254
    Stalinism, 48
    symbolism, 141, 142, 143, 144, 147–51, 152, 153
    title, 81
    war theme, 2, 45, 46–7
    and *You and Me* documentary, 9
Askoldov, Aleksandr: *Kommissar* (Kommissar), 7, 172n
Astrakhan, 3, 167
Auerbach, Erich, 90
Averbakh, Ilya, 58

Bakhmut (Ukraine), 2
Balázs, Béla, 49
Banerjee, Anindita, 105
Barnet, Boris: *Alenka*, 184, *185*
Bartunkova, Barbara, 135n
Baskakov, Vladimir, 168
beauty, 237, 238
Beginning of an Unknown Century (Nachalo nevedomogo veka) (omnibus film), 97, 109, 112, 158
    see also Gabai, Genrikh: *Motrya*; *Homeland of Electricity, A*; Smirnov, Andrei: *Angel*
Belorussia, 3, 131n
Belova, Valeria, 158, 167
Benjamin, Walter, 213–14
Bishkek (Kyrgyzstan), 240n
Bleiman, Mikhail, 22–3
Blind Cook, The (Slepoi povar), 20
Böhme, Gernot, 101
Boltnev, Andrei, 40

Bondarchuk, Natalya, 30
Brakhage, Stan, 139
    Dante Quartet, 145, 153
    Dog Star Man, 140–1, *141*, 146
    and Eisenstein compared, 142, 143–4
    Governor, The, 140
    on Shepitko, 145, 153–4
    and Soviet filmmakers, 145
    Window Water Baby Moving, 140, 145, 156n
Bresson, Robert, 257, 258
Breyfogle, Nicholas, 222n
Brezhnev, Leonid, 6, 225
Bulgakova, Maya, 21, 39, 49–50, 60, 64
Bulgakowa, Oksana, 142, 186, 187
Burstyn, Ellen, 25
Bychkov, Mikhail, 170, 171
Bykov, Dmitrii, 64
Bykov, Rolan, 186
Bykov (Bykaŭ), Vasil', 28, 247–52
    Crane's Cry, The (Zhuravliny krik), 249
    "How *Sotnikov* Was Written," 248, 250–1
    In The Fog, 247, 249, 251
    Monument (Obelisk), 249
    Ordeal, The (Sotnikov), 11, 44, 50, 77–84, 117, 133n, 249–50, 253–4, 259, 265, 266
    Quarry, The (Kar'ier), 251
    Raid, The (Oblava), 251
    Sign of Misfortune (Znak bedy), 251
    Third Flare, The (Tret'ia raketa), 249
    To Go and Not Return (Poiti i ne vernut'sia), 251
    To Live Until the Dawn (Dozhit' do rassveta), 249

Camino, Mercedes, 259
Carson, Rachel: *Silent Spring*, 228, 243n
Cawkwell, Tim, 263–4
censorship, 29–30, 31
    Beginning of an Unknown Century, 97, 112
    German and, 47
    Heat, 180
    Homeland of Electricity, A, 112, 168, 169
    You and Me, 7–8, 22–3, 39
Cerovic, Masha, 264
Chadaga, Julia, 174n
Chapaev (1934 film), 117, 118, 119
Chekhov, Anton, 42
    The Steppe (Step'), 225
chernukha: definition, 268n
Chernyaev, Anatoliy, 6
Chiaureli, Mikhail, 19
    The Vow (Kliatva), 187
Chukhnov, Vladimir, 126, 147
Chukhrai, Grigorii, 109, 112n
cinema of lyrical abstraction, 256–7

close-ups, 127
   Ascent, The, 49–50, 82, 84, 85, 88, 89, 124, *125*, 127–8, 130, 141, 253, 254, *255*, 256, *256*, 265
   Homeland of Electricity, A, 102, 106, 110, 165
Cold War, 146
colonialism, 221n
Congress of Cinematographers, Fifth (1986), 29
Coppola, Francis Ford, 25, 26
Costlow, Jane, 188, 195n, 254
"counter cinema," 180
Cousins, Marc, 9
Crimea, 3, 39

Daney, Serge, 65
Davydova, Tatyana, 171, 172
Dean, Martin, 135n
Deleuze, Gilles
   on affection-image, 252–3, 256–7
   on color, 261
   and direct time-image, 151
   on impulse-image, 261
   on lyrical abstraction, 257–8
   on rarefaction of the frame, 142
   on zero-gravity image, 230
Demidova, Alla, 29, 30
Demin, Viktor, 27, 29
diegesis theory, 99
direct time-image, 151
Dmytryk, Olena, 10, 61, 73
Doane, Mary Ann, 127
Dolin, Anton, 31, 43
Dostoevsky, Feodor, 87
Dovzhenko, Oleksandr, 2, 19, 145, 146
   Aerograd, 233
   Arsenal, 86
   Earth (Zemlia), 110, 118–19, 128, 184–5, 187
Draitser, Emil, 47
Dreyer, Carl Theodor
   and lyrical abstraction, 257
   Passion of Joan of Arc, The, 128, 253, 258
dubbing, 191–4
Ďurovičova, Nataša, 193

Ehrenburg, Ilya: *The Thaw*, 5
Eisenstein, Sergei, 146
   Bezhin Meadow, 169
   and Brakhage compared, 142
   essays, 156n
   "Form of the Script, The," 74n
Eisenstein, Sergei and Aleksandrov, Grogorii:
   The General Line (General'naia loniia / Staroe i novoe), 187
Ekran i stena (Screen and Stage) (newspaper), 31

Erley, Mieka, 183, 186–7, 195n, 226, 240n
Exeler, Franziska, 129–30, 131n, 135n
Experimental Creative Film Studio, 97, 109, 158, 168
Expressionist cinema, 256–7
Ezhov, Valentin, 57, 58, 72

Farewell (Proshchanie), 164, 216–19, *217*, *219*
   and the environment, 200
   location, 3, 216
   memorials, 28
Fay, Jennifer, 201, 202, 214, 215, 218
Fedorov, Nikolai, 114n
feminism, 8–9, 20–1
feminist cinema, 3, 140, 232
Ferree, Myra Marx, 14n
film festivals
   All-Union Film Festival, Leningrad, 20, 194
   Berlin International Film Festival, 28, 146
   Frankfurt International Film Festival, 194
   International Film Festival of Central Asia and Kazakhstan, 194
   Karlovy Vary International Film Festival, 20, 194
   London International Film Festival, 26–7
   Moscow Film Festival, 223
   Telluride International Film Festival, 25–6, 139–40, 142, 145
   Toronto Film Festival, 25
   Venice Film Festival, 23
Firsova, Dzhemma, 97
Fomin, Valerii, 14n, 30, 31, 168
Forman, Milos, 26
Foster, John Bellamy, 205
Frolov, Ivan, 205
Frunze *see* Bishkek

Gaag, Natalya, 170
Gabai, Genrikh: *Motrya*, 158
Gabrilovich, Evgenii, 74n
gender, 9, 10, 61; *see also* women
Gerasimov, Sergei, 184
German, Aleksei, 38–53
   and censorship, 47
   My Friend Ivan Lapshin (*Moi drug Ivan Lapshin*), 38, 40–3
   "Operation 'Happy New Year!'," 50
   and patriotism, 47
   and realism, 45
   Trial on the Road (*Proverka no dorogakh*), 11, 39, 43–5, 46, 48, 49, 50, 52, 53
   Twenty Days Without War (*Dvadtsat' dnei bez voiny*), 38, 44, 71
German, Yuri, 44
Gilburd, Eleonory, 5, 193, 194

Gimpelevich, Zina J., 249, 251
Glebova, Aglaya, 211
Goethe, J. W. von, 231
Golovskoi, Valerii, 119
Gorbachev, Mikhail, 6
Gorbatiuk, Sergei, 164, *164*
Gor'kii Central Studio of Children's and Youth Films, 183–4
Gosfilmofond, 172n
Goskino (film agency), 54n, 132n, 169, 172n, 193–4
Grey, Camilla, 145
Gurevich, Leonid, 168
Guynn, William, 253, 259

Heat (Znoi), 25, 164, *185*, *189*, 205–8, 224–9
    acclaim for, 20, 194, 205
    censorship, 180
    characters, 181, 185, 186, 190–1, 194, 206–7, 208
    dubbing, 181, 191–2, 193, 194
    ending, 239
    and the environment, 200
    ethereality, 229
    filming, 228
    and Hitchcock's *The Birds*, 228–9
    landscape, 184–5, 206–7, 224–5, 227
    location, 3, 39, 179, 205, 224
    modernity, 180
    nature, 218–19
    production process, 179–80
    sexual themes, 186–7, 207
    sky, 227, 232, 233
    soundtrack, 191
    and Virgin Lands campaign, 180–1, 183–93, 194, 226
Hirsch, Marianna, 167
Hitchcock, Alfred: *The Birds*, 228
Homeland of Electricity, A (Rodina elektrichestva), 7, 29, 97–112, *102*, *103*, *104*, *111*, 158–72
    actors, 100, 108, 168
    atmosphere, 99–101, 107, 108, 109, 110–11, 112
    censorship, 112, 168, 169
    close-ups, 102, 106, 110, 165
    cut, 102–5
    dialogue, 109–10
    electricity, 105–8, 164, 165–6, 167
    environment, 99–100, 101, 102, 103, 107–8, 109, 110–11, 112
    and history, 98, 99, 100, 106, 108, 109, 110, 111
    influences, 158–9, 169
    location, 3, 100, 102, 167, 168
    and memory, 159
    music, 106, 159
    origins, 97, 159

plot, 97–8
rain, 110–12
religious motifs, 102, 103–5, 165, 168
restoration, 158
and Soviet founding myths, 98–9
Howe, Fanny, 154
Hven, Steffen, 99

Ingold, Tim, 101, 112, 226–7, 228
International Association of Women in Cinema, 24
Iskusstvo kino [The Art of the Cinema] (journal), 21–2, 24, 29, 52, 57, 59, 181, 191
Iusupzhanova, Klara, 190, 194

Josephson, Paul, 182

Kaganovsky, Lilya, 10, 43, 123, 143–4, 180, 232
Kalatozov, Mikhail
    First Echelon, The (*Pervyi eshelon*), 180–1, 184, *185*, 186, 187, 190
    I am Cuba (*Ia Kuba*), 7
    Unsent Letter, The (*Neotrpravlennoe pis'mo*), 221n, 240n
    Valerii Chaklov, 233
Kapterev, Sergei, 181
Karavaichuk, Oleg, 67–8
Kardin, Vladimir, 21, 183
Kazak language, 192, 193
Kazakhfil'm Studio, 193; *see also* Alma-Ata Film Studio
Kazakhstan, 3, 28, 179, 182–3, 190, 203, 227
Kelly, Catriona, 6–7
Kheifits, Iosif: *Horizon* (*Gorizont*), 184
Khovanskaia, Valentina, 7–8, 131n, 132n
Khrushchev, Nikita, 5–6; *see also* Virgin Lands campaign
Khutsiev, Martin: *Ilyich Gate* (Zastava Il'icha), 7
Kierkegaard, Søren, 257, 258
Klepikov, Yuri, 221n
Klimov, Elem, 3, 28, 30, 97, 116–17, 134n, 158
    Farewell (Proshchanie), 236
    Larisa, 145
"kolkhoz films," 187
Konchalovskii, Andrei
    First Teacher, The, 191, 193, 194
    Siberiade (*Siberiada*), 236
Korchagin, Pavel, 183
Korzhikhin, Dmitirii, 100, 168
Kosygin, Alexei, 22
Kovács, András Bálint, 153, 156n
Kovalov, Olga, 29, 169–70
Kozlov, Denis, 5, 98, 182
Kracauer, Siegfried, 116, 201–2, 214, 221n
Kulidzhanov, Lev, 21, 184

Kulidzhanov, Lev and Segel', Iakov: *It Began Like This* (*Eto nachinalos' tak*), 186–7, 190
Kundialis, Algimantas, 29
Kyrgyz language, 190–3
Kyrgyzfil'm, 179, 180, 192, 194
Kyrgyzstan, 3, 20, 179, 206; *see also* Bishkek

Landsberg, Alison, 113n
Langlois, Henri, 22
Lazarev, Lazar, 77
Lebeshev, Pavel, 158, 234
Lenin, Vladimir Ilyich, 105–6, 159, 161
Leyda, Jay, 146
Lipkov, Alaxander, 29
Living Water (Zhivaia voda), 20
Loznitsa, Sergei, 248, 252
  Babi Yar. Context, 13
  In the Fog (*V tumane*), 31, 247, 248, 260–5, 264, 266
  Maidan, 13
Luddy, Tom, 140
Lugarić, Danijela, 73
Lukinskii, Ivan: *Ivan Brovkin in the Virgin Lands* (*Ivan Brovkin na tseline*), 187

Macauley, David, 234
McCauley, Martin, 182
Macheret, Aleksandr, 27
Makarova, Tamara, 21
Malevich, Kazimir
  Black Square ("Chiornyi kvadrat"), 145, 150–1, *150*
  White on White ("*Beloe na belom*"), 142–3
Malyshev, Vladimir, 31, 97
Margolit, Evgenii, 181
Markov, Moisei, 205
Masherov, Pyotr Mironovich, 116–17
Mazur, Liudmila, 195n
Medvedkin, Aleksandr
  First Spring, The (*Pervaia Vesna*), 183, 184
  Restless Spring (*Bespokoinaia vesna*), 184, 186, 187, 188, 190
memory, 69
  postmemory, 174n
Merleau-Ponty, Maurice, 230, 233, 234
Mezhelaitis, Eduardas, 27
Michelson, Annette, 140, 142, 143–4, 146
Mikhalkovich, Valentin, 27
modernism, 142, 153
modernity, 116
moon
  Apollo 11 moon landing, 223, 237
  Ascent, The, 237, 238, *238*
  and human culture, 237–8
Morozov, Pavlik, 183

Moscow
  Kremlin, 165
  Novokuznetsk Cemetery memorial, 28
  Shepitko and, 2, 3
  Twentieth Communist Party Congress (1956), 5
Moscow Film Festival, 223
Mosfilm, 2, 20, 28, 158, 184
Moskovskaia Nedelia (Moscow Week) (newspaper), 20–1
Motherland of Electricity, 22, 27
Mukaseeva, Karina, 26
Muratova, Kira, 9, 10, 38
  Long Goodbyes (*Dolgie provody*), 7, 63–4, 67, 69
Murnau, F. W., 145
musicals: kolkhoz, 187

Nagib, Lucía, 124
nature, 202
  Ascent, The, 218–19, 259, 260
  Heat, 218–19
  Shepitko and, 200–1, 203

Obertreis, Julia, 204
October Revolution, 7, 8, 97, 109
Ognev, Vladimir, 97, 169
Okeev, Tolomush, 191
Okudzhava, Bulat: "Sentimental March" (Sentimental'nyi march), 159
Olesha, Yuri, 97
Ol'shanskii, Iosif, 180, 191
Orlov, Dal', 31
Ostrovsky, Sergei, 42
Oukaderova, Lida, 240n

Panfilov, Gleb, 28
Pascal, Blaise, 257, 258
Pasolini, Pier Paolo, 121
  and cinematic free indirect theory, 78, 85, 88
  and *figura*, 90
Patti, Emanuela, 90
Paustovsky, Konstantin, 20, 97, 113n
Pavlenok, Boris, 24–5
Petrukhina, Nadezhda, 21, 39, 40, 41–2, *41*, 43, 45, 229; *see also* Wings
Platonov, Andrei
  "Homeland of Electricity, The" (opera), 170–2, *171*
  "Homeland of Electricity, The" (short story), 97, 99–100, 103, 106, 159–64, 167, 168–9
  Technical Romance (Tekhnicheskii romans), 169
Plotnikov, Boris, 31, 46, 82, 132n
Pohl, Michaela, 182–3, 190
Polyakova, Lyudmila, 82, 117, 126, 129

Polyantseva, Ana, 21
postmodernism, 153
Povolotskaia, Irina, 179, 180
Pozner, Vladimir, 109, 112n
Pravda (newspaper), 29
Proust, Marcel: *In Search of Lost Time*, 67
Pyryev, Ivan, 19
  Cossacks of the Kuban (*Kubanskie kazaki*), 187
  Tractor Drivers, The (*Traktoristy*), 187

Raizman, Iuli: *Pilots* (*Letchiki*), 233
Raksha, Yuri, 25, 259
Rasputin, Valentin, 28
  Farewell to Matiora (*Proshchanie s materoi*), 216, 217–18, 243n
Razloga, Elena, 193
realism
  German and, 45
  and production, 124, 126–7
  socialist, 43, 117, 119, 124, 146, 162, 233
Red Army, 241n
Riazantseva, Natalia, 11, 57, 58–9, 72
Richter, Gerhard, 218
Ricoeur, Paul, 69
Riefenstahl, Leni, 139
Rodchenko, Alexander, 210–11
Rogachevka, 159, *160*, 171, 172
Rojavin, Marina, 10
Rollberg, Peter, 180, 184, 189–90
Romm, Mikhail, 20, 184
Rostotsky, Stanislav: *The Dawns Here are Quiet* (*A zori zdes' tikhie*), 241n
Roth-Ey, Kristin, 193
Russia
  Civil War, 100, 105, 109
  electrification of, 105
  invasion of Ukraine (2022), 1
  see also Astrakhan; Moscow; Rogachevka; Siberia; Soviet Union; Voronezh
Russian State Archive of Literature and Art (RGALI), 22, 23

Scarry, Elaine, 235, 236–7, 238
Schneemann, Carolee: *The Interior Scroll*, 139–40
Schnittke, Alfred, 24
Schnitzer, Lyuda, 22
Scorsese, Martin, 25
screenwriting, 58–9
Sedelnikov, Gleb, 170
Segel', Iakov, 184; *see also* Kulidzhanov, Lev and Segel', Iakov
Seifrid, Thomas, 99–100
Seleznev, Yuri, 218
Semeryakov, Igor, 25

Senelick, Laurence, 42
Shalagina, Anna, 172
Shamshiev, Bolotbek, 190, 194
Shentalinsky, Vitaly, 169
Shepitko, Larisa
  achievements and reputation, 3–4
  on art's moral responsibility, 119
  Brakhage on, 145
  context, 5
  creative output, 31
  death, 3, 240
  early life, 1–2
  education, 2, 19, 184
  and emotion, 252
  and feminism, 8–9, 20–1
  films *see* titles of individual films
  and Hollywood, 2
  influences, 2–3, 146
  and landscape, 195n
  in London, 26–7
  and material realism, 201
  memorial plaque to (Lviv), 28
  and memory, 67
  and nature, 200–1, 203
  and patriotism, 47
  photographs of, 28
  post Perestroika accessibility, 29
  publications about, 27–8, 29, 30
  reputation, 27–8
  and sky, 223
  and Soviet myth, 52
  at Telluraide Film Festival (1977), 139, 140, 142
  TV programmes about, 31–2
  in United States, 25–6
  at VGIK, 19–32
Shipachev, Stepan: "Love is to be treasured," 63
Shitova, Vera, 27
Shohat, Ella, 221n
Shpagin, Aleksandr, 52
Shpagin, Andrei, 222n
Shpalikov, Gennadii, 7–8, 23, 74n
Shub, Esfir: *The Great Road* (Velilkii put'), 161
Siberia
  Angara river, 216
  Bratsk hydro-electric station, 216
  Virgin Lands campaign, 182, 203
Simonov, Konstantin, 45
Simonov, Nikolay, 170
Siranov, Kabysh, 192
sky
  Ascent, The, 234–9
  and closure, 239–40

Heat, 227, 232, 233
  political connotations of, 233
  Scarry on, 235
  Shepitko and, 223
  Tarkovsky and, 223
  Wings, 229, 230–1, 231, 233–4
Slavin, K., 183
Smirnov, Andrei: *Angel*, 97, 158
Solonitsyn, Anatoly, 39, 48–9, 82, 87, 88, 89
Solov'iov, Sergei, 58, 73n
Sontag, Susan, 154, 252
Sovetskie khudozhestvennye fil'my / Soviet Artistic Films (catalog), 181
Sovetskii Ekran (Soviet Screen) (journal), 21, 22, 29, 169–70
Soviet cinema
  artistic production, 6–7
  avant-garde, 142, 145–6, 187
  Bureau of Film Propaganda: *Larisa Shepitko* brochure, 27
  'counter-cinema', 123, 126
  crisis of memory, 159
  and electricity, 161
  and environmental decay, 236
  on-location shooting, 100
  screenwriting, 58–9
  scriptwriting, 11
  "socialist realist," 117
  status, 4
  Week of Work by Young Directors of National Republics, Paris (1967), 22
  see also Kazakhfil'm Studio; Kyrgyzfil'm; Mosfilm; Tadjikfil'm studio; Turkmenfil'm; Uzbekfil'm Studio; Virgin Lands films
Soviet Union
  and culture, 5, 6, 202, 226, 229
  environmental practices, 200, 202–5, 243n; *see also* Virgin Lands campaign
  gender equality, 8
  historical interpretations, 98, 100
  mythology, 52
  "new monumentalism," 181
  "stagnation," 6
  "thaw," 5, 38–53, 223–4
space race, 237, 241n; *see also* moon: Apollo 11 moon landing
Spitzer, Leo, 167
Sputnik kinokritika (journal), 29
Stalin, Joseph, 5
Stalinism, 98
  critiques of, 43, 47–9, 109
  and language, 110
"Steel Squadron, The" (war song), 41, 63
Stefanyk, Vasyl, 20
Steffan, James, 191

Steimatsky, Noa, 127–8, 130
Stepanov, Boris, 184
Stishova, Elena, 254
Stites, Richard, 180
Stolper, Aleksandr: *The Living and the Dead (Zhivye i mertvye)*, 45, 252
subtitles, 193–4
Suprematism, 142, 145, 152
Swinton, Tilda, 9

Tadjik language, 193
Tadjikfil'm studio, 193
Tarkovsky, Andrei, 2, 30
  Andrei Rublev, 223
  and Brakhage, 140
  Mirror (Zerkalo), 153
  on Shepitko, 117, 222n
  Solaris (Soliaris), 30, 139, 143
  Stalker, 236
Taubman, Jane, 63–4
Taubman, William, 220n
Tchernova, Irina, 264
Tobak, Esfir, 169
Todorov, Tzvetan, 129
Tolomushova, Gulbara, 192–3
Tripp, Alili Mari, 14n
Trouillot, Rolph-Michel, 98, 113n
Trusov, Yurii, 204–5
Tupitsyn, Margarita, 142
Turkmen language, 193
Turkmenfil'm, 193

Ukraine
  films shot in *see Wings* (Kryl'ia)
  Russian invasion of (2022), 1, 2
  see also Artiomovsk; Bakhmut
UNESCO International Colloquium "Women in Cinema" (1975), 24
United Nations conference on environmental protection (1972), 243n
Urusevskii, Sergei, 181
Uzbek language, 193
Uzbekfil'm Studio, 193

VGIK (All-Union State Institute of Cinematography), 2, 19, 31
Vaisfeld, Ilya, 26
Varda, Agnès, 9, 25
Varshavsky, Yakov, 27
Vechernyaya Moskva (Evening Moscow) (newspaper), 25
Vertov, Dziga, 146
  One Sixth Part of the World (Shestaia chast' mira), 143
  Stride, Soviet! (Shagai, Sovet!), 161

Virgin Lands campaign, 5–6, 182–4, 225, 227
  and environment, 203–4, 226, 229
  and populations, 189–91
  and propaganda, 183
Virgin Lands films, 180–1, 183–8, 189–90
  romantic subplots, 186
  sexual symbolism, 186–7
  see also Heat
Vizbor, Yuri, 28, 29
Voronezh, 170

White, Jerry, 145
  Dog Star Man, 141
Widdis, Emma, 161
Window is Opening Wide, The (Okno raspakhnulos'), 20
Wings (Kryl'ia), 4, 39–41, *41*, 57–73, *66*, 229–34
  authenticity, 27
  aviation, 40–1
  Chekhovian outlook, 42
  as a critique of Stalinism, 43
  ending, 239
  female protagonist, 10, 20, 21–2, 38, 39, 40–2, 43, 45, 53, 57, 59–65, *70*, 72
  and feminist cinema, 232–3
  gender, 60–2
  and German's *Lapshin* compared, 39–43
  interiority, 230
  location, 3, 39
  music, 40–1, 67, 70
  reminiscences, 65–73
  script, 11, 57–9
  sexual themes, 10, 61
  sky, 229, 230–1, *231*, 233–4
Wodening, Jane, 139, 140
women
  as directors, 20–1, 24
  as flaneurs, 10, 65, 233
  role of, 229
  see also feminism; feminist cinema
World War II, 44; *see also* Ascent, The (Voskhozhdenie)

Yampolsky, Mikhail, 71
You and Me (Ty i ia), 25
  acknowledgement of, 9
  censorship of, 7–8, 22–3, 39
  Demidova on, 30
  female protagonist, 10
  locations, 3
  Moscow State University audience, 23–4
  Vizbor's collaboration on, 28, 29
Youngblood, Denise, 44
Yurchak, Sergey, 6
Yurenev, Rostislav, 22, 23

Zakhi, Aleksandr, 21
Zalakavicius, Vitas, 22
Zarkhi, Nathan, 74n
Zharenov, Stepan, 160
Zubok, Vladislav, 182

EU representative:
Easy Access System Europe
Mustamäe tee 50, 10621 Tallinn, Estonia
Gpsr.requests@easproject.com